From
Cape
to
Cairo

Also by David Ewing Duncan
Pedaling the Ends of the Earth

David Ewing Duncan

From Cape to Cairo

An African Odyssey

W·N

Weidenfeld & Nicolson
New York

Published by Weidenfeld & Nicolson, New York
A Division of Wheatland Corporation
841 Broadway
New York, New York 10003-4793

Published in Canada by General Publishing Company, Ltd.

Portions of this book have appeared, in slightly different form, in *The Christian
Science Monitor* and Condé Nast *Traveler.*

Grateful acknowledgment for permission to reprint is made to:
Random House, Inc., for material from *Out of Africa* by Isak Dinesen, copyright
1937 by Random House, Inc., copyright © renewed 1965 by Rungstedlundfonden;
Christopher Hope, for lines from "In a Swimming Pool in a Garden in White South
Africa," *Modern South African Poetry,* edited by Stephen Gray, A. D. Donker,
Johannesburg, 1984; Houghton Mifflin Company, for an excerpt from *Letters of
Henry Adams 1858–1891,* edited by Worthington C. Ford, copyright 1930 by
Worthington C. Ford, copyright © renewed 1958 by Emily E. F. Lowes; and Andre
Deutsch Ltd., for lines from "Europe," by Mazisi Kunene, *Zulu Poems,* edited by
Mazisi Kunene, Andre Deutsch Ltd., London, 1970.

Care has been taken to trace the copyright owners of other material in this book
and to give full acknowledgment for its use. Any errors or omissions accidentally
occurring will be corrected in future editions provided the publisher is notified.

Library of Congress Cataloging-in-Publication Data

Duncan, David Ewing.
    From Cape to Cairo

    1. Africa—Description and travel—1977–
2. Duncan, David Ewing—Journeys—Africa.
I. Title.
DT12.25.D85   1989   916'.04328   88-36283
ISBN 1-55584-045-0

Manufactured in the United States of America

This book is printed on acid-free paper

Designed by Brush Horse Books

First Edition

10 9 8 7 6 5 4 3 2 1

To James Logan

Who knows better than anyone
that Ralph Waldo Emerson was right
when he said,
"Travel is a fool's paradise."

Contents

*Africa is a continent so saturated with human
history that the bones of people a million years
old sometimes appear in cracks in the earth.
Yet modern Africa is the youngest of
continents, barely older than I am at thirty. Its
fundamental history is being written at this
very moment. Not the slow, incremental,
predictable history of the West, but the raw-
nerved history of beginnings.*

*It is a continent on the ragged edge, where
everything—art, history, government, music,
everything—is tenuous and unformed. It is a
place where wounds gape open in a murky
dawn of violence and unknown possibilities,
like a spade upturning the earth, over and over,
reinventing life through birth, hope and
suffering. It is the expectant cry of a newborn
in the bush, the wanderings of the nomad and
the refugee, and the tap-tap-tap of a
Kalashnikov assault rifle in the hands of a
fourteen-year-old soldier. . . .*

*—Journal Entry
Lake Turkana
August 1986*

Preface

If you want to understand me
come, bend over this soul of Africa . . .
in the strange sadness which flows
from an African song, through the night.
                    —Noémia de Sousa

Years ago in Sudan I watched a child die. It happened in an Ethiopian refugee camp, a vast, stinking, unbearably hot morass of shanties and fleshless people. One afternoon, as riptides of humans swelled toward a food distribution tent, I stood with pale-skinned relief workers from my own country distributing white protein powder. A fellow from New Hampshire told me that the powder, which looked like talcum, was manufactured as a diet drink for obese people in the States.

I picked up a small plastic bag of powder and held it out to the closest person in the quiet mob. Spindly fingers snatched it away, reminding me of a battery-powered coin bank I once owned as a boy. I would set a coin in a slot and a grotesque, green hand would jump out of a door and grab it. "*Gotcha!*" the machine would say in a tinny voice.

After an hour or two, it became mechanical to hold out a bag and have it snatched ... *Gotcha!* I watched the refugees as I worked, astounded by the suffering, my mind reeling with stray, uncontrollable thoughts about life, death, misery, global inequities, fate and other imponderables.

Then my eyes caught sight of an infant riding in a cassock on her mama's back. The pink material is what first attracted my attention, a garish color against the earthen hues of refugees. The most remarkable thing about the girl was her eyes, large, glistening and pure, "eyes of gold and bramble dew," as the Robert Louis Stevenson poem goes. They were disarmingly peaceful amid that grim landscape of humans, baneful orbs that seemed to absorb the horrors of the world and reflect back only innocence.

I don't know the precise moment when the girl died. Perhaps she had been already dead for several minutes, for it takes some time for every part of the body to acknowledge the end. All I know is that as I stood there handing out American diet powder, her eyes abruptly turned to glass. Just like that they switched off, turning milky white, the color of cream in weak coffee. The girl's head, already bobbing like a yo-yo, went limp and fell backward. Several flies—Sudan is cursed with a particularly vicious variety—congregated in her open mouth and then crawled into her ruined eyes.

I was momentarily paralyzed, my brain and body debilitated by ... what? Anguish? Pain? Duplicity? I did not have any idea what I felt, or what I should have felt, being so fresh from America. But this was just as well, for I did not have the leisure to indulge in my petty agonies. All around me hands were reaching out, emaciated fingers looking precisely like the grotesque limbs on my coin machine.

"Mister," a ragged voice said, the tone insistent. "Food! Food!" The voice was attached to a hand, and it was tugging at my pant leg, demanding. So I gave it to him. And I drew out another packet and gave it to another set of hands, and they kept coming like that all afternoon.

How potent images can be that will not go away. They gnaw at us, they change us, they frustrate us, they drive us to embark on all sorts of wild-eyed journeys. After I returned to America I could not shake an Ethiopian child's eyes and other crowded visages I had seen on a journey that had taken me around the world. These faces haunted me as I settled down in Vermont to start a family and write my books. The questions kept coming and voices inside my brain begged me to go back.

In the spring of 1986 I said good-bye to my remarkably understanding wife and set off on a journey across Africa, traveling slowly and keeping my eyes open. Technically, I went as a gypsy journalist, in the sense that a book publisher and a newspaper were paying my expenses in exchange for a few scribbled pages and articles. But this was only a means to an end. It sounds a bit preposterous to call myself an explorer, but that is what I was, although my consuming interest was not in mountain heights and long rivers, nor was it a quest for data, statistics and fresh hypotheses.

My great unknown was far less obvious, having to do more with those imponderables that keep rattling around in my hopelessly restless brain—certain attitudes, morals, beliefs, fears and the old-fashioned notion of *soul*. My quest was, in a way, a repudiation of the tendency in our era to depend so much on numbers, theories and quick, titillating, journalistic sketches. I was looking for something deeper, for insights about human emotions and why people behave as they do—the rich, the poor, the student, the beggar, the politician. . . .

I chose Africa because it seems more than ever to be suited to a quest for human fundamentals. It is a continent where life and emotions are cut down to the barest essentials, where illusions of race, politics and history are being ripped apart and rebuilt at a breathless, often tragic pace. This is why I have chosen to present my journey in a novelistic fashion, to capture a place where hope, failure and brutality ripple across the surface like lightning, a place that must be portrayed—as much as I am able—with the language and brutal honesty of the poet.

What I saw in Africa was not particularly uplifting, although there were sublime moments of hope and even joy. Nor is everyone likely to agree with what I have reported on these pages, particularly those who still insist on treating Africa—to borrow a metaphor from Shiva Naipaul—as if it were a package marked FRAGILE: DO NOT SHAKE, BEND OR DROP. This is not to say that I am joining the new brigade of Africa Bashers who think they are doing the continent a great service by ripping it apart. On the contrary, I believe that Africa has been subjected to enough expert advice in the past century to last anyone for several millennia to come.

I chose my route through Africa as the best solution for a variety of personal requirements. First, the Cape to Cairo route spans the entire length of the continent, from sea to sea, which provided a necessary physical focus. It is also interesting from a historic standpoint, in that the Cape to Cairo route was once the major highway of Britain's Cape to Cairo Empire, perhaps the greatest absurdity ever attempted in the name of colonialism. And finally, it seemed to offer a fascinating cross section of Africa for an explorer of people's moods and attitudes. There were countries at war and those at peace, countries that had embraced everything from socialism to capitalism, and countries that ranged from desperately poor to relatively prosperous. There were Muslims, Christians, pagans, Caucasians, blacks, Arabs, Bushmen and various combinations of all of the above. The terrain included desert, mountains, bush and jungle.

I should briefly explain the origin of the "Cape to Cairo" term. It was invented by a Tory journalist at the height of the so-called Scramble for Africa in the 1880s and picked up by Cecil Rhodes as his imperialist battle cry. "I want only one thing," said Rhodes, "that is to see all the lands from Cape to Cairo painted in British red!" George Bernard Shaw, a master of uncovering humbug, later called it the "alliteration that launched an empire."

A young disciple of Cecil Rhodes named Ewart Grogan first walked the route in 1898, with the avowed purpose of "furthering the white empire in Africa." However, he spent most of his two-year journey gunning down wild animals—a fashionable enterprise at the time—and accomplished little else, other than spreading some fanciful lies about cannibals and other unsubstantiated native perversities. Grogan later settled in Kenya, where he continued as a crusader for the white cause, led a life of rampant promiscuity and founded the Thorn Tree Café in Nairobi, where pale, Western backpack tourists in Banana Republic khakis now congregate to drink beer, trade safari stories and buy hashish.

My mode of transport for most of the journey was the bicycle, the perfect tool for immersing myself in Africa. I want to make it clear from the beginning that I did not use the bicycle as an end in itself. I was not a bike fanatic who felt compelled to keep every gear shiny, every bolt screwed on tight and to grunt out every last inch of my route. The bike was merely a useful vehicle chosen because it moved slowly, but not too slowly, and because I enjoy—even crave—the sensation and relaxation of physical motion, being something of a latter-day nomad.

I traveled 7,000 miles through eight nations, following the Cape to Cairo route from the southern tip of the continent through South Africa, Botswana, Zimbabwe, Zambia, Tanzania, Kenya and Sudan to Cairo in Egypt. I carried everything I thought I needed with me on the bike, including the usual roster of tent, sleeping bag, portable stove and so forth. I traveled with two friends at different times. In the south Jim Logan joined me, an old friend who has pedaled with me on previous journeys. Jim is a tall, red-haired high-school teacher from Maine with the swaggering mustache of a true explorer. He is a teacher and a naturalist whose love of fauna and flora added a significant dimension to my primary interest in people. Another friend, Andy Shafer of New Hampshire, cycled with me in the north. Also lanky and red-haired, Andy has spent many restless years exploring the deserts of Africa in Land Rovers, but never before had traveled long distance by bicycle. Both Jim and Andy provided necessary injections of pragmatism and hard-won experience that were greatly appreciated. In the middle of my journey I traveled alone.

Although this book is nonfiction, I have taken certain minor liberties that the reader should be aware of. On occasion, I have provided aliases to protect the privacy or safety of individuals. I have attempted to write as accurate a depiction as possible of people and conversations based on notes and journal entries, though in a few instances I relied on memory.

Finally, for reasons of narrative flow, I have disguised the actual timing of my journey, which was conducted not in one continuous trip, but in two phases. The first phase, from Cape Town to Kenya, took place from April to September 1986. The second phase, through Sudan and Egypt, took place from April to June 1987.

David Ewing Duncan
Norwich, Vermont
December 1988

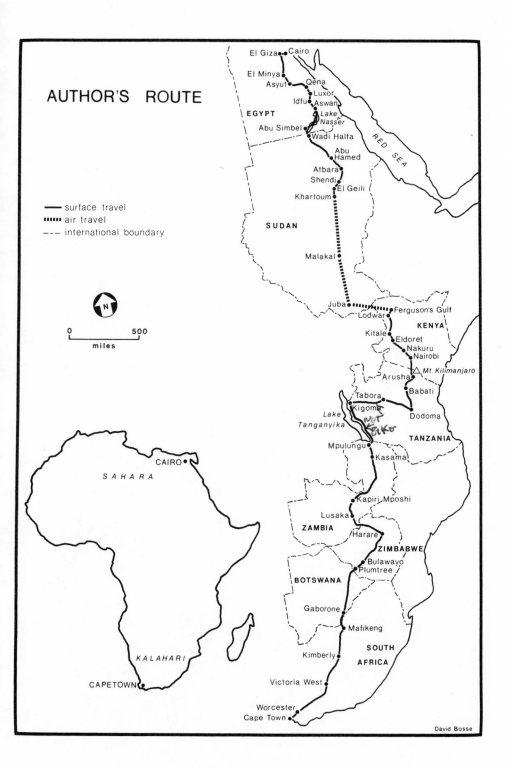

AUTHOR'S ROUTE

— surface travel
▪▪▪▪▪ air travel
– – – international boundary

N

0   500
miles

EGYPT
El Giza • Cairo
El Minya
Asyut • Qena
Luxor
Idfu • Aswan
Lake Nasser
Abu Simbel • Wadi Halfa
Abu Hamed
Atbara
Shendi • El Geili
Khartoum

SUDAN

Malakal

Juba • Ferguson's Gulf
Lodwar
KENYA
Kitale • Eldoret
Nakuru
Nairobi
△ *Mt. Kilimanjaro*
Arusha
Babati
Tabora
Kigoma • Dodoma
Lake Tanganyika
NOT EIKO
Mpulungu
Kasama
TANZANIA

Kapiri Mposhi
Lusaka
ZAMBIA Harare
ZIMBABWE
Bulawayo
Plumtree
BOTSWANA
Gaborone
Mafikeng
SOUTH AFRICA
Kimberly
Victoria West
Worcester
Cape Town

SAHARA
CAIRO •

KALAHARI

CAPETOWN •

RED SEA

David Bosse

I
South Africa

A Dry,
White Season

The worst lie was our hope.
                    —Patrick Cullinan

Waiting
Hungry for the flesh of tomorrow
                    —Wopko Jensma

Imagine that you are creating a fabric of
human destiny with the object of making men
happy in the end, giving them peace and rest at
last, but that it was essential and inevitable to
torture to death one tiny creature . . . and to
found that edifice on its unavenged tears,
would you consent to be the architect of those
conditions? Tell me, and tell the truth.
                    —Dostoevski

1 Twenty hours out of Boston my jetliner arrived, as expected, over Cape Town. From my godlike perch I saw scenes below of Caucasian bliss: whitewashed villas, beaches of tawny sand and hundreds of swimming pools, each one glinting like a fragile bead of blue glass. The poet Christopher Hope wrote:

> I am alone in a swimming pool in a garden
> In white South Africa.

A rotund Afrikaaner named Rolf Swart sat beside me. He insisted on pointing out sites, as if I were a child on holiday. The Cape of Good Hope, the squat, brooding Table Mountain, a harbor named after Queen Victoria . . . "You are looking at paradise on earth," he bellowed in the thin, pressurized air, a sloppy, suburban man who sold cooking utensils door-to-door. I imagined him at home sitting in a deck chair beside his own swimming pool, reading the sports pages and drinking lager beer.

Swart had boarded the plane when we stopped for fuel in Johannesburg; he was a perspiring, mildly offensive creature who had introduced himself by telling a crude joke about a woman and a goat. He then spent an hour trying to sell me a set of Teflon skillets, driving me mad with his shoddy sales pitch, a man who seemed carved not out of South Africa, land of steely-eyed Caucasian warriors, but out of some petty corner of America.

"Is it not beautiful down there?" Swart was saying. He bent over my lap to point out new sites, his breath smelling disagreeably of whiskey and tobacco smoke. I had asked him about the unrest in South Africa because I thought I should, and he was trying to convince me it was just a lot of rot spread by the Western media. "Man, do you see any trouble down there?" He had an Afrikaaner accent, which has a rough, Germanic timbre, a grating sound to a native midwesterner like myself, used to flat vowels and stressless consonants. "Do you see any riots? Any trouble at all? Of course not. I tell 3 you, your journalists have spread terrible, terrible lies about our country."

I asked him why the Western media would do such a thing, and he shook his head as if I were a hopeless dolt. "Man, it's so damn obvious. The whole thing is a huge conspiracy. Everyone here knows it, and I can't believe you Yanks 'aven't figured it out. It's the Russians! The Communists! They want our gold mines."

"Ah," I said, "so that's what it's all about?"

"Of course it is! Who else do you think is behind this unrest? It's a very clever conspiracy. No one ever said the Russians are stupid. They've got your media tricked, and now they're sending in foreign blacks to stir up trouble. See, *our* blacks want none of it. You'll see. I *know* our blacks. I grew up with 'em, and they're all right."

I couldn't believe my bad luck at being stuck next to Rolf Swart in that cramped space with no means of escape. It couldn't have come at a worse time. I was, after all, about to land in Africa to start a long journey I had been anticipating for years. This was supposed to be a moment for reflection, for meditating on all of those Big Questions a traveler is supposed to ask himself as he approaches that auspicious moment of arrival.

But here was Rolf Swart rattling in my ear. He was not giving me a moment's peace to collect my thoughts, which admittedly were confused anyway. "Look there," he shouted, "there's the Company Gardens! Have you heard of them? That's where the first Dutch settlers grew cabbages." I tried to shut him out as I peered through the scratched plastic window and watched endless suburbs and town houses and parks rush past below.

Then, abruptly, the scene below shifted and Swart's voice dissolved away. The suburbs disappeared and the jet roared very near to a column of black smoke. Beneath the jet everything was confusion. A sprawling shantytown had appeared, and in the near distance it was on fire, a sickening sprawl of cardboard and tarpaulin huts engulfed in smoke and red hedges of flame. Through my binoculars I could see spiderlike humans running as the blaze moved in huge waves.

I was stunned by this madness, this headline appearing in the flesh so soon in my journey. Swart was watching, too. The vision had put a stop to his tour. I could tell from his grumbles—it sounded like indigestion—that he was perturbed at this interruption, but I did not pounce on him and say, "Ah-hah, look down there!" For as much as I found him unappealing, I felt no victory that he was being proven so ridiculous.

Yet I was curious what Swart would have to say. As it turned out, he had little comment, indigestion being his most honest remark. Like most hopelessly content humans, he was prepared to deny everything. He merely frowned at this hint of turmoil, as if it had appeared on the TV news. "Those radical blacks are at it again," he groused while the scene below shifted from shanties back to suburbia. "They're trying to wreck everything we've built in this country. A cheeky bunch. They oughta learn some bloody discipline."

After landing in white Cape Town I checked into a one-star hotel, but I did not get too comfortable. I had no desire to linger in this city and neither did Jim Logan, my patient friend joining me on the first half of this trek. We wanted to stay only long enough to assemble our equipment and prepare for our journey. I was anxious to get under way. I had not traveled ten thousand miles to see a cloned Western city.

Yet I admit that the existence of a city like Cape Town held some interest for me, this little fortress of America in Africa, a tiny, perfect, white diamond bored into the forehead of a black, defiant face. It seemed a nearly perfect stone to the naked eye, each facet cut with skill and precision. In white Cape Town there was commerce, art, religion, intellectual discourse and a powerful sense of history. There was an undeniable quaintness in the bright, whitewashed facades and Old World feel of a city founded in the same era as the Pilgrims' landing in America. I found myself feeling an evanescent pleasure in strolling through palm-studded streets, eyeing sunbirds, jacaranda blossoms and attractive women in shorts and halter tops. I enjoyed the eclectic bookshops on Long Street and cozy cafés on Greenmarket Square. There was a bored, clean-cut feeling about the place that jarred me slightly, as if this city had been caught in a time warp of short hair, Bermuda shorts, gee-whiz grins and white knee socks. (Even the small scattering of punks and pseudobohemian artists on Long Street looked vaguely like Boy and Girl Scouts playing dress-up, their orange hair combed too neatly and their patent leather jackets out of date by several years.) But none of this prevented Cape Town from being a perfectly lovely illusion, a prototype of a type of paradise that once appeared all over white Africa, a sun-drenched utopia where the air was sweet with rhododendron and violets and Cape wine ran like honey.

Yet there was obviously a flaw in this smooth-cut diamond, a monstrous crack hidden to most Caucasians living happily inside the cold beauty of the stone. Was this crack called apartheid? Was it called imperialism? Was it called exploitation? I did not know. I'll leave the explanations to the experts. What concerned me was the human outcome of this maelstrom, the specter of violence and hate that lurked both inside and outside this little diamond.

Let me lay out the situation. The year was 1986 and the month was April, T. S. Eliot's cruelest month. South Africa was in its second year of a crippling conflict between black revolutionaries and the power-ful defenders of paradise. Over one thousand humans, mostly blacks, had been killed in twenty months of violence, nearly all of it con-fined to nonwhite areas. Thousands more had been beaten and de-tained. Each morning over coffee and eggs at my hotel, I read the latest body count in a small box on the inside page of the *Cape Town Times*. The numbers appeared like clockwork—two dead, eight dead, twelve dead, bludgeoned by *slamjoeks* during riots, blown apart by shotguns at a funeral, burned alive by tires soaked in gas-oline. . . .

One of the chief killing grounds in South Africa lay just outside of Cape Town, eight miles from my hotel. The place was called Cross-roads, the squatters' town I had seen ablaze from the jetliner. I had heard its name back home on the evening news, where it had become notorious in the late seventies during a series of forced evictions. Now Crossroads was in the headlines again because the police were mounting a campaign to eradicate what they called "radical ele-ments." However, this time the police were not using riot guns and dogs to track down revolutionaries. They were using a tactic much more subtle, a variation on the old imperial device of divide and conquer. There was a group of bitter Crossroads men known as "fathers," conservative parents and antirevolutionary blacks enraged by the specter of constant violence. They had recently organized to inflict vigilante justice on the revolutionaries, attacking known ag-itators and burning down their houses. The police, wanting to en-courage this trend, armed the vigilantes and then stood aside as fathers and sons battled all summer long for control of the shanty-town. When I flew into Cape Town, I happened to stumble on one of the worst battles of the season. The papers said eight died that day, although this was just a guess.

I tell this story because the memory of the inferno was still so fresh, and I was anxious to understand what savagery could unleash such horror. This was a major reason why I had come to Africa, to try to comprehend humanity's predilection for savagery in an era that seems particularly cruel. Thus, I was drawn to Crossroads. This is not to say that white Cape Town lacked in savagery, it is just that every effort had been made inside the gemlike city to smother ugliness and unpleasant questions. The whole point of apartheid is to maintain this image of utopia, no matter how bland and absurd it becomes.

So one morning I climbed on my bicycle (recently assembled from the plane flight) and headed toward Crossroads. However, I first had to stop at the central police station to get the required visitor's permit. Inside, the station was crammed with blacks waiting for word on detained relatives. These were not the tidy, silent, uniformed blacks that one sees waiting tables and sweeping streets in downtown Cape Town, but a motley, dusty, displaced group that came from the same world as the strung-out beggars I'd seen years earlier in Sudan. They were dressed in threadbare suits and over-washed dresses and carried their belongings in tattered shopping bags. Most held dog-eared, official-looking papers, gripping them tightly as if they were holding the very souls of their missing friends and relatives. They had the sad, enduring look of people used to being patient, a stupor that comes from a lifetime of waiting—for jobs, for food, for word about detained relatives. Waiting, waiting, always waiting.

I, likewise, had to wait to see the appropriate officer, only to be told curtly to go away, that he could not possibly issue the permit I required. When I persisted, a sergeant took over, then a lieutenant. Finally, a captain who was roughly my own age, height and hair color offered me a seat in a cubbyhole away from the din of the main room. He handed me a cigarette, as he might a suspect in a crime, and I gave it back to him because I don't smoke. He shrugged, lit up, filled the tiny room with smoke, and asked why I wanted to go to Crossroads. His voice was soft and patronizing.

When he heard I was traveling from Cape Town to Cairo he smiled wryly, assuming I was in search of the past. He suggested that I go to the Cape archives. In the archives, he said, I would find all of the history concerning my route. "Crossroads, I think, is irrelevant to your journey." I explained to him that I was more interested in the present and future than in the past, and he frowned. "I'm sorry," he said, "but I think you would have better luck at the archives. Crossroads is at the moment off limits to foreigners. Surely you have heard about the riots. It is quite bad in there right now, and we are under strict orders." He proposed that I see the other sites in Cape Town. "Have you been up the gondola on Table Mountain? From up top you can see just how beautiful our city is."

I walked out of the captain's office realizing that this city was not going to make it easy for me, a white foreigner, to escape its suffocating pleasantness. I passed again through the ranks of black supplicants, wondering what sort of people they were behind those stern, serious masks—laborers? teachers? mothers? revolutionaries?

Outside the station the sun beat down on my skin, still pale from my home in New England. I climbed onto my bicycle, a shiny, new, red mountain bike, and began to ride, pedaling fast and furious, trying to dissipate my frustration at being denied. It felt good to be pedaling—the rush of air, the blood pumping through my veins.

I rode back toward my hotel, but decided to take a longer ride. I kept going and headed downtown. I swung past the South African Parliament building, a ponderous, British colonial structure framing a glaring bronze likeness of Queen Victoria. (Nearby were other statues of white heroes, including Cecil Rhodes, Bartholomeu Dias and Jan Smuts.) I headed on toward Table Bay, past a canyon of glass office towers filled with white-collar workers, computers, telexes and ringing telephones, the brain center of the South African economy.

Beyond the skyscrapers I reached the warehouses and train yards beside the busy bay, where half of Africa still sends and receives its goods in trade. Zambian copper, Zimbabwean chromium, Botswanian diamonds, South African gold ... it all flows through here, despite racial enmity and talk of boycotts, because there are no other trade routes for the poor, landlocked nations of southern Africa. All of the railways and roadways from the former colonies lead here, to the mother city of white Africa.

I stopped for a moment when my tires touched the railway tracks, just before the water of the bay. This spot had some symbolism for my journey, the southern terminus of the Cape Town to Cairo highway. I won't dwell on the history of this infamous route. As I told the police captain, a historic replay was not my intention. However, this did not mean that I was uninterested in the colonial era. I was fascinated by one important aspect of white imperialism and settlement in Africa, namely, its utter failure.

To my mind, the whole enterprise smacked of the absurd. It was hatched much too late in the imperialist era, was pushed by singularly petty men and never even turned a decent profit. Economically, strategically and morally it came to nothing but a huge, uncertain, embarrassing muddle. Even as a site for white settlement, Africa never caught on outside of South Africa, and it would not have caught on there except for gold and diamonds. Throughout the rest of the British settler domains, stretching from the Limpopo River to Kenya, the population of whites never exceeded a million, a dismal failure for Caucasian dreamers who thought they could subdue millions of blacks and create a second North America. Yet this did not deter men like Cecil Rhodes, a megalomaniac's megalomaniac, who blustered about saying things like: "In Africa, think big" and "What was attempted by Alexander, Cambyses and Napoleon we practical people are going to finish."

Of course, one has to admire the tenacity of the would-be empire builders. With titanic effort, Rhodes and his minions gashed, rebuilt and bloodied half a continent in an effort to establish a string of little white utopias. They spent millions and killed thousands to make the Cape to Cairo Empire a brief reality. Salisbury, Lusaka, Nairobi . . . all of these cities I would pass through were hardly built and occupied before they collapsed under the weight of their own foolishness.

I climbed back onto my bike and left the railroad terminus, following the shoreline for a moment, then bearing away from the harbor. Traffic picked up as I left the water and pedaled onto a superhighway crowded with white and cream-colored sedans. A mile from the water the warehouses and factories along the bay faded into a series of nonwhite townships, sprawling complexes of battered apartment projects and storefronts reserved exclusively for mixed-race "coloreds" and Asians. These dismal enclaves stretched for miles behind tall, barbed-wire fences. Before the townships ended, the view on the right side of the highway had become obstructed by a dirt barricade. I knew this barricade. I had seen it from the plane.

When I left the police station, I had not intended to bike to Crossroads, but here it was, not one hundred meters away. When I stood up high on my pedals and looked through dips in the wall, I could see distant hills covered with makeshift shanties, a squalid mess of wood, tin and canvas.

Up ahead, just a few meters from the road, I saw a band of black children hurling stones at old bottles and road litter. I slowed down to watch as the rocks were carefully aimed and tossed, the face of each boy sunk in deep concentration. Of course, they saw me coming. They pointed and then ran in my direction, their faces blank, their hands full of stones.

Television images ran through my head. I had seen children like these on the news tossing gasoline bombs and burning people alive, wild, township warriors whipped into a frenzy by their hatred. I squeezed my brakes and slowed again, feeling terribly vulnerable on my bicycle. I knew it was ludicrous to be here, a white man on the edge of a violent caldron. Yet I wanted to stop. I wanted to talk to these boys, to test the veracity of my TV expectations.

I took a deep breath and stopped several paces away from the children. They moved toward me through a break in the fence, their faces taut and wary, their hands full of stones. It struck me that I could still make a break for it and ride like hell back to the white city. But I stood firm, determined to go through with this.

When the boys reached my bike, they stood still and stared, their faces impassive. I began to panic. Then I thought of my camera. I pulled it out of my knapsack. "Photographer," I said, "from America."

These were, it appeared, the magic words for kids growing up in a media fishbowl. Instantly, they dropped their stones and began chattering and behaving a lot like children everywhere. They laughed and pinched my tires just as kids have always done when I appear out of nowhere on a bike, pointing at the gears and hamming it up for my camera.

They knew almost no English, but the few words they did know said a mouthful: *petrol bomb, Nelson Mandela, American journalist* and *African National Congress.* They also knew by rote several slogans, including the Zulu chant *Amandle Kawage*—"Power for Freedom"—a slogan I had heard shouted at antiapartheid rallies I covered as a reporter in America. When I recognized *Amandle Kawage,* they repeated it loudly with fists clenched, laughing and acting as if this were all a wonderful game.

I tried to imagine these boys throwing gas bombs and burning people alive and could not, although I am sure they were fully capable of astounding cruelty and violence. I could see it in their eyes and in the grim visages of Crossroads behind the barricade. And why not? What did they have to lose? I had read the statistics. Even without apartheid, these Crossroads kids faced a dismal, Third World future of poverty and unemployment. An academic friend in Cape Town later gave me the numbers. At least thirty percent of the people in Crossroads were unemployed, thirty percent of the children were malnourished and education was virtually nonexistent.

One of the boys, wearing a black vinyl cap and a faded British Petroleum T-shirt, invited me to visit his home, which he indicated was close. Before I could answer, he and his buddies were pushing my bike up a steep path in the dirt wall. On top I saw at ground level what I had eyeballed from the air, a vast collage of shanties, ragged, sweaty humans and fetid pools of feces, urine and garbage. The boys began moving down the inside of the wall, but I hesitated, feeling the fear of one who has spent most of his life unexposed to even the potential for violence. The thought of joining boy revolutionaries in Crossroads left my stomach churning.

In the midst of my hesitation, the children abruptly shouted a warning and I saw fear cloud their eyes. Like spooked gazelles, they scrambled away, leaving me alone on the barricade. Then I heard an angry, almost hysterical voice behind me.

Turning around, I saw the muzzle of an automatic weapon pointed at my head. The weapon was held by a soldier in khakis and full combat gear. He beckoned me down from the barricade, keeping his rifle aimed. I saw more soldiers in an armored transport vehicle parked several paces away. One of them stood up, watching me with binoculars.

The first soldier began berating me in Afrikaans, switching to English when he saw my passport and papers. He was very young, probably no more than eighteen. He looked pathetically small in all his combat gear, his eyes barely visible beneath his steel helmet. His long-barreled automatic looked huge in his smooth, hairless hands.

My God, I thought, this was another child, conscripted to do battle with Crossroads kids only a few years younger, children battling one another on the squalid outskirts of paradise.

"Are you a fool?" the soldier shouted at me, his young, high-pitched voice quaking with indignation, his face contorted with authority and disdain. "This is not a place you are allowed to be. This is Crossroads! Those goddamned children will cut your white throat!"

2   Ten days after our arrival in Cape Town, Jim Logan and I climbed on our ridiculously overloaded bicycles and headed for the interior. Packed into bulging panniers and strapped on sturdy racks were, in all, the near equivalent of a small Western apartment on wheels, minus the television and faithful pet. We had tents, cooking pots, tire pumps, candle lanterns, a portable stove, numerous cassettes and books, a first-aid kit, water bags, sleeping bags, insect repellent and much more.

My bike felt as if it weighed ten tons as we set out, but I have a philosophy about training for these long trips. I don't. I realize this may irk some bicycling enthusiasts, but I have learned over the years that too much training is pointless, assuming one is in decent shape. My method is simply to get on my bike and start pedaling, resigned that for the first three or four days on the road I will wish I were dead.

The load we were hauling seemed absurd in a country replete with American-style supermarkets and the cleanest service stations I've ever seen. One old Englishman in Cape Town had said biking across South Africa would be about as challenging as pedaling across Wyoming, where he'd once attended a cattle convention. Yet I knew we would need every last dysentery pill and drop of iodine once we got clear of this rarefied white man's highway and penetrated the bush of Central Africa.

But first we had to get out of Cape Town unscathed and, according to certain white denizens of the place, this might not be easy. Our road to the north, the Stellenbosch Highway, passed by a series of colored townships where rioters and young revolutionaries had been randomly attacking cars and white motorists. Gasoline bombs had been tossed and gunfire exchanged. White Cape Town was terrified.

In our hotel dining room another burly Englishman had warned us about the Stellenbosch road. "You'll be hurt if you aren't careful," he had said one morning as we waited for a British breakfast of limp porridge and mangoes. "There are gangs of ruffians along that road just waiting for fresh white meat. They're real bad sorts, fellows 12 who'll attack in a minute if the police aren't about." He suggested that we get motorized transport out of town. "At least in a car you can outrun the bastards."

It seemed ironic that the entryway to paradise would be so frightening to these fellows, but irony was no comfort to two men on bicycles, especially after Crossroads. Neither Jim nor I planned to bike every inch of the way to Cairo. I was interested in Africa, and not in proving that I could ride, shout for help and dodge Molotov cocktails in a township, all at the same time. Nor did I feel an overwhelming need to grind out every mile just for the sake of saying I did it. On the other hand, we had enough biking pride that neither of us wanted to climb aboard a truck or bus before we even got started.

We checked with various authorities about the Stellenbosch Highway, and were told that the townships on the edge of the city had been quiet for several months. "The army's been doin' a good job out there," said a Texan at the U.S. consulate, whose job was to advise American travelers, issue new passports and notify next of kin. "They've been roundin' up everyone who so much as sneezes wrong out there," he added. "There's no one left to cause any trouble." So Jim and I decided to take a small chance and head out by bicycle.

The morning we left, the sun beat down hard on the tranquil city by the sea, making the biking hot and sweaty. At first, the highway was predominantly Western, a crowded street lined by British-era storefronts, offices and restaurants. The skin pigments began to darken, however, as we approached another leading edge between white Cape Town and the black townships. Gradually, storefronts became seedier and clothing less trendy. Patches of whites still appeared, usually behind the windows of speeding cars running the gauntlet north. These motorists seemed to be in a great hurry to get past this neighborhood, although from our perspective the speed and anxious faces hardly seemed justified in what seemed a completely normal street.

We felt in danger only once, when the highway we had chosen on our map abruptly took us away from the busy district of shops and into the middle of a housing project called Lavistown. The transition from an essentially modern street was startling. Just out of sight of the main white artery most First World details completely disappeared within a scant hundred meters. The road narrowed and the sidewalks became dirt paths. We passed grassless fields leading up to clusters of drab, gray apartment buildings looking like dozens of flat, unmarked tombs. Dangling laundry ropes spread across the face of each building like rigging on ghost ships, the shirts, trousers and dresses adding the only touches of color to this melancholy world. The buildings reminded me of the monolithic welfare slabs standing on the edges of Paris, Madrid and London, although they had a paltry, unfinished look, with no landscaping or human touches. These tombs had been built, I was later told, to house coloreds removed from those areas of Cape Town redesignated as "white." Nearly two hundred thousand nonwhites had been moved in twenty years from the center city, some from homes where their fathers, grandfathers and great-grandfathers had lived and died.

"I can remember when they announced the relocation policy," a colored office worker had told me in Cape Town. He was an administrative assistant for an American company, a university graduate who had spent his adolescence in a place like Lavistown. "My grandfather heard it on the radio, and he cried. It was the only time I ever saw him cry. 'They're going to take our house away,' he said. I was just a boy. I remember being very confused. We had a simple house in Woodstock, which for two hundred years was a colored neighborhood in the center of Cape Town. We had our churches there, our friends, a real history. And then came the apartheid men to move us out. What a stupid thing this was! I will never forgive them for what they did. They moved my old grandfather, and of course he died very soon after. Now a white family lives in our house in Woodstock, and they call it a white area. This is why those apartheid men are so foolish. I mean, why antagonize people who are content?"

In Lavistown, the pace slowed down several notches from the main highway. It was an abrupt warp of cultures, time and pacing. Mule-drawn wagons replaced automobiles and people walked with the languor of rural folk, though their faces had the intensity of city humans. Chickens pecked at the earth and dogs lay asleep in pools of dust. In the heat of day the place was nearly deserted, although the presence of two whites on bicycles attracted attention from sinister-looking gangs of children inhabiting dingy shadows and dark edges of apartment slabs. They stood warily, looking like the Crossroads boys when they approached me with their stones.

When we stopped for a minor repair on a brake, several teenaged boys strode up and stared, their eyes stark and livid. Their glares seared the dusty air like fire, and I thought of a gang of Palestinians on the West Bank who once mistook me for an Israeli. They had screamed at me in Arabic—acidic, bitter words that I did not comprehend, but could understand very well. But these boys in Lavistown just stared in icy silence, a terrifying glower that seemed much more violent than epithets or cast stones. The black poet Mazisi Kunene wrote:

> *Children have inherited the fire.*
> *They blow its flames to the skies.*

I wanted to somehow connect with the boys, to ask them to explain their hate, but I could think of nothing engaging to say. I asked them if we were on the right road. They remained silent and defiant. I felt like an idiot standing there, gawking and trying to *make contact*, the difficulty of my mission in Africa more clear than ever. All they did was stare, and for all I know, they're staring yet.

3 Outside of Lavistown, Cape Town mercifully ended and the countryside began with a blast of green. Neat rows of vegetables flared out like pinwheels. The air grew thick with the smell of leaves and soil being overturned, gratifying aromas after Cape Town's cloying sweetness. I felt released and free and strong despite the weight of my gear. I have always savored these moments of departure and breaking free. I tolerate cities and overorganized spaces for only a short time. (This is why I live in Vermont, for my life is something of an elaborate ruse to flee a society that is far too organized for my taste.) And there is no better way to escape than on a bicycle under my own locomotion.

I relished the earthiness and stopped frequently to breathe the moist, rich air, exhilarated by the sheer vastness of the landscape. However, as the day wore on, my load began to catch up with me and my legs and arms began to ache. Nor was relief in sight. The terrain began to tier, turning gradually upward, like the eastern foothills of the Rocky Mountains.

After a while we could see a massive, dark shape rising above the farmland, the wall of rock called the Cape Escarpment. We had talked about this "hill" for weeks as we prepared for the trip, and now we were faced with the reality: a three-thousand-foot monster rising as if to a continental divide.

We spent three excruciating days climbing a series of cold, steep inclines. The highway had been cut in the 1840s by hearty Dutch voortrekkers fleeing the English conquest of the Cape. These people, the ancestors of the present Afrikaaners, had a reputation for stoicism, now abundantly borne out by this steep, abusive road. The highway was etched in granite bluffs and flanked by sheer drops and breathtaking, barren heights rising to mountaintops far above our heads. In these raw, damp heights, watered by mist from the sea, we caught our first glimpse of storybook Africa when our roadside lunch was interrupted by a troop of baboons. They
16 dashed across the road and all around us, screaming as if they

were being attacked and glaring with expressions of arrogance and disdain.

At night, we slept in inexpensive roadside hotels, happy to find soft beds for our sore bodies. At one, the Hotel Brandwacht, in the village of Worcester, whose Dutch Reformed Church steeple seemed as high as the escarpment itself, we found a bar. Like other pubs in South Africa, it was segregated according to sex, a retreat exclusively for men. As in matters of race, attitudes toward sex seemed to have stalled in the forties or fifties. A fledgling woman's movement stirred in the cities, but the white male still ruled absolutely in the pubs of Worcester.

The Brandwacht pub was stark and masculine inside, reminiscent of blue-collar bars in my hometown of Kansas City. Three over-weight Afrikaaners sat at the bar while a lone Brit shot snooker to one side. The Afrikaaners said he was the local drunk, and humored him by getting up now and then to take a shot themselves.

A short, stocky farmer, the most gregarious of the Afrikaaners, greeted us loudly as we strolled into the pub, making fun of our cycling tights. "Ya ain't faries, are yah?" he asked. Just travelers, we said, out for a little bicycle hike. This made all three of them whoop and prompted the farmer to buy each of us a beer.

They started the conversation by asking about our trip, which got us into sports, a subject they were as keenly interested in as any American. They preferred rugby to cricket, "that English sport," which they said was for pansies. Football (soccer), they said, was all right, though not in a class with rugby. "My boy is a rugby player," said the farmer, half-drunk. "He's on the first team over in Well-ington."

After a while the discussion turned to the recent world boycott of the South African Springbok rugby team, an event that had attracted more media attention in South Africa than the daily body count. The Brandwacht men were angry and baffled by the boycott. "Ach, it's not fair to our lads to bring these sanctions against sports teams," said the second man, an auto mechanic. "They don't have nothin' to do with politics. They're just boys."

"That's right," agreed the third, a salesman. "If the Yanks or the EEC have a beef with us, they oughta take it out on the politicians, not on our lads."

The farmer shouted at Jim and me. "Why'd you Yanks do it, that's what I want to bloody know!" He spoke in a defiant, theatrical tone. "I ask you, man, why did they do it?"

"I'll tell you one reason," said Jim, feeling a little drunk and defiant himself, "because it's supposed to make you whites sit up and think about these sanctions. If the Americans want you to think hard about apartheid, isn't sports one way to get you to do it?"

"You have a point there," said the mechanic, the most evenhanded of the three. He ordered another round of beers and brandy chasers as he thought about what Jim had said. "It sure as hell made *me* notice. But, man, do you think it's really fair? We work hard. We're just average fellows, trying to raise families and make a decent wage. We got nothin' to do with this political bullshit. All I know is, these sanctions are comin' down hard on us, and I'm not just talkin' about the bloody Springboks."

"No offense to you boys," said the farmer, "but it makes me really mad when these foreigners start in with their sanctions and telling us what to do. 'Let the blacks vote!' say the liberals in America. Hell, let 'em come over here and tell us how that would bloody work."

"He's right, you know," said the mechanic. "We ain't blind. We know we got these problems. We know things ain't gonna stay the way they are forever. But I'll be damned if some pansy from America will tell me what to do. You know, the more they try to tell us what to do, the more they make us mad. They make us say, 'Hey, fuck you!' This is true, you know. Nobody likes to get orders from an outsider."

"Let me tell you," said the salesman, who had been trying to get in a word, "what these sanctions really mean. I lost a job and a wife because of this damned economy, and a lot of that is because of these goddamn do-gooders in the States who think they know what's best for us. You Yanks got this idea we're all rich over here. It just isn't so. I'm not rich. I'm selling bloody concrete bricks! I used to sell tractor trailers. There is big money in tractor trailers, but who can afford 'em now? I had to quit that line, and what happens? My wife of five years left me when the money ran out."

"Ach, she left you 'cause she was gettin' poked by another fellow," said the farmer. The salesman muttered something in Afrikaans and the mechanic and the farmer shook their heads in amusement.

They asked about blacks in America. Jim said that they were full voting citizens, protected by law from discrimination. He told them about black mayors, judges, congressmen, lawyers, doctors and businessmen.

"Then why do you hear about blacks livin' in Harlem?" asked the farmer. "Isn't it like a black township here? I bet there ain't no whites in Harlem."

"There may be a few, but not many," said Jim, the schoolteacher. I could almost see him standing in front of a classroom as he spoke. The men listened with great curiosity. "But the point is that blacks are not forced by the government to live in Harlem," said Jim. "They are there because of economics and history."

"And what about this one-man-one-vote?" asked the mechanic. "Does the black man in America have the vote?"

Jim nodded, and talked, as a good history teacher should, about the Civil War, Abraham Lincoln and the civil rights acts of the sixties.

"Well, I suppose you can afford to give 'em the vote," blurted the mechanic, "since there aren't as many of 'em as here. They're less than half of your people, right? I wish it was the same thing here. Then they'd get the vote; there'd be no problem there at all."

"Yeah, you blokes are lucky," said the farmer. "What are the blacks in the States, 'bout twenty percent? Here, *we're* twenty percent. I guess that's why you Yanks can let a few of 'em be mayors and lawyers. Here, we let one take over like that, and pretty soon they'll all be wanting to be mayor. Then the whole place'd go to hell."

I asked them why this was necessarily so, and the men thought I was joking. The farmer said blacks were uneducated and I asked why they couldn't be educated. He said because the blacks didn't want to go to school. And so the conversation went, with me asking why, and the Afrikaaners giving their answers.

"We spend good tax money on schools," said the salesman, "and they boycott 'em."

"Hell, sometimes they burn down their own schools," added the farmer. "It just don't make sense."

"But aren't you missing the point?" said Jim. "They're boycotting classes because of apartheid, not because they don't want to learn."

The mechanic rolled his eyes with exasperation. "Man, that word don't mean anything anymore. It's a dead word. Haven't you heard about Mr. Botha's reforms?"

"Cosmetics," I said. The drink was affecting me, too. "So what if blacks can sit on the same beach as a white? They're looking for basic freedoms."

"Cosmetics, the man says," groused the farmer. "I'll tell you about cosmetics. I got a little girl and another little one on the way. I ain't about to let a bunch of kaffirs take over and wreck things for my children, like they done all over the rest of Africa. This was a nice continent once, when I was a boy, back before you Americans let blacks become mayors and lawyers."

"Hear, hear," said the mechanic, "I remember driving up to Nairobi, 'bout 1960. Real nice drive, back then. Wouldn't do it now for a million U.S. dollars."

"What is it you men are so afraid of?" I asked.

"Afraid?" They all spoke at once, thinking my question was a challenge to their masculinity. "You're talkin' to three veterans of the South African Defense Forces," said the salesman. "Five years and a sergeant's rank and my share of action. All of us are soldiers. Afraid? We ain't afraid."

The air inside the bar was smoky and tense. I still had enough wits about me to know enough had been said, so I offered to buy everyone a beer. The salesman and the mechanic took the drinks, but the farmer, a stormy man with skin blotched brown by sunshine, said he was not through.

"One thing you foreigners don't understand is that we're tryin' to live here," he said, wagging a finger in my face. "Is that a fuckin' crime? You Americans carry on about the poor kaffir, but what about us? We ain't livin' like kings, yah know. You see this barkeep here? He's colored, and I'm a white. We make just about the same money— in a bad farming year, like this one, he might make more. But let me tell you the difference. That colored man gets a house on a ninety-nine-year lease for thirty rand a month.* His kids get free schooling, if they bother to go. And me? I got a thirty-year mortgage, costs me six hundred rand a month. I have loans everywhere, tryin' to keep up. On top of that, I got to pay taxes to support this colored man's thirty-rand-a-month house. Man, this is what apartheid has meant to me, supporting the likes of him while I keep paying and paying. In my eyes, it ain't fair, not at all."

"But isn't the colored man told where to live?" I said quietly, feeling this man's frustration, but unwilling to let his words go unchallenged.

"He doesn't have the vote either," added Jim, backing me up. "He doesn't have the freedoms you have."

"Fuck that," said the farmer, abruptly losing his fire and growing

---

* One rand = $.50.

weary. "I've got the freedom to go bankrupt and lose my house and family, that's what I've got."

The next morning we continued our steep ascent, moving like turtles alongside the quick waters of the Hex River. Vineyards filled these high valleys, divided by abrupt ridges of rock inhabited by baboons and swooping bateleurs. Toward the top of the escarpment, three thousand feet above Cape Town, the fertile valleys dwindled into narrow bands of malachite green in between tall bluffs of stone. We knew we were approaching the top, but the hideous incline seemed to go on forever as sweat soaked our bandannas and our legs felt like pulp being rolled through a sausage machine.

When we finally emerged onto the lip of the escarpment, we were too exhausted to go any farther. We stopped at a conveniently located trailer park, set up our tent, ate a peanut butter and jelly supper and fell asleep. Just before dawn I was awakened by a scratching noise and saw a baby-sized hand pass across our mesh window. A stack of pots outside fell with a crash. I sat up in time to see a baboon running across the park, carrying our food bag and screaming in ecstasy.

After the baboon I couldn't sleep, though Jim was still snoozing like a child. I climbed wearily outside, scrambling on hands and knees as the first streaks of ice-blue light broke over the horizon. The air was cold and smelled like frozen dew. My breath blew out as mist and the temperature turned my nose red. I assembled our small camp stove, pumped and primed it and watched it flare like a tiny bomb. I poured a tablespoon of ground Kenyan coffee into a filter— good coffee is one of my more harmless sins—and I set a percolator on the glowing yellow flame.

As I worked at simple camp tasks, the sun began to rise. Even in the low light I could smell and feel the difference between this place and the Cape. The air was drier and cleansed of the sea and the scent of earth. The wind here brushed lightly across my face, not like the heavier atmosphere down below.

As the coffee brewed and steamed, I watched the day appear in shades of violet and lavender, painted like watercolors against high, lean cirrus clouds. The sun rose slowly, pausing for a moment to bathe every rock and hill in gold. The terrain unfolded under this barrage of color and light. It was flat, expansive and arid, a lovely, barren plateau that stretches inland from the very tops of the Cape sea cliffs.

The coffee tasted as piquant as wine as I sat and stared, happy and at peace. For the first time since landing in Africa, I felt free of desperate people, desperate voices, desperate lies. It is true that I had come to see just those things, to experience life in its rawest state, but I needed these other moments of personal calm and disengagement. Cape Town, Crossroads, Lavistown, the Brandwacht bar . . . trying to make contact, for me, was an exhausting ritual.

That day I lived for bicycling, which meant I lived for the moment. Freed from the drag of the escarpment and feeling an odd power in my thighs, I sped like a wild cheetah through the empty land, a place the Bushmen called Karroo. It looked like southern Arizona, a place of space, rocks and abrupt volcanic ridges. I have always enjoyed this sort of country. Its immensity reminded me of the prairies where I grew up, those open, rolling lands where the horizon was always miles away. This sort of country brims with possibilities because it never seems to end. In its starkness is an honesty and a danger cloaked by tree limbs and underbrush in those deciduous regions where my family now lives.

Before long, the Karroo sun was a searing ball of flame, turning my skin red and raising beads of sweat. In the heat of the day the land was bereft of movement. The gerbil-like dassies and shrews we had seen earlier had taken cover in the cool shadows of the rocks, and the wind had died down to nothing. The lonely husks of wire grass stood absolutely still, knee-high stalks spreading their dead, white hairs across the rocks. This world looked so desolate and hushed it seemed desiccated, a place whittled down to its skeletal core, its flesh and blood corroded away by sun, wind and time. It had an odd, vestigial feel, a blasted antiquity where life once had flourished but then moved on.

In the Karroo one feels no resonance of life, only the absence of movement. Even a century ago great herds of wildebeest, impala and elephant roamed its ragged hills, nibbling green stalks after the annual rains and migrating north during the dry season. Humans lived here, too, though not in great numbers. This was the land of the Bushman, the short, yellow-skinned aborigine who spoke with clicks and lived constantly on the move, following the lightning in search of water and fresh game.

According to certain anthropologists, the Bushmen were one of the last peoples on earth to live in an essential harmony with the land, killing only when they needed food and using only what they needed for survival. This was a remarkable achievement if true, a life-style that modern man has been unable to rival despite theories, machines and enlightenment.

To be sure, the Bushmen had rotten teeth and bodies crawling with disease. And they produced nothing that will last—no monuments, cathedrals or palaces, although they did leave behind a few lovely, startling paintings of animals brushed on rocks. Yet they were supposed to be content, and isn't that the goal? Isn't that what all the effort at building utopias in Africa (and elsewhere) has been about?

The Karroo Bushman is now extinct, killed by guns, disease and sadness, it is said. There seems no adequate explanation for this loss. The history books talk about white and black expansion, about the coming of the modern world, and the unrelenting pressures of progress. One white African I talked to said the little yellow people simply failed to adapt to a cruel, Darwinian world, a theory still used to explain the extinction of certain American Indian tribes.

Today, a century after the Bushmen and great herds were destroyed, the Karroo has been dressed by its Caucasian masters in new clothes. Sheep and cattle roam land where eland and zebra once grazed. Scattered houses, barns and aluminum sheds rest on quiet knolls, and highways cover the earth with long strips of tar. But the biggest changes on the Karroo are the fences.

Rousseau said that the first man to fence in a piece of land, call it "mine" and believe he was right was the true founder of modern society. I wholeheartedly agree. Think of all the vexing fences, walls and barricades in the world and the troubles they have caused. We thrive on fences in the West. It is our common heritage. Fence this one in, that one out . . . throw up another barricade . . . hide behind your wall of invincibility . . . put *them* in that fence, make it like a cage . . . don't let *them* in here . . . this is *mine*, I *own* it, it is my right. . . .

There are many practical uses for fences—to keep sheep from wandering away and to prevent marauders from murdering us in our sleep. Even the Bushmen set up crude barriers and slept in trees to avoid lions, leopards and other carnivores. Yet what about these fences on the Karroo? As I biked, the shiny strands of wire marched endlessly beside the highway. I asked myself, as I pumped and breathed and sped along the road, what were these fences doing here? Keeping rocks from wandering off and dassies from murdering stalks of slumbering wire grass?

Not surprisingly, the whites we met on the Karroo were proud of their fences, built by fathers and grandfathers who killed the Bushmen, fought off the Bantu and simply said one day, "This all is mine." Pride long has been a way of life on the white Karroo. The farmers, ranchers and townfolk we met were rugged individuals who believed strongly in their efforts to domesticate this land, never doubting for an instant that they were anything but right. They seemed to say, as my own relatives used to say in Kansas, that "we've an obligation to do these things," to build fences, roads, railroads, electric plants and cities, "for us, and for our children."

Cities on the Karroo looked outwardly as American as Topeka and Wichita, with wide, cowboy-era streets filled with supermarkets, feed stores and movie houses. Victorian-era houses flanked the main streets and newer ranch houses spread like wildfire into the Karroo, each one with a garden and the glittering trademark of white South Africa: a swimming pool.

In a prosperous town named Victoria West, a sheep farmer named John Childs joined us one day for lunch in a hotel diner. He was lean, sunburned and gung ho about new irrigation schemes, dams and the latest in sheep technology. He had a great deal of pride in his little town. "Vic West is a lot like America, don't you think?" he asked in a drawl that seemed a strange mix of Yorkshire, Texas and Afrikaans. "I've recently returned from Wyoming," he added. "We sent a delegation over to check out what you Yanks are doing with your sheep." I admitted that the main street of Victoria West would not be out of place in Kansas. Childs was pleased by my response. "Man, I wish more of you blokes would come see for yourself how much we have in common," he said. "We're really just about the same."

I wondered. From the vantage point of main street Childs was right. But like many whites, he chose to ignore the fact that this was only half the story in Victoria West. Every town in South Africa, no matter how small, is actually two towns, one white and one black. And if there are any Asians or coloreds around they, too, have their own mini-dorps attached like dusty barnacles to the vibrant village of the whites.

Victoria West was no exception. The evidence was just beyond the Wimpy burger bar on the edge of town. After lunch with John Childs, I climbed onto my bike and rode down the white main street and there it was: a sprawling enclave of stark, gray huts surrounded by yet another sturdy fence, the black township.

It was typical of dozens I saw in South Africa, townships whose architecture and basic features had the unmistakable stamp of the master planner. From the Cape to the Limpopo River they had the same flavor of drab monotony, looking as if an assembly line had punched out each house from a common mold. The object seemed to be to create a *real town*, with churches, recreation halls and homes just as in the white town. But instead of ranch houses and swimming pools, the blacks inhabited bleak rows of tiny shanties bereft of decoration and greenery. They attended boxy, one-room meeting-houses instead of the soaring, contemporary chapels in the white man's towns. Their children played on concrete slabs rather than on grassy playgrounds and at football clubs. Like the apartment houses in Lavistown, the effect was oddly postindustrial and vaguely social-ist, a place designed for function.

I told Jim I was going to look around inside, and he said fine, he would ride ahead. I pushed my bike up to the gate and walked inside. Almost instantly I was surrounded by a life and vitality that belied the grayness of the master plan. Chickens, goats and dusty children swarmed around, the kids excited and chattering. Off in the distance some boys were playing soccer and some girls were singing songs. An older boy, named Stephen, about fifteen and wearing a bright blue overcoat, pushed to the front of my impromptu welcoming commit-tee and became my guide.

Stephen took hold of my free hand and held it in the warm, African style, leading me past houses arranged in rows like a mili-tary camp. Were these the thirty-rand-a-month houses the farmer at the Brandwacht bar had complained about? We passed by a commu-nity hall emblazoned with slogans that revealed two big preoccupa-tions here: VIVA ANC! and GOD IS GREAT!

I walked slowly beside Stephen, checked by the expectations and fears instilled at Crossroads and Lavistown. After three weeks in South Africa, I was keenly feeling the color of my skin. I hated myself for doing so, but how could I help it? One of the tragedies of

South Africa is that one cannot help feeling his color when he is out of his "designated area."

As we walked I was relieved by the ordinariness of life here. Near a brass tap, a woman in a bright red dress lathered and rinsed a basket of clothing. She hummed something as she worked. Nearby, a young girl hung up white sheets while holding an infant with a dangling head. On a bench in a sunny spot two men chewed biltong—salted springbok meat—and played what looked like checkers. The board was drawn in the hard ground. The pieces were bottle caps.

Stephen and I spoke as we walked, followed by a retinue of children and domestic animals. His voice was lively, quite the opposite of the resentful inmate's stereotype. He asked about my bike and about America, and his questions were detailed, concise and well thought out. He was a serious, intelligent boy, the sort who was probably good at math in school without really trying, and could explain trigonometry to his most befuddled classmate. He had bright eyes and an inquisitive demeanor.

I asked him what he studied in school. He frowned and looked down at his feet. "We do not go anymore," he said sadly, but with a trace of defiance and energy. I asked why he didn't go, remembering what the men at the Brandwacht pub had said about those "kaffirs" and their school boycotts.

"We do not go to school because of the Boer," said Stephen shyly. I sensed that he did not often talk to whites, and had never discussed this subject with any Caucasian. "They do not teach us what we want to learn. We learn the Boer's history and from his books only. We learn nothing about *our* people. The boys here say the schools are no good, that it is a place where racists lie and turn us against our people."

"Is this what you think?"

He nodded slowly, looking at the other boys following closely. "But there are some things," he whispered, "that I miss in the school. I like to read books. I read books at home now, but this is dangerous."

"Dangerous? To read books?" I exclaimed, feeling Stephen's shyness turn to anxiety. I looked at the other boys following us. A few were Stephen's age, watching me warily, boys on that razor-blade age between being children and revolutionaries.

"These boys boycott classes," said Stephen carefully. "They say to carry books is to be a sellout to the Boer."

I asked Stephen what books he read. "Charles Dickens is my

favorite," he said. "I read *Oliver Twist*, but it is very difficult. I read the easy version for children."

I told him I had some books with me and would be happy to give him one. I unzipped my handlebar bag and showed him the books I was reading at the moment: a Somerset Maugham novel and *Native Life in South Africa*, by the mixed-race writer Sol Plaatje. Stephen looked eager to finger the books, but hesitated.

"Surely, no one will mind if you look at these books?" I said, handing him Plaatje's book, which I told him was written by a member of his own race many years ago. He looked at Plaatje's picture on the back and said it would be acceptable, but Somerset Maugham was not.

"That is a white book," he said, "and I cannot read white books."

"But Dickens was white," I protested.

"I read him before, when I was in school. Now things are different. We read no white books here."

Stephen's house was in the middle of the township, painted off-white and stained by the reddish soil. An old man sat on the stoop, the boy's father. Resting in the heat, he appeared to be staring at nothing in particular, his posture uncaring and dignified with age. Perspiration rimmed his short, white hair. His head didn't turn until I said hello. He grunted, not caring one bit about a white American with a bicycle. Eventually he stood up slightly, his back bent, to touch my hand. Stephen was embarrassed. "He is old," he said. "Please forgive him."

I knelt down to look the old man in the eyes. He turned away, and I felt like an intruder. I asked him what he thought of the township. He cleared his throat.

"It is good," he muttered. "I do not complain. The government, he is good to us." I waited for more, but the man was staring at the clouds. I asked what he meant by "good" and he continued to look at the sky. "Long ago, this was a bad place. The houses were made of rocks and grass. The government, he brought us electricity and built these houses. I am an old man. I remember these things from before."

"But what about the fences?" I asked. "Do they bother you?"

"Sometimes yes, sometimes no. But I will tell you. Look at the white man. He lives behind fences, too." He smiled slightly at this insight, as if he had laid matters to rest and could now go on with his skygazing.

"Father," I said gently, using the African term of respect for elders, "are you happy here?"

"Happy?" He continued to look at the clouds.

"Yes, Father. Is this a happy place to live?"

He looked my way and said in a clear, ringing tone: "I have a house, I have a job and I have many fine children and one new grandson. These are good things. These are things that God has given me. I do not ask for happiness on this earth. Happiness is for angels in heaven."

"But what about happiness on earth? Is this possible?"

"Man, you ask too many questions. You are a white man. Why do you ask an old colored man about these things?"

"Because, Father, I want to know."

"I have told you," he said. "Happiness is in heaven, after we die."

He turned away again, but I had one further question. In America, I said, we tended to hear the views of those blacks who shout the loudest for the television cameras. I asked him what he thought of this unrest.

He looked hard into my face, his watery eyes peering at me for the first time with intensity. "Ach, now this is a bad thing. These young boys with this necklace.* These boys who are acting like criminals. They say they are trying to help me, but they do not know me. I am a man. I am a Christian. I tell you, they do not know me. I want no part of their crimes. I have a job."

"Do you wish the black man could vote?"

"Man, why do you talk nonsense?" He turned away. "I want no vote and no trouble. I want to be left in peace."

I asked no more questions, taking this as a cue to leave. As I pushed my bike toward the highway, Stephen took hold of my arm. His eyes were deep set and calm, yet his next words were intense, spoken low. He shooed away the younger children.

"Because you are American, I want you to know." His voice was as soft as a growl. "Man, my father is old," said Stephen. "He has a job. He has children. He does not understand. I have no job. I cannot go to school. I am told what to do by the Boer. What can I do? I have

---

* The "necklace" is an automobile tire doused in gasoline and ignited while around a victim's neck.

nothing to do. My friends have no work. So many boys are angry about this. We are angry at the Boer. We think that we must fight."

"You are angry about no jobs?"

"We are angry about everything," he said, though his eyes looked more sad than angry. "Angry about how the Boer has treated us. Our leaders, they talk about pride and dignity."

"And you believe you must fight?"

"Yes," he said slowly, as if he had thought a great deal about this. He seemed much more serious than a child ought to be, and I noticed that he did not mindlessly repeat slogans like other young revolutionaries. In Stephen, I saw a future intellectual, a thinker and possibly a leader. But what sort of leader? One with vision? Or an angry, disillusioned revolutionary? These were his formative years, the years when he and quiet boys like him were being shaped and molded by bitter experience. In the end, I think, boys such as Stephen will decide the future of South Africa, although it is still unclear whether they will act as warriors, madmen or agents of peace.

4 The Karroo outside the townships was a pleasant place for a white traveler, although the cycling, as we expected, was hardly challenging. As always, it was good to be close to the earth, though the earth here didn't speak very loudly, its history largely erased. The harshness and the mystery of the land were deceptive in this tame place.

I saw traces of Bushmen blood in colored faces, in the yellowish skin of a boy with a spinning top and in the lean frames of workers replacing steel sleepers on the rail line. Springbok occasionally appeared dancing across the hills, raised by farmers to shoot for sport and as a source for biltong.

Otherwise, the earth was still. I might truly have despaired had it not been for the birds that Jim frequently pointed out. No fence could stop the yellow-billed kites soaring on hot puffs of air, or the steppe buzzards crying "kreeee." In the morning Karroo larks hopped about on the stony ground, singing and chirping. Later a pair of lilac-breasted rollers would sense two cyclists and flee from perches on telephone wires, their brilliant coloring ablaze in the sunlight.

Unfortunately we could not fly, so we had to contend with those abominable fences. On breaks, we leaned our heavy bikes against them, drinking cool water from our bike bottles and munching peanuts and chocolate. At first, we tried to climb the barbed wire to see the land close up, but the fences were built tough. Further dissuasion came from ostriches. Farmers put these primitive birds on their land because they will go out of their way to attack human intruders with powerful, talon-tipped feet. They also attack the farmers, who have learned to grab the birds by their necks as they charge. This apparently immobilizes them, if you are lunatic enough to try it.

Fences were particularly annoying at night. As the sun set we looked longingly at the vast landscapes, marveling at them and wishing we could get inside. It was maddening that in all that space we were forced to camp on the narrow strip of Karroo alongside the highway. Sometimes we found picnic spots, but they weren't much better. About twenty-five yards wide, they typically consisted of two concrete tables and benches, a trash barrel, three or four sickly trees planted by the highway authorities and a sign: KEEP SOUTH AFRICA TIDY. At night we locked up the bikes with cables around fence posts. In the morning we used the fences as clotheslines to dry our dew-soaked tent.

Occasionally, we had visitors to our camps, people of the road. Truckers driving goods in powerful Mercedes rigs stopped and gave us cold beers. A busload of born-again Christians shared apples, candy bars and evangelical tracts written by Jimmy Swaggart, who had recently preached hellfire and raised cash in a Johannesburg stadium rally. There were still Swaggart posters pasted on telephone poles and concrete walls around the country, with a picture of Jimmy looking afflicted by the sins of the universe.

One evening a colored family in a mule-drawn wagon arrived at our picnic-stop camp. Constructed out of weathered planks, leather shock absorbers and automobile tires, the buggy-sized vehicle carried Jonathan Abrahams, his wife and two small children. A canvas tarp partially covered a mattress, table and vinyl trunks, everything they owned. It was an unusual sight on the slick, modern highway, blending not only past and present, but First and Third World.

Abrahams was small and his face flat and yellow like the Bushmen, whose ancient blood still swims in many South Africans. He smoked tobacco and dried roots rolled in newspaper while his wife arranged their camp opposite us in the picnic site. She tethered the two mules to our friend the fence and strapped cloth food bags over their ears. She lit a fire near a concrete table erected for Caucasians' picnic lunches. While I boiled dried vegetables and spaghetti on our camp stove, Mrs. Abrahams steamed a batch of mashed corn in a kettle.

Abrahams did not help his wife. This is the tradition in Africa, where women from time immemorial have performed domestic duties and men were hunters, warriors and storytellers. If we suddenly had fallen backward in time a century or two, and this picnic stop and highway had disappeared, Abrahams might have been returning from a hunt at this time of day, dragging a dead roan or gazelle hanging from a carved acacia pole, the beast's body still warm. Abrahams and his band of hunters would have been laughing and bragging about their roles in the kill, and singing poems to the spirit of the animal.

But Abrahams, born in the twentieth century of mixed blood, knew little or nothing about this sort of hunt. He was a farm laborer, trading his skills for a few rand, a hut and food for his family. Undoubtedly, he would laugh at my romantic Western fantasies about hunts and spirit poems. "I prefer this present to that past," he would say. But the present did not leave Abrahams with much to do on this night.

I wondered what he saw as he took long, thoughtful puffs. Did he see the beauty that I saw in the sunset and the stars? Did the cooling air feel exhilarating on his face? Could he know the confusions of living in a city, of war, of this desperate century? What did he think about? What did he know that I had no inkling of?

Abrahams was shy with us, partly because he spoke little English. After we each finished our suppers Jim and I asked him to come over for a sip of brandy. He invited us to sit around his fire, an African tradition we would enjoy many times on this journey. We got comfortable in front of the blaze as the night became cold. Fire was a salve for a biker disoriented by fences on the Karroo. It brightened my eyes and opened up the night. Above us, billions of stars shone, points of fire so plentiful they meshed into veins of light.

I remembered something Laurens van der Post once wrote about the Bushmen and the stars. To the Bushmen, the stars were the greatest of hunters, having "heart in plenty." At night, they believed the stars called their prey, making quite a racket as they hunted. According to a Bushman van der Post once knew, whose tribe is distinct from the lost Bushmen of the Karroo, the calls sound like *Tssik* and *Tsa* . . . *Tssik* and *Tsa* . . . van der Post, an Afrikaaner in his eighties, was raised on a farm north of the Karroo. He claimed that he, too, could hear the calls of the stars when he really stopped to listen. But he grew up in the old Boer tradition of living close to the land, a member of a race who called themselves "Africans" long before apartheid and suburban repasts, a people who lived, themselves, like ancient nomads in their earliest years.

I watched the stars and strained to listen for the *Tssik* and the *Tsa*, but all I could hear was the roar of silence and millions of distant crickets. To me, there was no *Tssik* and *Tsa* and no hunter's call. Why could I not hear it? For a moment I feared that the loss of the Bushmen might have killed the *Tssik* and the *Tsa* all together. But as the night wore on, I realized it was me. Growing up in a modern house with its cacophony of televisions, telephones and stereos, my ears were simply not attuned to the wavelength of *Tssik* and *Tsa*.

Perhaps something in my sensory perception had been lost from ancient times, when the skies were young and filled with magic. Perhaps I have paid a price for my knowledge, for my inability to believe without question and without analysis. For instance, I know that stars are concentrations of fusing gases compressed into balls of energy. I have studied physics and astronomy and have read about great telescopes that have identified and classified thousands of stars. I have entire libraries of information at my fingertips, containing theories, formulas and explanations. But what have these achievements meant? They have provided us with certain answers, many more questions and endless anxieties, all of which have drowned out the *Tssik* and the *Tsa*.

Sitting with us around the fire, Abrahams accepted our cheap brandy as if it were gold. He explained in simple English that he was a farmer traveling to a new job on a white man's farm. "I be no working many months," he said. "I hungry. Family hungry."

"How far have you come?"

"Many kilometers. One hundred. We go more. We go to work at this farm. It take many days."

I marveled at Abrahams's bravery. This was a significant expedition for his family, a grueling, Old World migration away from one life to another. It was a journey from a different time and space, something virtually impossible for me to comprehend. What motivated him? Did his movement have anything to do with that thin blood linking him to the past? Did he have anything of the nomad left in his genes after several generations of largely sitting still?

Abrahams would shake his head at my musings, offering more practical reasons for his trek, such as drought, unemployment and South Africa's diminished economy. As far as I knew he hated the idea of moving at all and preferred the security of a job and a laborer's hut beside a white man's farm.

I tried to ask more questions, but was frustrated by the barrier of language. In the end this was just as well, because the peaceful circle around the fire was not really a place for talking. It was a haven to contemplate the flames and try to listen for hunters in the sky.

5 Most of the road people we passed were black, families toting hoes and bundles of greens, young blacks in army uniforms waiting for buses and couples dressed for outings on their buggies. This was a slow, languid world baking slowly in the sun, something like what the Deep South might have looked like to Huck Finn floating down the Mississippi. Yet there was a darker side to these languid days, as there was for Huck and Jim. One Saturday afternoon a black man tried to grab my arm as I rode past. Drunk to oblivion, he leaped in front of me and tried to take a swing. Instinctively, I pushed him away. Like a rag doll he rolled down into a ditch, where he remained still.

"Baas, please, my friend not mean to hurt you," pleaded a slightly less inebriated friend, whose breath stank of *daga*—African hemp. "Man, do not call the police. He has a wife and many little children. They will take him away."

"Take him where?"

"To jail, man, what do you think?"

"But he didn't do anything."

"Hey, man," he said incredulously, realizing I was foreign and his friend was probably safe, "where you from, anyway?"

We seldom saw whites outside their towns. They shot past in autos and stood behind counters in gas stations and country stores. Far off the highway, down dusty side roads, we saw their houses and farms— cool, green clumps of trees standing out like oases on the Karroo. Each farm seemed like a tiny castle of serenity in this lunar kingdom, purely Western-looking outposts proclaiming the ethos of the Caucasian pioneer: independence, hard work and self-sufficiency.

The familiarity of this place, its attitudes, architecture and folklore, continued to make me feel uneasy. The pioneer, to most of my countrymen, is inexorably part of the American national identity. It is a major figment of our mythology, the settler slogging through the prairies leading a team of oxen; the homesteader hacking out a farm, a ranch, a city, a factory; and the more modern version of the pioneer as a tough entrepreneur struggling against the odds.

34

These are *our* myths, and yet they also are claimed by the whites of South Africa as theirs, a paradox. For here in South Africa, World Opinion has ordained that these myths are suspect, tarnished, evil. Yet how can this be? Are the same set of myths good in one place and evil in another?

Apartheid hung over South Africa like a shroud, affecting every observation, making it troublesome simply to say, "Look, there is a farm, and there is a farmer." There always seemed to be a further set of questions to ask. Is that farmer in favor of apartheid? Is he tainted because he has taken no action against it? Can we judge him so summarily?

These are not merely the idle questions of a traveler in a foreign land. This was not, say, India, where a sensitive Western traveler dutifully reports on issues that seem compelling, but remain somehow distant from his own experience. These Karroo people were drawn from the same stock as my own in America. Their ancestors got on their boats from the same docks in Europe and set out with nearly identical goals. Their grandfathers fought similar struggles, against natives and wild country, and their fathers felt the same pride as ours when their conquest seemed complete. "I used to watch cowboy movies when I was a boy," a middle-aged Anglo rancher told me. "John Wayne, Jimmy Stewart, Randolph Scott, Joel McCrea . . . you know, mate, these were my heroes. Wasn't till I was about fifteen or sixteen that I focused on the fact these movies were about America and not South Africa. Though I'd always thought Joel McCrea had an odd accent for a Scotsman."

Take, for instance, Hennie Bloem, a sheep farmer we stayed with near Victoria West. Bloem had all the basic ingredients of an American myth, the sort of slice-of-life subject that *Time* magazine might feature in its "American Scene" section, or that Charles Kuralt might include on his "On the Road" program. Bloem was a farmer who had struggled mightily, had won a measure of success and was struggling still. He was in his late fifties, a rugged, handsome man born during the Depression on a small farm in the Orange Free State, the great-great-grandson of a Huguenot pioneer. His ancestors had trekked by covered wagon from Cape Town to flee what they considered British tyranny and had fought like characters out of a Zane Grey novel to settle a new land. Bloem himself had at an early age left his poor and backward family farm and had become the first in his family to get a college education. He had joined the postwar rush into the cities, had married, had two daughters and had found work as an electrical contractor. But farming remained in his blood. For over twenty years he saved his money and, in 1975, bought ten thousand acres of the Karroo and set up a farm raising several hundred merino sheep.

Bloem would have had a good presence on TV. We met him as he was exercising a flock of homing pigeons beside a silver-aluminum birdhouse. The sun had burned his face and arms a permanent hazel brown. Broad wrinkles were etched across his cheeks. He had a powerful build, but patient eyes. He was what a TV producer would call a "strong, sensitive type."

Jim and I pedaled up his driveway late one day to ask permission to camp on his property. We were met by two young blacks in tattered clothes. They led us to the "house of birds," although it was awhile before Bloem noticed us, absorbed as he was in every movement of his birds. When he whistled them home they returned instantly to their cages, and he gingerly picked one up and expertly inspected its wings. Satisfied all was well, he let the pigeon go on a solo flight, a smile fitting neatly into creases around his mouth. When he finally saw us he insisted that we stay with him and his wife in their small farmhouse. "It's not often we get visitors out here," he said. "Why don't you just make yourselves at home?"

Bloem called his small ranch Tobakka Fontein. He gave us a tour of the grounds around the house. He showed us the barns, a small vegetable garden and the three small bungalows where his black laborers were housed in stark, but comfortable accommodations. As we walked he told us a little about the history of Tobakka, saying it was originally part of a two-hundred-thousand-acre ranch settled by a Boertrekker family in the 1830s. Bloem had purchased his portion of the old ranch from the original settler's grandson, an eighty-year-old living in Victoria West.

Bloem took us to the edge of his *fontein*—"place of springs"—and pointed out an ancient pear tree growing out of an even older stump. "This tree was grafted a hundred years back," Bloem explained, "by the old man's mother when she married. Her family gave her Tobakka because it was supposed to be the worst piece of land on the ranch. You see, she went an' married an Englishman. Back then, just before the Anglo-Boer war, that was like marrying the devil himself." He showed us the old Tobakka homestead behind his newer brick-

and-mortar home. The old home had no embellishments, just a simple coat of white plaster over Karroo-baked bricks. Bloem said it would have been preceded by a sod hut and then a rough stone shack. He wet his finger and rubbed the plaster, revealing a date on a brick: 1840. "Man, that was a long time ago," he said with his photogenic grin.

We continued to trudge about on the farm, listening to Bloem's slow, gravelly voice. Tobakka Fontein seemed light-years away from the unrest in the cities, from riots, bigotry and daily body counts. The main topics of conversation here were not apartheid nor politics, but the weather and the failing farm economy.

I could imagine, if this were indeed a piece for "On the Road," Charles Kuralt gently leading Bloem into the sad topics of the recession and the dry times. Kuralt would then ponder the possibility of a way of life being threatened and would show his famous empathy for a stalwart man pitted against the vagaries of the Fates. I could see the piece in my mind, with Kuralt and Bloem as they walked across his parched ranch, the crags and valleys serving as a dramatic backdrop for television.

This was the setting for one of Bloem's talks with Jim and me. He drove us in a pickup to the highest point on his land, an eroded rock ridge overlooking a dry, scarred river valley whose bed had been bone-dry for three years. Sheep with black faces hugged the ridges, picking at football-sized shrubs and flaxen-colored grass. When we arrived Bloem plucked a piece of grass out of the dry soil, rubbed it between two fingers and shook his head.

"Look at this," he said, "just a dry, dead stalk. Man, I don't know what we are going to do with this drought. It's been five years. This year we've had four inches of rain. Four inches only! Normally it's fourteen or fifteen inches by now."

Through a set of binoculars he scanned the hills, saying the cover was getting sparser. "We can't win in a drought like this." He sighed, kneeling down to feel the arid soil. "This keeps up, I'll have to round up the sheep and feed 'em store-bought mealies. That's bloody expensive. I make nothin' on the wool if I do that."

Bloem told us in a confidential tone that he was in trouble financially. "I don't want my wife to know," he said, "but I'm in debt up to my neck. We all are out here. We keep borrowing against the good year that never comes. I got two daughters in college, and mortgages, and the fellows who work for me. And on top of the drought we've got this recession, and all of this talk about foreigners boycotting our wool." He took a suck of his cigarette. "I've got a daughter studying agricultural sciences at university. I've always thought I'd leave the farm to her and her man, when she's married. Now I wonder if it will be here when the time comes."

At this point our "On the Road" segment would probably have drawn to a close if this were America, with Kuralt giving one of his well-known concluding comments about a man facing a dilemma with dignity and hard work. "It is a truly American saga," he would say with seriousness and compassion. Then there would be a long, thoughtful pause ... "This is Charles Kuralt reporting, on the road in ..."

But this was not America, and here in South Africa it is not enough simply to describe a man and his difficulties. Kuralt's audience would have demanded more. The central issue here was not recession or drought, but where this man sat on apartheid. Was he for morality or against it? Was he a bigot, a devil, a reactionary?

These are questions that we seldom ask ourselves, yet demand of a man like Bloem. But it didn't matter, because politics was on his mind anyway. Bloem, too, was preoccupied by this thing, this apartheid. He saw it as yet another large, unfathomable force threatening his existence as surely as did the lack of rain.

What was Bloem's opinion? Was he, like Rolf Swart, denying that there was a problem? Did he agree with the government, that the problem was something that could be contained with bullets and police dogs? Actually, he approached the unrest fairly straight on. In several conversations during our brief stay—over dinner with his quiet wife, while in his pickup truck, while walking on his land—he outlined his beliefs and fears, making it clear that he was deeply disturbed about apartheid, a surprising attitude for an old Boer farmer, stereotype of reactionary politics in South Africa. Here was an Afrikaaner calling the government a "pack of fools" for clinging to the old ways, saying that iron-fisted discrimination was "criminal" and was ruining the country.

I do not want to overstate Bloem's aversion to apartheid. He was certainly not about to embrace blacks as equal citizens, and he was disturbed about the prospect of a black government. Bloem was not of the black-boot school of big-time apartheid. His bias was the sort common in America before the civil rights war of the sixties, a bias of deep-seated attitudes and petty prerogatives. Yet nothing seemed hard and fast for Bloem in these troubled times, not even his prejudice. He was in a curious state of flux, reflecting a basic intelligence and willingness to bend if the wind became strong enough. Many of his assumptions about race appalled me, but it was this willingness to bend, to discuss change that I found compelling about Bloem. He had already crossed a line that few of his brethren seemed willing to cross. If he is not alone, then perhaps there is yet hope for South Africa.

"I'm terribly ashamed of what my countrymen have done," he explained as we ate a dinner of boiled meat and soggy potatoes, "the way we have dehumanized the blacks, treating them like cattle with these apartheid laws. Believe me, apartheid exists here, it surely does, and it has been a mistake. The problem is, how do you change this thing? How do you make it right? Apartheid has been going on all of these years; it cannot be changed overnight. This is the problem here.

"Let me tell you," he continued in a steady voice, "I have thought often about this, and I have come to believe that it is morally right and Christian to allow the blacks to have the vote. But they can't be allowed to run the country, not yet anyway. It's a matter of education and seeing where each of us fits in. At this present moment, these chaps working for me would run this farm into the ground. They would wreck everything. They might be able to run this farm someday, I'm not going to deny that. But it must be done slowly. If we are going to have a modern country and avoid going back to the Dark Ages, blacks must be modernized."

I asked him if he thought the government was committed to modernizing blacks. "I pray they are," he sighed, "but who really knows? Man, we have waited so long. It's a vicious cycle, because even if the government is committed, these black children don't trust them. They don't even go to school anymore. Man, this is bad. They must go to school if they are going to break out of this."

I told Bloem about my conversation with Stephen in Victoria West, about his complaints that the curriculum is stilted toward an Afrikaaner view of the world.

"I wasn't aware of that," answered the farmer. "They teach no native history?"

"That's the boy's complaint."

"That's regrettable," he said, pondering this information for a moment. "But it really doesn't matter. Even if the classes are a bit biased, they still need the education. If they are going to live in this country and advance, they need to learn. But many of these boys do not have even a desire to go to school. They have no goals, other than to do a job for a day. Those boys you saw by the birdhouse today, they have run away from school. I'm trying to chase them back. I drove them back last week, now they're here again. They whine and say they want to work. You watch 'em when we go outside. They'll be working like all get out, trying to prove their worth. Man, it's frustrating. They should be in school."

"But what incentive do they have?" I asked. "Right now the law doesn't even allow a black man to own this farm. If I were one of these black boys, I would be more likely to be interested in school if I thought it might mean a farm of my own. When you know the best you can do is become a simple laborer, it's difficult to . . ."

"Man, I have no argument with that," said Bloem, "except to say that it has to be done real slowly. I have no problem with these boys coming up someday and offering me money for my farm, provided they have the education to understand the finances and the science of sheep farming."

"Have you ever told them that?"

"No." He frowned. "Man, it seems so unlikely at this point, I would be a fool to go and tell them the farm might be theirs someday. That would really do me in. They would never work again. No, it's going to take some time."

Just before we left Bloem, he took us once again out on his ranch. We joined him as he searched for a lost sheep. He didn't say much, having already, I suppose, said far more than he was normally inclined to. Yet at one point he stopped on a high point on a ridge, standing in the hot sun, his eyes absorbing the sky and the land.

"I sometimes wonder," he said in a low voice, "if all that is happening is a part of some grand plan. There is this book called *A Dry, White Season*. Have you heard of it? It's written by a South African. Well, I've never read it, but I have thought about the title and wondered if it doesn't fit, if we whites have done something terribly wrong and we're being punished for it. But, really, I don't believe this. I am not a religious fellow; I mean I don't go to church. But I do believe in God, and I believe that He tests us all the time. He makes some years good, and some years bad. This is the way life is. It's in the Bible. And man, you know, it's up to us to be up to His challenge."

Unfortunately, Bloem was an exception among the Boer farmers we stayed with in rural South Africa. Typically, we would ride up their long, winding roads and knock on their doors, asking if we could camp on their land. Almost always, they initially behaved like Bloem, inviting us to stay in their houses and share their meals. But the conversations and basic attitudes were much closer to the stereotype of the stubborn Boer. Like Bloem, they tended to view the unrest as just one of myriad problems, although, unlike Bloem, they made a point of strongly defending the status quo. I was reminded of a description Mark Twain made in 1897 in *More Tramps Abroad:*

He is deeply religious; dull, obstinate, bigoted; uncleanly in his habits; hospitable, honest in his dealings with whites, a hard master to his black servant; a lover of political independence, a good husband and father; not fond of herding together into towns, but liking the seclusion and remoteness ... and silence of the veldt; proud of his race's achievements in South Africa ...

In my encounters with rural Boers I found Twain's description still true. However, most Afrikaaners are now as sensitive about cleanliness as Americans; they also are rich, and they have a great deal more to fear.

This fear seemed at first glance to be buried deep out in the countryside. However, if one looked closely, there were blatant signs of nervousness—barbed-wire fences, pistols bulging under jackets and a plethora of large guard dogs that terrorized us on the bikes. And, if one looked even closer, there were more frightening undercurrents swarming beneath the surface of tranquillity, dark, ominous moods that one had to experience to comprehend truly.

Late one afternoon, at the end of a particularly exhausting day of cycling, we were looking for a campsite. It was getting late, and the fences were particularly constricting, affording only a meter or two of open land between the pavement and the barbs. This was toward the end of our South African sojourn, and Jim and I were terribly weary of this daily search for a piece of land on which to pitch a tent, it being beyond belief that so much wire could be stretched across this country.

As the sun began to fall we came to a driveway, where we stopped to scratch our heads. Did we want to turn toward that farmhouse on the hill? Could we tolerate another discussion about the weather and cheeky blacks? These visits, though initially interesting, were becoming tedious.

As we turned up the gravel path, all I could think of was my rubbery legs and an overwhelming desire to sleep. I hoped the farmer would not prove overly talkative. I saw that this farm looked like the usual little fleck of paradise on the veldt—the cool, green lawn, the blossoms and the black boys hanging about on the edges. When the farmer reached out a massive, sunburned hand to greet me, I expected this stop would be more or less like all the rest.

The farmer's name was Tom Greig. He had a compelling personal story, not unlike Hennie Bloem's and thousands of other Afrikaaners. They had come from similar roots, in Greig's case a poor farm in the Transvaal. Like Bloem, he had gone to college, lived in town for a while and then returned to the land. He had saved his money and bought a tractor business in a small town on the northern veldt. He lived nearby in a rented farmhouse.

The Greigs seemed nice enough when we arrived. They reminded me a great deal of my own family in Kansas. The land here was similar—we were now on the veldt north of the Karroo, where fields of corn, wheat and beans spread across the country. The Greigs' house was something like mine growing up, with the same appliances and comfortable furniture. A color television stayed on nearly all the time, whether or not it was being watched. Tom Greig even had two boys two years apart, like my brother and me.

Yet everything was not blissful for the Greigs. They were in even worse financial distress than Hennie Bloem, and it was this topic that dominated the conversation at dinner, served soon after Jim and I arrived. Apparently, the tractor store was near bankruptcy, a point that clearly distressed Tom Greig, who probably would have preferred to discuss something else in front of strangers. But Mrs. Greig, a lively, round woman with the tongue of a gossip, would not let the topic go. She did almost all of the talking, since Jim and I were too exhausted to do much more than chew and keep our eyes open.

"Five years ago," she spoke as the rest of us half-listened, "when Tom bought the store, farming around here was booming. We did very well. Then came the drought. But around here, we're optimistic by nature. We bought up inventory for three years and sold everything on credit. Man, the drought is still going, and this recession, and those bloody boycotts. Nobody can afford to pay us back." She rattled on, the type of person who seldom takes a breath. "The farmers are struggling to stay afloat. We can't give away tractors. We have been surviving off selling parts and repairs, but even those are slacking off. People are beginning to wait longer for parts to save money, and they're patching things up best they can."

Finally, Mrs. Greig paused. Her husband seized the moment to switch the conversation to more pleasant family matters. He asked his elder son about college and his twelve-year-old about the soccer team at school. This sort of talk continued after supper when we moved into the den, leaving the dishes so we wouldn't miss the latest episode of "Dallas." Mrs. Greig served ice cream and, during lulls in the action, she and the boys quizzed us about American television— the new programs, stars and rather detailed questions about game shows, most of which we couldn't answer, not being big television people.

After "Dallas," we menfolk settled into the living room for an after-dinner beer. Greig sat back in an overstuffed chair and lit up a cigarette, a handsome man with feathery eyebrows, deep-set eyes and a sturdy chin, the profile of an astronaut or a Marine colonel. (He was an officer in the SADF reserves.) His arms were strong, his muscles firm from hard work.

I sat down feeling content after my hot meal and looking forward to sleeping in a real bed after several days in a sleeping bag on the hard ground. I was enjoying my half-drunk, half-exhausted state, and found myself getting annoyed when Greig began to talk about the bloody weather and the economy. Soon, I thought, if my luck held, I would have to suffer through another dissertation on reactionary politics.

"It's true what my wife said about the tractor store," Greig was saying, having warmed up to us since dinner. "We'll have to sell the business soon, or we'll go bankrupt. Man, the prices just keep going up. Two years ago a new tractor went for twenty-five thousand rand. This year it's fifty-two thousand! How can anyone afford an increase like that?"

"It's ridiculous!" agreed his wife, who was clearing off the table nearby.

Greig looked at her and stroked his chin, as if he knew it was useless to attempt getting a word in edgewise. When she returned to the kitchen he continued, going into considerable detail about his company and the political situation, as if he had no one to talk to but strangers. As he talked, his words became more harried and intense as he worked himself up. "I sometimes ask myself why this is happening," he said, his voice turning into a whispered hiss, a disturbing noise for a quiet, family man in his own den. "I don't believe for a minute it's coincidence." His voice was now very low. I leaned forward so that I wouldn't miss whatever he had to say. "It's a conspiracy, that's what it is." He paused to let this sink in. "You Americans have no idea what is going on here. These blacks are being organized by the Communists. They give 'em guns and ammo. The Communists already have most of Africa, and look at how they've destroyed everything. Now they're after our goldfields and mines."

This opinion was nothing new in South Africa. Rolf Swart had said essentially the same thing. But Greig's tone and countenance were different from the smug Swart's. They were laced with a fiery bitterness.

I asked him how he knew it was a conspiracy, and he said he had heard the details in a speech by Terry Blanche, leader of the Afrikaaner Resistance Movement (called AWB, after its Afrikaans name). I should have guessed that he had not come up with these notions on his own, that he was mouthing the hateful words of South Africa's leading white supremacist. (The AWB has a small but vocal membership, numbering only about fifty thousand in a white population of five million, but their ideas are shared by many more sympathizers such as Greig who are not members—farmers, blue-collar workers and other whites demoralized by recession and distrustful of the most cosmetic reforms.)

Greig recently had attended an AWB meeting led by the charismatic Blanche. Listening to the neo-Nazi leader rail on about conspiracies and pride, Greig had absorbed the AWB's populist, bigoted notions as his own. They fit neatly into his own fears and offered a tidy scapegoat for failures that he refused to blame on himself, fate or whatever dark, unfathomable forces are at work in his country.

"Blanche spoke to us about being proud of our Afrikaaner heritage," Greig said. "He said that people overseas are trying to make us out to be criminals. Well, they're wrong. I'm damn proud of my country and my people. We came here and settled this land. It was just a bunch of naked heathens here before that—you know, the Bible in one hand and a rifle in the other. We fought like hell. It was a matter of survival then, and still is. We will never give up!"

He went on in that hissing voice. "The kaffir is incapable of doing anything beyond menial work," he explained. "Oh, some of them can do better, maybe one in a million, or possibly two in a million. I like this president in Bop,* although I've been told he has a little white blood in him, so that may explain why he's so civilized. But he is an exception. In general, it's a waste of time to do anything to raise the black. What we are doing now is half-educating them, which makes them think they know more than they can ever know. They think they can do more than they are capable of. We would all be better off if the black remained stupid."

He was ranting now, so I just sat back and listened. He called the Botha regime a "pack of sellouts." "They are giving away everything," he bellowed, "all of the gains we Afrikaaners fought for with our blood for all of these years. Have they forgotten the wars we fought? If they aren't man enough to stand up to these blacks, they should stand aside and let the army and police handle it. They know what to do. Clean up those radical blacks. Get tough, man. If the government doesn't soon, the army may do it anyway, without Botha's permission."

I finally broke in, interjecting what I thought was a rather critical point of logic. "But aren't you concerned about the population difference?" I asked. "My God, man, it's six to one against the whites."

Greig looked at me as if I were some sort of fool, and didn't answer for several moments. Then he opened his mouth and slowly said the following words: "Yes, of course, that is a problem, but there's a simple solution. You shoot the lot of them. Even up the population, make sure there are no more of them than there are of us. . . ."

"I know what you are thinking," he said. "That this sounds like the Nazis and the Jews. But this is different. This is survival I'm talking about. It's us or them."

As he kept talking, I became fixated on his eyes. Here I saw the cold passion of a man driven to the brink of madness, the colorless

---

* "Bop" is the pronounceable nickname of Bophuthatswana, a native reservation that became a so-called independent country in 1980 recognized only by South Africa. Its first and present president is Lucas Manyane Mangope, considered a sellout by most blacks.

savagery that lurks deep down in every human being, but is usually held in check.

"We're ready for the fight," Greig continued. "Do you want to see how ready we are?" He got up and headed down a hallway. I followed and watched as he opened a locked closet. Inside was a gun rack holding three automatic rifles and several hunting rifles. He had carefully wrapped pistols in plastic bags on the floor and stacked crates of ammunition neatly on steel shelves. Greig pointed out a box of grenades on the top shelf and four gas masks with spare cartridges. Bulletproof vests hung from a rack in the back.

"All the farmers out here are armed," he said. "We all know what's coming. This place is going to be a bloody Armageddon."

6   The Orange was the first river with water we saw in drought-stricken South Africa. A dark, textured band of green stood up against the desert on either bank, a ribbon of life after the Karroo. Little egrets buzzed the shallows. Below the highway bridge Jim sited a malachite kingfisher scanning the blue-orange water. For nearly an hour we watched, marveling at his concentration. He finally dove in headfirst and emerged with a squirming fish, an ancient rite of killing and survival observed.

That day we lived for biking, racing toward the North Cape and, in a few days, black Africa. We were lean, our skin hardened and tan. It was a glorious day, with bateleurs and lilac-breasted rollers filling fields with specks of color. Not far from the river the land began to change from the Karroo desert to savannah bush. Tawny grasses began to cloak the rocky ground. Violet blossoms with yellow, nickel-sized stamens grew in profusion by the road. We saw for the first time a trademark of Africa: scattered acacias with flat tops and horizontal branches. This was a battle line of sorts, drawn between the desert and the grasslands. Actually, it's more of a slow rout, since the desert is clearly winning.

That night we erected our tent beside the broken porch of a large, abandoned farmhouse. We locked the bikes inside a broken chicken coop. The usual gardens and trees had died, their husks littering the vacant yard. The place felt dead, the house long ago painted red and white, now peeled and veined with cracks. The seasons had rusted farm machinery and crushed the windmill's slats. Africa is littered with similar ruins—colonial-era mansions, farmhouses and factories collapsing into the bush. However, this sort of abandonment was unusual in the tidy confines of South Africa. Was this house a victim of the drought? Was it a harbinger of things to come?

We set up our camp in the usual way, with our portable stove fired up to cook cold meat pies. After coffee, we took a long walk, hoping to get a good sighting of Halley's comet. We happened to be in South Africa at the time of peak sightings. Tonight was a "five" night—the best. In 1910 Halley's came so close to earth that it became visible in   47 daylight. The world watched in awe, with fanatics claiming it was the end of the world.

In 1986, Halley's was neither apocalyptic nor awesome. It appeared in the early evening as a smudge near the eastern horizon, a tremendous disappointment. Astronomers explained that this year Halley's was farther out than seventy-six years ago and was facing our planet head-on, which obscured the long, dazzling tail. Yet even this was an omen to some. I met one Afrikaaner who claimed the comet's lackluster appearance was a bad sign for whites in South Africa. "Even the damn stars are against us," he sighed.

A few days later, the Karroo faded completely into the southern African prairies, a land of dry, brittle savannah and bush that would dominate the landscape for most of my African journey. In May, it was nearly winter in the Southern Hemisphere, and people waited anxiously for the coming of the annual rains. For five years these rains had failed or had sputtered in brief, violent, nearly waterless storms. Unfortunately, this year the soothsayers and weathermen expected more sputtering and little relief.

However, one afternoon the usually clear skies became grizzly and overcast as black clouds gathered above the expanses. The fields of grass and corn and wheat began fluttering in a cool, uncertain wind that made my bare legs shiver. It was the sort of wafting temperature—hot and cold—that forces a biker to take a pullover on and off every few minutes. Coming from the Midwest, I recognized the sky signs as the day blackened like nighttime and the birds disappeared. I kept an eye out for a building or a farm for shelter, but none appeared. Jim and I often rode far apart, and today he was at least a mile ahead. On his bike was the tent, our only shelter.

The storm began as storms do on the American prairies, with the wind suddenly growing still and giant droplets splattering. I kept pedaling, shifting into my highest gears, hoping I'd catch Jim and the tent. Lightning flashed and thunder cracked. I thought of the Bushmen, who in ancient times spent most of the dry season searching for lightning, which signals the direction of the coming rains. Even among the rural Afrikaaners lightning was traditionally a holy thing, a force of nature to be feared and respected. However, this particular lightning was getting a bit too close. The crashes were deafening, as if God was hurling together great pieces of metal and then, as the noise echoed across the waves of grassland, He seemed to be crinkling the metal as a human would crinkle wastepaper.

The pace of the rain quickened. The droplets fell faster, raising a fine mist around my tires. The wind, once fickle, gusted and then held. Of course it blew in my face. After years of cycling, one accepts the gross inequities of constant headwinds with good humor. Somewhere I read that when twigs wiggle, the wind is blowing at about three miles per hour; when *branches* wiggle, it is five or six miles per hour. But the *trees* that day in South Africa were wiggling, meaning the wind speed was approaching twenty-five miles per hour.

Then came the hail. Caught in a rush of roaring projectiles, I took a full load of ice bird shot in the face. Ducking, pointing my helmet into the barrage, I couldn't take it anymore and steered my trail bike off the road. Standing on the pedals, I rode my bucking mountain bike down a muddy gully over slippery rocks, finally losing control and crashing into a fence. Barbed wire cut into my arm. Carefully, ignoring the clamor, I extracted a barb from above my elbow. I yanked a plastic tarp off my rear load and erected a makeshift lean-to against my bike resting against the fence. I washed out the bloody wound with bike bottle water and dabbed it with a clean bandanna. Then I donned a pullover, sweater and sweat pants. Locating a small bottle of brandy, I splashed some on my cut and then down my throat. Wound and throat burned in unison.

In my little shelter, I watched the silver threads of rain and hail fill the sky. The strong spirits warmed my gut. Amber mud-water rushed in rivulets along the fence, upset by the obstacle of my bike. I wondered what happened to the birds during storms like this. I mean the smaller birds—the rollers, barbets and swallows. I didn't worry about the larger birds. Safe on an upward bend of air, the kites and eagles no doubt soar above the thunderheads, cawing and angry to be cut off from their prey, but dry and secure in that bright, dazzling world where heaven seems so close, and anything solid is out of sight.

The brief storm did little to alleviate the drought. This was amply clear the next day when all traces of the thundershower had been absorbed into the soil. However, just as we were hunkering down for another hot day on the road, we suddenly entered a busy, prosperous farming community. Like a dream, barns, silos and cultivators were scattered across fields of corn, soybeans, wheat and cotton. Sunflower blossoms the size of record albums grew wild along the fences.

The center of this unexpected garden was the town of Jan Klempdorp, a new enclave whose boxy, plastic architecture resembles kibbutzim in Israel. This was no coincidence. This project, an experimental irrigation scheme called the Falls' Irrigation Project, was launched twenty-five years ago as a joint project between Israel and South Africa, whose governments have joined forces as world outcasts to develop the Cheetah jet fighter, an atomic reactor (and bomb?) and dozens of dams and factories. This project utilized water from the nearby Vaal River Dam to irrigate almost seventy-five thousand acres of once-dry savannah. The land was administered by a corporation and divided into privately purchased segments: thirty lots of 2,200 acres and twenty lots of 1,500 acres. The assistant town clerk of Jan Klempdorp, Mr. J. C. W. Weyers, told me in a boosterish tone that this was the largest irrigation project in the Southern Hemisphere, what he called "the wave of the future for Africa."

"The Israelis provided the technology," he explained, "using their experience in Palestine."

Falls is so far only a wave in the white future. This is significant because the project happens to abut a large native reserve—a "tribal homeland"—known as Taung, home to nearly two hundred thousand blacks crammed into a territory about four times the size of Falls, which is home to fewer than three hundred whites.

I asked Weyers about Taung and he said he was disturbed about its proximity to his project. However, he was happy to have such a massive pool of labor to fill two thousand farming and domestic jobs. "We certainly have no labor problems," he said. "Each kaffir working here knows that he had better behave, because there are ten more kaffirs waiting for his job just over the border. And, with this drought, those kaffirs need whatever job they can get."

I asked him if it bothered him to be living amid so much prosperity beside an island of poverty. He misunderstood the thrust of my question, thinking that I was asking about issues closer to his mind, those of personal safety and the unrest.

"Ja, man, it bothers me plenty. These people over there, so far, they have been peaceful, with no incidents, but you never know. The agitators are up in the cities. But these kaffirs breed like flies. We have asked for more police, as a precaution, because we're having a real problem these days with vagrants coming down and stealing crops and such. They come every day and beg for work. Some days we have to round 'em up and take 'em back by the truckload.

"It's a serious problem," he continued in his friendly, small-town manner. "I wish the government would listen to us and move the whole lot of 'em up to one of the other homelands, as far away as possible. For one thing, have you seen what they've done to their land? Man, it makes me sick. They've wrecked some really good land by overgrazing and poor management." Weyers shook his head, as if two hundred thousand unemployed people required by law to live in Taung were somehow derelict because they were unable to turn their land into another Falls' Irrigation Project.

It took over an hour to reach Taung from Jan Klempdorp, but when Taung appeared, it did so even more abruptly than Crossroads had in Cape Town. One moment we were cycling through rows of ripening corn, quiet and alive, and the next moment the land was brown, desolate and ugly. The two worlds meet in the crux between two hills, one side green and lush, the other a gentle swell of dry, exhausted earth. The effect of the two rounded, elliptical hills was of two pieces of fruit set against each other, one ripe and luscious, the other rotten.

Inside Taung, the dead land was cluttered with concrete houses topped by rusty tin roofs. As in the townships, each yard was divided into small, equal lots, exhibiting again the state socialism that has been forced onto the black population by a government that claims to be defending democracy in Africa. We passed by children, chickens, goats and a few cows lolling about in the sun while women tended steamy fires and walked beside the road carrying everything from firewood to plastic cartons of gasoline.

In my mind I tried to categorize this place. It seemed neither Third nor First World, but something in between, a limbo. The soil had the exhausted look of a poor country, the children were ragged, and the animals lean and wiry. Yet the uniformity of the small, dirty houses had the stamp of a master planner, a disconcertingly modern touch as sullen and drab as Lavistown and welfare enclaves everywhere. In these places, even small children look grown up and bored.

As I biked, the sun baked the earth at noon, and this corner of Taung above Jan Klempdorp was still. My gears clicked, slightly off

kilter, an empty noise in the desolation. I stopped near a house close
to the road, hoping that a woman and her two boys would come over
to talk. Once again I faced the traveler's task of trying to *make
contact* in a place where I had no connections and no ready affilia-
tion. I was too embarrassed to climb over the highway fence and
violate their space by going over to them. I felt I needed an invitation,
or a guide such as Stephen at Victoria West. After a few futile minutes of standing and staring awkwardly, I called out to them. The
boys, sitting in the shade of a chicken coop, looked in my direction,
their dusty faces revealing nothing. They stared for a moment, and
then returned to doing nothing.

I remembered the eager young faces in Crossroads, the confronta-
tion in Lavistown and the sad eyes of Stephen. With fists raised, the
Crossroads boys had shouted: *Amandle Kawage!*—"Power for Freedom!" Yet here in Taung the faces were blank.

Were these boys also angry? Eager? Sad? Did they raise their fists
and demand freedom? Politicization runs deep among nonwhites in
South Africa, but it seemed the slogans and raised fists had somehow
missed this lonely spot in Taung. These are people we have heard
nothing about in the media, their plight overshadowed by the violence of burning townships. They were people whose lives seemed to
have withered from disuse, shorn of pride and purpose. How did they
live each day? Had they been born merely to endure and die?

I shouted again to the boys under the tree and they turned away,
but not in anger or disregard. They merely turned away, lay down on
their backs and closed their eyes as if going to sleep. I climbed back
on my bicycle and slowly made my way through Taung.

After a while it dawned on me that these people seemed to be
waiting, but waiting for what? For their next meal? For checks to
arrive from fathers and sons working in distant mines? For the sun to
go down? For a revolution? For happiness? For the Second Coming of
Christ? I picked up my pace, for limbo had suddenly become too
much to bear.

7 After Taung we reentered white South Africa. Once again the scenery shifted back to expansive pastures reserved for corn, fat cattle and sheep. Farm compounds and well-watered gardens reappeared on distant knolls and white farmers waved from Nissan pickup trucks. Yet I could not concentrate on this gorgeous land. I was thinking ahead to Botswana and black Africa, whose border was fast approaching to the north.

Yet South Africa continued to plague my thoughts. I tried to draw some conclusions about this first phase of my journey. I had met my share of reasonable people in South Africa, but I had a sense that reason was fast becoming a thing of the past. The madmen and the haters seemed to be rising across the land.

A black South African I know in the States once told me that the key to understanding his country is to realize the role of hate. "Hate is our god," he said, "a god that knows no color bar. Hate has been our father, our mother and our teacher for so many generations it is now part of our genetics. We worship hate, and I'll tell you what this means. It means we are always ready for violence. Violence is always an option, always lurking around the corner. I say this even for whites in their nice suburbs, because they cannot hide forever from the hate in their own genes.

"You ask me if I have hope for my country," he said, "and I will give you an answer you do not want to hear. I have no hope at all, except for what can possibly emerge from war, after the millions have died and the hate has finally been washed away by blood."

I thought of these bitter words as I biked through the warm, exuberant fields of South Africa's high veldt and I wondered, even after all I had seen, if things could really be this bad. In America we are raised believing in compromise and talking things out. We grow up operating under the assumption that reason, at some level, is going to win over chaos. Yet what happens when reason is extinguished by fear and words become worthless?

In the end, a visitor to South Africa is staggered by the spectacle of a country about to commit suicide. It may take years, even decades, 53 before the entire drama is played out. The whites are more powerful than many observers in the West surmise. They are not about to roll over and give in, not with their Cheetah fighters, machine guns and wide veins of gold. Nor are the blacks. They have potent weapons, too, with their bitterness, boycotts and the raw inevitability of sheer numbers. It may take them awhile, but they have the ultimate weapon in the knowledge that one day victory will be theirs, even if the war must be fought with stones and gas bombs and millions killed one by one.

Still, the question remains: Why does this have to happen? Are the men who run this country so obstinate that they cannot grasp the reality of what is coming? Are they so wedded to their guns and psychology of fear that they would rather destroy their country and half of Africa than give in? And what of the blacks? What will they do with this nation they call Azania once the bombs have stopped falling and the bodies have all been laid to rest?

II
Botswana

Hallowed
Land

*The land eluded the colonial era. The forces of
the scramble for Africa passed through it like a
huge, destructive storm but a storm that
passed on to other lands. It remained black
man's country. It was a bewitched crossroad.
Each day the sun rose on a hallowed land.*
                                        —Bessie Head

*There is a sense of wovenness, a wholeness in
life here; a feeling of how strange and beautiful
people can be—just living.*
                                        —Bessie Head

1 Before leaving South Africa we had one final task to perform: passing through customs. The border station was divided into two sections—the front for whites and prominent blacks, the back for the tens of thousands of migrant blacks who come yearly from as far away as Tanzania to dig gold and diamonds in South Africa. It is an incessant back-and-forth migration that is generations old, the last vestige of the days when a string of white colonies worked as so many links in a chain binding the continent's resources, including men, to the largest commercial enterprise Africa has ever known.

Every railway, city and road Jim and I saw on this part of the Cape to Cairo route, from the Limpopo to deep inside Central Africa, was a legacy of this entity, this White Africa, Inc., whose mark is still evident long after its imperialist superstructure has melted away. Its force remains as permanent and unstoppable as a river, notwithstanding boycotts, sanctions and rhetoric. This migration continues for the simple reason that the jobs are still in South Africa, the economic powerhouse of southern Africa. And, if you ask the migrants, which I did, they will tell you that they do not like working in an apartheid society, but for them it is not a matter of politics. They do not talk about liberation and revolution. These terms make them nervous. Instead, they talk about wages, steady work and hungry families back home in the bush. They are a part of the machine, and they know it, and South Africa knows it, and they will tell you that there is nothing to be done.

In the front section of the customs house, facing the highway, Jim and I were led into a comfortable room and asked to sit down while our papers were being processed. A South African soldier joked about our bikes and gave us the usual unasked-for advice about "kaffirland." "You're leavin' civilization behind, mate," he said in a one-white-to-another tone of voice. "You'll need all the luck yah can get."

While we waited for our passports I walked outside and saw a busload of migrant workers disembark on the Botswanian side of the border. They were directed by soldiers into a series of holding pens, each cage wrapped in ten-foot fences and topped with barbed wire. Loudspeakers were mounted atop steel poles and guards carried automatic rifles. I wondered why the South Africans felt they needed these Gulaglike fortifications. Was it intimidation? A precaution against terrorists slipping through?

Ironically, the soldiers directing the workers were black themselves and wore the uniform of the Republic of Bophuthatswana, another one of those astonishing fictions hatched by the apartheid mind. And such a pathetic mind, this apartheid, and so simple to ridicule, for here we were in a supposedly black country, yet the voice over the loudspeakers was white and the words Afrikaans, a language that was incomprehensible to most of the workers in the pens.

I leaned against a tall, leafy *mupane* tree beside the nearest cage and watched the faces of the workers. In the blistering sun they waited with the patience of ancient Africa to be manhandled by the Bophuthatswana guards, searched, fingerprinted, issued identity cards and released to waiting buses. The dusty, rural men looked uncomfortable and out of place in the sterile, concrete cages. Their clothing was colored the hues of the African soil, in browns, blacks and grays. A few bright swathes of polyester broke the monotony, turquoise slacks and old mauve T-shirts. One man wore a New York Yankees sweatshirt.

When the guards released a group of workers to board a waiting bus, a Botswanian miner named Lawrence paused to admire my bike. His powerful hands, stained the color of coffee by hard work, rubbed lightly over my handlebars and panniers. He laughed, filled with a drink or two that mitigated a tough countenance and made him talkative. I asked him if this was his first trip to South Africa.

"Oh, no, man, I be coming now eleven years." And did he miss his family? "Ja, of course. It is hard work. I have eleven children." He grinned, and I wondered if he drank to make the journey easier, or if he just drank. "One for each year in the mines."

And what did he do at home, I asked, besides making babies?

"Ah, making babies, that is hard work!" His laugh rumbled. He was speaking playfully, a simple, ebullient man who didn't seem to mind a situation I would have found intolerable. Didn't he deplore his situation? Didn't he want to change it?

Apparently not. He said he was not politicized and did not want to be, that this only leads to trouble. "I work in the mines," he said, still smiling, "and when I am home I make babies!"

I asked him what else he did at home. "This and that. I build huts. I work with my father's cattle. Mine is a quiet village, not like Johannesburg. I like the village best. I know the people and there no man bothers me. I have my family and my children. I drink beer with my friends.

"Ah, man, but we have no money there." He frowned, but still spoke in a straightforward tone, as if these things were simply a part of life and must be accepted. "People are hungry," he said, "so I go and work in the mines for the Boer. I do not like to go to South Africa. At home [in Botswana] black men, white men, all men are the same. Here the Boer thinks he is a lion, the king of all the men. Lions and Boers, man, they make me nervous, so I stay out of trouble. I have made a career in the mines of staying out of trouble."

He spoke of his farewell party in his village the night before. "Man, it was so beautiful. I played such beautiful guitar. You have heard our African music?" He pantomimed the strumming of a guitar and sang a half-drunk line from a Tswana tribal song. His voice was rich and deep, a Muddy Waters of the sub-Kalahari. "I am singing about love," he explained. "It is a love song. We Tswana are known for our good music. Last night, we sang and danced and drank beer in my village. It was the beer we brew in our village, a sweet beer, so fine! It has been made for many years—hundreds of years, I think. In the mines, the beer is made in a factory. They put the beer into a can. This is robbing the beer of its soul. To me, it is a crime to take the beer and put it in the prison of a can."

Apprehensions disappeared on the Botswana side of the border and everyone became instant friends, as if the ordeal of South Africa had initiated us into some grand fraternity or secret club. The mostly female guards treated our arrival as a party, teasing us about white skin that burns so easily. They made suggestive remarks about our cycling tights and the anatomical features highlighted by stretched Lycra.

Since it was nearly dark, they asked where we planned to sleep, the nearest town being over fifty kilometers away. When we mentioned camping, they became abruptly serious, warning about lions in the bush. We thought they were joking. Fresh from South Africa, where lions are as much a danger as grizzly bears in Kansas, we waited for the teasing women to smile. They didn't.

That night we erected the tent on open land off the highway for the first time since arriving in Africa. Fences still lined the road, but they were much more tentative here than in South Africa, loose strands of wire sagging on weathered posts. It was simple to slip a bicycle underneath and revel in the wild, uncultivated, untidy bush stretching off in every direction. Thorny vines, pungent *muunga* trees and dense underbrush cloaked the land in a great, nearly impenetrable tangle of flora. We pushed the bikes back into the bush until we could no longer see any asphalt or electric wires or fences and then erected the tent behind a hedge of "wait-a-bit" brambles, a nasty shrub with fishhook thorns that cut deeper and deeper as one thrashes to get loose.

Being so close to the "wait-a-bits" was a major distraction for us as we moved about at dusk, but we had our reasons. "Lions probably do not like brambles," I said to Jim, certain that entire armies of vicious cats were waiting nearby, poised to attack. I considered strategies. Should we make lots of noise and scare them off? This works for bears in the Rockies. But what if noise attracts lions?

Jim was infuriatingly cool in the face of imminent danger. He said it didn't matter. "Noise or not, they'll know we're here. And, if they're hungry, we're dead and there is nothing we can do about it. So let's forget about it and fix dinner." He began chopping up onions for a soup. I opened my Buck knife to slice tomatoes, noting how pitiful a six-inch-blade would be against a half-ton killer.

Lying awake in the tent that night, I swore I heard cat screams. *Grrrr . . . Grrrr . . .* As I drifted off into a half-sleep, images of the weeks in South Africa played through my head. I stood again with the black boys atop the Crossroads barricade and sat again in the living room of Tom Greig. Perversely, my subconscious mind placed Greig and the boy revolutionaries together in a great, empty space. Each was armed with a six-inch Buck knife. Lions growled everywhere. Greig and the boys began to circle each other, and, as they drew closer together, they began to shed their human forms and were slowly transformed into hideous shapes hot with blood and ready to strike. They growled and hissed like maniacs and attacked and lunged and stabbed until I woke up in a sweat, startled and terrified in the middle of the bush. I lay there afraid to go back to sleep, the air outside the tent abuzz with noise and my brain a knot of apprehensions.

At dawn the sun glowed green through the fabric of the tent, a fresh light, and I realized that I must have slept peacefully for at least part of the night. Yet the dream was still vivid, lodged in my mind. I tried to shake it off. Climbing outside I saw a thick layer of dew glistening across our gear and the nearby "wait-a-bits." I took a short walk in the fresh, ethereal air, stepping over vegetation and spying the first sunbirds of the day.

Up on a rise I could see the immensity of the bushland. It stretched on for miles, changing in the far distance to a hazy beige as the green faded into the sands and scattered bramble of the Kalahari. I stood transfixed, my mind caught in a moment of dreamtime, a refreshing sensation after my nightmare. Deserts have always had this power over me. Like stars, they offer unknown expanses that both defy and enlarge the puny imagination of a single human.

I felt a shudder run through me as I recalled my nightmare. I closed my eyes to drive away the thought, and then opened them again. In front of my face, just two inches away, I concentrated on watching the dew burn off an acacia branch. I touched the point of one thorn and felt its sharpness and I kept pressing until it broke the skin. It probably was a pathological thing to do, but the pain somehow felt cleansing, a pinch after a nightmare to make sure the world was real. When I pulled my finger back I squeezed it gently and watched a bead of blood spill out of the wound. It dropped quickly onto the earth, a tiny spot in Africa watered by my sweet, innocent American blood.

Back on the road, the bush quickly gave way to a forest of small *mutowa* trees, which produce a milky, rubbery sap still used by the Tswana as a cure for blackwater fever. The trees clung to abrupt ridges appearing on either side of the highway, a trough between the South African border on the right and the Kalahari on the left. A strong, hot wind blew down this trough, making our going slow.

Life on the road that day was languid and peaceful and utterly *African* after the infuriating familiarity of South Africa. Lean men led leaner cattle along roadside paths, dusty and acrid so close to the desert. Small, barefoot boys played games beside the pavement as they watched herds of goats and hoed the ground around scattered stalks of maize. Crops were grown in the traditional style, meaning spread out randomly in clearings in the bush. It was not a terribly efficient way to plant, but it was a relief after the hyper-tidyness of South Africa to see stalks arranged by whim.

The first town we reached was Lobatsie, a market town where herders from cattle posts all over Botswana come to sell their animals and buy new stock. The poorer herders, who had walked on foot for days from parched ranches in the desert, had erected makeshift camps and cattle kraals around the town. As we approached the town we passed their shanties, made of cardboard, grass, planks and plastic. In one of the larger kraals I stopped to take a drink of cold water from my bike bottle.

This was during the heat of the day, when sane Botswanians were resting in the shade. So I dropped my bike in the rust-red dust and joined a group of herders sitting under a canvas tarp. Their shanty was attached to a makeshift shop selling kerosene, rope and refreshments. At least a hundred head of cattle shouldered each other in a nearby pen. The proprietor of the shop, a local man from Lobatsie, wore mirrored sunglasses and a Baltimore Orioles baseball cap. His first question concerned cattle. He asked how many I owned.

"I don't own any cattle," I said, knowing that cattle means wealth in Botswana.

"No cattle?" He looked incredulous. "Man, it cannot be true. Americans are rich! No cattle?"

I explained that not all Americans own cattle, that we have other ways to measure wealth. "We buy cars and videocassette recorders and occasionally put our money into banks."

"Ach, and we, too, have banks. But how many cattle do you own?"

"I'm trying to tell you, most Americans do not own cattle. We have other things we own that are as valuable to us as cattle."

"Yes, I understand. I speak English, as you can see. My question is, though, why will you not tell me about your cattle? Here in Africa, we are proud of our cattle. My father owns many cows. I freely tell you. I would take you to see our cattle if they were nearby, but our cattle post is far from here."

"My uncle once owned some cattle," I finally said, seeing that my lack of cattle was distressing this fellow and his friends. It was true that my great-uncle Bill had long ago owned a ranch where he raised

Angus on the edge of Kansas City, but the farm was sold years ago to developers who slaughtered the Angus, mowed down the grass and earned a good deal of money erecting ranch-style houses beside an artificial lake.

"There, you see, I knew you had cattle." He beamed, explaining to his friends that I was one of them. They shyly shook my hand in the Tswana style, touching with their left hand the elbow of their outstretched right hand as if they were handing me a gift that was too heavy to hold in one hand. In ancient Tswana society, the heavier the gift the greater the honor.

Lobatsie itself was announced a mile farther on by an incongruity lingering from British colonial days, a rusting sign decorated with the city's coat of arms. Behind the sign we passed a few old, tin-topped bungalows fading into the bush. Then Jim and I emerged into a crowded street of rough, wooden storefronts, another enclave reminiscent of the old American West. However, after the bland, suburban dorps of white South Africa this was a rawer, less sterile place, a town stained with the sweat and dust of real living.

Behind one storefront was the Lobatsie Hotel and pub, run by an ex-Rhodesian I'll call Mattie (I've forgotten her real name). In her face I could see the quintessential white pioneer, cheeks and forehead and chin carved by hot sunshine and Africa, a countenance that could have been plucked from the early days of almost any old Caucasian frontier, whether in America, Australia, Canada or Africa. She stood in command of a cozy, essentially white pub where we stopped for lunch. Mattie's patrons were a leathery group, most of them anachronisms from the era when nearly every white man in Africa wore baggy shorts and white knee socks. A dozen of them occupied stools in Mattie's pub, a cast of cronies arrayed like buzzards on a knobby branch.

"You boys want lunch, you'll have to pay for it," growled Mattie as we sat down. She was cleaning the already shining counter with such vehemence I thought she would break through the top. We assured her we would pay and were soon served a gigantic lunch of mutton, chips and ale.

As we ate, I chatted with some of the customers at the bar, who told me they had been coming to Mattie's pub for years. I asked if blacks ever came, and one man said, "Of course, mate, this is a black country. But most of us who come here, we're white. Which is not a big thing, you know, in this country."

Most of the men were, like Mattie, ex-Rhodesians who had escaped to Botswana during the civil war in the seventies. They talked with sadness about giving up farms and businesses and leaving friends behind, yet each was happy with his decision.

"Man, I just got sick and tired of the war," said one of the men at the bar. "I came down in seventy-seven, when the rebels burned down my barn and nearly burned down my house. Man, I figured it was just too close, that God was tryin' to tell me something. There comes a time when a man's got to say, 'Look here, let's stop this nonsense and get back to livin'.' So I gathered my family and came down here."

"But why Botswana?" I asked, intrigued by a country where these old imperialists could wallow in such tranquil anonymity.

" 'Cause it's the best friggin' country in Africa," said Mattie, still scrubbing her counter. "It's a decent country where no one cares a bit about white or black. The blacks run the government, but they leave us alone. They're a good sort, not like that bunch up in Rhodesia. And we can still live the old life here. I can run this pub and not worry 'bout getting shot or sayin' the wrong thing or whatever. I ain't rich, but I'm still alive and kickin' hard, and that's about all I'm after."

"And we're still livin' in Africa," added one of the leathery men. "Man, that's worth somethin'. Some of my friends from Rhodesia are back in England sittin' in one of those clubs and drinkin' scotch all day, wishin' they were back in Africa. That's a sentence for execution in my book."

"Hear, hear," said Mattie. "When I left Rhodesia I thought about goin' to England, and I am damn glad I didn't. Have you seen the weather there? Gray and rainy, that's what it is. And the place has been run by pansies and socialists so long there's not much left to admire, despite what Mrs. Thatcher has done."

"I also coulda gone to America," Mattie went on, "but you blokes are just too damn stuck on yourselves. I see all these women in your television programs, with their fancy hair and shiny dresses. And the men . . . well, the world's full of pansies. Besides, America's too far away. So I came down here to Bechuanaland. Haven't regretted it since."

O ver the next several days I met dozens of whites and blacks who had escaped from tumultuous countries to find peace in Botswana. I met a former South African diplomat who quit his country to protest apartheid, a former SADF fighter pilot who had grown weary of dropping bombs in Angola and a mixed-race Mozambican who had seen half his family killed by whites and the other half killed by blacks. I met anthropologists, shopkeepers and authors who all had come to a country that one woman called "an eye in a hurricane."

As we traveled along the quiet, dusty highways I kept asking myself, why Botswana? What was so special about this Texas-sized country on the Kalahari? How had it avoided the tensions and bloodshed that have plagued every country on its borders?

Actually, the answer is quite simple. When Europe carved up Africa a century ago no white power wanted Botswana. It was desolate country with poor soil, no gold to mine and virtually no rainfall to break the monotony of hot, dusty days. Dr. Livingstone, who traversed the country several times, called it "the most God-forsaken territory in southern Africa."

Yet Botswana did have one asset the Europeans coveted, something that helped rather than hindered its status in splendid isolation. This asset was a strip of land stretching north from Lobatsie along the edge of the Kalahari, a corridor of green that happened to be located between two intractable obstacles to white settlement in Rhodesia: the desert and the then independent Boer republic of the Transvaal.

All of the leading powers in southern Africa coveted this corridor, called the "Missionary Road" by Livingstone, because it was the gateway to Rhodesia and Central Africa. The Boers wanted it to stop the Portuguese and the British, the Portuguese wanted it to stop the British and the Boers and the British wanted it so they could continue their march to the north and the ultimate goal of a Cape to Cairo Empire.

Fortunately for Botswana and the Tswana people, the least offensive combatant won—that is, the British. And, in order to protect this valuable corridor from everyone else—including their own wild countrymen in South Africa—the parliament in London made the unusually enlightened decision to declare the entire region a "protectorate" in 1895. This meant that Europeans could have free access to the Missionary Road in transit to Rhodesia and the north, but were barred from settling or owning land in Botswana. The protectorate proclamation was a godsend to the Tswana. It ensured their isolation and sequestered them from the white maelstrom that soon swept past them into Rhodesia.

For seventy years the protectorate stood inviolate as the British reluctantly ruled a desert country they really didn't want. They tried to give it away on a number of occasions, to Rhodesia and to South Africa, but fate always intervened. The Foreign Office spent these years sending out junior Foreign Service officers who whiled away their time doing what British administrators did best: building roads, playing cricket and drinking gin. Meanwhile, the law of the land remained with the Tswana chiefs and those ancient tribal customs that did not overly offend Victorian conventions. This was a miraculous situation, unique in Africa, a country free of bitterness and hate. Bessie Head, the brilliant black South African novelist who herself escaped to Botswana, summed it up by saying that Botswana was a "bewitched crossroad. Each day the sun rose on a hallowed land. . . ."

2 Late that same afternoon, Jim and I arrived in Gaborone, the capital of Botswana, after a long afternoon ride made longer by Mattie's mutton and ale. It was nearly dark when we reached the first wave of mud and thatch rondavels. Smoke from cooking fires glowed violet in a gathering sunset as people went about the business of living: stirring pots of steaming meal, drinking cartons of cheap "24 hour" beer, fathers playing with sleepy children. People were walking home from the center of the small city, most of them government workers in a town where there is no other real industry. They strolled with the slow, determined gait of people who seldom ride in automobiles.

The rondavels lasted only a kilometer or two, possibly the smallest and neatest capital shantytown in all of Africa. But this was typical of Botswana, where everything organized by humans is small and scaled back. Botswana is first and foremost a desert country, a nation of a million souls that has not yet made a break with its ancient ties to a harsh and unforgiving land. Over eighty-five percent of Botswana is uninhabitable most of the year, a wasteland of sand and scrub and vistas of beauty and death.

It seemed only natural that Gaborone would reflect the mentality of a desert people whose currency, the pula, means "water." It must be the most unpretentious capital in the world, a sprawling, dusty, quiet town of broad avenues, squat, functional office buildings and a central square with a movie theater, bookstore, post office and hotel. Most of the buildings are the color of sand and earth and some Gaboronans, I was told, actually prefer to live in rondavels of mud and thatch rather than concrete and tin. I did not entirely believe this, although a young journalist explained to me that thatch is cooler than concrete houses, something I later found out for myself. "Have you ever sat under a tin roof in the heat of day?" he asked.

Gaborone had little charm and no style, other than a desert swarthiness, but it was a city that worked. This was evident almost immediately as we passed through broad intersections and well-lighted streets. In Gaborone I saw none of the costly monuments and 67 gaudy skyscrapers that fill so many desperate African cities. Instead, Botswana seemed to have concentrated its limited resources on such unglamorous items as telephones that work, reliable electricity and buses that run more or less on time.

"Gabs," as the city is affectionately known, was not always such a marvel. It was Africa's newest capital city, founded just twenty years ago, when this forgotten nation abruptly found itself an independent state. When Botswana was born it had no urban areas at all. Nor did it have any of those other things considered essential for modern, instant nationhood: an electrical grid, factories, soldiers, political parties, telephones. The only paved road was a two-mile stretch of asphalt laid for a visit from King George VI.

Most Westerners who cared about Botswana predicted at independence it would be a permanent basket case. But they were wrong, because it takes more than concrete and guns to make a country. "The naysayers thought we would fail," a Tswana chief told me, "but they did not understand the soul of our people. We are a stubborn people. We fought hard against the white man, so we would not be swept away. We paid for this by getting none of the white man's roads and cities, but, I think, the price was worth it. Ask any black man in Africa what he values most, roads or dignity, and he will tell you with a loud voice: *dignity!*"

The numbers tell the story as well as anything. Let us see what they have to say. Since independence the economy has grown an astonishing eleven percent each year. Per capita income has risen almost eight hundred percent, from $80 a person in 1966 to almost $620 in 1986. This may seem low on a worldwide scale, but it is far above most African nations.* Tarmac roads now span the country from the Limpopo River to Zimbabwe, and the nation's all-important cattle count has risen from under a million in 1966 to over three million today, a three-to-one cow-to-person ratio. "That's the largest meat-to-man ratio in the world," said Ove Neilsen, chairman of the Botswana Meat Commission.

People I met in Gaborone were understandably proud of their country's achievements, which have been largely ignored by a world intent on depicting Africa as poor and bankrupt. Foreign experts talked excitedly about the success of Botswana's small-scale approach to development, its focus on small businesses and basic

---

* For example, Kenya at the time had a per capita income of $309, Tanzania, $200.

infrastructure. Bankers pointed to the low national debt and what may be the highest credit rating in Africa, a double-A.

The president and vice president and other political leaders beamed during interviews in their small, refreshingly modest offices. Vice President Peter Mmusi, a short, roundish character with wide eyes and a manager's quiet mannerisms, spent most of our interview spewing more statistics than I would ever care to know. "Our goal is to expand small businesses and light industry," he said gleefully. "We are devoting more development money for infrastructure and cities. The budget is over sixty million pula for roads alone. . . ."

But it was the smaller success stories that spoke loudest in Gaborone. Take Nicolas Jacobs, the twenty-six-year-old owner of a one-room shoe factory. In 1980, Nicolas had arrived in Gabs from his village without a job and just a seventh grade education. Three years later he opened Pilane Clogs, taking advantage of government programs that provided low-interest loans, business training, and subsidized work space. "This year, I made $1,000 profit on $15,000," he told me proudly, sitting behind his ledger book. Nearby, his four employees cut and sewed leather strips onto prefabricated soles.

He was a lean, quiet man who talked a great deal about his family. He said he was using part of the money to build a house for his mother, whom he was moving up from her village. "Next year," he said, "I will export my shoes to Zimbabwe. This will, I hope, increase my profits."

"And what will you do with the extra money?"

"I will rent another room and hire more workers. And I will build an extension on my house for my children."

As I wandered about in Gaborone, talking and watching, I could not help but be impressed by what I heard. Yet I have to admit to a grudging skepticism about all this rose-colored talk. I suppose that I am, like many half-fallen optimists, at least a part-time cynic. And Botswana does have a downside or, to be more precise, it has a dark angel. This downside can be summed up in just two words: South Africa.

As a poor, landlocked nation hugging the northern frontier of Africa's economic colossus, Botswana depends almost completely on South Africa for manufactured goods—everything from trucks to paper clips. South Africa provides Botswana with fuel, guns, concrete and food. It employs almost ten percent of the population in its mines and factories, a source of income for individuals that is often the difference between survival and starvation.

This dependence has become a political nightmare for the pragmatic Botswanian government, caught between radical black neighbors to the north and the increasingly paranoid white government to the south. President Quett Masire, a quiet, diminutive man, bristled when the topic was brought up during an interview with several visiting journalists—and with reason. If Masire speaks too harshly about apartheid and South Africa, he risks the very real wrath of his southern neighbor, who has attacked Botswanian targets with bombs on two occasions during raids against supposed ANC targets. Yet if he speaks too softly he risks dishonoring the unwritten code of South Africa bashing that has become a well-worn groove in African rhetoric.

"It is a difficult path we take with our southern neighbor," President Masire said, carefully choosing his words. "Our neighbors to the north tell us we must disengage from South Africa, that we must join in sanctions to defeat the evil of apartheid. But I tell them this is not possible. How can little Botswana do this thing? How can such a poor country take on this rich country? We can deplore apartheid and join our brothers in calling for its end, but it would be suicide to do much more."

Masire was asked if he feared a war in southern Africa, and he smiled grimly, saying that he could not read the future. "But," he added, "the situation is deteriorating. Things are getting worse."

And what will war in South Africa mean to Botswana? Can Botswana avoid being drawn in?

"No. If it comes to war, and I pray it does not, then Botswana will not be spared." His voice became almost a whisper, and I sensed even in this undemonstrative man a sadness at the prospect that his hallowed land might be in danger. "That will be a terrible day," he continued, "for it will mean the end of all we have accomplished and the end of all our dreams."

3 Jim and I spent several days in Gaborone, resting from the tensions of South Africa. I arranged a scattering of interviews, most of them newspaper assignments, but spent much of my time lounging with expatriots and Botswanian students in the President Hotel. We drank lemon juice on an open veranda overlooking the city square, watching people and lazy pools of dust swirling in the hot sun. It was a pleasant time to be alive, a moment of tranquillity for a weary traveler.

However, as the time for our departure drew near, we were assailed by regrets. Our projected course along the Missionary Road did not dip into the true Kalahari, it merely skirted its eastern rim. For weeks Jim and I had been journeying along highways sanitized from the wild. "We are so close to the Kalahari," Jim said wistfully. "It is one of the last areas of undisturbed wilderness in sub-Saharan Africa. And I'm not going to get to see it."

But Gaborone, being a nexus of opportunities for the ragtag traveler, soon came through. Just as we were despairing over the lost Kalahari, we ran into a white hunter named Neville Peake in a Gaborone pizzeria where expats hang out nibbling on soggy but presentable pepperoni and drinking ales and spirits. He astounded Jim and me by offering to fly us out to one of his safari camps in the Chobe National Park area on the western edge of the great desert. He had seen us cycling into the city and had heard about our trip to Cairo and said we were "the ballsiest lunatics I've met the whole damn year."

Neville Peake was a character Rider Haggard might have conjured up: *the great white hunter with a heart of gold*. He fit neatly into this old African stereotype right down to the cocked khaki cap, macho gait and gentle smile. "You should see Africa the way it used to be," he said with bravado, consuming a large whiskey chaser in a gulp. "The *real* Africa. Hell, we've got to get you away from these milk-toast restaurants and fancy hotels and out into the goddamned wilderness."

Neville quickly made the arrangements, and two days after his 71 invitation, Jim and I were happily boarding a Botswana Airlines Fokker Friendship headed for the deep Kalahari, to a camp situated on a tributary of the Zambezi River near the border with Namibia and Angola. Actually, I hated the copout of traveling to the wilderness by plane, but the flight did reveal something that is impossible to appreciate from the seat of a bicycle—the hugeness of the Kalahari, its flanks curving like a fisheye against the horizons of the earth.

Even from the air the Kalahari does not look like a desert. The undulating surface is covered by knee-high bushman grass, stubby thornbushes and an occasional acacia or terminalia tree. If we had come in the wintertime, during the brief rainy season, the grasses below would have been a bright yellow-green. The great mammal herds, attracted by the water, would have spread out across the land by the millions. But we were flying over the Kalahari during its driest months, when game is scarce and vegetation burned brown and black. Waterless riverbeds, remnants of an ancient watershed, cut jagged troughs across the land. Stray zebra and antelope hung about on the edges of the beds, resting under withered trees. Jim, who had read about these things, said these animals would likely die. "They haven't kept up with the main herds," he said, his face pressed against the plane's window. "They're probably already way up north, where we're going. That's where the water is."

Jim and I landed in the desert town of Maun, from which we were scheduled to be taken by bush plane to the camp. Neville's contact met us at the tiny airport, a woman from Los Angeles wearing multiple trademarks: a Banana Republic T-shirt, Reebock tennis shoes and Vuarnet sunglasses. While we waited for the flight, she took us to the Duck Club bar, a mock-thatch tavern and burger joint that looked like a Southern California tourist trap. The place was filled with more Great Whites waiting for clients, ruddy Land Rover tourists and more amply labeled women from the States. Everyone was drunk, alcohol being as prevalent here as heat and dazzling women.

I was curious about what had attracted these women to the place and asked Neville's contact—she was called Candy or Katrina or something like that—what she was doing in the middle of the Kalahari. She said she had come to Maun with some friends on a hunting trip and simply decided to stay. But why?

"Because the men here are real men," she said. "Not the wimpy types we have at home. Jesus, these guys can kill things with their bare hands. No fooling, I've seen it. My current boyfriend once ripped the head off a snake."

A few minutes later we were airborne again, this time in a six-seater Cessna. The pilot, a former South African fighter pilot named Mike, was young and reckless—"a real man," as Candy/Katrina would have it—and gave us a run for our money. At one point we dipped so low we were nearly even with the tops of parched trees that rushed past at over a hundred and fifty miles per hour. Mike screamed over the buzz of the prop. "This is an old riverbed," he shouted, "that's why there're trees. Hey! Did you see that? Elephants at three o'clock. What! You didn't see? Well, hell, we'll have to go back!"

Zoommmm, twist and tuuuuurn . . . my stomach is in my socks . . . "See that big ole male! Look at the tusks! And the baby— he's a real young one!"

We climbed up to five hundred feet and continued racing above the bush, cruising like a motorboat with a wake into enormous herds of wildebeest and zebra, which scattered like confetti below us, stampeding and kicking up the dust of the Kalahari.

"Hey! Do yah see that?" shouted Mike.

"See what?"

"It's a bloody lion!"

Zwishshsh, swerve and dive . . . rushing at a hundred feet off the ground.

"Hell, there he is!"

I could see a great cat loping along below, running slowly but obviously frightened by this noisy bird.

We continued our swoops and turns most of the way to Neville's camp, although at one point Mike nearly lost us. We had just climbed back up to two or three thousand feet when Jim noticed a Marshall eagle flying close by, its seven-foot wingspan resting on a fast-rising blast of air. I could see the bird's eyes just a few meters away, a look of wild arrogance, rage and freedom. We slowly gained on the Marshall as Mike opened up the throttle. Then, just as we were about to pass him, the eagle suddenly tucked in his wings, swerved and took a steep dive, falling like a bullet under our plane. Mike, Jim and I swiveled our heads in unison to follow the magnificent bird. This is where we made our mistake.

Marshall eagles, as Jim later observed, always travel in pairs, and the male we had been watching was no exception. As he fell away from the plane toward the ground, we suddenly heard a thud and a scream and felt a violent shudder. All eyes swiveled back to the front of the plane, the source of the racket, as we looked in horror at a mass of blood and feathers and warm guts being flung off the prop against the windshield and wings.

The former fighter pilot's face went pale as he scanned the grass-lands below for a site to crash-land. He radioed his position as the plane began to lose altitude and the engine sputtered. Then, to our relief, the blood began to clear from the windshield and the pilot gingerly pulled up the plane's nose. We watched, the atmosphere in the tiny cockpit tense, as Mike studied his instruments. Slowly, his color returned. "Man, we're okay!" he announced, though he said the prop was skipping and would have to be repaired back in Maun.

The Cessna limped onto Camp Linyati on the edge of the Chobe National Park, rumbling to a stop on a grass runway cut like a tidy scar out of the thick bush. A Land Rover waited for us as hot sun-shine bleached everything white except white skin, which turned red and then brown. A lanky, bearded fellow in a floppy bush hat greeted us by shouldering an elephant rifle and holding out a massive hand, another African myth in the flesh. "Name's Map," he said. "I'm your guide." He introduced his wife, a silent South African named Kathy, and John, his Ngami driver, a shy, sensitive, servile yet tough man who reminded me of Isak Dinesen's "natives" in *Out of Africa*. John saluted smartly and ushered us onto the Land Rover equipped with padded seats bolted high above the bed. They provided a tall view of the land above the grass and shrubs. Map offered us Cokes and, as we sped away, pointed out a small herd of roan grazing and alert a half-mile off. "Damn good sighting for this time of day," he said. "It's a good omen for yah, fellows, a damn good omen."

Map Ives, our guide for the next three days, was a sinewy, gentle man who seemed perfectly at ease discussing Rousseau or Pascal while carrying an elephant gun and stalking a leopard. He reminded me of Denys Fynch Hatton, Isak Dinesen's lover in *Out of Africa*, although there was nothing aristocratic or imperious in his manner.

Yet like Fynch Hatton, he was here in this wilderness quite deliberately, having made an existential decision to abandon what we call civilization. He said he hated to leave even to go to Maun for supplies. His mission, he said, was to learn everything there was to know about this small piece of land, a goal a nomad like myself admired greatly.

Like most whites in Botswana, Map had escaped from somewhere, and in his case it was Rhodesia, where he had grown weary of the civil war and "humans killing one another for no good reason." This repugnance at man's capacity to kill ran deep in Map and, I think, had broken his own predilection toward wandering. He had traveled a lot when he was younger, having been born and raised in Liverpool, from which he quickly escaped to make the rounds through Asia, North America and Africa. He had finally settled in Rhodesia before the civil war, where he fell in love with wild places and began his slow divorce from humanity.

As we drove through the dense, tangled bush, I asked Map where he got his nickname, and he said his fellow game rangers in Rhodesia had given it to him on account of his good tracking sense. His army unit had kept the name, because his abilities extended to tracking human prey.

"Shhh," he said, "see that?" He pointed up into a tree and we saw a vulture alight on a dead branch, its bald head the color of dried blood. Map thumped once on the roof of the cab and John stopped the truck. Another vulture landed, and then several more, swooping in and dropping their feet and braking with wings drawn in tight to their bodies.

"What does it mean?" I whispered, suddenly realizing where I was, deep in a fastness of bush and desert three hundred miles from the nearest town. I breathed in the dry, vaguely rotten odors and felt a warm breeze blow across my face. My God, I thought, I'm in *Eden,* or at least a reasonable facsimile.

"Shhhh," repeated Map, holding up a hand. I followed his eyes, gazing in narrow slits into a patch of knotty, golden bushman grass. "There," he said, "lion! They've got a kill!"

"Where?" Jim and I said at once, straining to see through the thick grass. Then I saw it, a long, dirty yellow creature, its haunches matted with burrs and its face soaked in blood. Then it disappeared back behind the grass.

"Can we get closer?" I asked, caught up in the hunt.

"Nope," said Map, "sorry, but they're already gone. The kill was a small one, maybe a warthog or a mongoose. Just a snack." He leaned down and spoke in Ngami to John, who carefully drove the truck into the thick grass. Map jumped up on top of the hood and surveyed the land, looking for the remains of the kill. Then he pointed at a splotch of blood on the ground. "That's all that's left, just a little blood." He looked up at the vultures cackling and vying for space on the old tree. "Sorry, fellows, but there's nothin' left. They even ate the bones."

A half hour later we arrived at the entrance to Camp Linyati, which I expected to be a modest group of tents or shacks planted on the shore of the Linyati River. After all, Neville had said this was "the *real* Africa."

Neville was either joking or had lived a very charmed life. The camp we drove into that afternoon was no five-star Hilton, but it was about as comfortable as one would hope to find in the middle of nowhere. It was the sort of camp where the likes of Bror Blixen and Theodore Roosevelt would have felt at home. *The Grand Old Safari.* The tents were made of bright green canvas and outfitted with beds, feather comforters, washbasins, flashlights and full linens. In back was a thatch hut for taking a shower with water heated by burning logs. In the morning, tea was served in bed on china with sugar and cream in sterling silver servers.

Meals at Linyati were prepared in a fully equipped kitchen and served in a rustic, homey mess hall decorated with antelope and buffalo trophies and the skull of a seventeen-point impala. A refrigerator was stuffed with soda and beer, and the black servants were experts at preparing everything from a stuffed chicken to a Manhattan on the rocks. Upon arrival, Jim and I were handed cold gin and tonics and roasted nuts. A servant gave us seats beside the river and we watched the sun drop and illuminate the feathery tops of reeds and papyrus as hippos slid into the water and impala screamed from the woods nearby.

Predictably, it was Americans who were behind this African fantasy, and it did not surprise me that the Americans in question hailed from Texas. Map told us that Linyati is one of a dozen camps built and paid for by a group of bored oil barons with a penchant for Hemingway's *Green Hills of Africa.* Buying concessions from the Botswanian government, which is always ready to make an honest buck, the Texans and their guests were allowed to shoot a limited number of big game animals at exorbitant rates. Neville, back in Gabs, had given me a list of bounty fees to be paid for this increasingly rare privilege. How much was a pound of flesh in Botswana? Leopards headed the list at $1,600. Lions cost $1,000. Baboons, the African pest, cost $40, although I hardly think they would be a challenge sitting and squealing overhead in a tree.

These bounties were charged on top of a $1,000-a-day fee charged by the government and additional fees charged by Neville and other professional hunters. We met a hunter from Wyoming in Maun who had just unloaded $60,000 for three weeks of hunting. Apparently, he was a good shot, as his leather cases were stuffed with pelts to mount on his walls back home in Laramie.

Although fascinated by the hunting mentality, and sharing an affinity with hunters in their love for wild things, I have never had a desire to kill those wild things. I had made this clear to Neville, who unexpectedly agreed with me. "I enjoy the chase," he said, shelving for a moment his mock-machismo, "but no longer get a big thrill out of the killing. That's why I stay in Gabs and Maun and manage the business. I'll let the younger hunters lead the slaughter."

Map, too, had grown weary of killing. That's why he was sent specifically to Linyati, one of two photo safari camps organized by the Texans. "I don't really mind hunting," said Map. "It's natural for man, the carnivore, to want to hunt and kill for food. But, hey, let's do it like it's meant to be done. Let's come here and get the feel of the land. Let's walk about, study the trees and birds and find out every detail about the animals. Let's admire them, show them respect. Let's throw away our watches and our hurry-up mentality.

"That's why I'm the guide at Linyati and not one of the hunting camps," he added. "I get disgusted by the killer who sweeps in here and checks off his kills like a grocery list and then goes home. Man, that's just immoral."

I asked Map how he could tolerate even photo safari tourists, and he said it sometimes wasn't easy. "I prefer solitude, and some of these people are truly difficult," he said. "But I am not ready to become a hermit, and the business gives a chance to live out here rather comfortably."

We spent three days motoring in our magic Rover across the bush, tracking antelopes, lions, and elephants. Map, Kathy and their servants entertained us along the way as if we were Old World aristocrats. We dined on chicken Kiev beside a pool brimming with hippos and ate barbecued steak within spitting distance of at least ten thousand wildebeests and zebras. At night we retired to long, steaming showers, high tea and French wine served as ten thousand feathery communal reeds across the river refracted the sunset. From the stoops in front of our tents we could see baboons squawking in the trees and herds of grazing red lechwes, a small, umber-colored antelope seen nowhere else in the world.

One evening before dinner we were sitting and drinking wine when, abruptly, the baboons in the tall, dark-leaved garcinia trees began madly screaming. Map quietly set down his drink and reached for his rifle. "Something's inside the perimeter," he muttered. "Probably a leopard. I saw some prints this morning." He rose, a slinking animal himself, and waved for us to follow. "Don't walk on twigs," he whispered, "and keep low."

We crept into the forest of fig trees and tangled acacia, a lush growth fed by the Linyati. Tracing a "hippo highway" cut by hippopotami on feeding runs, Map crouched to inspect a set of fresh cat prints. As we stalked on, the sun set and the air cooled and the forest burst with the exotic noises of nighttime. I felt an electric shiver and a sense of danger that I found stimulating, an emotion that combined innocence, fear and savage possibilities. "Follow me closely," said Map in a low voice. "If you see anything, whatever you do, don't run. They'll chase you if you run. Just stand still if they come at you and let me get off a shot. If I miss, then, well, you might as well run. But no need to worry, I'm a damn good shot. Got that way in the war, you know, with blokes shooting at *me* all the time."

We tracked the leopard as the sky turned golden, but he escaped into the bush. The baboons—their humanlike faces frozen in smirks of disgust—settled back into fighting and squealing overhead. I expected to head back to the camp, but Map kept walking, heading deeper into the wilderness.

Little unseen rodents and reptiles scampered and slithered in our path as we penetrated farther and farther into the darkening bush. I might have been worried, except for the newfound sense of fear and excitement that made me want to keep walking, or stalking, like a hyped-up primitive. Up ahead we saw another family of roan, which ran away in terror. Map guessed they must have smelled us. "We must smell pretty awful," he said, " 'cause they run away so fast. Even the animals that have never known man, they run away." He stopped and put a foot up on a log and gazed into the dense thicket.

"I've thought about this," he said. "Why do these animals run from us? We're puny creatures, and if you take away our guns, we're pretty helpless. I've come to believe these animals are smarter than we think. They somehow know Homo sapiens mean danger. Maybe it's in their genes, because we have been here in Africa for a long, long time. Whatever it is, they somehow know, even way the hell out here, that we are more dangerous than our scrawny, hairless bodies might suggest. Even the lion fears man. He's got to be starving or insane before he tangles with the most dangerous species on earth."

Map believes that humans are more like other animals than we care to admit, that we have certain animal senses. "You feel anything right now?" he asked as we stalked along the hippo highway. "I mean, do you feel the electricity? I swear, even before I came out here from the city, this place was already familiar to me, I mean deep down. Deep inside our brains, we have instincts developed long before cars and air conditioners. A city man here for the first time can sense when a lion is nearby. I've seen it happen.

"The problem is that we are unlike other animals," he continued, "because we are never satisfied with our niche. You know, things worked pretty efficiently on this planet before we came along. The whole planet was like Linyati, wild and free and functioning in harmony. Back then, everything had its purpose. But what is *man*'s purpose out here? I'm not talking metaphysics, I'm talking *function*. What is his function? Why can't he just enjoy all this and shut up and quit while he's ahead?"

Map suddenly stopped and waved us down behind a wait-a-bit bush. A guttural roar shook the sky. I braced myself, expecting a lion and wondering if I could really stand still if he charged. But it wasn't a lion. Instead, an impala burst through a stand of elephant grass. Looking crazed, he ignored us, swinging his great head of horns and emitting horrible, pained bellows. Map pointed to his left, where a half-dozen female impalas serenely grazed. "Poor fellow," whispered Map, "he's rutting and the fillies just don't care." He laughed. "Man, that ever happen to you?"

At dawn on our last morning in Linyati, John took us out into the river for a cruise on a double-decker powerboat. It was a crisp, sun-drenched morning. Sunbirds swirled in the papyrus reeds. Slaty egrets soared in our wake. Monitor lizards slid quietly into the water and hippo bubbles exploded on the surface. Across the river, on lilies the size of steering wheels, a spindly bird with feet as long as its body snapped at insects. Map told us the bird was a lily-trotter, and noted that this bird had made a big difference for the white army in the Rhodesian war. He reached way down in the water and tore off a lily leaf.

"See how delicate this is? You can poke a finger through it with hardly any pressure at all." I took the thick, slimy plant and tore it with no effort at all. "Some of my mates in the army, like me, were trained naturalists. When the war got serious, the blacks started planting mines. They blew up trucks, tanks and lots of people. Man, this was a big problem, as you can well imagine. So we blokes got together and asked ourselves, 'What are we going to do?' "

He told us to watch the lily-trotter as it walked across the pads. "Why doesn't he fall through?" Map asked. " 'Cause his weight is evenly distributed over those wide feet. A mine is triggered by weight. We learned from the lily-trotter to construct huge, wide tires to put on our minesweepers, tires so wide that the weight per square inch was less than what triggered the mine. Even you blokes in America use these big tires on your minesweepers, and you can thank that little bird."

I asked Map if it bothered him, about nature contributing to warfare. He said it did bother him, but it couldn't be helped. "Man is a warrior species," he said, "and we have used and abused nature to create our weapons and make war. But I recognize that war is part of human nature, part of our dissatisfaction. We want what others have, so we try to take it. But we don't stop there, like animals do. If an animal needs food, he takes from the environment, but he takes only what he needs. A man takes and takes, and then is unhappy 'cause he doesn't know what to do with it all. I saw this happening in that war I fought in, and it made me sick. Whites wanted to screw over blacks, blacks wanted what whites had, and they were going to kill each other over their greed and hate. This is why I got out of there and why I have made my own peace out here. Man, let them have their wars and bombs and bullets. I'll take life out here any day. It's brutal, but at least it's fair."

The boat continued trolling down the stream, when the peace of this mythical Africa was broken by a sharp noise. A rifle shot cracked, then another. The lechwes on the opposite bank looked up, startled, deploying by instinct so that they could peruse every approach to the herd. Map stood up and grabbed his rifle.

"What is it?"

"Poachers," he said, pointing out a trail of smoke on an island in the marsh. "Those rifle shots were a signal we're coming. See 'em! There they go!" Two figures in the distance, carrying what looked like automatic weapons, scurried across an open stretch of bush into the woods. A dozen carcasses, bloody meat left after skinning, lay in a heap beside the poachers' fire. Map said to be prepared to hit the deck if the poachers started firing again.

"Are they good shots?"

"Look at that heap of meat," said Map as he cocked his gun, "and you tell me."

III
Zimbabwe

On the Brink

*Who loves the sun enough to throw body and
soul there?*
                    —*Tchicaya U Tam'si*

*We were happy that we won the revolution. We
danced and sang. We drank beer. Then we
woke up in the morning and the rainbow was
still over the hill.*
                    —*former Zimbabwean guerrilla*

1 We arrived at the Zimbabwe border on the Shashi
River at sunset. The journey from Gabs had been a hot, poetic ride
along the rim of the Kalahari, six days of dry sunshine, blood rushing
through my legs and remote camps in the bush. It had been a mesmerizing, quixotic trip, a traipse through an African Brigadoon, and
now it was over.

We paused for a water break at the bone-dry Shashi, resting uneas-
ily in an idyllic picnic spot built long ago, when the river had water,
Zimbabwe was Rhodesia and whites felt safe eating fried chicken in
these parts. We didn't linger. Guerrillas, leftovers from the civil war,
inhabited the rugged Matopo hills to the east of the Missionary
Road. They had been murdering people by the dozens, being especially fond of attacking whites and foreigners. Two years earlier they
had kidnapped six Western tourists and tortured them to death,
burying their bodies in shallow graves in the bush. Just ten days
before we arrived they had gunned down an Irish priest at a nearby
mission as he weeded cabbages.

Nobody was completely sure who these guerrillas were or what
they were doing. Several months earlier, in a brightly lit cubical in
Washington, D.C., a pale, humorless man at the State Department
had briefed me on the situation. He had multiple Ph.D.s and had
devoted most of his life to deciphering secret cables and marking up
maps with pink and blue highlighters. He said that "certain field
observers" suspected the guerrillas might be South African agents
trying to disrupt their cheeky neighbor to the north. Other sources
suggested they might be nothing more than bandits, former rebels
bored with homelife and looking for a thrill.

"But we, of course, discount these theories," said the State Department man, pulling out a map and a batch of smudgey cables from
under a stained coffee cup that said I LOVE DAD. "We know there is
more to it than that. We believe these men are tribal dissidents."

He related the most likely theory in a droll, professional voice,
providing me with considerably more detail than I cared to know. He
explained in dry diplomatese that there are two major tribes in the 85

country, the minority Matabele in the south and the majority Shona in the north. The Matabele and Shona had fought together against the whites in the war, but had had a falling out when the Shona won the first elections in 1980 and attempted to dominate the minority Matabele, their traditional enemy and modern political foe. Thus began a spiraling conflict in the remote bush where we were riding, involving shadowy dissidents, repressive government troops and a disturbing rise in those human rights violations Africa too often specializes in.

I later met a black Zimbabwean cobbler, crippled by a land mine in the war, who offered another explanation for the violence in the Matopo Hills. He told me with complete seriousness that the guerrillas were not men at all, but spirit soldiers unleashed by the long civil war, ghosts who thrived on violence and bloodshed. "They are our evil ancestors," he said, sitting in a concrete hut and sewing a snakeskin wallet. "They were released because of the hate and will not be defeated until the Second Coming of Christ."

The sun continued to fall as the sky changed to gold, then pink, then darkening blue. Jim and I pedaled hard up a series of steep hills. I was exhausted, wanting only to get off my machine and sleep. Yet fear has a way of keeping one motivated. We had been warned repeatedly about this road and now it was getting dark. *Where the hell was the border station? How far did we have to ride?*

I had met an ex-Rhodesian soldier named Marvin in South Africa, a bitter, bigoted man who had spent most of the war fighting guerrillas in the Matopo. He had written some crude but startling poems, including one about guerrilla warfare. The words stuck in my mind.

> *The bushes in Rhodesia have eyes.*
> *Bushes are where the snipers hide,*
> *Where they plant the mines so that*
> *Little white girls explode like milk pods.*

We kept biking fast as darkness fell. I couldn't help but feel my white skin glowing like plutonium, as it had on occasion in South Africa. Heavy bush, black and menacing, pressed in on either side of the highway. We pedaled and pedaled, round and round. Breaths came long and deep. The arms of giant candelabrum trees, half cactus and half tree, swayed like demon centaurs in the wind. The bushes have eyes, Marvin had told us. A long uphill slowed us down to a frightening crawl. Animals screamed and nightjars buzzed past, black shadows launched from the pits of Mordor.

Abruptly, a spotlight sliced the night. Up ahead I saw the silhouette of soldiers with rifles standing in beads of light. Then came the outline of a flag and a building. Safety?

We had one more hill to climb before reaching the lights at the border post. With our destination in sight I felt the heavy weariness of a long day on the road. I could see the guards ahead and looked forward to being enveloped in light and warmth.

However, as we reached the crest of the hill, the soldiers began to shout. "Hurry up!" they screamed behind spotlights and raised rifles. A few meters from the station two scowling men ran toward us with heavy submachine guns that seemed to be growing out of their arms. When they discovered we were Americans they brusquely grabbed our handlebars and bellowed at us to move faster, turning the last few meters into a mad, burlesque scramble for the lights.

I assumed that the soldiers had come out to protect us, but this was only partially correct. At the station an officer berated us for being out on this road after dark, words we certainly deserved. His grim, efficient soldiers then searched our bikes, bags and our pockets. "Where did you come from in South Africa? When did you enter Botswana? Where did you go? What proof do you have that you went to these places?" I asked what this was all about, and they looked incredulous.

"Man, surely you heard about the raids. We are looking for spies."

"What raids? What spies?"

"From South Africa. We are looking for the men who raided Harare."

I explained that we did not know about any raids, that we had been on the road in Botswana for the past few days.

"Three days ago, man!" he said. "The South Africans attacked."

I later found out that SADF agents had planted a time bomb in a former ANC office in downtown Harare. At the same time they had attacked other supposed ANC targets in Lusaka and, incredibly, in tiny, defenseless Gabs. "We are looking for suspects," the officer continued suspiciously, as if spies would be foolish enough to travel on pedal bikes. "Now, tell me again why you were in Botswana. . . ."

When we entered Zimbabwe during the summer of 1986 the country was supposed to be at peace and enjoying an economic boom, despite the tribal problems in the south. I had read about record maize crops, tobacco drying beautifully in the sun and a massive program to construct new highways, electrical stations and housing. Zimbabwean factories, built by stubborn whites during years of sanctions, were cranking out everything from toothpaste to machine guns. African specialists in the West, apparently overlooking the south, had proclaimed the country the latest miracle-nation in liberated Africa, that year's success of the decade.

Judging from the media excitement over the end of the black-white conflict in Zimbabwe, hopes were running high for a nation of warriors turned farmers, politicians and businessmen. Indeed, they seemed to have done a number of things right in their first six years. The new black government, led by an acclaimed rebel-intellectual named Robert G. Mugabe, had managed such a thorough rapprochement with the whites that many former colonialists were moving back, bringing with them their expertise and capital. In the realm of the economy, Mugabe—an avowed Marxist—had astounded everyone by acting almost capitalist, apparently learning from the many mistakes of African nations that had moved too fast into socialism. The results had been a steady rise in income and life-style for most Zimbabweans—particularly those in the Shona-dominated north— in an era when Africa as a whole had been backsliding economically for years.

When we arrived in the nearby town of Plumtree, soldiers in full combat dress stood on corners and patrolled in jeeps and personnel carriers. We pedaled carefully and quickly, as if on some sort of mission ourselves. Indeed, we were—to get away from these fellows with their guns. I had been before to armed towns poised on the lip of simmering conflicts, although this one seemed particularly outrageous, since by all accounts the dissidents in this area numbered less than one thousand men. Yet here were all these soldiers, thousands of them, making this small farm town seem like Northern Ireland.

In the morning the soldiers were still on patrol, swaggering through the streets with the grave, self-important expressions of warriors. They exuded an impervious authority that I always find distasteful, a grim officiousness that makes everyone so nervous I wonder who is most intimidated, the enemy or the populace they are supposed to be defending.

I asked the Indian manager of the Plumtree Inn if it was normal to have so many troops in town. "There are always soldiers about in Plumtree," he said, speaking in a British accent that was so thick it sounded like a parody. He sat in a stark office wearing a polo shirt and pressed trousers. His mustache was waxy, his complexion the color of a thick Spanish wine. "They've been here in one form or another for close to fifteen years, since the civil war began. Of course, the color of their skin has changed, but I swear they're wearing the same uniforms."

Did all of this military bother him?

"Not really. I suppose one gets used to anything after a decade or two, although these blokes can be a bit unpredictable at times. You know, shooting up villages in the bush and that sort of thing. And they're taking this raid business a bit too far. From what I've heard, the South Africans only blew out an empty office or two. Nothing truly serious. In my view, it is almost embarrassing what little damage they were able to cause. You would think that the mighty South African Defense Forces could manage at least a whole building."

He pointed toward the morning paper, the *Bulawayo Chronicle*, whose lead story told about a white farmer arrested in connection with the raid. "The government seems so bloody nervous about this thing. They're arresting everyone that even blinks an eye the wrong way. Such a bloody shame. Take that fellow they arrested. He lives not far from here. They're arresting him because he owns a truck that looks like the one the raiders may have used. As far as I can tell, they're chasing shadows." He shook his head. "Silly blokes, these blacks, a paranoid bunch."

"And what about the whites when they were in charge? Were they paranoid, too?"

"They were even worse," he chuckled, twirling his waxed mustache. "You know, they fought that war for swimming pools and maids. I'm serious, mate. That's what they used to say when they came in here. 'We're in it for the swimming pools.' " I remembered that certain South Africans had said the same thing. "Well, look at what's happened," he went on. "They gave up to the blacks and what do they get? They get to keep their bloody pools. The whole country is lunatic, if you want to know my opinion. It's a pity, though, because it's such a nice spot. That is, if people aren't shooting at one another."

I finished a plate of soggy eggs and toast at the hotel and took a stroll around Plumtree. There wasn't much to the downtown, a cluster of dusty, whitewashed shops with dark interiors smelling of grain, kerosene and mothballs. A small bookstore sold socialist periodicals and Zimbabwean schoolbooks with glossy photographs of the prime minister and other heroes of the revolution. "I'm sorry we have nothin' more," said a white woman with more wrinkles than my own grandmother, who has spent most of eighty years in the sun of West Texas and Georgia. The woman, a lifer in Rhodesia/Zimbabwe, was clearly embarrassed by issues of *Soviet Life* and *Communist People's Daily.* "This is what the government sends us to sell," she explained in a whisper, as if she was afraid of being overheard. "You want any real books, we got a few of 'em in the back. I got Sidney Sheldon, P. G. Wodehouse, Ian Fleming. . . ."

Few people in Plumtree wanted to talk about the dissidents. Who would, I thought, with all these troops running about? But they didn't mind talking about cattle, crops and the drought. And everyone had a favorite team going to the world cup in Mexico City— Zimbabweans of all fleshly hues, like South Africans and everyone in the world but Americans, are mad about soccer. However, the general mood during a morning of small talk was one of forced normality, of pretending that this was merely a languid farm town on a hot, stuffy day. It was what we used to call a dog day in Kansas, except that here even the dogs seemed uncomfortable and alert as they lay in pools of red dust under shade trees.

While waiting for a local branch of Barclays Bank to open, I met a woman on the neat lawn who told me she was frightened by the soldiers. A teacher at a nearby secondary school, she had recently moved down from Harare and was shocked by soldiers and rumors of killings.

"I would never have left Harare if I had known," she said, speaking in the same anxious whisper as the old lady in the bookstore. She kept glancing over at a nearby soldier guarding the bank. "There are no soldiers like this in Harare," she added. "It's real nice there. These troops remind me of when I was a girl, when there were guns everywhere." I asked her why she was whispering, and she said there had been arrests. She had even heard of beatings, but these were only rumors.*

Over at the train station platform a young black worker did not whisper. He was angry and wanted to talk. "I do not like what is happening," he growled while loading bales of raw cloth onto a dolly. "The war is supposed to be over," he said, speaking so loudly that he made *me* nervous. There were soldiers nearby on the platform. "I tell you something. My father lost his legs to a mine in the war. He stepped on it while walking down the road to meet me at school. I saw him just after. Ach, it was terrible. His legs were ripped apart like paper, just like paper. I was so angry. The ZAPU men,† they said it was the whites who planted the mine. The whites said it was ZAPU. Man, I did not care! My father lost his legs!

"Then there comes this peace settlement," he continued. "I say 'hallelujah' and 'praise the Lord.' The people are happy. We celebrate. Ohhhhh, it was a good time! But it was a lie. There are these dissidents and now these soldiers. Now we got this war again. I am Matabele. I do not like what the Shona are doing to the Matabele. But I got a family and I want to live, only to live. The war is supposed to be over. We are supposed to be at peace."

* According to human rights reports issued by the U.S. State Department and Amnesty International, the government in Zimbabwe had employed systematic beatings and torture in Matabeleland, mostly in remote areas. They had also indiscriminately arrested and detained hundreds of Matabele, including several political leaders.

† Zimbabwe African People's Union (ZAPU), the Matabele-dominated party in the south. During the civil war ZAPU fielded one of two liberation armies, the other one being the Zimbabwe African National Union (ZANU), dominated by Shona speakers from the north. ZANU is now the ruling party in Zimbabwe.

2 Later that morning in Plumtree, Jim and I wheeled our bikes over to a bakery on the main street. We bought sticky buns and waited for a large blue truck to come and pick us up. We had been invited to spend a few days on a white farm named Manifest, about forty miles to the east. The invitation had come from a Rhodesian barkeep, a fellow named Bradnick, whom we had met in South Africa. His brother and sister-in-law owned Manifest and he insisted we look them up. "Man, you've got to see a real colonial farm in old Rhodesia," Bradnick had cooed, a ruddy man with a distant smile. "Ah, it's the old life, and it ain't goin' to be around forever."

The Manifest truck arrived as the heat rose to a searing temperature around noon. A large, bald, black man named Milo hopped down from the cab and gripped our hands. He wore a crimson jumpsuit with a marking from the Bradnick farm. Two subordinates, also wearing red jumpsuits, strapped our bikes on the long flatbed of the truck. Cartons of supplies, everything from mealie meal to bales of wool, were stacked high in the back. Milo explained that on the way to Manifest he was going to be dropping off weekly supplies at several village stores the Bradnicks owned.

As soon as we pulled out of the center city, Milo began to talk, answering our questions in a deep, thoughtful voice. Milo was a calm, muscular man whose laugh was easy and his words direct and genuine. He was not the usual African one hears about in the Western media, meaning that he was not angry, loud or despairing. His talk was about life, children and raising a family, a relief in this tense corner of Africa. "I am a family man," he said in a low rumble, adding that he disliked politics. "I am mostly interested in just living."

As we pulled out of Plumtree, Milo pointed out the old whites-only section, with its South African–style brick homes and gardens. " 'Bout half these houses are owned now by blacks," he said. "It is amazing how the new big men move so fast into the old big men's houses."

We came to the former blacks-only township, a sprawling concentration of the same concrete row houses that had appeared in Victoria West and other dorps in South Africa. Yet here the township had a more congenial feeling, with houses spread out and decorated with trees, hibiscus blossoms and fresh paint. And there were none of the fences we had seen in South Africa. "Yes, when the whites were in charge, there were fences," said Milo. "A black man couldn't even go into downtown Plumtree without a pass."

I asked him if things were better now that blacks were in charge.

"Ach, man, that is not an easy question," he said, mentioning the troubles with dissidents and government troops. "Before we had that war, and now we have all of this arguing between the politicians. And the bush, it is not safe. This is bad.

"I think I miss the old days, really, when Mr. Smith ruled," he said to my surprise—a black man preferring Ian Smith to Robert Mugabe. "He kept things calm for a long time, at least until the war got real bad. For the Matabele, Mr. Smith's government was better than the current one. With this one-man-one-vote the Shona outnumber us. They are in control now. It is their country. They get the big jobs in the government, and you know what that means. They give jobs to their families, to brothers and sisters and sons. They keep out Mr. Nkomo and his people."*

Milo kept talking as the pavement ended on the edge of Plumtree and we began rattling along on a rutted, hard-packed byway in the bush. It was a lazy, pleasurable ride, despite apprehensions that guerrillas might be lurking about. Cattle fields appeared interspersed with large stretches of brambles. This country had not enjoyed the rains that had apparently soaked northern Zimbabwe. In fact, Matabeleland was suffering from the same drought we had seen since the Karroo.

Milo continued reminiscing about the "old days," telling us about life under Ian Smith, a man whom Joshua Nkomo once called the devil himself. "Mr. Smith gave the Matabele more food subsidies and development money than this current group in power," he said. "I don't know everything about this. I am not political, but I know for a

---

* Joshua Nkomo is the leader of the Matabele and was coleader of the rebellion with Robert Mugabe. Nkomo lost the election for prime minister to Mugabe at independence in 1980. Since then relations have been tense between the two. At one point, Nkomo left the country when Mugabe accused him of supporting the dissidents, an allegation he denied. However, when I arrived, Mugabe was trying to convince Nkomo to join him in a single party so that Zimbabwe could become a one-party state.

fact Mr. Smith gave us more for roads and irrigation. I have seen this difference. When we get out near Manifest, I'll show you a dam Mr. Smith was buildin' for irrigation. It's been stopped now, I heard, because no money was sent by the government. Why was this dam stopped in this terrible drought? We need the water. It don't make sense.

"Mr. Mugabe sends food when we have a bad famine," he added. "He is not a bad man. But there are hungry people right now in Matabeleland, and that never happened in the old days. I don't know what Mr. Mugabe's group is doing with the money. Maybe they're putting some in their own pockets."

I asked about discrimination under Ian Smith. Hadn't this bothered him? Wasn't it better now? "I did not like the discrimination in the old days," he said, "but that, it was changing. It was not so bad at the end. Mr. Smith was abolishing the discrimination. I am a black man; I think it is good to have black men in big positions, but things changed too fast. How can we say one day the government is white, then one day black, when there has been no preparation? Look at what is happening, with these dissidents and this trouble between Mr. Nkomo and Mr. Mugabe. This is a big mistake. We should have gone slower. Things might have been better."

After an hour of driving we stopped in a small village, Empandeni, to resupply one of the Bradnicks' general stores. While Milo and his men unloaded supplies, Jim and I took a walk. Milo warned us not to go off the main trails through the bush. "It is not safe here," he said. "There are probably no dissidents, but please be careful."

We stayed within sight of the truck, walking across a broad, dusty cattle field toward a lake that was almost dry. The land here was as quiet as any I had seen in Africa, with scattered mud-daub huts, languid children and a few cows emaciated by the drought. Near the lake we ran into a farmer who spoke only a few words of English. "Drought," he said, sweeping the thirsty land with a gesture like a conductor. "Bad year. Bad crops. We pray to God. God save us. Praise God."

Back at the truck I asked Milo if villagers here were getting enough to eat. In the human rights reports, I had read that as many as thirty percent of all southerners suffered from malnutrition. "With this long drought I am sure there are hungry people in this village," said Milo, his face grim and concerned, like a father's. "See that old man?" He pointed at the man we had talked to. "Man, he has no meat on his bones. He is so thin. In the old days, Mr. Smith would have sent these people help by now. But this group in Harare . . . I do not know. Do they care about the Matabele?"

We arrived at Manifest late in the day, when the sun was turning the bushlands gold and red and pink. The main compound appeared through a break in the tangled acacia, a prosperous cluster of beige, red-roofed buildings, two or three barns and pens filled with cattle. In the center of the enclave was a garden with weeping willows and blossoms.

It was a lovely, tranquil scene, a vision from an *Out of Africa* dream, except that the entire compound was surrounded by a series of tall fences, which made it seem more like South Africa. Barbed wire had been strung in bunches across the fence tops. It reminded me of kibbutzim near the borders of Israel. As we drew closer I could see other articles of warfare—an armored pickup truck, sophisticated antennae for communications and a bunkhouse where hired militiamen stepped outside to check us out.

Milo told us that several whites had been killed in the area by dissidents, including a farming friend of the Bradnicks who was ambushed while out driving on his land. Manifest was on alert because of a recent dissident killing at a nearby Catholic mission. "Other day, they shot a priest," he said. "Shot him dead while he was off in the fields."

Quentin and Jay Bradnick were waiting for us when the truck pulled up in front of Manifest's main gate. They immediately took charge in a rural way, helping us unload the bikes and directing the workers. Quentin, nicknamed "Atom" for his swift legs when he was younger, said we were insane to be biking all the way to Cairo. "Damn Yanks," he grinned, "you're all a bunch of lunatics."

He and his wife showed us into a rustic bungalow behind the main house and offered drinks. "What'll you boys have?" asked Jay, a short, sunburned woman with gray eyes and a mischievous grin, a sprightly character to meet out in an area where whites were being used for target practice. "Beer? Brandy? Whiskey?"

"What do lunatic bicyclists drink?" ribbed Atom, a male version of his wife: short, burned and as insouciant about dissidents as she. I was taken aback by their calm, and blurted out "beer." Within seconds, an old servant in a white coat and battered fez appeared. "Here are your beers, master."

Atom and Jay Bradnick were farmer-soldiers, second-generation English born and raised in Africa. It was Jay's father, J. Skinner, who had built Manifest in 1923. Like thousands of others, he had come to Rhodesia to flee the squalor of urban England. At the time, according to Jay, Manifest was dense bush, as untouched as Linyati. She told me her father had worked like a "damn mule" to carve the farm out of the virgin bramble. He cut roads, erected fences and built a rough house topped with corrugated iron. At first he had intended to completely clear the land for cattle, but decided along with other ranchers in the area to tear out only the thorny acacia while leaving the *mupane* bramble intact. *Mupane* leaves are sweet for cattle, the Bradnicks explained, and grow better than other cover in these drylands. Skinner had started with about fifty head of cattle, mixing them with wildebeest and antelope already there. Leopards and lions also stalked the land, that is until Skinner shot enough to make the survivors wary.

Today, sixty years and one war later, the Bradnicks are among the last white holdouts in this area, and they're hanging tough. Atom and Jay have four adult sons, three of them former Rhodesian soldiers. Their second boy, A.J., was living on the farm and said he hoped to inherit it someday. He was a wiry, intense man with a wife and new baby. He lived in a cottage behind the main house, the cottage J. Skinner built for Atom and Jay when they were newlyweds.

The Bradnicks' oldest son worked as a mechanic in nearby Bulawayo. The two younger Bradnicks lived in South Africa, one at university and the other chased away from the Matopo by black neighbors. "His wife was a died-in-the-wool racialist," explained Jay. "She treated blacks badly, ordering them about and the like. So they were threatened by the local blacks and left. You know, it's damn hard for some whites. We were racialists for so long, some blokes can't adapt to the new situation."

We spent four days at Manifest, relaxing, lazy days, a holiday in a colonial time warp that bordered on the unbelievable. It was as if we had dived into the middle of a tale by Elspeth Huxley. There was a medieval sensation of danger, of chaos lurking at the gates. We were living in a fortress-castle with outer walls of steel, a neat, ordered fiefdom where the benevolent Lord and Lady and their clan swaggered about carrying machine guns like cutlasses, while flashing playful grins worthy of characters in a Dumas story. Even the presence of murky rebels—which in this fairy tale were the dragons that no one ever sees—seemed part of the adventure. There was a certain tension underlying the fantasy, but I found the situation invigorating rather than frightening, a constant drama beating at the edge of every activity. It was impossible to get bored at Manifest.

During the daytime the Bradnicks supervised the business of the farm, working beside black laborers wearing crimson coveralls. They did chores that reminded me of my uncle's ranch on the edge of Kansas City, leading cattle to and from pens, restocking barns with feed, organizing inoculations of animals and repairing farm machinery in a workshop off the barn. One afternoon A.J. and a veterinarian friend from Bulawayo counted pregnant cows. Black workers grabbed each beast while others pushed them into a collaring device. With the beast immobilized A.J. or the doctor would push his arm into its vagina. "I feel the fetus—is that a fetus?" asked A.J., who was trying to learn the technique.

Whenever anyone left the compound area, at least one of the private militiamen went along as escort. Each morning we took a group walk into the bush to look at birds and wild animals. The militiamen wore green, unmarked fatigues, carried American G-3 automatics and never said a word, stalking in the bush fore and aft. The Commercial Farmers' Union, a farmers' advocacy group, had provided these men to farmers living in dissident areas. The government had trained them as part of an employment scheme for former guerrillas now out of work. "It's damn ironic," said A.J., "that I was shooting at these fellows a few years ago. Now they're protecting my wife and child."

At night, after the chores were done, we gathered on a broad, screened-in porch. Insects buzzed and bounced off the wire mesh and the blackness beyond hung heavy. During these evenings we forgot about dissidents as we drank and played long bouts of darts. Atom was once the dart champ for all of Rhodesia and got a mischievous thrill out of whipping two novice Americans at a game appropriately called Killer.

One night I got Jay and Atom to be serious, for I knew there was more to life at Manifest than fairy tales. I knew there must be a deeper devotion to ... what? To Africa? To survival? To the land itself? After another bloodbath at the dart board, where Atom won my house, all my money and my firstborn son, he and Jay sat back in wicker chairs and began talking about life as whites in Matabeleland.

"To make it out here, there is one simple rule," said Atom, sitting on an overstuffed chair and smoking an American cigarette. "You adapt. When you stop adapting it's time to cash it in."

"And we follow a few simple rules," added Jay. "You always travel armed, you don't leave the compound after dark, and you just go about your business and don't muck around in other people's affairs. It's not an easy life, but there are some wonderful trade-offs. Aren't many people back in England who could live like this."

"You learn to live and let live," said Atom. "We don't even know who these dissidents are. And, really, we don't care. We just try to stay clear of 'em. Hell, to be honest with you, they're not such a bother compared to before. We survived the war and that was much, much tougher."

"Don't get us wrong, though," said Jay. "We aren't wild about living with security fences and all this rot. We'd prefer to be left alone in peace. But I guess we're used to it. In some ways, it's better than a lot of blokes thought it would be. The hard-core racialists at the end of the war said the blacks would kill us and take away our farms. A good lot of whites up and left everything rather than have it taken away. But we just couldn't see up and leaving everything we worked for. This land, man, it's a part of us."

"So we're stickin' it out," Atom said, a note of pride in his voice, "and I'm bloody glad we are. I think the government realizes the importance of whites here, at least so far. Those who left, they got compensation, but it wasn't much. The government offered me twenty-seven thousand Zimbabwe dollars for this farm.* 'Right,' I said, trying not to laugh, 'and it just cost me forty thousand Zimbabwe dollars to electrify the place!' "

I asked who got their neighbors' land when they joined the "chicken run," what the whites called those who fled the country during the war. (The phrase is being revived in South Africa.)

"Blacks got the land," said Jay, pouring herself a fresh drink of whiskey. "They live in these cooperatives. It's some sort of socialist arrangement along African lines, or so the government says. We used to call the coop lands Tribal Trust Land—native reserves, you know.

* $1 Zimbabwe = U.S.$.50; Z$27,000 = U.S.$13,500.

We have cooperatives on two sides of the farm, land that used to be white."

"Are they good neighbors?"

"I suppose so, given how many of them there are and the fact they're overgrazing their land. A.J. has had problems with 'em cutting our fences. Other day he found fifteen kilometers of fence cut. Jesus, was he sore. He found cooperative cattle on our land and found out whose it was. Fortunately, the government sided with A.J. They fined those fellows thirty Zimbabwe dollars for each head on our land. I'm happy to hear they're upholding the law, but it doesn't sit well with our neighbors. With this dissident situation, you never know what's going to happen. Some of these incidents with whites, I wouldn't be suprised if it's racialism in reverse. Some of them, you know, they say they fought the war to get rid of all the whites and they're real sore we're still around.

"I'm not being racialist, mind you. I think we whites made some really lunatic mistakes over the years. We weren't at all fair. That's accepted by most of us who stayed. But I do hope they don't drive us away, 'cause we have something to offer. We have the know-how to make this country work. Most of the blacks in charge know this, but it makes 'em very unhappy. They'd love to make this a socialist country, to split up the land and such, and kick us all the way back to Britain. But they've seen what happened in other black countries. They kick out the horrible, capitalist whites and change everything overnight. Okay, but what did they get for it? Chaos and disaster, that's what they got. You'll see when you get up north into Zambia. Mugabe's bunch doesn't want that to happen here."

On our final afternoon at Manifest, A.J. took me on a drive deep into the Matopo, the rocky hills that jut up on the edge of the Bradnick farm to spread across the southwestern flank of Zimbabwe. Accompanied by the veterinarian (I think his name was Alan), militia and two other Bradnick guests, we raced along a maze of cattle trails walled in by tangled hedges of acacia and *mupane*. Impala mingled with the cattle, wild, beautiful creatures standing out like nymphs among troglodytes.

As the sun began to fall, A.J. drove us to the highest point on the ranch, a bald rock overlooking miles of Matopo. He pointed out the sites. To the northwest was World's View, a huge rock where Cecil Rhodes, the most pompous man ever to live in Africa, is buried under a large cap of bronze. "Rhodes was the fool who started it all," mused A.J., "but if it hadn't been him, it would've been someone else."

To the east he pointed to a nook in the rocks where the Pioneer Column had passed in 1890, a motley group of settlers and trigger-happy troops sent up to invade Rhodesia and launch the white man's rule. "The funny thing was," said A.J., "these pioneer fellows were heroes when I was in school. But they aren't heroes here anymore. No way, man. They're the bad ones."

When the sky became too dark to see well, we broke out some beers—alcohol seemed as pervasive here as flies and sunshine—and pondered the sunset. Alan and A.J. pried off the bottle caps with spare gun clips, something they had learned while in the army. The militia said that they, too, had learned to open beers with gun clips during the war. Moments later, former enemies pried open each other's beers.

The sun was slow setting at this elevation, spreading in a full array of color across the sky, a scene that demanded silence. Each of us found a spot on the large rock where we crouched and watched and said nothing, listening to the land.

As the sun dropped, A.J. sat immobile beside me, so still that I was reminded of Bedouins squatting on distant dunes. The intensity in his frame had vanished as he soaked in the last traces of pinks and golds. As it became nighttime, his silhouette seemed to meld into the stars. He was completely comfortable and at home, a man who said he wanted to raise his baby son on this land. He seemed like an impossible figure sitting there, a man drawn from an era that has faded away so thoroughly that it was hard to judge it as a present phenomenon, one that could be called good, evil or indifferent. He was a living anachronism, a character drawn from a colonial memoir, not true flesh and blood. And I wondered, how long can a character in a memoir survive on this continent?

I didn't want to bother A.J. in his revelry, but I had a question. Did he, I inquired, consider himself an African? It seemed to me this was an important thing to understand, for if he did, he might be safe, like certain white settlers in Kenya who will always stay no matter what. He remained still for so long I thought I had made a mistake in breaking his silence. But A.J. was thinking with the patience of a man who has been forced to make real decisions.

"This place is in my blood," he finally muttered, whispering in a low voice so as not to disturb the night. "I'm not sure, though, if I can truly call myself African. The war did that, the bloody war . . . I saw blokes die, friends of mine. I can't forget that. But I am a part of Africa, the land. It is the land that is part of my blood. And if I have anything to say about it, I'll never leave."

On the way home A.J. raced through the dark bush. The guerrillas operated in this area. I felt, along with the others, an icy apprehension. We sat tensely in the bed of the truck, bouncing and jostling, the cold wind of the Central African plateau blowing through our thin shirts. We felt foolish having stayed out so late, and Atom's voice crackling on the radio sounded worried, which did not make us feel any more comfortable.

Abruptly, a shadow crossed our path, a black shape rushing in front of the truck. A.J. swore and stomped on the brakes, but he couldn't stop in time. The thud sounded like a man getting slammed in the stomach with a baseball bat. The militia hopped off and deployed. The rest of us ducked and waited, our heartbeats barely muffled by the noise of the night.

When no guerrillas appeared, A.J. stepped into the headlights, swimming with nightjars and insects, and saw that he had hit a young cow. He touched its wet neck, blood gurgling out of a wound in its throat. Lying on her side, with eyes wide open in terror, the animal twitched and heaved. Blood stained the broken grille of the truck. A.J., distraught, crouched down to cradle the animal's head. He cursed himself and talked gently to the wounded beast, oblivious to anything else. Alan put a hand on A.J.'s shoulder. "It happens, man," he said quietly as we stood around the man and his animal glowing in the lights.

"I know, man. I'm mostly mad at my stupidity. I was goin' too fast." A.J. muttered his words and stroked the cow and told her to be calm.

"It can't be helped," said the vet. "You know she's a goner. You know what we've got to do. You gonna do it, or do you want me to?"

"You do it."

A.J. touched the young cow again and then moved aside. Alan gingerly laid the muzzle of his G-3 on the animal's temple, now completely soaked in blood. She looked up at A.J., mewing with pain and confusion. A.J. touched his friend's shoulder.

"I'm sorry, mate," said Alan, "but you know she's a goner. You understand. It's the way things are."

3 One hundred miles northwest of Manifest farm, poised on the edge of the anarchic crags and ridges of the Matopo Hills, is Bulawayo, the former capital of the Matabele Empire. Before the European invasion it was a city of kraals, cattle, smoky fires and Impi warriors. This had all changed in 1893, when the last Matabele king, Lobengula, was routed by Maxims and shrapnel—the newest inventions of a war industry busily gearing up for the twentieth century—and his kraals were replaced by polished streets of British bungalows, colonnaded shops and neat rows of jacaranda trees.

Today Bulawayo has been reconquered by the grandchildren of the Impi, but they have not yet had time to make their presence felt. Visually it remains a bland, suburban Xanadu born out of a colonialist's dream, a whitewashed, gleaming, Western metropolis that Evelyn Waugh once described as a "dull town with flowers."

We arrived in the hills above the city late in the day, having taken a lift from A.J. through dissident country. (The Bradnicks had insisted that we not pedal this stretch.) From our vantage point we could see Bulawayo's broad streets, tallish buildings and the eel-like tracks of Africa's largest railway yard. Acres of trees and parks and, yes, flowers wound serpentine through the city. I was reminded of an old adage, that Rhodesia was a suburb masquerading as a nation. Even the old townships, those old symbols of segregation and bitterness, had a hint of gathering suburban bourgeoisie with rivers of green, television antennae and dozens of community swimming pools softening the steady rows of concrete and corrugated tin.

Yet I wondered if this was merely an illusion of dullness and tranquillity seen from a distance. As we well knew, there was a war of sorts going on just an hour's drive south, where the bush had eyes and the streets of Plumtree were filled with troops and nervous people. Would we see the same thing in Bulawayo, or was the war confined only to the bush? And what about those reports of prosperity? Would we see evidence of the postindependence boom in Bulawayo?

102   As we cycled into town, having bid A.J. a warm good-bye, I saw no

visual manifestations of war, other than a few rusting armored trucks in a used-car lot. No troops patrolled the roadways nor guarded trim government offices, banks and police stations. But neither was Bulawayo the boomtown one might expect in a newly liberated nation. There was none of the bustle and synergy I would later see in Harare, where the streets were packed with prosperous workers and the skyline was dotted with cranes and construction superstructures. Bulawayo was obviously a prosperous city, or at least it had been under the white regime, but now it was eerily still, almost as if there *were* troops lurking about.

Of course, a conflict doesn't have to be erupting in the streets of a city to make its presence felt. Wars, uprisings and the like have a sobering way of altering moods far away from the actual fighting, particularly when the feud in question is a slippery, vague malevolence that few people fully understand.

"The problem is the Shona," a black businessman told me over drinks at Gray's Hotel downtown. He whispered as he spoke, telling me that the government had spies everywhere. "They have caused this sadness to fall over our city. They have deprived us of our fair share of development resources. They do not provide bank loans to our businesses. In this way, they hope to destroy the will of the Matabele people. This is absurd! All they do is arouse anger and fuel these dissidents, whoever they are."

Jim and I didn't stay long in Bulawayo, agreeing with Waugh about the flowers. The morning we left was steamy as we climbed up a gradual rise through townships and suburbs thick with gardens and palm trees. It was a pleasant, albeit hot ride until the edge of town, when we reached a dreary industrial area of brick kilns belching rust-colored smoke.

For miles Jim and I passed what seemed like endless stacks of bricks. Yet life existed here. Shadowy figures moved among the kilns, their gray squatters' huts made of tin, adobe and cardboard. This was the first spot in Zimbabwe where I had seen this sort of squalor, yet another dark edge to this land of hope.

In the midst of the smoky world of the kilns, I stopped to talk to one of the ragged shadows walking along the road, a young teenager named David Mamamba. He had recently come from a village in western Matabeleland looking for work in the city. His possessions included a small bag of clothing and a knobby stick, a club with a heavy, rounded end. "I am sometimes attacked on the road," he explained, "I am a boy alone. This knobby stick is for protection."

David said he left his village because people were hungry and the land was no good. "I have no future in the village," he told me, speaking in a simple English he had learned at a government school near his village, "so I come to this place to find a job."

I asked if he had been successful and he sadly shook his head. He kicked the red clay dust with a bare toe calloused from years of going barefoot in the bush. "I am just a dirty boy with bad clothes," he said, "so no man will hire me."

"But you speak English," I said. I had read that one of Zimbabwe's postwar achievements had been in education. Surely, I thought, this skill would help him find work, even in the depressed job market in Matabeleland. But he said it did not make any difference, that there simply were not enough positions. This is a great paradox in Africa, that so many countries have been reasonably successful at education, but have no jobs for the mobs of half-enlightened teenagers swelling cities where there is already high unemployment.

"If things are so bad," I said, "then why don't you go back to the village?"

"No, I do not go back. There is nothing in the village. I have no land. My parents are divorced. My father is in another place. My mother live with my grandfather. He tell me to go away. There is not enough food. I will stay here. I will find a job."

I asked what kind of job he was looking for, and he said "any job." He had tried at some factories, at the railway station and at the welfare office downtown. He looked pathetic standing there in that apocalyptic world of choking red dust, this boy who symbolized the yearnings and bitter realities of so many Africans. I didn't know what else to say, so I asked him what he would do when he finally got a job. Would he get a house in the township? Buy some new clothes?

No, he said, "I buy a motorbike, and a guitar."

"Why a guitar?"

"They do this guitar in my village." He smiled for the first time and, when his serious mask broke apart, I saw that he was a very young boy, no older than twelve or thirteen. "We used to sing," he said. "My father, he sing. He do this guitar. It so beautiful."

"You miss the village, I think."

"Yes." His childlike countenance dissipated into more permanent, adult lines of hardness and impassivity. "In the city, few men smile. It is hard to find food and a place to sleep. I know no man. In the village I know every man. Here I live in the bush like an animal. In the village, you need only build a small house, maybe out of sticks. You grow your own food, when it is not a drought. It is a simple life."

"It sounds like a decent life, really," I said.

He shook his head, and I felt his despair, this boy who was willing to work, who was not a freeloader, who was even optimistic about finding a job despite the odds. "Yes, but I have nothing in the village. My father is gone. There are old men who tell me to do this and that. It is a small village, far away. I want to make money and have a good life and not live like the old men. I will work at any job. If a man give me a job, I will work very, very hard."

Beyond the pallor of the kilns, we broke clear of the city and entered an expanse of dry bushlands and scattered cattle pasture-land, another dusty, silent, calm land. The drought was still in evidence, with dry riverbeds of white stones and soil as hard as concrete. This parched, thorny landscape would change little for almost twenty-five hundred miles along the Cape to Cairo route, with the exception of northern Zimbabwe, with its miraculous dousing of rain.

As always, it was a pleasure to be back on my bike, with all the possibilities of the road. Up ahead, Jim stopped and hurriedly pulled out his binoculars. I stopped beside him and he pointed at a thigh-high, gray bird with large legs strutting in a field of bushman grass and thornbushes. It had a regal, yellow mask and plumes jutting from the rear of its head like a crown. "He sees something," Jim whispered excitedly.

Suddenly the bird flared its wings and struck at the ground with its long, powerful feet. It jumped backward and I got a glimpse through my own binoculars of a struggling snake twisting and jerking. Then the bird struck again, arrogance and confidence in its eyes, a killer who killed out of instinct and not out of hatred, pettiness or pleasure. After the attack it seemed to grasp the snake in its talons and shake it, to make sure it was dead. Then it began to eat, joined by its slightly smaller mate.

Along the highway to Harare we passed a profusion of small, shabby villages, bottle stores and gas stations. About sixty miles north of Bulawayo, toward the end of our first day out, we came to the village of Bembesi and stopped for a break at a white-era monument beside the road. I was attracted to this plaque because most of these old memorials to Caucasian glory have been removed and scrapped by the black government. Once, I was told, they had covered Rhodesia like similar monuments cover former Indian country in the United States.

This particular marker told about a horrific battle between invading Caucasians and the Impi warriors of the Matabele in 1893, days before the whites seized King Lobengula's kraal at Bulawayo and crushed the Matabele. I suppose the monument was saved because it not only glorifies the colonials, it gives an unusual amount of credit to the bravery of the Impi.

The battle had occurred nearly a century earlier, almost precisely where I was sitting and drinking water on a hot, silent afternoon. The plaque said that as many as a thousand crack Impi, Lobengula's finest divisions and his last chance, died within the space of several hours, their bodies piled in heaps on the trampled grass. Most of them were mowed down by six brand-new Maxims, sent up by Cecil Rhodes, guns that fired a gale of bullets into Impi regiments whose armor consisted of lion's fur and cowhide shields and charms that were supposed to turn bullets into water. No white died that day. I was reminded of a jingoistic ditty popular in Britain at the time:

> *All we know is we have got*
> *the Maxim gun and they have not.*

Today, the field where the Matabele armies made their last stand had been thoroughly absorbed by grass and maize. Cattle grazed there, and a few goats. Not too far away a group of ragged village boys—young David Mamambas?—played soccer beside a herd of goats. Their ball was made of paper and cloth scraps compressed and wrapped with string. It was surprisingly effective, a product of rural ingenuity.

I walked over to the boys, hoping to ask some questions about the history of this place, but they were young and spoke only a little English. Besides, they were much more interested in soccer. They began showing off, grabbing the ball and doing tricks. They bounced it off their toes, knees, chests and foreheads. One boy kicked the ball in my direction and I hit it with my head. As the ball sailed through the air the boys squealed and laughed and grabbed for it, tumbling across a former battlefield soaked in their grandfathers' blood.

Before I knew it, we had been playing soccer for over an hour. The sun was beginning to fall and we had no place to stay for the night. The boys indicated that we should ride ahead and sleep in the main village of Bembesi, which was close by. So we climbed on the bikes and followed the sprinting boys to a large village of concrete, tin shacks and round huts.

We arrived on a Friday afternoon after work. Half the village was celebrating the end of the week, drinking, talking and dancing in and around the single beer hall, a conspicuous building in the middle of the scattered huts. Our appearance caused a sensation as people crowded around and touched our gears and tires, chattering questions. A small man named Albert, wearing a neat green suit and tie, welcomed Jim and me to Bembesi. He apologized for all the fuss, explaining that many of the younger villagers had never seen a white man up close.

Albert said he worked for the Zimbabwe National Bank in Bulawayo as a teller and was home for the weekend. The green suit was his Zimbank uniform, which he proudly wore in the village as a sign of success. He invited us to spend the night in his family's kraal.

However, as he led us toward his house we were stopped by a large man wearing a polo shirt and what looked like a puka shell necklace. He said he was an off-duty policeman and told Albert that we must first check in with the commanding officer at the police station. "It is only a formality," the puka-shelled man insisted, leading the way through a crush of villagers.

The police compound, heavily fortified by the white regime during the war, was walled in and wired with strings of heavy barbs. A small, ridiculous-looking cannon from the British era stood in ceremonial readiness beneath the new Zimbabwean flag. The puka-shelled man took us into an office, but neither the commanding officer nor his assistant was on duty. A lesser officer sat in the commander's chair, a man who was obviously unhappy about being here on a Friday night.

"What are these two whites doing here?" he asked Albert in a curt, irritated tone. "Are they friends of yours? Is it true you were taking them to your house?"

Albert was uncomfortable, as most people are with blathering officialdom. He said that he had just met us outside the pub. The acting CO ordered him to go, after berating him in a local language. Albert wished us farewell and exited the compound. This left us suddenly alone to face an irate policeman who obviously did not want us there. He said that we must go back to Bulawayo. "You are not allowed here."

We explained that we were hours away from Bulawayo by bicycle and said we didn't want to cause trouble. "We just want a place to sleep," said Jim, who was as exhausted as I was after a full day of cycling. "We have a tent. We could sleep right here in your compound."

"That is impossible," he said sharply, "it is against orders." Then his voice became more suspicious and he began asking us policelike questions while perusing our passports and inspecting our bike bags. "What's this?" he suddenly asked, looking at my passport. "You have been to South Africa? You did not tell me this! When were you there? Don't you know we had these raids!"

This launched a new round of questions that ended with him asking us who we *really* were.

"You have our passports," I said, hoping this wasn't going to get out of hand. "I am *really* a writer and Jim is *really* a teacher."

"Passports can be faked!" he shouted and pounded his fist on the desk. "How do I know you are not troublemakers sent by the racists in South Africa? How do I know that you are not terrorists? Tourists do not come to Bembesi. This is not a tourist sight!"

I tried to explain that we were touring the country by bicycle and had just happened to appear here at dusk. Jim asked again if we could camp in the compound. "You can watch us tonight," he said wearily. "We will leave in the morning, and you will be rid of us."

This set him off. He began haranguing us about our stupidity for being in an "unauthorized place." We were "idiots," "fools" and "stupid whites" and he should lock us up, he said. As he continued to shout abuse I became afraid that he just might convince himself we *were* spies. The newspapers had been filled with stories about enemy agents and terrorists in the aftermath of the South African raid. I fidgeted, sitting on a crude bench in an interrogation room. I knew that part of the problem was our skin and our foreignness, an odd sensation for a white man.

Fortunately, the acting CO eventually grew tired of his own voice, realizing that words would not make his problem go away. So he instructed another officer to try and raise a superior on the radio. As we waited, a patrolman dragged in two drunks wearing clothes recently torn. One man had blood running out of his nose, but was too besotted to notice. The officer had subdued his prisoners with what seemed like excessive restraints—chains around their necks and legs and a metal rod locked into handcuffs. The patrolman explained to the CO that the drunks had been fighting. When one interrupted, he was kneed by the officer in his kidneys, a painful thing to watch, especially in our position.

After a while, the radio crackled, but the CO could raise no one in authority. So he shouted at us some more. The radio crackled again. Someone yelled on the other end in a native language. Then something odd happened. As he turned off the radio, the officer turned to us and smiled. "I have spoken to my commanding officer," he said, his voice suddenly amicable. "And he said that you are welcome to sleep here in our compound. He said that we are to assist you in any way that we can."

I can only guess that the man had been ordered to be friendly. He became a gracious host, offering us sodas and insisting that we sleep in the compound's officers' club. Nothing more was said of spying and terrorism, although it was clear that we were to stay in the police compound for the night.

Our host sent a subordinate to show us our quarters in the officers' club, where a servant brought us soda and beer. The club was an unfriendly-looking haven where white soldiers under virtual siege toward the end of the war had spent their off-duty hours drinking and shooting darts. Their bawdy attempts at brightening the concrete walls remained six years after their surrender, but the decor was fading and breaking apart in an early stage of postcolonial decay. A beer tap handle with a plastic naked woman had cracked in half. Above the bar a poster of a busty woman was fading into primary colors, her breasts light blue, her nipples green. The battered dart board, beside a scratched chalkboard, was laced in broken spiderwebs. Whoever was in charge of cleaning up had different priorities from the white soldiers'. The corners were filled with dust and the counters needed a good scrubbing. The sit-down toilet, the ultimate fixture of the West, was stopped up, perhaps for good.

4 Three days later, Harare appeared on the Bulawayo road between two hills cloaked in bright, green grass and yellow hibiscus blossoms. It was a vision that must have seemed like Eden to the whites who invaded Mashonaland nearly a century ago. Behind these hills the first group of settlers had raised the Union Jack in 1890 and named their camp Fort Salisbury, after a British prime minister who never set foot in Africa. One of the settlers, writing in his diary, called this verdant glade a "white paradise on earth," words I had heard before in Africa.

Today the land behind Harare's hills is covered with acres of townships and smart neighborhoods, parks and gleaming high-rises. Even from a distance I could see evidence of a boomtown as tall cranes swept the China-blue sky and cars and people clogged the streets. It was such a blatant contrast to Bulawayo that I might have been in a different country. This was a city that radiated confidence, brashness and impatience, a capital in the full throes of transition and newness that made Bulawayo and the south look like an orphan left behind in all the fuss.

As we reached the busy downtown streets we had to be careful to avoid the stampeding automobiles and overflowing sidewalks. At one point we had to get off the street altogether to avoid a speeding convoy of black Mercedes limousines accompanied by howling sirens and a police escort. "Another minister going out for lunch," a white man in a greasy jumpsuit muttered before melting into the crowd.

Jim and I arrived in the city at dusk and checked into the first cheap hotel we could find. The Oasis was situated on a street of rusty bungalows in a working-class neighborhood near the railroad yards. It was a comfortable and inexpensive inn with no atmosphere at all, a perfect cipher in a city hell-bent on becoming as modern as possible. Even the rooms had the antiseptic smell of an American economy inn, a nauseating familiarity that made me feel as if I had just gotten off an interstate on the edge of Anytown, USA.

110   That night, in the Oasis's grim, Naugahyde-bound café, I got my

first introduction to the fervor and optimism I had heard about but had not yet experienced in Zimbabwe. As I wearily ate a watery bowl of fish and chips, a boy about twelve years old asked to join me. James Ledaba was only slightly younger than David Mamamba, but was significantly better off. He said he lived on this street and hung about in the Oasis looking for foreigners to corral into a chat. "My parents say I talk too much," he said with a precocious grin. He was a pixieish fellow whose shy, unpolished enthusiasm reminded me of Pip in *Great Expectations*. He blurted out that his father was an officer in the army and his older brother was "going to be the richest businessman in Zimbabwe." He asked me the usual questions about America and then turned to his favorite topic, which happened to be Harare, a city he unabashedly called "the greatest city on earth."

Though I was exhausted, even inclined to be irritable, I was taken by James's innocent adoration for his hometown, something I had not seen since talking to certain whites in South Africa.

"Do you see how wonderful Harare is?" he said, flapping large eyelashes and taking me up on an offer of a cola. "It is an exciting moment to be here. We are building a new country. Have you heard what our prime minister has said? Zimbabwe will be the first country devoted to justice and dignity for men. This is good, don't you think?"

"We have a new tobacco auction house," he said proudly, sounding as if he were about to list all of his toys, this boy who represented the future of a nation even younger than he was. "And we have a new convention center, and many new buildings. You *must* go see them."

"I will," I said, trying not to sound as weary as I felt. I asked him if he wanted something to eat and he ordered a piece of chocolate cake, a piece of apple pie, a sweet roll and another cola. When I asked if this was too much sugar, he assured me that his mother would approve. How could I in my condition argue with such a boy?

I spent eight days in Harare, chasing after another elusive African paradise. The city was impressive, though there were a few oddities. For instance, there were almost no books in the bookstores, which tended to be filled with more Russian and Chinese periodicals glorifying the sort of socialism Prime Minister Mugabe no longer claimed to embrace. There was also a touch of vulgarity in some of the new buildings and monuments, particularly the new convention center. It looked like a massive, mirrored spacecraft, an outlandish extravagance in such a country.

Yet I did spend several pleasant days walking about in the streets of Harare, sipping beers in British-style pubs, watching Eastern European and Cuban movies ("released by our brothers in international socialism," said a pamphlet), and returning again and again for Szechuan chicken at the Blue Dragon, the best Chinese restaurant in Africa. The people, too, were pleasant, and if they were not quite as exuberant as James Ledaba, they seemed generally pleased with the situation in Zimbabwe. Blacks were pleased because they had won the war and the whites because they had been allowed to stay and keep their money. The city was almost unnaturally saturated with goodwill, brotherly love and the sort of polite tolerance one would expect in these honeymoon years.

This goodwill continued as I made my rounds in Harare for my newspaper. I found that Zimbabwe's successes were predictably easy subjects. Exuberant government leaders, white and black, gave me long lists of enviable statistics until I was buried under an avalanche of good news. Even a white MP,* a former colleague of Ian Smith's, said that the blacks were doing a better than expected job. "We got our complaints," he said somewhat dourly, "but it could be much, much worse."

Nevertheless, there was something a bit off about all of this back-slapping and benevolence. Perhaps if I had entered Zimbabwe through Harare, as most foreigners do, I would have been completely taken in by all of the activity, and would have shrugged off those "rumors" of problems in Matabeleland. But I had felt the tension and fear in the south, and had seen hunger with my own eyes.

Regretfully, I got few straight answers from the authorities. When I began asking tough questions of various leaders and officials, a remarkable thing happened. The flow of information stopped. My interviews were canceled or postponed, and I was asked to limit my questions to "germane topics." I was astounded by this behavior in a country that claimed to be open, free and tolerant, Africa's newest democracy. The authorities became so suspicious that I was assigned a government "minder" to follow me about with a tape recorder and notebook.

Western diplomats I met sloughed off this behavior as the inex-

---

* Under the constitution that ended the war in 1980, the whites were guaranteed twenty seats out of a hundred in Parliament, a provision that would be gradually eliminated over time.

perience of a young nation, a passing phase. I hoped they were right, although I wondered if it didn't go deeper than that. "The government hasn't yet realized that they don't have to be scared of everyone who disagrees with them," said one diplomat, a ruddy fellow who liked to take hikes in the bush and was an expert on native baskets. "It's what we tell them about torture, that it is silly to put a bag of water around a man's head to determine his guilt. Laws, openness and fair trials can work much more effectively. When they realize this, why, the paranoia will go away!"

"Right," I said, hardly finding the diplomat's analogy about water bags reassuring. I have seen enough of this world to know that paranoia is not something that goes away quickly, nor does it usually facilitate the creation of laws and openness. Paranoia seems akin to greed in the sense that, once touched, the feeling never goes away and one must have more and more.

Though rebuffed by the government I still managed to arrange a few interviews on my own, although it became more of a matter of endurance and frustration than anything meaningful or informative. After a boring conversation with the president of the Commercial Farmers' Union, I asked my minder why exactly she was following me around. She was young and smiled nervously most of the time, but her answer was direct. "They don't want you causing any trouble," she said.

"They?"

"The Ministry of Information."

"I see," I said, feeling very tired. We continued to talk as we walked through the streets on the way to my next interview. My minder was a curiosity in liberated Africa, a woman who dressed and acted like a spoiled Western girl. She had a costly coiffure and was dressed in an expensive, but tacky dress. Her fingernails were painted red to match her lipstick, and she spoke in a throwaway tone of voice that reminded me of teenaged girls who inhabit shopping malls in the States. She told me she had gone into the minder line of work because she wanted to be a journalist, although this comment, like all her others, lacked much commitment. "I learn by watching foreign journalists at work," she said, chewing gum manufactured in East Germany.

"But how can you learn anything when the ministry will not arrange any appointments for me?" I growled, feeling ornery first that she was here at all and second because she was so insubstantial. It seemed a contradiction, to make the point of sending out a minder, and then having the spoiled daughter of some minor official show up. Maybe it was me. Maybe I was considered just a tiny threat, so they didn't need to send out their heavies.

"Our leaders are very busy," she said, echoing what her boss had said. "They cannot always keep appointments."

"But I have plenty of time to wait," I said, telling her that it was difficult to report on a country if the leaders were unwilling to be interviewed.

"But we don't like you Western journalists," she said, "you print bad things about our country."

"Bad things?"

She looked shy again. "The Western media are always criticizing our leaders."

"How do you know I am going to criticize your leaders?"

"I have heard about the questions you asked," she said.

"But they were merely questions!"

"They were *critical* questions."

"And what is wrong with criticism, if the facts warrant it?"

"Criticism is not healthy in a developing country," she said. "We must devote our energy to saying positive things. Uplifting things. We cannot afford to always be arguing and criticizing."

"That sounds like slogans," I said. "Do you believe what you just said?"

"Yes, of course," she snapped. "Have you heard what our prime minister has said on this matter? Our country is new and weak. We cannot afford to be tearing it down like the Western media do all the time. Your countries are established and developed. Here in Zimbabwe, we need time to build a strong country before we can begin to criticize."

"But what if your leaders make mistakes? What if you disagree with them?"

"We do not disagree," she said. "And our leaders do not make mistakes."

I had to shake my minder only once, on my last night in Harare. I had arranged an interview with an opposition leader who did not want a minder present. He wanted the meeting to be "top secret," in the words of his nervous aide. He requested that no names or locations be mentioned. The arrangements were made through a shadowy contact in an office in Harare, a man who told me to meet him in front of a certain restaurant at a certain time.

I waited at the unnamed restaurant for over an hour, feeling as if I were in the middle of a spy novel. This feeling did not diminish when a black Mercedes pulled up and my "contact" rolled down the electric window a crack and told me to get into the back. I slid into a leather seat beside two quiet, thuggish men in dark suits. They were busily puffing European cigarettes, filling the car with smoke and saying nothing. The contact made me promise again not to reveal any names or locations. He made me swear to God to keep this promise, although God I'm sure could not have cared less.

The evening went on in this cloak-and-dagger fashion as we seemed to drive around in circles, I suppose to confuse me in case I was captured and forced to reveal the leader's whereabouts. (Actually, thoughts of water bags on my head did cross my mind. I had to keep reminding myself that I was going to see a prominent opposition leader, a public man, and not a criminal.) Finally, we arrived at a nondescript office "somewhere in Harare" (the contact's words), where I sat in an empty room and drank burnt coffee and waited for Mr. X to appear. After two hours it was clear the man was not coming, a fitting ending to this frustrating city.

On the way back to my hotel the contact apologized for his leader's no-show, hinting that there was more intrigue than met the eye in the disturbing world of Harare politics. He seemed inclined to tell me more, but I was no longer interested. I asked to be taken forthwith to the Blue Dragon, where I planned to meet Jim so we could drink Mai Tais and plot our escape.

IV
Zambia

Human
Failings

and today's bitter cloud
is a moment's pain
which the rain must dry.
                    —Marcelino dos Santos

The night roars on
one dies of love for the stars . . .
Certain great ideas
now obsolete
the night roars on

                    —Tchicaya U Tam'si

When does a man fail? He never fails if he
believes. Yes, even a man who has lost
everything.
                    —Kenneth Kaunda

1 Perched high above the Zambezi River is the Clouds End Hotel, a failing white beacon deep in Central Africa. After a fast, sweaty, uneventful ride through the prosperous fields of Shonaland, we spent our last night in Zimbabwe drinking gin and tonics in the cozy Clouds End pub, the walls covered with moldy animal skins and portraits of disbanded white rugby teams. The men in the yellow photos seemed pleased with themselves in a cocky, imperial sort of way. A fire crackled in a rough stone fireplace.

Clouds End seemed an appropriate place to end one phase of my journey and to contemplate the next. For nine weeks we had been cycling through nations that bore at least a passing resemblance to America. The roads had been paved, the autos made in Japan and the cities and towns reasonable reproductions of those I knew back home. Old Africa had cropped up outside of parks and remote territories only a few times, in the guise of a stray wildebeest or a postcard-quality grass hut in Botswana. New Africa, the post-colonial Africa of tumultuous change, had begun to appear more often, although it remained shadowy and hidden from the naked eye. The abyss, thanks mostly to South Africa, lay gaping, a possible future. But so far the specter of conflict had remained subdued enough to keep alive at least a superficial sheen of peace and prosperity along the southern third of the Cape to Cairo route.

As for the biking, it had been embarrassingly easy. Riding on smooth asphalt roads I had repaired only three punctured tires. Amenities such as cold Coca-Cola, fresh steaks and clean inns had been plentiful.

But come tomorrow, the moment we crossed the Zambezi, the influences of my race would become less apparent. The carbon-copy U.S. cities and highways built years ago by whites were going to be altered—tempered, changed and in some cases destroyed by strident republics formed twenty-five years ago at the height of Africa's liberation mania. Zambia, Zaire, Tanzania . . . across the swirling, primordial waters of the Zambezi, we were about to enter Central Africa, a region exhausted by years of unkept hopes.

Oddly enough, as we drank gin and contemplated the future, the only true bigot I met in all of Zimbabwe sat beside me on a Clouds End barstool. The object of his venom was Zambia, which he insisted on calling "Northern Rhodesia," a name that had expired two decades earlier. Apparently, he had lived there as a colonialist in the capital of Lusaka. "Owned a feed business," he said, "that is until the fuckin' kaffirs stole it."

"Man, you're makin' a big mistake goin' over that border," he said. "That country is the pits. It was once a fine place, 'fore the kaffirs ran it into the ground. Man, you're talkin' the Dark Ages over there. They made me sell out my business, back in sixty-nine, said it was for the good of the people. Rot, I said, all rot. Only good it did for any 'people' was to the bunch in power. They pocketed a few quid, all right. Then they ran the bloody thing into the ground, the stupid kaffirs. They knew nothin' about feed. Nothin'! And they still don't."

"When was the last time you were in Zambia?" I asked, having talked to too many mindless bigots in South Africa, many of whom had not been to black Africa for twenty years. But this fellow had just been over to Zambia. He was stopping in at Clouds End on his way back to Johannesburg.

"I was in Lusaka just today," he said, speaking in a chummy, let's-be-pals-and-put-down-the-uppity-niggers kind of voice. "Shit, I'm still sellin' 'em feed." He chuckled. "They botched it up so bad over there they asked me—*me*, the bloody imperialist—to come back and save their skins. And they're payin' me good money—dollars, that is, not that trash currency of theirs. Way I see it, the kaffirs can't bloody do without me."

"Do you often use the word kaffir over there?" I asked.

"Naw, course not. I keep my bloody mouth shut over there on that side of the river. It ain't healthy to go spoutin' off, yah know."

As he laughed, we heard someone behind us clear his throat. One can tell a lot from a cleared throat. I inferred from this one a man of girth, sophistication and extreme irritation. I also suspected he was not Caucasian.

"I'm not sure if it is healthy to go 'spoutin' ' over here either, my friend," said a deep voice. "Perhaps you have forgotten, sir, whose country *this* is." The bigot slowly pivoted to face a six-and-a-half-foot black man standing with legs spread and arms crossed.

The bigot stiffened in his seat. What could he say? He was utterly alone. I wondered if he would hold his ground and fight back, but he did not. Like most bigots, he was a coward.

"How right you are," he finally muttered, and then hastily made his way out of the bar and probably all the way back to Johannesburg.

2 The next morning, we left Clouds End at dawn and glided at top speed down the Zambezi Escarpment. I enjoyed the cold, crisp morning air and longed to get to the river and out of Zimbabwe. This country left me feeling weary and sullen, steeped as it was in contradictions and unanswered questions, a nation teetering on the brink. And I still did not know whether to despair, to wait for fate to run its course or to ignore my apprehensions and join in the cheerleader's chorus of hope. In a larger sense, these are the choices we Westerners have for most of Africa, despair, apathy or encouragement—a passive, futile set of choices.

I tried to put Zimbabwe behind me as I anticipated the approaching border, always an enticing benchmark for a traveler. As we dashed down the slope of the escarpment I saw that we were headed for what looked like a diversion from strictly human affairs, a valley teeming with crowded, rounded tops of jungle arbor. I could see the mists of dawn lifting above the floodplain, a green-gold veil of dankness, steam and passion, a vision of ancient Africa untainted. At the bottom of the hill the valley became a fortress of spindly hissing trees, baobabs and the tallest *mupane* I had ever seen. We slowed down to a crawl to absorb this unexpected patch of wild country, the first bit of truly primeval flora we had seen outside of parks on our Cape to Cairo highway.

Baobabs shaded our road, their branches looking like twisted sausages, their bark like sagging flesh. Black-shouldered kites swooped low through the branches and babbits chortled. Small, unseen mammals and lizards scampered through the dry, paperlike grass, making slithery noises that made my skin crawl. Before long we would see impala bellowing as they rutted, an unearthly noise.

Within a few minutes Jim had stopped to watch a gathering of kestrels and vultures in a baobab far off the road. He took out his 'nocs, as he called his binoculars, and was grinning with delight. "Look at that," he said, pointing at the birds in the baobab, "they're watching a kill, waiting to scavenge a bit of meat. Must be a lion down in the bush—'bout eight hundred meters from here." Through my own 'nocs I could not make out any predators through the brambles, but it was intoxicating to think they might be there.

We watched for a while as the carrion birds, their heads the color of a blackened corpse, stirred and jockeyed for position on the baobab. Finally, one bird dropped toward the ground, its wings flaring out like a parachute. A moment later the entire tree emptied as if by prearranged signal.

We passed on through the forest. None of our maps indicated that this area was a park or a reserve. Yet steenbok antelope grazed just off the road, perking up every muscle in their supple bodies when we got too close, their faces like teddy bears'. Elephant dung lay heaped on the highway, the freshest mounds steaming in the cool, morning air. At one point a herd of impala abruptly rushed across the highway, dozens of them jumping in arcs all around us. I felt their life-force radiating, tickling my skin.

Much later, I found out why this patch of ancient forest had been preserved. The reason had nothing to do with any preservation movement or sudden enlightenment about the animal kingdom, but rather with human warfare. During the Rhodesian conflict this area had been a kind of Ho Chi Minh Trail, a conduit for rebel supplies coming in from secret bases in Zambia. This activity had, of course, offered strong disincentives to human habitation and modern development. A former Rhodesian soldier, dying of drink and bitterness in a Nairobi bar, told me weeks later that he had spent several months on patrol here in 1978.

"Man, it was a hellish place back then," he said with red-rimmed eyes, a defeated soldier who described himself as a man "wrecked by war." He was grateful to meet someone who wanted to talk about his lost conflict, a topic he said nobody in Nairobi cared a whit about. "Certainly not my ex-wife," he said miserably, telling me he had married a white Kenyan during the war. She had abandoned him soon after and had taken their son away to England.

"You had mines and sharpshooters hiding in the bush all along the Zambezi," he explained. "Nighttime was the worst. See, we'd go out at night to try an' catch the rebels crossing the river. We'd walk through miles of thick jungle movin' and squirmin' with all sorts of animals, lions, leopards, everything. The rebels, they'd use these little dugout boats and fill 'em full of supplies and try to cross the river. We'd wait for 'em to reach our side and then pot 'em, one by one." He acted out the image, a drunk aiming a finger at liquor bottles on the back wall of the bar. "Pow! Got one! Pow! Another! It was very, very nasty stuff, indeed. Pow! Pow! Pow-pow-pow! We used infrared scopes, you know. We had all the latest gadgets."

The Zimbabwe side of the Zambezi valley is only twenty miles wide, but we took the entire morning to bicycle through it. We had planned to move quickly here, because we wanted to make Lusaka by the end of the day. But all our plans were forgotten as we became mesmerized by the forest.

We frequently stopped. Once I left my bike against a tree and walked alone into the woods. Bones marked a dozen kills, white scowls of elephant and buffalo skulls surrounded by scattered broken femurs, bits of vertebrae and loose teeth. Small mammals scurried unseen in the thorny underbush. I felt light-headed and alive, as I had in Linyati, although the electricity here was more genuine. I had flown into Linyati on a private charter, falling out of the comfort of the sky into a camp erected for our entertainment. In the Zambezi forest, I had arrived by bicycle under my own locomotion. I felt less of an interloper, armed only with my senses and imperfect knowledge.

The forest threatened only once. It happened when we came around a bend in the road and suddenly found ourselves in the midst of grazing elephants. My first reaction was to grab my camera, but I never had a chance. The lead bull, all seven tons of him, raised his trunk in a shattering bellow. He was only about thirty meters away, close enough so that I could see every detail of his face.

Have you ever seen the eyes of a bull elephant about to charge? The sharp, tiny, black marbles open wide with fear. This happens just before he lowers his head and starts his attack. Map, at Linyati, had warned us about startling an elephant. "And whatever you do," he had said, "do not ever get between a bull and his calves."

With a frightened group of females and calves to our left and the bull to our right, I forgot my camera and watched as the elephant gathered his bulk and charged. I braced myself as Jim, who was behind me, screamed at me to run. But I knew there was no point in running. A bull has a gait of eight meters and can move faster than thirty miles per hour.

I felt none of the clichés of those who have faced imminent death. Nothing flashed before my eyes. Instead, I felt an overwhelming acceptance, an almost welcome sensation that *here*, at last, was something completely honest, an ancient animal defending its family. The world was reduced to such a basic certainty that I felt no fear or remorse.

Miraculously, the bull veered off from his attack and ran crashing back into the woods. His family crossed the road in front of me and followed the bull into the forest. I stood stock still, feeling a peculiar lightness and clarity. Dropping my bike against a tree, I sat down and drank an entire liter of water. Facing imminent death makes a fellow thirsty. I had read that somewhere. Now I knew it was true.

A mile from the elephants our primeval odyssey ended, and it was back to reality, in this case a small, neglected border post stained by decades of sweat, rain and bloodshed. Vestiges of the recent war were strewn about amid piles of junk—rusty spools of barbed wire, an abandoned armored vehicle overgrown with brambles and what looked like armored duck blinds near the river. ("We'd wait for 'em to reach our side and then pot 'em, one by one," the ex-soldier in Nairobi had said.) This place was called Chirundu, and it had an atmosphere of Conradian jungle decay, a tiny, brackish blight on the edge of a pristine world. Everything was darkened by age and blistering sunshine. Yet the small shop next to the customs house seemed modern enough inside, filled with packaged candy bars, comic books, plastic toys and other bounty of postwar Zimbabwe.

Several heavy trucks were waiting their turn in line for gas, most of them heading south to Cape Town with loads of copper ingots from Zambia. Baboons, fattened by contact with man, scurried across the trucks and begged for food with their usual insolent sneers.

The truck drivers hooted when we told them where we were going. Most were blacks from South Africa, although the truckers who came through Chirundu came from everywhere in Africa. This was one of their spots to congregate along the highway, where they stopped to talk, drink, sleep and gas up their rigs. For them, Chirundu was like the Super Trucker Gas and Eats stop on the edge of Kansas City, and this route through deepest Africa was as common and mundane as a run in the States from, say, Chattanooga to Omaha.

"Man, have you seen the roads over there?" asked a Zulu driver

named Matthew, pointing across the river. He leaned against a corrugated wall near the gas pumps, joking with a half-dozen other
drivers, tossing bits of food for sport at the baboons. Matthew looked
American in a blue jumpsuit, tennis shoes and a purple cap. He
offered us a bag of Cheese Doodles, a puffed cheese snack. "You
fellows, you aren't taking those things 'cross the border, are you?
Man, don't be ridiculous. That road be like it was bombed. It looks
like a man hammered away the asphalt. They do not take care of
roads over there."

"This Matthew, he is right," said another driver. "It's very bad, not
like over here. It will take me four hours to make Harare from here. It
is . . . hey, Matthew, how many kilometers from here to Harare?"

"Four hundred," said Matthew.

"Over there," the other driver continued, "it takes three or four
hours on those bad roads to go eighty kilometers to Lusaka. In my
lorry, I go only fifteen, twenty kilometers per hour. Real pitiful."

The men invited us to share lunch and a bottle of spirits with
them, but we were in a hurry. Our plan had been to make it to
Lusaka, but we had spent most of the morning in the forest. "You're
thinkin' on makin' it to Lusaka *today* on those push-bikes?" said
Matthew. "Ach, it is lunacy on those roads over there. You will not
make it."

I showed the truckers the fat tires and reinforced frames on our
mountain bikes, but they were not impressed. Matthew pulled an
unmarked bottle of brandy out of his truck. "Man, this will be so
fine, the way to spend an afternoon in this heat. You stay with
Matthew and his friends. We drink. We talk."

I was tempted, but Jim and I were feeling compulsive about reaching Lusaka. We said good-bye to the drivers, finished with customs
and headed toward Zambia.

The Zambezi Bridge appeared down a small hill, a surprisingly
modern structure in the middle of a jungle, its arches of steel glittering with a coat of silver paint. Pedaling across we stopped to gaze
at the murky, gray river, whose waters had begun as runoff from
the war-torn hills of Angola to the west and would be delivered
into the ocean from the equally war-ravaged heights of Mozambique
in the east. But this has long been a river of blood. In the last century
the Zambezi served as a highway for slave traders and later for

conquering imperialists. Just a decade earlier this entire river had bordered warring nations, with the exception of that little miracle called Botswana.

As we crossed the bridge the Zambezi moved fast and furious, bruised by swirls and eddies and shaded by steaming ferns. Jim sighted a fish eagle overhead. We stopped to take a look as it soared and circled in a slow, cruel circle, searching for fish.

Suddenly, we were jarred by a sharp noise. A shot! It was coming from the Zambian side of the river, where a soldier was waving frantically at us with a large gun. Other soldiers were running out of a small bungalow toward the bridge and toward us. We stood still, too stunned to move. Were those lunatics actually shooting at us?

In Zambia, the soldier who had fired the gun wagged his finger at us, shouting about security, bridges and spies. But he did not seem very serious about it, grinning as he spoke. I wondered if he was drunk, but decided he was just desperate for a diversion in what must have been a boring post. I asked him why he had fired the shots. "To get your attention," he said gleefully, letting loose another short blast into the air. He thought this was funny and we laughed because he did.

In the customs building, another soldier took his job more seriously. He said he wouldn't let us in the country. The problem was purely bureaucratic. To enter Zambia one needed to pay a small visa fee. "And it must be paid in kwacha!" said the official, kwacha being the Zambian currency. The problem was we had no kwacha and the border post had no bank to exchange our U.S. dollars. Naturally, the official's solution was to send us back to Zimbabwe.

We were about to start arguing when the officer's superior appeared out of a back office. He was a small, weary-looking man in a sweat-stained shirt and tie. His eyes had the glint of an intellectual, an unexpected sight among grimy soldiers waving rifles. When he heard about the trouble, he kindly offered to give us the necessary kwacha himself. I wanted to give him U.S. dollars in return, but he waved the money away. "You will repay me by speaking English with me," he said with a tired smile, adding that he had attended the university in Kenya. This surprised me. A minor post such as Chirundu seemed an unlikely place to find a foreign-educated African. I asked him why he was here, and he said it was a matter of opportunities.

"We are a poor country," he explained, "whose one success has been education. We have many educated people. Many Zambians have been to university, but unfortunately there are no jobs for so many. I might leave Zambia and work overseas. Many have done this, but I want to stay. I want to help my country, so I go to where I can find a job.

"I will go back soon to Lusaka," he added hopefully, "and I will get a better job in the customs department. This place is only a temporary job." But he admitted that temporary already had been five years, a long time, I thought, to be drowning on the edge of the universe. He reminded me of one of those unfortunate, petty officials marooned on the Congo River in *Heart of Darkness*. What sort of country was this that had such little use for this bright, educated man? I asked him what he did out here.

"I perform my duties and read books and take a bus to Lusaka to see my wife and children every two weeks." But didn't he find this life-style hard? "I am serving my country," he said, though he hardly sounded convincing. "At least I have a job. In Zambia, this is something. Many men have no job at all."

Jim and I rode up a small rise from the customs house, past an enclave of makeshift huts and muddy paths. We pedaled past a row of people sitting outside shacks and doing nothing. Their dark, absorbing faces glared at us but revealed no emotion.

We stopped in one of the dark, ramshackle shacks to buy supplies, but found the food bins were empty. I asked an old man inside the store if he had any vegetables or meat. He had mixed Caucasian-Negroid features and wore the white skullcap of a Mohammadan, the first evidence that we were on the southern edge of the Islamic sphere in Africa.

He squinted and spat a wad of something—tobacco?—onto the floor. He looked sinister standing behind his counter in the darkness of the store, his skin sagging in wide wrinkles and his hair growing in white patches around his ears.

"We have some little food," he growled, "but it cost you many kwacha. You want?" He spat again just below my feet. "We have only some few potatoes and tomatoes. And some plantains and mangoes." He grunted a command and a boy, also in a skullcap and dirty white tunic, appeared with a chipped wooden crate. A few withered potatoes and tomatoes rattled around amid chunks of rock-hard soil.

The Mohammadan reached down under his counter and produced two labelless tins thick with dust. 'This is meat in a tin," said the old man, "beef and chicken. Very, very good." He used an already dusty robe to wipe off the cans. "Very expensive," he added. "You buy? One hundred kwacha."

"How much for the vegetables?" asked Jim.

"One hundred kwacha," he said, as if he liked the sound of this number. At the time, one hundred kwacha was about twenty dollars, a gross overcharge.

"That is too much," I said. "How much does this really cost?"

"This is only food here in this village," he insisted, enjoying what had to be a rare chance to truly haggle in this poor, desperate village. "We have this drought. Very bad times."

"But there was plenty of food over in Zimbabwe," I said.

"Ah, yes, but that is over there. You are over here now. They are a rich country. We are poor."

"Why is that?" I asked. The old man thought this question was an attempt to bargain him down. He narrowed his eyes to the narrowest slit.

"It is this drought, I told you. We have no food in the drought. That is why these foods cost much money."

"But here you are, right beside a river," I said, catching on to the haggling game. "How can you be having a drought beside a river?"

"Because we have no irrigation," he said, "and have no way of bringing river water to the crops." He swore that this was the truth and implored me to buy his food. He lowered his price to one hundred kwacha for the veggies and the canned meat.

"Why is there no irrigation?"

"We have no water pumps," he said warily, wondering what I was up to now. He lowered his price again, but I was not paying attention to the haggling anymore as I thought about this startling news that a village beside a river was in the midst of a famine. I was thinking about Egypt. In that faraway country I had seen a potential solution to the problem of irrigation on the Zambezi. Along the Nile there is a wonderful network of wooden hand pumps and Persian sail wheels that use the wind and human and animal muscle to pump precious water into the fields. It was a simple technology. The machines had been perfected by the ancients three thousand years ago and used effectively ever since. If it could work so well on a desert, why not rechannel a few dollars from some other more dubious Zambian development project and apply it to a program of constructing Persian wheels? With so many places in Africa that have no chance at all, it seemed perverse to let this fertile valley, built upon layers of alluvial soil from the Zambezi, go to waste for want of water when a huge river flowed a few meters away!

I knew nothing about the politics and logistics of transferring the Persian wheel to the Zambezi. I have no university degree in development theory. However, I occasionally see in my travels a solution that seems so obvious I must venture to blunder a suggestion. And so I will. The Persian wheel! Bring it forthwith to the Zambezi!

As I posed my seemingly random questions to the Mohammadan, I ended up talking him down to fifty kwacha for the veggies. I paid him in Zimbabwe dollars, which to him was worth a great deal more than the kwacha. The old man seemed disappointed that we did not want the tins; he must have been trying to sell them for years. But he accepted our money, a hefty sum that was the equivalent of about seven U.S. dollars in a country where each person statistically earns $47.50 a month.

On leaving the Mohammadan's store, we again ran the gauntlet of empty faces. They stared as they had before, unnerving expressions that combined with my weariness to rob me of whatever enthusiasm I earlier had felt. I knew that Zambia was having serious problems—what with the drought and the decline of their critical copper industry. And I was well aware that I would find little encouraging news in this butterfly-shaped country. Yet I had not expected to be slapped in the face with this degree of despair hardly an hour after my arrival.

At the edge of the border shanties we pedaled into another forest and began to bike up and down through the foothills of the northern Zambezi Escarpment. We were still cycling fast, hoping that we could make it to Lusaka by nightfall. So I wasn't paying much attention when I came bursting off a downhill and nearly crashed into a roadblock.

I didn't see the gate or the smoldering signal fires or the soldiers until I was just a few meters away. I slammed on my brakes and barely stopped in time. A gruff officer, hysterical with rage, waved a pistol at my head and screamed commands: "Get off that bicycle! You stupid man, why did you not stop?" Another soldier roughly frisked me for weapons. "Tell me why you are here!" demanded the officer, a disheveled, unshaven man who looked like a terrorist. "Where is your passport!" A dozen soldiers in ill-fitting uniforms aimed weapons at me, including a machine-gun nest with a heavy-caliber gun across the road.

As the officer shouted at me, Jim appeared at the top of the hill, moving at top speed. The officer screamed for him to stop. Jim, his head tucked low, was unable to brake in time and had to steer off the road and around the roadblock. The soldiers ran out to block his path, their guns on their shoulders ready to fire.

"Wait! He's stopping!" I shouted.

"Shut up," yelled the officer, telling a soldier to watch me while he ran up to Jim hollering and chastising him for trying to "escape" the roadblock. He accused us of being South African spies working with the agents who had attacked Lusaka, Harare and Gaborone three weeks earlier.

Then, with no explanation, he let us go.

After that we rode slowly, feeling drained and slightly paranoid. Soon we were obliged to go slower still, as the highway began to deteriorate. Matthew, the Zulu truck driver, had been right. First the pavement became crumbled along the edges, then rutted and pot-holed, and finally chopped up into sharp-edged islands of asphalt jutting randomly above gravel ruts. This place looked like a spot where a battle had been waged, with the victor being incomprehensible neglect. Fortunately, the fat tires on our mountain bikes* held firm against the assault of rough edges and sharp pebbles, although the bumps and batterings made me feel like I was riding a pneumatic drill. Agagagagaga . . . jitter, jitter, jitter. . . .

The bicycling was tedious and I soon became irritable, focusing my wrath on the Zambian government. How could they allow an asset like this highway to self-destruct? As I steered through the rocky channels I struck upon another development idea—why not employ those people at the border to rebuild this road? I had seen this sort of scheme work in Nepal, where mountain highways are maintained in rugged but satisfactory condition by peasants who live along the way. Each village is paid a fee and assigned a stretch of highway. The wage is a pittance, but it is more than nothing, which is what most of them made before the road came through.

* I want to mention Fuji bicycles, who donated our cycles, because they performed so well on this horrendous road and throughout the trip.

(Later, in Lusaka, I heard the actual details of what had happened to the highway. Apparently, the road had been slated for a major resurfacing job for at least fifteen years. It had begun as a development project sponsored by the United States. Then the Zambians decided to internationalize the project because the Americans were imperialists. This effort was stalled when the civil war in Rhodesia flared up and the Zambezi River valley became a battlefield. Finally, at the end of the war, the project fell back into the lap of the Americans, who held it up because they didn't like Zambia's radical economic ideas. Finally, in 1982, several million dollars were provided by Washington in grants and loans. Contractors were chosen, materials gathered and workers hired. However, none of this resulted in asphalt actually being laid. There were rumors about a corrupt official who diverted the money to a personal mansion and other officials with Swiss bank accounts—and on and on it went.)

A few miles into this wretched stretch of highway we passed a reminder of the colonial era, a picnic stop overgrown with weeds. Neglect had shattered the concrete table and the whitewash was cracked and peeling. A rusted sign buried under a tangle of grass conveyed a touching Western notion: KEEP THIS HIGHWAY TIDY. Farther on another faded sign announced a picnic stop in a small petrified forest. I tried to imagine bands of holidaying Rhodesians picnicking here, Norman Rockwell families stopping for a bite and a pleasant hike in search of fossilized trunks and limbs lovingly maintained by the white authorities.

After the petrified forest we continued our struggle along the battered highway, which soon turned steeply up the northern slope of the Zambezi Escarpment. Food became a major concern as the afternoon wore on. We had eaten for lunch what the Mohammadan had sold us. It was obvious that we would not make it to Lusaka by nightfall, so we began to look for villages. When no villages appeared, we began to look for trucks and cars, but the road remained empty. Even the jungle was oddly silent, with no animals and only small birds. I was later told that large mammals used to be as plentiful here as they were on the Zimbabwe side, but in recent years had been shot by human beings looking for food.

We did have emergency food supplies packed on the bikes, bouillon cubes and powdered oatmeal, but we didn't savor such meals. Nor were we thrilled about camping in this oppressive woodland, particularly after the roadblock incident. Then we spied a sagging hut of saplings and twine. A faded white cross hung above the doorway and a sign with sloppy white letters: SALVATION ARMY. Next to the church was an abandoned grain storage hut on stilts, empty and rotting.

A mile down the road I was relieved to see an actual human, and then several others and a cluster of round huts, a village. There were only two modern buildings, a colonial-era post office and a more recently built tavern. Attached to the post office was a red British postal box. The name of the village was stenciled in sun-bleached letters: ZEEMBAZEEMBA.

The post office was under a eucalyptus tree in the middle of a dusty common. Dour women in colorful wraps sold a few overripe plantains and vegetables on a table near the road. Thin chickens pecked at the hard dirt while old men squatted in the shade and watched us without interest. We used sign language to ask about food and a place to sleep. Several lively boys, the only creatures with energy we had yet seen in this country, dashed off like hungry rabbits to find someone in authority.

Soon a shirtless, barefoot man in cutoffs and a red cap appeared. He looked like a disheveled camper from, say, rural Arkansas. "I am Anderson," he said with an easy languor, "son of the village head-man." We asked if we could camp in the village and he said that only his father could grant this permission.

We bought eggplants and bananas from the women and set out to find the headman of Zeembazeemba. Pushing the bikes down a broad path, we entered a timeless world of cone-topped huts, cattle pens and naked children tending smoky fires.

Other than clothing and a scattering of plastic pots, the twentieth century seemed to have sidestepped Zeembazeemba. I saw no electric wires, no telephones, no radios, no engines and no running water. The people defecated in the bush and fetched water from a stream a mile away. Zeembazeemba seemed as deeply embedded in this land as the river and the baobabs we had seen, a village whose lines of ancestry had not been severed by colonial or postcolonial attempts at enlightenment.

Anderson finally found his father. The old man welcomed us with beer-drenched breath. He then fell asleep, but not before telling Anderson to put us up in a nearby cattle pen. This seemed like an odd place until Anderson explained the reasoning. He said the tangled acacia fence offered protection from wild animals and thieves. Besides, we were honored guests, and it was only right that we be treated with the same devotion and care as Zeembazeemba's all-important cattle.

While Jim set up camp with several young villagers watching intently, Anderson and I took a long walk to fetch water from the stream. He took my hand in the African fashion and we walked slowly through the village fields.

Anderson was proud of his English, telling me he had learned it in the Salvation Army school we had seen along the road. He told me the school, one of the few connections between Zeembazeemba and the outside world, had been closed for some time for lack of funds. "I am the headman's son," he explained, "so I must learn English. The headman is the government here. I translate and write papers for my father. It is an important job."

I smelled cut maize and wheat, familiar scents from summers on an uncle's farm in the Midwest. The fields were planted haphazardly in the traditional style, the stalks of corn stunted and brittle-white from drought. A few tired women hacked at the maize. They chopped in the same methodical motions as the women sweeping and spreading dung in the village. The women stacked their felled stalks into neat tents.

"As you see we have a poor crop this year," said Anderson. "You know of the drought? We will not have enough maize to feed the village."

"What will you do?"

"Some men from the village, they work in the mines and in the city. They will send money to this place. We will buy food if we have enough money."

"And this will feed everyone?"

"No, I think not. We will be hungry this year."

"What do you mean?"

"Some years, we have more to harvest. When the rains come. We keep enough mealies for our people and sell the rest and buy nice things to eat. Now, we eat no nice things. No meat and no vegetables. We eat mealies, but only a small amount. One cup instead of two. The elders of the village decide these things. Sometimes we kill a goat, but we need the goat for the milk."

"But the land here seems like good land. Why do you not plant more?"

"Ach, man, what a question. Are you a farmer in your country?"

"No."

Anderson knelt and picked up a clod of red soil. He crumbled it between his fingers. "This is dry," he said. "We have water in the stream, but how can we get this water up here? We have no machines for bringing up the water. We have no fertilizer. Man, we are so poor. We cannot afford these things."

Anderson talked on, telling me that another problem in Zeembazeemba was a lack of manpower. "Our men, they go to the city. They go to the mines to find work. We have no strong men here to work on these problems."

"But, Anderson, you are here."

"Yes, I am the headman's son. I will be headman, so it is my duty to stay." He said he had been to the city, and that he wanted to go back. "In the city, I see films and meet new people. The women, aha! There are many women, do you know?" He was in touch with the village, but he was bored because his mind had been awakened just enough that he craved to see more, to be introduced to the rest of the universe. He therefore looked down on the ancient life and thought of it as an impediment. But Anderson was not going to leave Zeembazeemba. He had his duty. "I will be headman soon. My father is old and sick. I must stay here."

I asked Anderson if there was any way he could see to improve life here. He shrugged and said yes, but with a gloominess that reminded me of the Chirundu customs man. I asked about the government. "They long ago sent fertilizer and helped us, but they have disappeared. We do not trust the government men.

"We are alone," he added. "No man," said Anderson, "is going to help us. We have learned this, to depend on no man. This is the old way in our village."

3 A white farmer named Bruce Skinner drove us into Lusaka the next morning, after several futile hours cycling uphill against waves of broken asphalt. Skinner's Toyota pickup was half-loaded with tiny plants from Harare, Virginia-flue-cured tobacco. Skinner owned an estate north of Lusaka, one of four hundred white farms settled before independence and still gathering harvests after two decades of black rule. "I'm going to make a go at tobacco," he said, a vital, warm man whose father had come out to Northern Rhodesia from South Africa in the 1950s. Skinner believed that tobacco could be the boon Zambia needed to start the long climb up from its dark, economic chasm. "We've got a good bit of donor money comin' in to get tobacco goin'," he explained, "including some dollars from you blokes in the States."

Jim and I loaded the bikes aboard Skinner's pickup, being careful not to damage his tender hopes. Within an hour we were on the outskirts of Lusaka, a swollen, dusty city that passed by as endless heaps of makeshift shanties, concrete huts and listless apparitions trudging along. The people looked like refugees fleeing from a war, Tolstoy's desperadoes.

Soon the slums ended and merged into a neighborhood of shopping arcades and finally into the old colonial district of unkempt parks and mansions, empty streets flanked by blank, medieval walls. Each concrete bulwark was topped by barbed wire and broken glass. Private guards, many armed with submachine guns, stood outside heavy, metal gates. Hints of the inner sanctums leaked through these defenses, here and there a spray of brilliant jacaranda or an overhanging branch of eucalyptus, Britain's imperial tree.

Skinner insisted we join him for gin and tonics at the Lusaka Club on the fringe of the colonial zone. The club was a sun-worn bungalow with an orange roof and parched playing fields. When we arrived a team of cricketers were playing in bright white uniforms. They looked miserable in the heat, their billowing outfits giving them the look of puffy, insignificant clouds blowing across the lawn.

The dining room accosted us with a rush of machine-cooled air that made the shabby interior musty and uncomfortably cold. An obsequious maître d' in a formal white coat met us at the door. Bruce Skinner, both powerful and familiar, was received with a flourish, while the farmer's bedraggled guests, dressed in muddy Lycra tights, were given a head-to-toe regard of contempt.

At lunchtime the faces at the Lusaka Club were a mix of white and black. The whites were businessmen, diplomats and farmers. There were also several "reliefers" sitting around the cozy tables, directors and subalterns of worthy organizations in town to help solve the AIDS problem, revitalize the economy and perform other tricks with smoke and mirrors. The blacks' professions were harder to surmise. Most wore dark, formal suits and imported leather loafers. Their expressions were dour and slightly dangerous, like minor mafiosi, with stone-carved frowns and intimidating girths. They drank prolifically, their place settings surrounded by small heaps of beer bottle caps. I guessed they were upper-level bureaucrats, since the government runs everything in Zambia and no one else can afford such copious appetites.

After lunch Skinner drove us to the Ridgeway Hotel, another fragment of colonialism near the downtown core. It was a quietly efficient hotel permeated by a faint odor of mildew, the result of introducing air-conditioning to an old building in the tropics. The Ridgeway was a bit pricey for me, but Skinner said it was one of the few hotels with functioning telephones, which I needed for my newspaper work. (This turned out to be only partially true. It sometimes took an entire morning to raise a dial tone.) The white desk clerk insisted we pay in hard currency, telling me that the kwacha was "more worthless than used toilet tissue."

Waiting for our room, we sat in the Ridgeway lobby—another watering hole for reliefers and overdressed elite. On an empty chair, I found a copy of the *Times of Zambia*, a smudgy, six-page paper controlled by the government. The front page was devoted to the comings and goings of the president (flower show, farmers' cooperative and speech on the need to sacrifice for one's country). Other features included an editorial on the menace of South Africa, Hagar the Horrible, "25 Years Ago Today" and the usual sports news.

Lusaka, the city, seemed as inebriated and weary as the elite in the Lusaka Club. It was desperately poor, stalled between two conflicting visions of utopia—the colonial town, once a paradise for several hundred whites, and the Marxist-inspired city of the post-colonial era. Both visions now lay in ruins, with numerous great public projects and heroic monuments scattered like so many carcasses amid the usual British sprawl.

An Ernest Hemingway character once was asked how he had gone from great wealth to bankruptcy. "Two ways," he said. "Gradually and then suddenly." This is essentially what had happened in Zambia. This country was not always the wasteland that confronted me in the summer of 1986. At independence, Zambia had been one of the richest and most promising nations in Africa. If a poll had been taken among African aficionados of that day, Zambia would have been placed just below the heady ranks of Nigeria, Guinea and Kenya. It seemed to have everything those halcyon days required—a small population, fertile land and limitless natural resources.

Zambia also had an enticingly radical and charismatic president, a former missionary teacher named Kenneth Kaunda, who briefly became a hero to the now-faded international humanist set. His plan had been simple—to buy happiness on earth. This was to be achieved by building a benevolent state apparatus that would provide not only spiritual leadership for the people, but would distribute the wealth so that everything—food, housing, education, clothing—was free, or close to it.

The key to Kaunda's scheme was copper. During and just after the colonial era, Zambia was one of the major suppliers of this precious metal. In a good year, copper brought in over a billion dollars in foreign earnings, a substantial sum in Africa. But worldwide copper prices plummeted in the mid-seventies, derailing Kaunda's already overstretched juggernaut and plunging the country into a deep depression.

By the summer of 1986, when I arrived, Zambia was destitute. The statistics were numbing. Foreign earnings had dropped to half their level from the early seventies. The gross national product was sharply down and falling. Half the population was unemployed, although this statistic was a guess made by foreign embassies, as the government was too embarrassed or too disorganized to print such data. Inflation was over one hundred percent and rising. Those "quality of life" numbers we Westerners take such stock in, what Jimmy Carter called the "misery index," were in a free fall, with life expectancy down, disease rates up, infant mortality up and food output in some areas below minimum nutritional needs.

Not even Kenneth Kaunda, who once called himself the most optimistic man in Africa, could deny such stark evidence. Just before we arrived in Lusaka, Kaunda had muted some of his liberation rhetoric and admitted to making certain mistakes, an extraordinary confession for an African leader—some would rather imprison and torture hundreds of dissenters than admit a single error. Kenneth Kaunda could be accused of being a hopeless romantic, but he was not stupid. If he wanted to keep the money coming in to pay his army and those workers any dictator must keep loyal, he had only one place to turn—those lousy capitalist banks which had always bailed him out before. But the era of easy credit was long over and the banks were in a nasty mood, what with $500 billion already out in Third World loans and little prospect of ever seeing most of it again.

So the banks—led by the now loathed International Monetary Fund—descended on Zambia like TV preachers among sinners. They sent teams of free marketers unleashed during the height of Reaganomics to coax Kaunda into capitalism. Like the previous generation of left-leaning Westerners who had preached "centralize," this new breed of Westerner preached "privatize." Kaunda, a desperate man, had reluctantly gone along.

The bankers' new religion did have some merit, as even Kaunda admitted. "It is wrong for the state to do everything for the people," he said. "This causes stagnation. There must be some way to spur individual initiative within the context of humanism, to reward those who work hard and punish those who do not." However, the bankers' radicalism was proving to be as wrongheaded as Kaunda's own revolutionary bungles. It wasn't that reform was unnecessary; it was just that things were moving too far too fast. What the people needed most was moderation, not another zealot's cause.

With the bankers' prescriptions in place less than eight months, the people were still suffering. The misery index was sinking to yet new depths, with inflation raging and hunger on the rise. Young men in Lusaka's markets complained bitterly of no future as the heaps of beer bottles grew higher on tables from the Lusaka Club to the shabbiest beer hall in the slums. Yes, it was true that the reforms were restoring some sanity to Zambia's chaotic spending binge. But at what cost?

I later met a Catholic priest in a city north of Lusaka whose face became livid at the mere mention of "reform." He was Eastern European but had lived for forty years in Zambia. The priest's skin was pale and fleshy, his eyes tired and drawn—a dedicated, anxious man who spoke in a holy rage about "those lunatic leaders who are killing the people."

"It is criminal what these leaders are doing," he said. "How can the peasants and the workers eat? Overnight, with these so-called reforms, their money has become worthless. Everything they need to live has become too expensive to buy. Do you know that bread has increased in the last year from forty ngwee to one and a half kwacha? Petrol is up one hundred percent! And do they raise the wages? No! It costs a week's wages for an office clerk to buy two cups of maize. The people are starving. There is suffering. And the president, he tells us we must sacrifice. Pah! He is living in a nice home. His friends live in nice houses. Who is doing the suffering?"

To prove his point, the priest insisted that I see a real "starving" person. He led me down a hard-packed trail along a swampy maize field and into a smoky grouping of mud-daub huts. The usual chickens and skinny dogs scattered at our approach. The priest gently sat down beside a woman tending a fire. He said she was twenty-two, but I could hardly believe it. She reminded me of refugees in Sudan, her face pinched and sallow, her back bent and her eyes weary. She had a nine- or ten-month-old baby wrapped around her back. Nearby, a toddler was being washed in a tin pan by an older girl of about eight or nine. The children were skinny, but not emaciated. A small portion of mush steamed above the fire. The priest talked to the woman in her native tongue.

"This woman, she has been abandoned by a no-good husband," he explained. "It is so very common here. I have known this woman for her whole life. She has these children here that you see. And she has another little baby girl. I have asked where is this baby, but this woman will not tell me. I will tell you where the little girl is. She is off in these fields somewhere, dying of starvation. This woman—I do not blame her. She has made a decision that many women must make. They have not enough food for every little mouth, so one must be sacrificed. It is an ancient custom here in bad times. Do you understand? They leave one out to die."

He asked me to come along and look for the little girl. We searched through the corn and on the edges of a black, polluted swamp. The priest grew more agitated as we searched, tearing away piles of brush and looking up in trees. He called the girl's name—it sounded like *Anania.* "Anania!" he cried in his mouselike voice. But we found no trace of the little girl.

Back at the village, the priest pleaded with Anania's mother. His voice sounded like a child's, one who cannot ever get the grown-ups to listen. The woman remained impassive, with a shell-shocked expression. She muttered a few words that sounded like a prayer, but would not tell him where the child was hidden. I felt the priest's anger and then his frustration as he threatened, cajoled and then begged. In my Americanness I was prepared to help any way I could, to beat the fields, to raise an army of searchers, to contact the presidents of a dozen international relief agencies. But the priest said it would do no good. "Look at these people," he said, his rage finally spent. "They are so weary and so desperate. They do not want to do this thing, but it is a tradition when all else has failed. And, you see, in a cruel way it is logical if there are too many mouths to feed. They have been abandoned by their government, so they revert to the old ways. They know no better. I threaten them with the wrath of God, but they fear hunger more than they fear God."

One morning I went to visit Kenneth Kaunda in his State House office. I found him ensconced in a cozy study that might have been transported from Oxford or Harvard Square. There was an antique globe, oil paintings in heavy frames and built-in mahoghany bookcases. Kaunda owned a large collection of books on economics, philosophy and theology, many of which I suspected were censored for public dissemination. I saw Lenin's collected works standing near Adam Smith's *The Wealth of Nations* and a hopefully unprophetic collection of works by Thomas Robert Malthus. Gifts from favorite state visits—that great prerogative of presidents, dictators and kings—lined the walls. These included a plaster bust of Bobby Kennedy, a samurai sword from Japan and a sensitive ivory statue of a woman and child. A much-thumbed Bible lay open on the president's desk.

Kaunda—he is called "KK" by nearly everyone—was dressed in his trademark safari suit and silk ascot. In his right hand he held a flashy white hankerchief, a traditional symbol of chiefs in Africa. His white hair stood on end, three inches thick, as if he had stuck his finger in an electric socket. It was a wild coiffure that appeared along with KK's let's-be-pals grin on posters, billboards and kwacha notes all over the country.

Since I was interviewing him for my newspaper, I asked the usual questions and he gave the usual answers. He spoke about the suffering of his people and his reluctance to initiate the IMF reforms, freely quoting the Bible and his own doctrine of humanism—a mix, he said, of Christianity, socialism and "liberal ideals." He was painfully sincere, or else an excellent actor.

"We were very romantic," he said. "We wanted to make the people happy. We thought we could do this by providing them with everything. We discovered this was wrong, that the state cannot do everything." He was quite frank about socialism's pitfalls, saying that it breeds corruption in leaders by giving them too much power, while encouraging laziness among a people used to having things for free. He had recently embarked on a highly publicized effort to cure both ills—a purge of corrupt officials and a program of slogans and rallies to "energize the people."

Here is a snippet from our hour and a half conversation:

DED: *Zambia is embarking on a tough program of economic reform. Will it work?*

KAUNDA: *These recent years have been difficult. Our economic health is not good. The people are suffering, especially those in lower brackets. This is the battle we must fight, the battle against poverty and its offshoots—hunger, disease, ignorance, crime and above all exploitation of man by man.*

DED: *But what if the suffering gets too great? Will you stick to the IMF measures?*

KAUNDA: *If the suffering gets too great, they will be revised. Everything must be fluid, subject to adjustment at the appropriate time. You see, the secret of our success over the past twenty-two years has been the acceptance of God's creation and our belief in the importance of man. I am telling the people honestly about these reforms, that they are necessary now. We are all Zambians. We are building a country. When I speak to the people, I say 'One Zambia,' and they answer, 'one nation.'"*

We spent much of the interview talking about South Africa, the topic my newspaper was most interested in. At the time, South Africa's unrest was on the tip of every media tongue in the world. Kaunda was a firebrand on the subject; he was eminently quotable as one of the few original leaders of black independence who had not been overthrown or killed.

"I'm normally a very optimistic person," he said, "but for the first time, I am very pessimistic indeed. Everything we have talked about today—Zambia itself!—is threatened by South Africa. I see the whole avalanche coming down very soon. Ten years ago, I predicted that the political volcano was going to erupt with so much lava. Hundreds of thousands will die. I do not want to believe this, but I do. Tragedy can be averted, but those in Pretoria with the power to act have not acted. They will not, I am very afraid. But we have the spiritual and moral power on our side. They have the economic and military power, but we are mobilizing the international community to fight this. Right is might, not might is right. The blacks won the rest of Africa against the colonial oppressor using the force of morality, and we shall win the last battle against South Africa."

When I asked him if he expected more raids by South Africa, he looked away from me toward a contingent of the local press recording the interview. Kaunda, like many African leaders, seldom ventures forth in public without his reporters and television crews. Our discussion would undoubtedly appear on that evening's news broadcast and in the next edition of the *Times of Zambia*.

"The situation with South Africa is grave," he said to the cameras. (I had been told that he often uses interviews with foreign journalists to make important announcements.) "I have this very morning put my small security forces on alert against possible aggression by South Africa." He said this with the dramatic flare of a great actor, raising his white hankie in the air as if it were a spear or a Kalashnikov.

"Do you have reason to believe South Africa will attack again?" I asked. "If so, when?"

"I do have evidence," he said somberly, lowering his handkerchief, "of a coup attempt sponsored by South Africa." The local pressmen gasped. Strobes flashed. Kaunda looked crestfallen, a father who has discovered an erring son.

"What evidence?" I asked. "Have there been arrests?"

"Yes, there have been arrests. My office will issue a full report shortly."

After the interview ended, Kaunda lingered like a close friend to say good-bye and wish me luck on my bicycle journey. Then he rushed off with a covey of young aides dressed just like him in safari suits and ascots. I followed the president and his look-alikes to an awaiting train of limos—painted a good-guy shade of white rather than the usual black—and a sizable police escort. Then Kenneth Kaunda was off to make another speech.

A dour aide led us out across the pleasant State House grounds, once the British governor-general's lawn. It reminded me of Caucasian gardens I had been seeing since Cape Town, resplendent with sweet-smelling blossoms, broad-leafed trees, white verandas and tame pea-cocks and impalas. Behind the main mansion was a nine-hole golf course, proof that even a man of the people must have his fun.

As we approached the State House gate, the grounds became filled less with flowers than with troops in combat gear. Truckloads of them drove past while others stood guard behind the fortresslike walls. Kaunda cannot be blamed for turning his grounds into a garrison. Nearly thirty heads of state have been assassinated in Africa in the past thirty years, while only one or two leaders have died peacefully in their sleep. Yet seeing this splash of cold, African reality indicated that there is more to Kaunda than his warm, grand-fatherly performance might suggest.

That afternoon, Jim and I cycled out of Lusaka, passing through acres of slums in the northern precincts of the city. It was a dan-gerous stretch of highway, where thieves and murderers were known to prey on travelers. We tried to pedal through without stopping, but after two hours, we were exhausted and needed a break. We stopped at a bottle store on a side street not far from the main highway. Makeshift concrete buildings lined the dirt street, with heaps of sour-smelling garbage piled between the structures. The walls of the bottle store itself were blackened with soot. The proprietor told us a gang of drunken boys had set the place on fire one evening when the store ran out of beer. He seemed blasé about the attack, exuding that inexplicably calm fatalism of common people living on the edge of an inferno. After all, the structure had survived, a bit charred but still intact.

Inside we met an angry young man, the sort who gave Kenneth Kaunda good cause to surround himself with high walls and Ka-lashnikovs. He said the president should resign or be killed, and that he would do it himself if he could afford a gun. These were dangerous words, but he did not seem to care. "That man has made everything bad," he said, fuming about the lack of jobs and all the rest.

As I watched the young man's face, I realized he was no man at all, but a boy of fourteen or fifteen. As he talked in simple English I watched his angry eyes and realized that I had seen this boy before—

on the Crossroads' barricade, in Victoria West and on the outskirts of Bulawayo. He was a boy who heralded a generation of new Africans who have grown up in places like this hell on the edge of Lusaka, boy-men in their early teens who constitute half the population of Africa, a growing rabble of youth being cheated out of even the slim hopes their parents embraced.

It is these children we should mourn if we are to grieve for Africa. They have had no proper childhood amid the rubble, denied the traditions of their grandfathers and the "new" Africa their fathers once believed in. Even if Africa eventually pulls itself out of its morass, it will be the children of the future who will benefit, and not these feckless souls.

After the bottle store, we reached the farthest outskirts of Lusaka after climbing a steep hill. I stopped and looked back at the city, gauzy and stinking of poverty. Up ahead I saw a metal archway set up for some long-ago-consummated ceremony, the sort of monument built because leaders from Caesar to Kaunda seem to get a thrill out of passing under them. It seemed fitting that a rusting arc de triomphe would wave us out of Lusaka, and that this hulking ruin would be plastered with old posters of Kenneth Kaunda, his perpetual grin and electric hair faded into blurry blues and greens.

4 Outside of the capital we joined the Great North Road, named by British Empire builders anxious to link up Northern Rhodesia with Tanganyika, Kenya and eventually Cairo in the north. Cut by the British South Africa Company less than eighty years ago, this highway pushes into the heartland of Zambia's two natural treasuries, the rich veins of copper and some of the most fertile farmland in Central Africa.

British Empire builders once had big plans for this corridor. In the twenties they had cleared out any natives with the bad luck to be living here and had embarked on their usual routine of hacking out roads, post offices and raw frontier towns. However, this dream was more of a dud than most in colonial Africa. As it happened, the settlers simply never came. And why should they have? The area where Jim and I were cycling was about as remote as any in Africa, a territory separated from the ocean by hundreds of miles of rugged terrain. In the early days copper was the only reason anyone bothered to come at all.

Eventually, a few settlers came, the types who thrive in the farthest hinterland. But the total number of whites in the entire colony never exceeded seven thousand, ruling a nation of six million blacks. Today, with copper nationalized and whites excluded from most sectors of the economy, their numbers have dwindled to less than one thousand. Nearly all are farmers.

They have been allowed to farm for two reasons. First, because they grow almost half the food in Zambia. Second, because Kaunda's obsession with factories and planned cities meant that he never got around to breaking up the white estates. His lack of interest in agriculture has been devastating to black farming. As we saw in Zeembazeemba, most villages are subsistence at best. Thus, Zambia, one of Africa's most fertile and least populated countries, remains dependent on several hundred eximperialists to keep them from starving.

Most of the white farmers live on large plantations along the
146 Great North Road, where they have quietly prospered despite the

collapse of the Zambian economy. We saw the first farms emerging over a rise just north of Lusaka. The sight was startling. Abruptly the bush was transformed into smooth, tidy rows of maize, wheat, oats and tobacco, watered by irrigation pipes lacing the land like silver snakes.

This abrupt vision of plenty, appearing like a dream after the slums of Lusaka, seemed an ambivalent blessing as I pedaled along in the hot sun. On the one hand, the farmers here should be commended. Yet what did this say about KK and his revolutionaries? I thought of Anderson in Zeembazeemba. All that man and his village needed was a water pump and some fertilizer. How much money would it have taken to make that little village work? What percentage of some idle factory?

We spent our first night out from Lusaka on a farm called Frangella, staying with a white foreman and his wife. Ronnie and Anita Tarr had recently come up from Zimbabwe to seek their fortune in the new atmosphere of economic reform. "I was damn bored in Zimbabwe," said Ronnie. "My father has a farm near Harare, and I got too many brothers fightin' over the land when the old man dies. So I said, 'To hell with it' and I got Anita and we comes up here to give things a try in Zambia. There's opportunities here with these reforms. We're savin' our money so we can buy us our own farm one day."

We arrived at Frangella just before dusk, in time for Ronnie Tarr to take us on a sunset walk through the nearest fields. As the sky turned pink and then gold we strolled past the house of the owner, an original settler whom Ronnie said spent most of his time in Lusaka and Harare. We walked through a large gate and into a field just cleared of crops. It smelled pungent, mingled odors of fertilizer, moist soil and animal dung.

Ronnie pointed at the long, neat coils of dirt. "I just got in the oats," he said with the pride and matter-of-factness of a lifelong farmer. "Pulled 'em in off of three thousand acres total. Man, they look great. They're over there, in the blue silo. Next I'm goin' to put in wheat."

He talked about the reforms, offering a positive assessment I had not yet heard. He claimed they were a godsend to commercial farmers and other private businessmen. "These reforms makes farmin' profitable up here for the first time in years," said Ronnie. "They've freed up the foreign currency so we can buy what we need to modernize. And they're finally payin' us close to what our costs are. Before, with all that socialist bull, the government just didn't pay enough for what we're growin' here. Said they wanted to make everything cheaper for the people. Well, that's real charitable of Mr. Kaunda. I mean, I'm all for helpin' the African. But you gotta pay what things are worth. It's real simple. We gotta pay for seed and tractor parts and water pumps." He looked around at the farm in the dusky light and spat. "Man, we grow food for half the country, and you don't do that unless you get paid for it."

That night at Frangella we ate a simple African meal of maize and goat meat with the Tarrs, whose small house suggested what Africa must have been like during homesteading days. Everything was designed for self-sufficiency. They had a small generator for electric lights. Heat in the house came from acacia branches and charcoal trees collected in the bush. Food was grown on the farm or shot in the bush. Anita was a master at pickling and preserving and salting away months' worth of basic foods. She also did all of the sewing. They had no television or stereo and their small radio was broken. They were saving money to buy a new one.

"It's a hard life," said Anita, a plain, frail woman who looked more like a librarian than a pioneer. She seemed lonely up here, away from her friends in Harare. Her two boys were in boarding school in Zimbabwe. "It's a little dicey up here for children," Ronnie explained, "and they ain't got a decent school." So Anita, a dutiful, but frustrated wife, spent her days doing chores and writing letters to her children and friends. She also painted pictures—simple, childlike watercolors of little boys and friendly, smiling animals. When I asked about her boys, she looked forlorn and answered like one of those suffering, wholesome women that fill Charles Dickens's stories: "I wish they were here. Oh, how I wish it!"

After supper, we drank Ronnie's whiskey and heard about his plans for a move even deeper into the wilderness. He said he was thinking about going to Mozambique, where the war-torn government was desperate for experienced farmers to come and take over the old Portuguese plantations abandoned at independence. I could see the look of the nomad in his eye, the man who is never satisfied with sitting still. "I hear they're askin' for white farmers," he explained after a deep swig of spirits, his voice becoming excited. "They're havin' a hell of a time with their farmin' there. They had some Communist farmers come out from Czechoslovakia and take over some of them old colonial farms. (You know, those fellows over there are all tied in with the Russians.) But the rebels chased 'em off. See, them Czechoslovakians ain't used to farmin' while they're gettin' shot at, not like we Rhodesians were durin' our war. You know, carryin' the hoe and the rifle at the same time. Well, I hear they're offering ex-Rhodesian farmers a hundred thousand dollars each to come to Mozambique and set up a farm."

"But, Ronnie," said Anita in a tremulous voice, "you don't know nothin' about farmin' in Mozambique."

"Ah, I'm not worried, woman." He took another drink and grinned the vagabond's smile. "That's what God gave me these brains for, what it's all about. Aye, I'll learn. For a hundred thousand U.S. dollars I'll learn anything."

"But I thought we were goin' to stay here for five years and go back home."

"Ah, listen, this place isn't at all what I thought it'd be like. It ain't no good, this country here. We'll go to Mozambique and make us some real money. Then we'll go home, I promise."

The next morning, a few miles north of Frangella, the white farms abruptly disappeared, yet the pace remained brisk in this comparatively prosperous area of Zambia. It was as if we had stumbled into an entirely different country. Faces here were animated, children laughed, and the African sky spread overhead like the underbelly of a bluebird. Trucks carried workers from field to field, children walked in gangs wearing school uniforms and vendors stood beside the road selling fat tomatoes, plantains and charcoal.

At lunchtime we reached Kabwe, the first major mining town along our highway. On the outskirts dust and smog began to spread over the bright sky. The dark, bizarre machinery of a major mine appeared through the haze like great erector sets: towers, elevator wheels and conveyer belts. Slag heaps hugged the road like long, gray-powdered ridges above a valley.

On the edge of town several hundred schoolchildren were holding a demonstration against South Africa. Antiapartheid and pro-Kaunda slogans were scrawled on banners as civic leaders spoke from a raised platform. It reminded me of similar demonstrations in America, except here the enthusiasm was not at all spontaneous. It did not have that rebellious, counterculture edge that makes such protests seem glamorous and slightly dangerous in America. In Zambia, the government itself claims the mantle of the rebel, which makes these gatherings part of the establishment rather than a swipe at the status quo. Consequently, the Kabwe bash was about as thrilling as a Republican rally in an all-Republican neighborhood. The children were bored and looking for a diversion, which we unwittingly provided. The moment we arrived, two white cyclists on red eighteen-speeds, a portion of the young crowd broke away from the monotony of the speakers and gathered around us, squawking questions, laughing uncontrollably and pointing at our ridiculous-looking tights.

Our brief burst of celebrity, however, ended as abruptly as it started when the denizens of authority rushed to the rescue of their erring children. "You are disrupting our meeting!" said a flustered school teacher. "You do not belong here! You are foreigners. This is for Zambians only!"

So we moved on and came to downtown Kabwe, which consisted of a single street of shops and a couple of side streets, a surprisingly small core for a city of at least fifty thousand people. Yet the small downtown in this comparatively wealthy part of Zambia was at least well stocked. A shop named Bargain Sales, Ltd., listed its products on a frontier-style facade: "Gent's suits, sports jackets, trousers, shirts, shoes, dresses, radios, watches, blankets, suitcases, beds, mattresses and furnitures."

Our stop in Kabwe was a quick one. We found a small, grimy restaurant, ate meat pies and took only a short rest. We had no particular reason to want to move fast that day, but we were again feeling compulsive, enjoying ourselves back on a decent road where people were healthy and normal.

Outside the restaurant I ran into a small boy playing with a homemade wire truck. He entertained us by roaring his toy vehicle up and down the wooden sidewalk. I took his photograph and climbed onto my bike and took off.

I mention the boy and the photograph because of what happened next. As Jim and I pedaled out of the town a carload of men drove up and tried to push us off the road, shouting like maniacs for us to stop while waving their hands menacingly. Who the hell were they? What did they want?

Since neither Jim nor I wanted to stop and find out, we steered off the paved road and onto a dirt path along the highway, where the car could not follow. Here we pedaled like Olympic stars, raising plumes of dust, hoping the car would give up the chase. But they kept at it, and the outcome was inevitable. They finally lunged their automobile off the highway and across our path, cutting off Jim, who nearly collided with the careening automobile.

Jim and I were furious. "You could have killed us!" I shouted. Our unknown assailants were also fuming. A brusque man stepped out of the car and loudly demanded to know why I was taking photographs in Kabwe.

"Photographs?" I asked, taken aback by the apparent non sequitur (I had forgotten about the boy with the truck). "What the hell are you talking about?"

"In Kabwe!" He waved his hands as if I were an idiot. "I want all your photographs. I want your film and your camera and your passport."

"Who are you to ask for such things?" I asked. "Are you a thief?"

"You are truly thick," said the man. "I am a policeman. It is illegal for you to take photographs. I am going to confiscate your film and cameras."

I asked him for identification, and he blew up even more, threatening to take me back to the police station. I showed him my photography permit, knowing full well that these papers offer no guarantee of anything. I read a passage from the permit regarding photography, which it said was legal anywhere in Zambia except for train stations, bridges and military installations. I added that in Kabwe I had been photographing children and toy trucks—surely, I insisted, this was not a security risk. He perused my permit and showed it to his colleagues.

"We have new restrictions since this permit was issued," the man said, acting a bit more professional. "The security forces are on alert. The racists in South Africa may attack us at any time. All photographs are temporarily banned. Please take no more photographs while you are in Zambia."

We didn't realize it at the time, being on the road and out of touch, but the news of a possible attack by South Africa was spreading like wildfire across Zambia. Kaunda, a master communicator, was turning up the full wattage of his charisma to spread the alarm of a coming invasion, energizing his people over the state-controlled media with calls for patriotism and resistance.

This was not good news for us. It was a rotten time to be cycling through Zambia. When a country feels it is about to be destroyed by an army of white, blond, blue-eyed warriors, it is not propitious for people who fit that description to be traveling about. As we biked north of Kabwe it became clear that the country indeed was absorbing its president's urgent message. *Look out for spies,* warned the papers. *Watch for suspicious people, unusual happenings,* admonished the radio. How unusual and suspicious were two Caucasians on funny-looking push-bikes?

Apparently, we were unusual enough to be stopped again a half hour north of Kabwe by nervous troops at a recently raised roadblock. Again, my papers saved me from having my cameras and tape recorder confiscated, although it took a great deal of patient negotiation with officers primed for finding trouble. I wondered how many roadblocks it would take until my equipment was actually taken. Jim and I, being the gruesome, gallows sort, placed a bet. I said three more roadblocks and the cameras would be history. He said two.

"We are on guard for spies from the racist regime," said a young soldier at the next roadblock, standing beside a smoking tin of oil. "The country is getting prepared to smash the racists," said another.

The situation was made worse by our knowledge that this insanity was in some ways justified. Kaunda undoubtedly was whipping up patriotism to help out his faltering regime, but there also was a great deal of truth in what he was saying. South Africa indeed was looming like a great, dark shadow over southern Africa. Not only was the body count continuing to mount in South Africa itself; the SADF had just launched several raids against its neighbors, including a full-scale invasion of southern Angola. It seemed clear to everyone—Zambians and American cyclists alike—that the defenders of white South Africa were in a particularly vicious mood, and that they were capable of doing just about anything.

Our sympathy with Zambia's situation did little to mitigate our own troubles. In three days of cycling we were stopped and searched four times by security forces, although somehow neither Jim nor I won our bet. (My papers worked surprising wonders, although there were close calls.) Maybe it was my own gloomy mood, but even the people themselves appeared less friendly along the road. They seemed to be ignoring us or even glaring at us, which made Jim and me even more nervous as we began almost unconsciously to bike faster.

At first, I thought that time might mitigate the situation in Zambia, but time only seemed to make things worse. Three days north of Kabwe several soldiers burst into our hotel room in the middle of the night. The place was called Kapiri Mposhi, a town on the crossroads between the Great North Road and the highway to the copper belt. The soldiers descended like Furies, screaming incoherent questions and accusing us of being white spies as they ransacked our possessions for nearly two hours.

The next morning Jim and I tried to place a call to the U.S. embassy, deciding that it was time to get some accurate reading on what was really going on in Zambia. Was it safe to keep going, or should we return to the capital? Was South Africa really about to attack Zambia? I felt all eyes on me at the local exchange when I asked to place the call. Were these people suspicious of a call to the U.S. embassy? The papers were full of misstatements about America's supposed support of South Africa against the front-line states.

The call did not go through, although several other people successfully placed calls to Lusaka that morning. This made us more nervous and suspicious. Why had the call not worked? Was it deliberate, or merely the horrendous condition of the phone system? We asked the post office operator to keep trying, and he promised to send a boy to fetch us at the hostelry if the call went through. So we returned to our room and began to collect everything we could find suggesting that we had been in South Africa. We either burned the items or slipped them into envelopes to mail home. In my journal, which I did not trust to the mail, I marked out any reference I could find to South Africa with a black marker.

We had planned to depart Kapiri Mposhi by bicycle later that morning, but decided to wait and try the embassy again. Neither of us felt enthusiastic about cycling in a nation suddenly gone mad. Our trip through Zambia was only about a third complete. We still had seven hundred fifty kilometers—ten days of cycling—before reaching Lake Tanganyika, where a weekly steamer would haul us to Kigoma in Tanzania. This seemed like a phenomenal distance given the current hysteria and our general feeling of exhaustion after three months on the road.

Before leaving America, Jim and I had agreed that we were not going to be fanatical about the biking. So we made a decision as we nervously burned our papers, to forgo biking for the next three hundred miles or so and seek faster transport away from this chilling environment.

So Jim checked train schedules while I strolled down to the local United Bus Company (UBZ) garage to inquire about buses. The train seemed the best option, so we bought two tickets for the next day to Kasama, a northern Zambian city about two hundred kilometers from Lake Tanganyika. Hopefully, in this distant town, the invasion mania would be less acute and we could bike again in reasonable safety.

I spent the rest of the day strolling around Kapiri, happy despite my anxieties to have more time than usual to glimpse a small town. I did not want to appear too curious and arouse suspicion, so I didn't talk to many people, although there were several who seemed friendly despite the general mood. One fellow, a shopowner, told me he thought the "alert" was a lot of bunk. "It is something the president does so the people forget they are poor," he said, "and so the people forget that they cannot afford to buy food." He stressed *"the people"* with great irony, as if he had once believed in these words, but was doubtful of them now.

I discovered that about five thousand people lived in Kapiri Mposhi, a town that was a primitive version of those interstate jungles that appear at major intersections on America's highways. Kapiri was built on the axis of Zambia's two major trade routes, the south-north road and railway connecting the minefields to the capital and the south, and the east-west road and railway connecting Zambia to Tanzania in the east and Zaire in the west. It was primarily a transient's town, a stopover for miners, truckers, railroad hands and general travelers.

Downtown Kapiri had a bedraggled look to it. The only modern building on the main street was a plastic-coated Zambian National Bank building, looking out of place with its modernity, a fast-food-restaurant design appearing amid cowboy architecture. It probably had been raised during the boom time in the seventies, its condition a sad reminder of the country's rapid decline. Its white facade after just a few years of neglect was blotched by rust and dust. Its colors had all faded, and its interior amenities like air-conditioning had long ago ceased to function.

Behind the storefronts I found a market inside thick concrete walls, another government effort that went awry. The concrete walls were crumbling and the neat rows of cubicles that were meant to be enclosed shops had never been finished. After only a decade, the market looked more like a ruin than a wave of the future. It reminded me of abandoned Arab desert forts I've seen, where ragged families make their homes amid the wrecked walls.

Still, the Kapiri Mposhi market was a colorful, active spot, a refreshing diversion from anxieties. At the entrance, boys were roasting peanuts and an ancient man in an Arab's white tunic was operating an antique Singer pedal sewing machine. "We sew everything" said his scrawled sign. Inside, vendors sold clothing, including T-shirts with Kaunda's smiling face. (One said KAUNDA IS MESSIAH, a shirt the vendor said had not been selling well recently.) Other stalls sold everything plastic—combs, buckets, bags, shoes and saucers. The colors were blinding and exotic in a place where browns, grays and blacks predominated. One boy sold old Western LPs, their covers limp with moisture and age. On one album cover, a young Barbra Streisand looked vaguely sexy in a fifties, kittenish way, her hair arranged in a Doris Day, pixie hairstyle. On another album the Jacksons crowded into a photograph, with Michael and his siblings wearing uniform, two-inch Afros, as if they were trying to be hip, but not too hip. And then there was Marvin Gaye.

"I like Marvin best," said the boy in the stall, making the point that Marvin was black and a hero to all Africans. He refused to believe that Gaye was dead. To prove the point he cued up "Let's Get It On" on a battery-powered record player. "See, Marvin is not dead!" He sang along, cocking his head back and doing a little dance.

That night, we rode to the Kapiri station, a gargantuan structure towering over a cornfield on the edge of town. The station was part of a one-thousand-mile railway built for Zambia and Tanzania by the People's Republic of China. Conceived at the height of the Rhodesian war, the project was intended to provide Zambia an alternative to trading with the white regimes to the south. Against all odds, the TAZARA (Tanzania–Zambia Railroad) has been a moderate success, though the Chinese are unlikely to ever see the $400 million they donated to their brothers in revolution.

The Kapiri station was painted light blue and green, oddly serene colors in the bush. Even odder was its size. As we rode closer, I was sure that distances were playing tricks on my eyes. Most of Kapiri's population, I thought, could fit in there, and many more if they were stacked vertically. But there was no trick. It *was* vast, and trimmed with neat landscaping and walkways better suited, perhaps, to Beijing or some other gentle city. The road leading up to it is gravel and rough and rural African, and then, suddenly, there is a smooth concrete road, broad steps and an urbane-looking passenger platform with gentle, curving lampposts and flowerpots filled with the tawny stalks of dead plants.

Perhaps the designers thought that this station would so change the destiny of this dusty town that the rest of Kapiri would catch up to its imperious style. The whites fell for this reasoning, so why shouldn't the Chinese and the Zambian government? Build a railway and change everything, Cecil Rhodes himself had said, although Central Africa had resisted even this formidable dreamer. Now the blacks have had their turn at wishful thinking, although the verdict is not yet in. Perhaps, one day, this railway will indeed make Kapiri Mposhi a large, wealthy, tranquil city in Africa.

But meanwhile there is this absurd monolith sitting out there in the middle of the bush, a black pipe dream that is already beginning to melt back into the rugged landscape. After fifteen years the huge windows were mostly broken and the soft, asbestos tiles inside were encrusted with black dust. Cobwebs hung in unreachable corners and the soft, pastel paint was cracking and fading.

As we tried to board the train, a soldier demanded that we wheel our bikes into the police post in the station. My hopes for a quick escape became dimmed as once again a gang of hyped-up officials began barraging us with incoherent questions. Apparently, the captain in charge knew all about our movements in Kapiri, including our inquiries at the bus station, our letters mailed home, our attempted phone call to the embassy and my chat with the boy in the market about Marvin Gaye.

The officers shouted their questions, and the scene became more and more incoherent. First they focused on me, then Jim, then me again. Then they brought in a British woman with a backpack who was apparently also waiting to board the train. They began searching her pack and shouting at her, somehow reaching the conclusion that she and I must be husband and wife because we both had on wedding rings. I tried to argue against such powerful logic, but they never did fully believe me.

After half an hour of escalating nonsense, an army major came and chastised us for coming so late to the train. He said it would be impossible to search our bikes and gear in the time remaining before the train departed. I told him we had been sitting here for the last forty-five minutes, which had been plenty of time to inspect us.

"That is impossible!" he said. "You have only just arrived! Don't you know that you must have a security check? Don't you do this in your own country? Surely it is the same in your country, you stupid boys."

"You mean you are not going to let us on?" I asked.

"We have a very bad situation now in Zambia," he explained, his tone becoming suddenly apologetic, "with terrorists coming in from South Africa. But do not worry. There will be another train in four days." He smiled as if this should be reassuring. "And do not forget to come in time for a security check!"

Back in town, we searched for cold beers, feeling exhausted and frustrated. Kapiri had a chaotic nightlife, with its large transient population and the sort of local riffraff that seem to appear like weeds in such places. We stepped inside a dingy disco in front of our hotel, a makeshift structure literally vibrating with the loud thumps of country and western.

The inside was laced with pulsating Christmas lights, a garish mimicry of a Western dance hall. Inside, men and painted prostitutes danced and swirled in a gauze of tobacco and hemp. It seemed like an awfully serious business. No one smiled. A few men without women danced drunkenly in hops and twirls, grave-faced Africans stumbling through steps reminiscent of traditional free-form dances. A man at the door offered us a woman, *Daga*, and a beer, in that order, but we accepted only beer and found a place to stand beside the bar, where another woman tried to seduce us by fingering her nipples through her thin dress.

I have seldom been to a place that seemed so joyless, unless one counts the Ridgeway Hotel, where rich Zambians went to drink and find women. There was a Western edge of pointless hedonism, of postindustrial despair, blending with a languid, despairing fatalism that can be so distressing in Africa. I thought about trying to talk to someone, to find out why everyone seemed so unhappy. Was it the lack of jobs? The economy? But the music and the despondency seemed so crushing we could not bear it any longer.

Back at the hotel, the noises of copulation and drunken brawls in nearby rooms kept us up most of the night. We finally gave up on sleep at four A.M. and passed the rest of the night playing gin rummy, until the army came at their usual time to search us. By now we knew them well enough. They were no longer abusive, but joked with us and accepted an offer of beer and peanuts. When they left, Jim said, "Dave, we've got to get out of here. We can't play gin rummy forever. Particularly if you continue to win."

5 The next morning we tried our luck with a public bus, and waited most of the day for it to appear in a lot across from the disco. "When will it come?" we asked, as skinny prostitutes watched us from across the road and occasionally whistled. "Soon," said the always patient Africans sitting with us in the dust. We spent the morning playing more gin rummy and batting away a particularly nasty strain of large, black fly.

Finally the bus came, a ramshackle vehicle piled high with bundles of every description. It had once been a Fiat bus—that much I could tell from rusty insignia on the back. Its sides were battered, its tires bald, its windows cracked and its engine sputtered as black soot spewed out the exhaust pipe. I marveled that it even functioned. We hoisted the bikes atop a roof rack already piled high and then climbed inside, stumbling over suitcases, canvas bags, human appendages and chickens. The only unoccupied seats seemed conspicuously empty, located directly behind the door. The reason why they were empty became immediately clear. Whoever had the misfortune of sitting there automatically became keeper of the door. The folding door of the once-tidy bus had long ago lost its ability to open and shut itself, and apparently it was beyond the bus company to fix it. So it was secured by a scrap of old tire, which the keeper untied and retied each time our traveling caravan stopped.

The Fiat soon was rushing through familiar African country, though the bush and light woodlands were thicker and less developed than I yet had seen on the Cape to Cairo highway, broken only occasionally by huts and scattered maize. Every two or three hours we stopped in a former settlers' town. Typically, a village of round, African huts surrounded a wide street of four or five frontier shops and a half-dozen crumbling colonial bungalows. Years ago the shops had been whitewashed, but more recently they had been painted in turquoises, crimsons, yellow-greens and violets. They were strung out along the main streets like strings of colored beads.

The bouncy, twangy tunes of African rock and roll blared from tavern doorways, reminding me of summer evenings in Mexican villages, where colors are also bright and the air hot, sleepy and remote. It seems as if something is about to happen in such a place, but never does, and a man begins to suspect that the heat is playing tricks on his expectations.

In one town, Serenje, the bus broke down for three hours, which gave Jim and me time to get reasonably drunk in a former British pub called The Half Moon. Inside, the walls had been painted over in cartoon images of smiling Africans in Western clothes, drinking beer and dancing. Underneath a painting of a white mermaid with luscious breasts sat a middle-aged prostitute. She seemed a regular fixture in this local pub, a pudgy, middle-aged Mae West character with a saucy tongue. The clientele sat and laughed and drank, rural fellows out having a slightly naughty time after supper, old friends gossiping and telling the same jokes over and over again.

As a biker, I thought I would hate the bus. I expected it to be impersonal and much too fast, like a bullet slashing through the country. I had seldom traveled by motorized vehicle in the Third World, so I suppose I was feeling a bit superior to it all with my biker's airs. But I was wrong. This particular bus, with its slow progress, breakdowns and entertaining rabble of passengers was not the least bit impersonal. I was reminded of the medieval pilgrimage, where strangers from all stations in life were thrown together on a common trek toward redemption, the ultimate metaphor of the journey. We were not bound for Godhead in our Fiat, nor would Chaucer have thought us as interesting as his Canterbury folk, but we had a cast of characters that made for a pleasant three-day trip.

The driver was our nominal leader, a silent man with bulbous cheeks and a grin that always seemed on the verge of a long, self-deprecating laugh. Behind Jim and me sat a warm, no-nonsense woman named Phoebe, a secretary in Kapiri Mposhi who tried to set us straight on everything from the economy to the natural superiority of women. And then there was Joe. He sat two seats back from Phoebe, a machine repairman who could quote the Preamble to the U.S. Constitution and most of the Declaration of Independence. He was something of an expert on Abraham Lincoln, whom he admired, like many educated Africans, as the author of the Emancipation Proclamation. There were also two miners across from us. Jim taught them five-card stud. (The second day these two fellows had a fistfight over who won a game, and only stopped when the driver began laughing and calling them women for fighting over a card game. This set off Phoebe, who said that women were far too intelligent to indulge in such a stupid pastime as cards.)

Inside our Fiat, we felt safe from the paranoia engulfing Zambia. We talked lazily about Abraham Lincoln, Phoebe's no-good former husband, the finer points of poker and the difference between African and American beers ("African beers have taste, American beers do not," I said, an assessment the Africans loved).

I asked Phoebe what it was like to be an educated woman in Zambia. "I do not complain too much," she said. "I have a job and make money. I have gotten rid of my bad husband. This is important for my children. But women are still ordered about by men, and this I do not like." She frowned. "But I do not think this will be changing much. This is the way things are in Africa."

"Why do you think that?" I asked. "You have been telling us that women are better than men. Then why don't you assert yourselves? Why don't you try to change things?"

Phoebe grinned, as if I were a child. "Because, as I said, this is Africa."

"But that sounds terribly fatalistic," said Jim.

"Of course, it is! Africans are fatalists, don't you know? I can believe women are better than men, but that does not change anything. You see, we do not have great expectations like you Westerners."

"It's true," said Joe, whose large, oceanic eyes seemed to take up about a third of his hairy face, giving the impression of a kindly cartoon character. "Man, look at Lincoln."

"Ach, not him again!" said Phoebe.

"Now, now, listen! Lincoln, he had expectations. He wanted to free the black man, to win the war and to get on with making America this great country. We Africans, we have no such expectations."

"But why?" I asked, having been perplexed for some time by this most un-Western phenomenon. "What is wrong with having great expectations? There is so much here that could be done." I waved at the bush out the window. "Look at all this empty land. Why aren't crops growing here?"

Phoebe laughed gently, and so did Joe. "That is why you Americans run the world," she said sarcastically. "You see this bush here and you want to make it into a farm or a factory. I ask you, why do you want to turn that bush into a farm? Why do you want to run the world?"

"I don't want to run the world," I said, "but I have seen hungry people in Zambia."

"It is true," said Joe, "but Africans accept these things. It is part of life. Some times are good, some bad. In the end, it is a balance."

"He is right, this man, for once," said Phoebe. "Africans accept life as it is. In this land, people most years grow enough food to eat. They build a house to live in. This is enough. We do not have to be the world leaders. It is too much work to run the world! It is hard enough to raise children and earn a little money to eat. Why do Americans work so hard? It is not healthy, I think."

Conversations rose and fell in the cocoon of the Fiat, interrupted by naps and hours spent staring out the dusty, rattling windows, mesmerized by rushing shapes. Sometimes Jim and I joined the two miners for a game of poker, but I think they were working in cahoots, because they always won. (These victories delighted the entire bus.)

Our fellowship deepened when our cocoon was violated every few hours by army checkpoints. Typically, young soldiers in steel helmets would come aboard and order us off the bus. Outside, we were told to form into three lines: men, women and whites. They then searched each of us and went carefully through the bus.

Phoebe and Joe said checkpoints were common in Zambia, but not these rude and thorough searches. "This is new since this latest news about South Africa," said Joe.

As white foreigners, we were always questioned the longest. "Have you been to South Africa?" the soldiers would shout inches from our faces. They generally ignored the luggage in the racks, and only once discovered my cameras. This time I came very close to losing them simply because one obnoxious soldier fancied them for himself. There was no pretension of security risks or confiscation. "I take these," he said, "you get another, okay? You American. You rich. You get another." Thankfully, his commander did not see things his way. He ordered the young soldier to return my things, which the boy grudgingly did.

In the middle of the second night the Fiat's generator died. The driver, still jolly and talkative, kept going on the deserted highway without headlights in the bright African moonlight, rushing into the darkness at seventy miles per hour. It was an eerie ride, silvery and mysterious, with the usual nightjars diving about, their silhouettes murky against the glowing pavement. Periodically, the engine died and the driver had to rouse the male passengers to stumble out of the bus and push until the engine took. None of the passengers complained. "What is the point of complaining?" said Phoebe. I told her that in America it was unlikely that paying passengers would get out and push a bus in the middle of the night. "But why?" she said in disbelief. "Buses break down. What do they do when this happens? Just sit and wait?"

Early on the third day our crippled bus pulled into Kasama, capital of the northernmost region of Zambia. In the crowded, squalid central market we had to abandon our beloved Fiat to an unsavory-looking mechanic clutching an old wrench. Jim and I considered bicycling from here to Lake Tanganyika, about two hundred kilometers away. After the warmth of the Fiat the situation seemed less grim in Zambia, and we were anxious to see some of this remote country on the bikes. Besides, Phoebe told us there was a great downhill above the lake, a vertical drop of nearly two thousand feet.

Our optimism about a relaxation of tensions was premature. We didn't realize that Kasama was just about the worst place to be at that moment. A few days earlier a bridge had been blown up by saboteurs. The entire population was roused, expecting any moment an invasion from the south.

As Jim and I discussed our travel plans, a tall man in a powder blue coat asked to see our passports. He was loud and demanding, but said he was not a policeman. As he spoke, a small crowd gathered, but I didn't think much of it. This was a common occurrence in places where eighteen-speed bikes are a curiosity. Yet people did seem unusually serious. They were pressing in so tightly that we were having a hard time getting air.

When we declined to give him our passports, he became hysterical. "You are South African spies!" he screamed.

"What?" I stammered, feeling a sudden chill.

"Spies! Spies!" he shouted as the crowd pushed in with ugly expressions: They split to let a policeman through. He asked what was happening, and the powder blue man loudly insisted that we were South African spies and must be taken to the police station for questioning. The policeman looked at the people and at us and realized that he was in over his head. Yet he looked at our passports, showed them to the man and attempted to persuade him that there was no reason to arrest us. I admired his courage and professionalism, but a silent, unfathomable pitch of anger had been reached by the people in the Kasama market.

"Those passports can be faked!" bellowed the powder blue man. I put my hand on his shoulder to reassure him. "We want to be friends," said Jim.

He angrily slapped me away. I was startled by the intensity of his violence. I was drawn to his eyes, and was horrified to see the extent of his rage. With a shudder I realized this man *hated* me. It was such a powerful emotion being slung at me that I stepped back in dismay. *He hated me,* and there was nothing I could do to change his mind.

The die, it seemed, had been cast, although this was all happening too fast. "Sir, we are merely travelers," I was saying, trying to calm the lunatic in powder blue. But as I spoke, the crowd was swelling from dozens to over a hundred and perhaps more. They scurried from alleys and shanties into the open space of the market. We were becoming a small, Caucasian eye in a hurricane of enraged faces. The policeman fled when the first tentative rocks and sticks began to fly. We held on tightly to our bikes, the nausea of fear welling up in our bellies, our backs against a low wall that provided some protection. "Spies! Spies! Spies!" shouted the mob.

"Take them to the station!" Powder Blue shouted. I felt hands grabbing me and my bike, lifting me high into the air to carry me across the market to a waiting flatbed truck. A fist punched me in the ribs and someone struck my head.

I was not going to give in easily. As we were lifted into the truck, I squirmed and fought. "Where are you taking us?" I bellowed. I was as angry as I was frightened. I had some grossly misplaced conviction that this couldn't be happening to me. No, not to *me!* Not a reasonable, fair individual like myself! I sympathized with their fears about South Africa. I loathed apartheid as much as the next fellow. But what did this matter to the mob?

The crowd cheered when we dropped into the truck bed. Enthusiastic members of the mob jumped aboard and I began for the first time to truly panic, realizing at the very least I was going to get beaten up. Then, abruptly, a siren blasted the marketplace. Everyone scattered as a police Land Rover rushed through the people. Soldiers armed with automatic rifles deployed around the truck. The would-be lynchers, including Mr. Powder Blue, fled into the crowd. I breathed a guarded sigh of relief, never imagining I would welcome the arrival of the Zambian police. Moments later we found ourselves sitting in the Rover and pulling into a fortified police compound.

The mob chased us, but stopped at the gate. "You are safe now, my friends," said one of the police.

The police compound was yet another remnant of the colonial era. There were two one-story buildings, one shaped like a U turned on its back, and the other a straight line resting on top of the U like the dictionary symbol for a long vowel. The long building was the jailhouse, the bottom of the U the main booking room, and the rest of the compound was offices, interrogation rooms and toilets. Long ago, the station must have looked like something out of a Graham Greene novel, complete with tidy gardens, flowers and fresh paint. Yet little of this stodgy Britishness remained. The courtyard gardens were overgrown and filled with heaps of junk, everything from tires to a rusty engine block. Each object was labeled with a weather-worn "evidence tag" attached by a wire. The toilets had been clogged for years. One of them had been cemented over. However, I could still see the faded initials of the imperial police painted in large letters on the roof—NRP, Northern Rhodesia Police. After twenty-five years of independence, no one had bothered to paint them over.

Jim and I were led into the commanding officer's office by police dressed in neat if slightly threadbare uniforms. S. M. Nchiminga (the CO) and three colleagues welcomed us to Kasama and asked if we were hurt in the market imbroglio. We told him we were a bit shaken but physically unharmed. We felt relieved by Nchiminga's geniality, and answered several of the usual police questions about our trip.

Nchiminga then turned and whispered to his colleagues, a dour pregnant woman, a sneering detective in a paisley, three-inch-wide tie and a tall, friendly-looking man in what looked like a naval commander's uniform. I leaned over to say something to Jim and Nchiminga screamed loudly for me to shut up. His abruptness startled me. He then shouted an order to a guard by the door.

"Separate them!" he commanded, his friendly demeanor having disappeared.

"But, sir . . ." I said.

"Shut up," he retorted. Then to the guard: "Do not let them speak! They shall be interrogated separately. Take them to separate rooms." Jim, meanwhile, had been taking out eyedrops for his contact lenses, an innocuous act that elicited a fantastic response.

"Stop him!" shouted the detective in the paisley tie. "He is trying to take poison!" The guards scrambled to grab the villainous drops, nearly tripping over each other in the effort.

"Those drops are for my eyes," Jim started to explain.

"Silence!" bellowed Nchiminga. "You are South African spies. You will be held for questioning."

"South African spies!" I stammered. "But, but ... that is nonsense! What proof do you have?"

"Take them!" he shouted.

I was led to a small room and told to sit on a bench, where I was incarcerated most of that first morning. The hours were excruciating. I had nothing to do. It was dark and I had no idea what the hell was going on. I remembered reading somewhere that detainees in an Argentinian prison tried to pass the time by thinking of pleasant things. I thought of Vermont, hikes through thick stands of pine, my wife's embrace, a crackling fire, a glass of wine. . . .

As the hours passed, I took each of these thoughts and mentally lined them up like a shell collection so that I could study each memory. Yet they seemed so distant in that bleak room I soon began to despair. Would I see my wife again? My own little paradise in the hills of Vermont? Somehow, I had to learn to shut down my mind, if I planned to remain sane.

By the time I was fetched for interrogation, my anger was beginning to rise, although I knew that I must keep it in check. I demanded that Nchiminga inform the U.S. embassy that we were being detained. The greatest fear in these episodes is that no one in the outside world knows you have been arrested.

"You want me to call the U.S. embassy?" said Nchiminga. "But you said you are a writer. Now you are saying you work for the U.S. government? Perhaps you are a spy of the CIA? But, then, they work for the South African racists."

I tried to explain to him that Zambia, like most nations of the world, had signed a treaty that required them to inform the appropriate embassy when one of their nationals was arrested.

"You are a liar!" said the pregnant woman, whom I grew to dislike intensely. She hardly asked anything, but frequently piped in like a parrot, echoing Nchiminga's "Liar."

I tried a different tack as the questions continued, suggesting that they check my papers. But they said they had searched my bike and knew all about my "faked" papers.

"Then why don't you call the Ministry of Communication," I said, referring to the authority that had issued my permits, "and check with them?" I mentioned my interview with President Kaunda and suggested that the State House could verify who we were. "With a simple phone call you can clear this up," I insisted.

"That is clever," said the man with the paisley tie, the thug of the group with his passionless eyes and hulking presence. "You would have us believe that you interviewed the president when we know this is a lie," he said, "so why should we bother the State House?"

I told them that I had proof I had interviewed the president, a cassette tape. "If you will let me go to my bicycle, I will get the tape and play it for you."

"Let you go to your bike?" said the man in the paisley tie. "Do you think we are stupid? What do spies carry on their bicycles? Bombs? Poison? We are not finished inspecting those bikes."

"When will you be finished?"

"Shut up!"

I spent most of the afternoon alternating between interrogations and the void of the dark room. Then, sometime around three or four o'clock, I was led into the booking room of the station. On the way, I passed a jail cell with bars up high, close to the roof. I saw a pair of white hands reach out of the bars and realized that Jim and I were not the only Caucasians in this place. This gave me a really bad feeling. "Help me!" said an accented voice. It sounded French.

In the booking room, I was told to sit on a wooden bench. It was not a comfortable seat, but I preferred it to the dark room. Here it was light and I could watch the police go about their routine business. I could see a street out in front, lined by trees and flowers. Later, Jim was brought in and told to sit beside me, although we were ordered not to talk. It was a relief to see my friend unharmed. He also brought bread, apparently taken off the bikes. We ate in silence.

It was a lazy afternoon in the Kasama police station. The desk sergeant spent most of the time drinking coffee and, being a decent sort, gave us each a cupful. He recorded a half-dozen arrests in a large leather book over the space of four hours. There was a dispute among a prostitute and two male customers that seemed to involve a child. Then there were two men arrested for fighting and a boy brought in for poaching. Once, the sergeant's men beat a black prisoner with a small club. The blows seemed routine, almost boring to the police. Blood flowed from purple lips and burst from wounds on the victim's legs. Since the episode occurred in the Bemba language, I did not know the man's crime, or why the police felt compelled to beat him, but it was a chilling thing to watch, particularly in our position.

After a while a Frenchman was brought in to sit with us on the bench, a friend of the man whose hands I had seen in the jail. The desk sergeant had told me these Frenchmen were arrested for blowing up the bridge, acting as if there were no doubt they were guilty.[*] I slipped him some bread. He said he hadn't eaten much in the past three days.

The Frenchman seemed on decent terms with the sergeant, who gave him a copy of the *Times of Zambia*. France was playing in the world cup that year, and the sergeant was a soccer fan. The Frenchman asked if the sergeant had seen his friend.

"He is in the jail."

"Yes, I know. He is all right? May I talk to him?"

"No. He continues to refuse to talk to us."

"I tell you, he speaks no English! You speak no French, so that is that. Don't you understand?"

"How come he speaks no English?" The sergeant was humoring him. "It is the world language."

"French, too, is a world language," the Frenchman said. The sergeant smiled as if he were talking to a fool.

"You are of course lying," he said. "Why does your friend not talk?"

"Half of Africa speaks French," said the Frenchman increduously, his Gallic honor piqued.

"You are only making it difficult," said the sergeant pleasantly. "I do not want to see your friend hurt, but he must talk!"

The interviews continued that night and the next day. They covered a wide range of topics that often had nothing at all to do with my alleged spying. I usually ended up giving long speeches, trying to explain such things as American electoral politics and the ins and outs of publishing a book. Much of this talk I purposely designed to bore them, but they kept having me come back for more.

---

[*] Later, I found out that the two Frenchmen were wildlife workers on contract in Rwanda. They had been driving south to Zimbabwe on holiday and had had the misfortune of driving a Land Rover painted the same color as Zambian Army vehicles. When South Africa raided Zambia, their agents had used similar vehicles. The Frenchmen also had touch-up paint for their Rover and a ladder to climb up on the roof rack. Similar items were used by the actual raiders. All of this "evidence" bode very badly for the Frenchmen, and also for us, since Nchiminga seemed to think we were in cahoots.

Most questions were asked by the man in the paisley tie and Nchiminga, with the pregnant woman shouting "liar" every few minutes. I later recorded some of these conversations in my journal. The words below are taken directly from my scribbled notes.

ON FREE ELECTIONS IN AMERICA

In one session, they were suspicious of my Americanness. They believed that America supported the South Africans.

"You are American," they said, "and America supports the racists in South Africa."

"But I do not personally support South Africa's government," I said.

"What! You oppose your government and your president? That's impossible."

"But I *do* disagree with my government's South African policy. Many people in America disagree with our president. I voted against him in the last election."

"Impossible! This is absurd! Vote against your president? How can that be possible? Here we love our president. No one speaks against him!"

I then gave a small lecture about American democracy and the concept of free elections. . . .

ON PUBLISHING IN AMERICA

"You say you are writing a book about Africa," they said. "Who are you working for? What have they told you to do?"

"I am working for myself," I explained, "under contract with a publisher."

"This is nonsense! Who pays you? Surely it is the government. Do they not publish the books in America? Do you not work for the government? They must know what you are doing."

I gave a short discourse on the First Amendment and free enterprise, speaking at least a half hour of gibberish which they carefully copied down. Then they asked how I was paid and, as I was becoming tired of the questions, I gave them another speech, a twenty-minute lecture on the technicalities of book publishing, including contracts, royalty structures, subsidiary rights. . . . I spoke until I was exhausted, and they jotted it all down until they became so bored I was dismissed.

ON THE HISTORY OF THE CAPE TO CAIRO ROUTE

"You say you are following the Cape to Cairo route," they said, "but it does not come through Kasama. So why are you really here?"

"But the Cape to Cairo route does come through Kasama."

"Liar! How can you prove it?"

"I have read books."

"What books? Where?"

I named about twenty titles, and mentioned that most of them included photographs.

"You have photographs of Kasama? That is illegal."

"These photos were taken years ago."

"Where are they? You must bring them all here. They must be destroyed! They are illegal!"

Late in the evening, Jim and I were allowed to get our bedrolls off the bikes and told to sleep behind the sergeant's desk in the booking room. The Frenchman and two thieves were put in jail cells. When I asked to go to the toilet, I was taken under armed guard to the sit-down toilet reinforced by concrete. It was filled with years of excrement. "Do you use this toilet?" I asked.

"No," said the guard, "it is broken." He led me to a nearby room with the more sensible African-style toilet—a hole in the ground with a bucket of water.

In the middle of the night we were awakened by more beatings. Someone was being struck repeatedly just a foot or two from my head. The victim wailed and begged the police to stop.

"Don't look," said Jim in a whisper, "don't look."

In the morning, two more whites were detained, a Norwegian and his Austrian girlfriend. Like us, they were mobbed when their bus stopped in the market. The Norwegian was furious over his detention, saying he was born and raised in Zambia and would call Kaunda himself if he wasn't immediately released. I tried to tone him down, having learned from experience that there was no point in locking horns with these people, but he kept at it. I was afraid he might make it worse for all of us.

Later in the morning, when I saw Nchiminga, he was in a foul mood. He was quite frustrated now that he was awash in white foreigners. "You are all spies!" he shouted at me, as if I were the leader of the whites, "and you will admit it sooner or later." I caught his meaning, knowing it is common practice in many countries to beat confessions out of those prisoners with the bad judgment to insist they are innocent. I decided to play on the CO's frustrations and offer him a saner way out.

"You can be rid of us right now if you let me play the tape of the KK interview," I said. "After all, if I have been a guest of the president, and he finds out you arrested me, will you not get into trouble? It would be so easy to play this tape."

I expected him to deny my request again, but he surprised me. "Yes, yes," he said, "get it! Get this cassette!"

An hour later, I played the tape for the assembled interrogators. When they heard the voice of their president welcoming Jim and me to Zambia, their jaws dropped in unison. Then came a remarkable transformation. Nchiminga stood up, shook my hand and smiled. He welcomed me to Kasama, as if nothing unusual had happened. He offered to take us out to lunch at a local restaurant. "Please come tonight and stay at my family home," he said. "I would like you to meet my father."

"Then you are going to release us?" I asked.

"My friends! You were never arrested! We merely have to be careful." His smile was so patronizing it nearly swallowed his face. "I'm sure you understand."

We declined his invitation, saying that we would like to board the first bus available going north. I then inquired about the other whites being held, insisting that they also be released. Nchiminga frowned and asked if we knew them before coming to Kasama. I answered no, but said they obviously were not spies.

"They will have to remain for further questioning," he said flatly. "We will arrange a bus for you."

Later that morning the paisley tie and the man in the naval uniform escorted us by foot to the bus station at the market. A crowd still was hanging about from the episode with the Norwegian, so armed guards came along in one of the more bizarre hikes I have ever taken. Four policemen formed our guard, carrying automatic hand pistols and Kalashnikovs. They deployed in a square formation with Jim and me in the center, pushing our bikes beside Paisley and the navy man. Over a hundred Kasamites pressed around us, their faces glaring, their hate hanging in the air like a powerful force. The entire crowd remained eerily silent as we walked slowly down a road lined with crumbling colonial bungalows and shacks sweating in the heat.

"I hope you are not offended," Paisley abruptly said in the midst of our anxious march. His small, peevish eyes scanned the throng, searching for any untoward movement. His fingers grasped a large revolver like a gangster. Paisley's face, scarred by tribal markings, was subdued but fierce. As an interrogator, he had been particularly abusive, hinting that he would make us confess. And I had watched him casually punch at least four local prisoners. Now this savage wanted to have a chat, and the topic was, of all things, morality—and the humanism of Kenneth Kaunda.

"We are very worried about South Africa," he said in a low, mechanical voice as he stalked along. "But I want you to understand, we are all brothers. Black and white, we are all one. This is what our president teaches. This situation is not racial. Do you know the philosophy of our president? *The Dignity of Man. Tolerance Towards Human Beings of All Races.* These are our president's slogans. We in Zambia believe in the morality of man, in human rights and in the love of God."

He talked on as he scanned the mob. His words flowed monotonously, a mindless recapitulation of Kaunda's sentiments. This man was a thug, an official whose acts blatantly subverted Kaunda's teachings, yet his voice rattled on in utter disregard of their meaning, his finger poised all the while on the trigger of his weapon.

Soldiers stopped us five more times along the hundred miles between Kasama and Lake Tanganyika. Once a roadblock officer shouted: "I want those whites taken now to the station!" Fortunately, Nchiminga had scrawled out a note certifying that we had been "screened" in Kasama.

"Yes, I know Nchiminga," said the officer. "We will allow you to proceed. I am sorry to inconvenience you, but we had two South African spies come through here last week posing as Frenchmen. It is very bad. They tricked us into letting them go. It was Mr. Nchiminga that found them out. He is a hero for finding these spies."

Late in the afternoon we arrived in Mpulungu, a small town on the southern shore of Lake Tanganyika. When we disembarked we were surprised to see Phoebe run over from a nearby market to embrace us. She said she had been very concerned about us. "I am so happy you are safe. I have been praying for your safety."

Riding into town, we found a telex office and sent a message to the U.S. embassy in Lusaka:

TO USA CONSUL FROM DAVID DUNCAN AND JIM LOGAN, CAPE TO CAIRO CYCLISTS: *Detained two days in Kasama. Released today unharmed. Have arrived safely in Mpulungu. Please advise foreign travelers to expect trouble on Great North Road.*

The message included details about the other whites being held with a request to inform the proper embassies.

Later, we learned that dozens of white foreigners had been arrested in Zambia after Kaunda's announcement of a coup attempt. Overnight, a calm, friendly country had erupted into a caldron of xenophobia. White tourists had been taken to jail for taking snapshots of old buildings, for mailing "suspicious" packages and for no reason at all.

As for the other whites arrested in Kasama, they were held for six weeks by Nchiminga and his officers. Six weeks! Later, in Nairobi, I read a short article about the incident in the *International Herald Tribune*. It reported that several "white tourists" held in Kasama had been released after Kaunda received personal entreaties from François Mitterrand and the prime ministers of Norway and Austria. "The detainees said that they were beaten and deprived of food," said the *Herald Tribune*. "No reason was given for their arrest," concluded the short article.

The Cape of Good Hope,
originally called the Cape of Storms,
a more appropriate name
in these tumultuous times.

Hennie Bloem, an Afrikaaner farmer
we stayed with, was a man buffeted
by drought, recession
and almost unfathomable change.

Ready to shove off in Cape Town.
Jim Logan, who was crazy enough
to join me on the first half
of the journey, stands to my left.
We were never again this clean
and tidy in Africa.
(Photo by Peter Stanford)

The Abraham family,
who shared a camp with us
on the Karroo in South Africa.

Kids in the black township
of Victoria West, South Africa,
near where I met Stephen,
the boy who refused
to read Somerset Maugham
because he was a "white" writer.

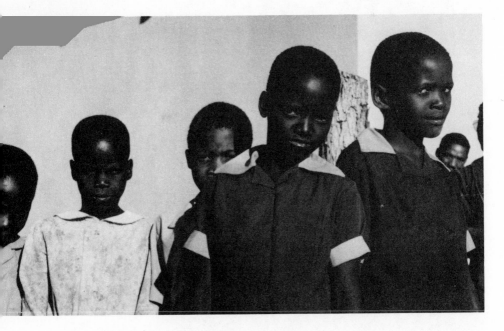

Fixing a punctured tire on the Kalahari in Botswana. Although the road was decent, when we pushed off into the bush to camp, acacia thorns wreaked havoc on even our thick-skinned mountain bike tires. (Photo by Jim Logan)

Jim is riding on a long, long road in Zimbabwe.

Guitar boy, spotted near the Bembesi battlefield in Zimbabwe.

Quentin "Atom" Bradnick, son of a Rhodesian pioneer, stands among his cattle on his fortress/farm in the Matopo Hills of Zimbabwe.

Zebra and wildebeest running under a baobab tree near my campsite. It's dusk in the Serengeti, and the air is electric with energy as the bush shifts into night.

This sign stands outside the city hall in Eldoret, Kenya, and points the way to my starting point far to the south. I didn't have the courage to look for the mileage sign to Cairo, which was also still well into four digits.

Pausing in a Nile village to chat and drink "cha
(Photo by Andy Shafe

Cycling on the Sahara. Note the road
(or lack of road) and the dust storm.
We are lost and nearly out of water.
(Photo by Andy Shafer)

Andy Shafer, my companion in North Africa,
stops to consult an Egyptian boy,
probably about the location
of the nearest shop that sells Stella,
a local brew.

Finished at last,
I pose like a tourist
in front of a great pile of stones at Giza.
Sprawled out below me
is my long-sought destination:
Cairo.
(Photo by Andy Shafer)

V
Tanzania

*The End
of
Something*

hear my burning cry o heavens!
hear the lament
of a disillusioned soul
in this land of ravaged hope
                              —Amin Kassam

1 Two stone lions in Mpulungu guarded the Red Lion Disco, known as the Red Lion Pub in colonial times. On each lion's face the ferocious countenance of empire still glared pathetically at a fading street of rust-stained bungalows, the beasts' features softening as they eroded into lumps of pulpy stone.

Inside the disco-pub we drank warm, moldy-tasting beer in a room painted electric blue. Jim and I were waiting to board our steamer to Tanzania, scheduled to leave that afternoon. We took our drinking seriously, feeling edgy after Kasama. Across the room a half-dozen dissipated Africans drank near a loudspeaker blaring American rhythm and blues. The men were surrounded by the usual empty bottles and bent metal caps. One man was arguing in a slurred voice with a prostitute in a tight pink dress. She seemed to be soliciting him, although neither was the least bit enthusiastic.

We sat as far away from the Africans as possible. They seemed perfectly harmless, though in our state of mind, we wanted nothing to do with them or, for that matter, with anything African. If there was a low point of our journey, this was it. I was so shaken that even the drunks in the Red Lion Disco looked suspicious to me, as if they might turn me in at any moment.

We finally boarded the Lake Tanganyika steamer just as the sun began to dilate before setting across the lake. To my surprise, I discovered that our ship was none other than the *Liemba*, launched by the German Empire when the century was young. I had read about her in a Nairobi museum—how she had been manufactured in Prussia just before World War I, hauled a thousand miles overland from Dar es Salaam to the lake and then almost immediately lost to the British, along with Tanganyika itself, when hostilities broke out. Now, more than seventy years later, it was still in service, magisterially skirting the lake's desolate shores and slowly disintegrating into rust and decay. Much of the hull was already badly stained, an orange-umber color. The passenger decks were deteriorating into a 175 slumlike squalor, and the engine sounded like a man with emphysema—*a-wheeza-a-wheeza-a-wheeza* . . . Long ago, the European builders of the *Liemba* had declared that she was but the first of a great fleet of ships that would ply Lake Tanganyika. But now, here she was still alone, another symbol of that era when the white man played God in Africa.

While we waited to set sail, I leaned against a rusty railing on the passenger deck and watched gangs of perspiring, barebacked workers transferring cargo from the dock to the ship's hold. This was a long, grueling process. Everything was being loaded by hand, a string of workers passing bundles along like a fire brigade. It was a pitiful sight, as the men were laboring in the shadows of several large, abandoned cranes from the imperial era, machines that had unaccountably been allowed to fall into disrepair. I remembered what Cecil Rhodes once said about Mpulungu, that it was going to be another Chicago, and the lake another Michigan. "I see cities all around that lake," Rhodes said, "European cities . . . with factories, docks and parks with flowers." He was so confident that he ordered the construction of a pier, against which the *Liemba* was resting.

As I watched, two Mercedes-Benzes roared onto the dock. Their sleekness and the clean hum of their engines jarred against the gathering gloom of Mpulungu. I asked a Tanzanian crewman standing nearby what these fresh black autos were all about. He sneered at the cars and shook his head, explaining that they were being shipped up to Tanzania for the "big men"—government officials—in the capital of Dar es Salaam.

"The cars have come from South Africa," he said contemptuously. "It is supposed to be illegal to trade with the racists, but here they are anyway. But, as you can see, the big men do not really care about the boycotts. It is all talk. The big men want this Mercedes, and here it is."

When the engines finally revved up for departure about nine P.M., I was half-asleep inside our cabin. I would have been fully asleep except for the heat. Lake Tanganyika is much lower in altitude than the drier bushlands we had become accustomed to and at the lake's lower elevation the full fury of the equatorial climate suddenly descended. The worst place to be in this climate is in any enclosed space—for instance, in a cabin on a ship.

Fortunately, I had anticipated this problem—or, to be more precise, I had humored myself into believing I had. While still in Lusaka, I had asked the *Liemba*'s agents if the cabins had fans. "Yes, there is one such cabin," a thin man in a chartreuse coat had told me. "It is a special cabin for a special price," he had said as I handed over a hundred extra kwacha. "It have such a very, very good fan."

Actually, Mr. Chartreuse was not completely lying. There *was* a fan in my cabin, at least the remains of a fan—a tangled lump of machinery bolted to the wall above my bunk. Yet all was not lost. There was a large window in our doorway that allowed a faint breeze to blow into the cabin. Its screen had been partially gouged out, affording an even better flow of air. Of course, this also made it possible for mosquitoes, flies and other unidentified insects to flow freely into our cabin, to say nothing about the easy access afforded to larger, uninvited guests.

Once we were under way I could think of nothing but sleep. Normally I would have taken a look around the ship before retiring, but I have seldom been more exhausted and less curious, having failed to get a decent night's sleep since leaving Lusaka. This didn't mean I had any illusions about the possibility of sleeping in that casketlike cabin. Not only were the heat and humidity in the cabin suffocating, but a rooster was cackling somewhere in the third-class section, accompanied by a series of unsettling clanks and whirrs from the nearby engine room and the *thump-a, thump-a, thump-a* of a cassette player in the next cabin.

In the midst of this carnival I lay on my bunk brooding, reminding myself that at one time I had actually looked forward to this steamer trip. Back in Vermont, it had seemed a romantic notion, taking an aging African Queen across a remote lake in the middle of Africa. "Yes," I had told myself beside a fire smelling of birch and cedar, "sailing on Lake Tanganyika will truly be *living*."

The worst thing about this sort of *living*, now that I was doing it, was that it gave me an inordinate amount of time to indulge in morbid introspection. Not only was Kasama still hanging over me, there was also the little matter of my immediate future to worry about. I somehow had to rally myself and regain the enthusiasm that is my fuel on these long treks. Unfortunately, this was not proving easy, for even though time seemed to have slowed down to a dead crawl in that oppressive space, the seconds were still ticking off toward the next phase of my journey. I was three days away from

Tanzania, another unpredictable country that had long been a cause of anxiety.

I didn't want to denigrate Tanzania before I had even set foot in the country, but I had heard a number of disquieting things about the place. Not only was Tanzania, like Zambia, in desperate economic straits, it was likewise renowned for its paranoia and xenophobia. Even the U.S. State Department, an organization usually loathe to criticize, had issued a long list of warnings about travel in Tanzania. "Local officials have been known to detain tourists on suspicion of spying for South Africa," said a Travel Advisory, "and have often failed to inform the U.S. embassy. Anyone traveling to South Africa should employ extreme caution." And then there were the rumors I had heard from other travelers. These stories raced through my head as I lay in my bunk, about the Canadian couple detained for six months because they were wearing clothing manufactured in South Africa, and about the German cyclist who was detained for five weeks because he couldn't speak English or Swahili. And then there was the time another Canadian was imprisoned for over a year because he joked with a local official about being with the CIA. . . .

2 We spent three days on the *Liemba*, uneventful days filled with attempts to sleep, more gin rummy (we were getting quite good at it) and long interludes when I stood as still as a zombie against the ship's railing, watching the empty shores roll by and feeling the balmy wind against my skin. To my great surprise, I began to enjoy the lazy tranquillity of the trip—the steady movement, the rushing of the lapis-blue water and the high-pitched song of the air. After a while, even the heat and humidity became a kind of salve, working like a powerful tranquilizer to reduce my overactive mind into a happy, stupid torpor. Maybe I was just exhausted, or maybe the great patience of Africa was finally having an effect on me. Despite my earlier misgivings, I ended up enjoying that slow, peaceful journey up that long, dagger-shaped lake embedded in the heart of Africa.

Our journey on the *Liemba* was over far too soon. On the morning of the third day, after the sun had risen in its usual blaze of oranges and reds, I stood on the roof above the bridge as we entered Kigoma harbor. It was a poignant sight, watching the old German vessel return to its berth in a town that the kaiser's empire builders had boasted would one day rival the great cities of the Rhineland.

The arrival of the *Liemba*, the only large ship on the lake, was still a big event in Kigoma, though there was not a white face left in the crowd. At least two hundred people swarmed onto a crumbling concrete pier stretching about a half-mile along the bank. A few children dove into the cold, oily waters to splash around. Behind the crowd, ranks of large warehouses stood abandoned, their rusted hulks collapsing. Someone had attempted to gloss over the decay by painting several huge cranes a bright, phosphorescent green, a color that I could not look at too long without going blind.

From the harbor, Kigoma rose up a steep, shaggy hill, a city frayed as thoroughly as Mpulungu by neglect and humidity. The predominant colors were heavy greens, rust and every shade of brown. At the top of the hill rows of old Teutonic and British bungalows were perched among date palms and mimosa trees. Below the bungalows a 179 large, graceful railway station dominated the north side of the bank like a medieval castle. One could tell it was not designed by Englishmen. It had none of the squat ponderousness of British imperial architecture. I was taken aback by its gentle lines and sweeping arches, a poetic style that seemed at odds with my image of Imperial Germany, land of Wagner, goose steps and grim, monocled nobility. This felt more like the Germany of Schumann and Mendelssohn, though how it had ended up in the middle of Africa was beyond me.

While the ship was serviced and took on cargo, Jim and I disembarked to search for lunch. This was to be a special meal for the two of us, for Jim was parting company with me that day after nearly four months on the road. Originally, he had planned to accompany me to Nairobi, but we were several days behind schedule and his wife was already waiting for him in Kenya. Therefore, he had decided to take the *Liemba* on to its final landfall at Bujumbura, the capital of Burundi, where he would fly on to Nairobi. Meanwhile, I planned to travel alone across Tanzania.

We stepped off the gangplank and passed through a phalanx of customs authorities. Given the rumors I had heard about officials in Tanzania, these dour faces made me slightly anxious, although they behaved professionally enough, searching our bags and stamping our papers and sending us on our way.

After customs we followed our fellow passengers up the hill toward the old train station, where we found a market of makeshift shops and an unexpectedly frenetic swirl of people selling and buying everything from hemp rope to black market colas. Most people in the market were dressed in Arab garb. The men wore white tunics that they somehow kept clean despite the dust and moist air, while the women wore robes decorated in dazzling swathes of red, blue and yellow. I was told that this predilection for color had been introduced long ago by swashbuckling Arab slave traders, most of whom fancied the bright costumes of Persia and Turkey for themselves and their women. Whatever the origin, it was nice to see such color after the somber hues of southern Africa, where dull, English-inspired browns and grays predominate.

I was surprised as well by the intensity and energy of the peddlers and their bickering customers, given the heat and Tanzania's precarious financial health. This place was positively bursting with a raw, powerful energy that I had hardly expected in a country famous for its draconian socialism.

"Hey, mister, ten shillings for a cola," shouted a nearby vendor. "No, mister, over here," bellowed another, "only nine shillings."

"But what about socialism?" I inquired of the first peddler. He answered with a wily grin I would see often among the hawkers of Tanzania.

"Yes, we are a socialist country," he said. "That is what the government says, but that is politics."

"But all this seems quite capitalistic," I said.

"This? Capitalistic? Ah, that is not a word we use in Tanzania. No, we prefer to call it *business*, my friend. But enough of this talk about politics! Hey, you buy cola? I give you very good price, the *best* price."

"Don't buy from *him*," shouted another vendor, who had been trying to interrupt. "I give you cola for eight shillings. Best price in Kigoma!"

"Seven shillings," said the first man, "and I also give you ice."

Jim and I ate mashed corn and spiced goat meat in the shadow of the old German station. Sun and sweat had blanched the station's once vivid trim of maroon and beige, the colors of the old imperial East African Railways. Remnants of once-brilliant awnings hung in tatters high above the ground. When I went inside I saw fragments of the British halcyon days lying bruised and discarded. There was a shattered red telephone booth—that ubiquitous symbol of England—with ancient dialing codes to London and Liverpool printed on yellowed paper. The phone itself had long ago disappeared. Signs to various classes of waiting rooms still hung from the rafters after twenty years of egalitarianism, though no one paid them any mind, poverty establishing a crude equality that no amount of laws and edicts could have accomplished so thoroughly.

In a corner of the lobby a tarnished brass plaque announced that Kigoma had won the "Tidiest Station Award" in 1965. Obviously there had still been some Englishmen about that year, though the country had been independent for four years. I can imagine the colonists being properly competitive for these little prizes right up until the end, with the man in charge of tidiness saying, "By Jove, we've got to keep this station clean and neat, or we'll lose the bloody contest!"

Jim and I spent the afternoon drinking beers and napping on the terrace of the Kigoma Railway Hotel, a hostelry on the lake shore. It was a melancholy afternoon, a time for reminiscing and playing our final hands of gin rummy. Soon, I was saying farewell to my old friend, a man who has suffered my company on many journeys, a companion whom I would sorely miss as I faced the prospect of traveling alone.

Jim was taking my bicycle and most of my gear with him to Nairobi. In Tanzania I planned to travel in a more sane style— bumming rides, walking a little and taking trains and *matatus*— African bush taxis—when necessary. This had been a difficult decision, but one that seemed most appropriate for a number of reasons. There was the matter of no real road and few towns between Kigoma and Dodoma, and my chariness about cycling alone after Zambia. For the next one thousand kilometers, I was giving up biking, although I hardly expected public transport in Tanzania to be any more comfortable than sitting day after day on a small, hard seat. I was, in a way, looking forward to moving light and lean, a first for me in the Third World. In Nairobi I planned to climb back aboard my bike and cycle the rest of the way to Cairo in the north.

After seeing Jim off, I took a walk along the lakeside road in the hot, late afternoon sun. It felt good to be stretching my legs after several days of enforced idleness aboard various vehicles. I hiked a good distance along the lake as the sun began to drop and bathe everything in orange. At this point I looked out over the water, across the capped waves flickering in slivers of white, and saw a ship in the distance—the sad, rust-colored *Liemba*. I stopped and watched the thumbnail-sized steamer disappear into the haze of the lake, and with it my longtime friend.

To travel east from Kigoma, I had three options—bus, truck or train. A Catholic priest in Kigoma advised me to take the train, saying that the road was almost nonexistent and buses infrequent. However, he said not to expect much. "That railroad is in awful shape," he said. "It derails all the time, and the engines are in terrible condition. Really, I'm surprised that it functions at all." When I told him I had originally planned to bike the route, the priest could not stop laughing. "My friend, that road is worse now than it was when Dr. Livingstone came through."

I had a difficult time spotting the right train in the sprawling railroad yard. Dozens of junked coaches and boxcars lay strewn across a large, red clay field, most of them abandoned and rotting on long-unused tracks. I walked down the steps behind the old German station and began walking through shallow canyons between strings of cars, stepping over stinking heaps of garbage and several sleeping indigents. The place reminded me of vacant lots I have seen in New York City—tracts of land piled high with burned-out autos, junked appliances and piles of rubbish that will probably still be there a million years from now.

Stepping through that yard was grueling work in the afternoon heat, particularly because none of the carriages I saw seemed the least bit functional. Nor did I see any evidence of passengers or crew for a train scheduled to depart in less than an hour. Finally I asked one of the indigents, a man dressed in a loincloth and a Dodgers T-shirt, to direct me toward the Dodoma train. He pointed a lean thumb at a nearby string of cars that looked as derelict as all the rest. "Dodoma," he grunted, holding out a calloused hand for baksheesh.

As I advanced toward the train I was joined by three barefoot boys carrying a tray of barbecued starlings, a Tanzanian delicacy that is supposed to be the equivalent of hot dogs in America.

"Meeester, meeester," said the boys, "you buy bird? Meeester, meeester, you buy bird?"

"No bird," I said. "No like dead, burned-up fowl. Do you have any hot dogs?" I smiled like a buffoon, hoping to drive them away by appearing to be insane. "I'll have mine with mustard, relish and ketchup," I said.

My ploy failed. I should have known I would need a more convincing stratagem than mere madness to beat back the entrepreneurial spirit of a determined Tanzanian. (Could this really be a *socialist* nation? If it was, then the government was ignoring an extraordinary asset.) The boys started over again with their shrill cries.

"Meeester, meeester, you buy bird? Meeester, meeester, you buy bird? Meeester, meeester, you buy bird . . . ?"

So I bought one of their damn birds.

But they didn't stop there. They wanted to see me eat it. "Meeester, meeester, you eat bird. Meeester, meeester . . ."

"All right, all right!" I bellowed. I held the thing with one wing between two fingers as if it were a dead mouse, trying to determine which parts might be edible. Finally one of the boys broke the suspense by biting off the head of another bird and spitting it out. He then greedily munched the breast, threw away the bones and wings and grinned. Since there was no way I was going to bite off the head, I took a tentative nibble on the breast as the boys squealed—this was great entertainment—and encouraged me to eat more. The thing tasted like charcoal, so I threw it on the ground with a satisfied noise and fled down the track.

As it turned out, the Dodoma train was on the other side of the yard, although its condition was only slightly better than the cars indicated by the indigent. I assumed I had the right train because a diesel engine was attached, a locomotive that seemed to be preparing to leave at some point, perhaps even that afternoon. But I was not holding my breath. The machine was emitting sparks and smoke out of a hole in its side and moving not at all. Several men stood about, one of them holding a wrench the size of a bazooka, but no one actually did anything.

I stood and watched the engine cough and sputter until it got so hot outside I was driven to board the train to get out of the sun. In the dank corridor of the first-class car I nearly stumbled over an old man on his hands and knees. At first I thought he was a Muslim praying, but he was only sweeping the floor. As my eyes became accustomed to the dark, I saw that he was wearing a uniform that once had been white, but now was silver-gray with constant wearing. An insignia on his breast said EAR—East Africa Railway. He identified himself in broken English as the first-class porter, saying that he was preparing the train for the passengers. "I be doing this job since 1956," he said. "I work first with the British man. He train me good."

His feeble efforts hardly left the dirt disturbed, though it seemed important to him to make the attempt. He was a proud old fellow, undoubtedly on the edge of senility. "I clean this carriage every day for so many years," he said, his smile opening into a single row of yellow teeth. "You want to give me big tip? The British, they always give big tip to the cleaning boy."

My compartment was at the end of the corridor, but when I turned the doorknob nothing happened. It just spun around, its catch broken. I began to push on the door, trying to force it open, when an angry black face appeared from the inside through a small, sliding window. It had a mustache and wore glasses. A cigarette dangled from its lips and its neck was wrapped in a collar and tie—ridiculous garb in steamy Kigoma. "Yes?" said the face unpleasantly. "What do you want?"

"I believe I'm your compartment mate," I said.

"That so?" He sneered, scrutinizing me from head to toe, noting my bedraggled appearance. "You got your ticket?" I held it up against the window. "All right," he said, undoing a homemade latch, "come on in. And hurry, please!" He then did something very peculiar. The moment I walked through the door he stuck his head out and took long looks both ways down the corridor, as if he was expecting someone or was afraid he might have been followed. Then he shut and locked the door. He seemed so agitated I wondered if he *was* being followed. This seemed like a perfect setting for some overblown train thriller—the old coach, the Peter Lorre character puffing nervously on a cigarette, the innocent traveler—or was he as innocent as he looked?—stumbling into the middle of some sordid episode of international thievery or espionage.

The scene was completed by the condition of our roomette. Not only was it dark and dilapidated, but this fellow had sealed every outlet to light and air. The corridor door was locked and the window shuttered and secured with a makeshift bolt. The only light entering the room came from several broken slats in the wooden shutters, which pierced the thick air like the beams from movie projectors in a smoke-filled theater. To complete the *film noir* milieu my cabin mate sat on the edge of the lower bunk sucking on his cigarette and staring at me.

"Name's Arnold," he finally muttered, as if he had decided I might be okay. He introduced himself as a middle-level official with the railroad on a monthly business trip from Dar es Salaam. "Usually, I take an airplane," he said, "but you know, we have this fuel shortage, so I must ride this awful train."

"Say, do you mind if I open the window?" I ventured, hoping to get some air before I suffocated.

"Yes, I do mind," Arnold snapped.

"But isn't it, well, a bit stuffy in here?"

"Stuffy? What do you mean . . . stuffy?"

"Smoky, hot, dusty . . ." I was getting impatient.

"Oh, you do not like the smoke?"

"Not really. At least not in a sealed room."

"Then perhaps you prefer to be robbed and beaten?"

"How's that?" I said, sensing that I was about to get to the bottom of this little mystery.

"Don't you realize," he said, "that there are criminals on this train? They will come in here and rob us if we do not protect ourselves. They are everywhere. We must keep the door and window locked. They go after the first-class passengers, you know. I personally have been robbed twice. Once, they put a knife here." He pointed to his jugular. "And they threatened to kill me."

So this was it. Arnold was merely another variation on the familiar "paranoid petty elite" theme. And he saw not the slightest irony in the spectacle of an official of a decrepit railroad being forced to ride the end product of his own incompetence, an experience that clearly terrified him. But such is life in socialist Tanzania, where a satrap in a rather conspicuous suit and tie cowered in a first-class compartment surrounded by peasants he feared and detested.

The train soon filled up with ordinary Tanzanians. They appeared about two hours after the scheduled departure time, as if by prearrangement, wedging themselves into every nook and cranny inside and on top of the train. This included the first-class corridor, which became so crammed that my companion and I could not open our cabin door. When I tried, Arnold chuckled and said it was not worth the effort. "Haven't you heard?" he said. "In Tanzania, our president says that we are all equal. This means that you and I must share the first-class corridor with the common people."

"It appears to me," I said, "that you do not have much choice."

As the train set off across the arid plains east of Kigoma I quickly tired of Arnold's complaints, and decided that it might be the lesser of two evils to venture outside our compartment and take my chances with the masses.

Unfortunately, just as I was getting my bearings in the passageway, the train abruptly jolted, stopping dead with such force I was knocked off my feet and thrown on top of a sleeping band of Swahilis. The result was a huge tangle of humans, baggage and clothing that was not righted until I was able to raise myself above the heap. At the same moment a cursing man also raised himself up, angrily coming at me. Then he noticed I was a *wazungu*, a "white man." His murderous scowl suddenly turned to a wily, familiar smile. "*Wazungu!*" he exclaimed, perched precariously on top of some luggage. "You want to buy some blue jeans? I have the best. Do you want exchange dollars? I have best rate!"

"It's a derailment," said Arnold. "These engineers are so incompetent. They do not know how to drive these trains."

"How long will it take to fix?"

"Who knows?"

"I'm going outside then," I said.

"Outside? But there will be many thieves. You must be careful. These men, they like to rob whites. They think you are rich." He lay back on his cot and lit another cigarette.

Outside, the last edges of twilight were fading and the temperature was rapidly dropping. I relieved myself with several other men behind a tangle of acacias. I noticed that all of us, Caucasian, black and mixed, were all one color—beige—covered as we were from our toes to the tops of our heads with dust.

After my pee I began investigating the land around the train. I walked about a hundred meters from the tracks so that I could hear the low throb of nightjars and watch the stars appear above the bush, spilling out across the sky. I was joined by a young soldier who I had spoken with before leaving the station. He was no more than seventeen or eighteen, an enthusiastic boy who presented a nice contrast to the Tanzanians I had met—the raucous entrepreneurs and the dour Arnold.

We had a rambling discussion over the next hour or two, walking under the brilliant sky. He told me he had been assigned to the train to guard against thieves. Thinking of Arnold, I asked if thievery was a problem. The soldier shrugged. "We have so many breakdowns," he said, "and the people are very poor." I asked if he carried a weapon.

"No, we are very careful with weapons in Tanzania. We keep them in another car." He held up large black fists. "I use these.

"My father is also a soldier," he told me proudly, explaining that his threadbare uniform had once belonged to his old man. "My father, he joined the army so he could leave our village and see the world. I have done the same. It is a good job, and I have seen many places. I have been to Dar es Salaam and to Kigoma and even once to Zanzibar. And my father, he went to Uganda in the war, so far away!* Someday I will visit Kenya, I think, or Uganda. This is my hope. And maybe, someday, I go to America." He asked me to tell him about America. When I told him it was bigger than Tanzania, he scoffed. "No, Tanzania is so big! It must be the biggest country in the world."

Later that night, after the train was under way again, Arnold and I were about to go to sleep when I heard a loud knock on the door. "Porter! It is the porter!" said a singsong voice outside.

---

* In 1979, Tanzanian troops invaded Uganda to overthrow Idi Amin.

I slid open the window and, sure enough, there was the old man I had met earlier. "It's the porter," I said to Arnold.

"Of course it is! Are you going to let him in?"

I released the lock and the porter lunged into the cabin as the train jerked to one side. He fell on the floor in a mess of bed sheets and blankets marked with EAR. His appearance was, I thought, a minor miracle. How had he made it through the throng in the corridor? Where had these bedrolls come from? I gave the old man the tip he had asked for earlier. He smiled coyly, a true Tanzanian, and asked if I could tip him in U.S. dollars. "I prefer hard currency," he said.

3 The train rolled into the central Tanzanian city of Dodoma nearly a day late. Arnold, still ensconced in his smoky cell, said in a parting comment to watch out for "dirty urchins" selling things. "They will rob you very blind."

I disembarked through the compartment window after fifty-eight hours aboard a train that had been stalled longer than not. Arnold handed down my rucksack, shouting at the hawkers in Swahili to keep away.

Once on the tracks, I had to negotiate through yet another rabble of indigents. Such homeless paupers had appeared in every station since Kigoma, sitting listlessly in the dust. A few of them were employed as food vendors, children who rushed up to accost me with more dead birds and other delicacies. But by now I was savvy to their considerable persuasion, having discovered that Arnold was right about one thing. The only way to avoid being hawked to death in Tanzania was to feign haughtiness and simply walk away.

Across the street I checked into the Dodoma Railway Hotel, built by the British and maintained in Spartan cleanliness by the Tanzanian government. I was obsessed with the idea of a shower, my first since Kapiri Mposhi twelve days earlier. But when I turned the water knob nothing came out. "Sorry, meester," said the man at the front desk, "no water until evening." So I went into the hotel's pub and ordered a beer. "Sorry, meester," said a small waiter in a stiff white jacket, "no beer available until evening."

"What about a soda?"

"Sorry, meester."

I had to settle for warm, yellow-tinted water, which I treated with a purification pellet. A few minutes later, I saw a group of officious-looking men in suits drinking cold beers. "They are big men," whispered the waiter, as if this were all the explanation I needed.

"And cold beer is available for them?"

"I am sorry, meester," he said, looking as if this were all beyond him, "but we have no beer available until evening." 189

I had stopped in Dodoma for two reasons. First, because the road north to Nairobi and Kenya runs through the center of town, and second, because this city was something of an anomaly in post-colonial Africa, one of the few large-scale, planned-from-scratch cities in emergent Africa. Launched during the first flush of independence, Dodoma was the brainchild of President Julius Nyerere, another schoolteacher/intellectual with big ideas in Africa. "Our object is to create a new order in Africa," he had said when he announced his plans for the city, "based on simplicity, justice, equality and humanity. And Dodoma will be its capital, a city absolutely devoted to man."

I already had seen a number of white dream cities along the Cape to Cairo Highway, and had noted what had become of them. But Dodoma was the first purely African attempt on my route. I suspected that it probably had gone the way of most other big ideas in Africa, but this did not assuage my curiosity. What did a city built on *simplicity, justice, equality and humanity* look like? What sort of architecture had been employed? How did the people dress? Was this indeed a more just society?

Before I began looking around, however, I wanted to have a hot shower and decent night's sleep. I was much too tired to go tramping about in even the most perfect city, my mind being occupied solely by temporal concerns, such as when these people were going to get around to bringing me a beer and water for a shower. (I had a feeling that the Big Men were not having to wait for *their* showers.)

It was evening before the sheepish waiter from the pub arrived in my room with three cold beers. *Nirvana*, I thought. "And, meester," he said with a grin, "the water, it is working now." He walked into the bathroom and turned the faucet. When he held out his hand for a tip, I grudgingly gave him five Tanzanian shillings. He held out his hand for more. I told him irritably that he could get his tip from the Big Men, who had gotten their beers four hours earlier. He looked deeply shocked and went away muttering something about *wazungus* and their odd ways.

The water rushed steamy and hot over my skin as my anxieties melted away. I scrubbed off dirt that had been accumulating for almost two weeks. It was caked on my skin in layers, and I imagined that I was removing each layer according to its geographical location, working my way down from the train journey to the *Liemba*, Mpulungu, Kasama, the bus trip, Kapiri . . .

In the morning, I felt like a new man. As I sat drinking tea in the hotel dining room, I found myself looking forward to exploring Dodoma. My body still felt tired, but the languor of the past few days was losing out to that unfathomable inquisitiveness that has long afflicted me. After a second cup of tea I pulled myself up and headed outside into the coolness of the morning.

What can I say about Dodoma? As I walked toward the center city I secretly hoped that a city born of such high ideals would not prove to be an utter flop. *Simplicity, justice, equality and humanity.* Like most people, I wanted to believe in the validity of these words, and could not be blamed if I harbored some tiny wish that the Dodoma project might have accomplished *something.* Nyerere's lieutenants had been at work here for over thirteen years and were, according to the original plan, supposed to be close to completion.* They had spent hundreds of millions of dollars in grants and loans—nearly a billion dollars, according to U.S. State Department officials. They had shipped in thousands of workers and countless trainloads of materials.

Imagine my disappointment when I left my hotel and found a small, sleepy town of aging markets and houses sprinkled with three or four squat high-rises, perhaps a dozen paved streets and a grotesquely large cathedral—a Renaissance Revival nightmare that looked terribly incongruous in the middle of the bush. I saw no socialist Eden, no happy masses and no visual manifestation that I could readily identify as *simplicity, justice, equality and humanity.*

As I walked about in the hot sun I tried to make some sense of what I saw, to place fragments into the framework of a master plan, but I could not. Perhaps I was hopelessly biased by my Western predilections for straight, clean lines, but I saw no rhyme nor reason in the willy-nilly scattering of modern buildings, paved streets and shops. They simply appeared here and there, apparently quite randomly, suggesting a half-developed, clumsy company town grafted onto a dreary rural slum.

* The new Dodoma was supposed to be completed by 1993, meaning that all government offices, legislative departments and foreign embassies were to be moved from Dar es Salaam to new facilities in Dodoma. In 1986, only two ministries and the prime minister's office had made the move. There was a new foreign embassy village under construction outside the city, as well as a number of agricultural projects to the west.

Here was the Ministry of Development's high-rise office building on a lazy street of crumbling Arab and British-era arcades. And there was Nyerere's party headquarters, painted turquoise like a seedy inn in Atlantic City, rising near a dirty, dusty market inhabited by hawkers and the usual dogs, goats and chickens. Near my hotel—the only hotel in town, built long ago by the hated imperialists—was the prime minister's office. It was located not in one of the new socialist edifices, but in one of the very symbols of imperialism that Nyerere professed to abhor—an old fortress built by the Germans and ringed by the sort of troops and weaponry that reflects a reality quite apart from dreams in Africa.

As for the people in this "model" city, they numbered no more than ten or fifteen thousand, hardly the throngs one might expect in the capital of a nation of twenty-two million. Nor did I see much evidence in faces and clothing styles that this was perceived as a chief city. I saw a few bureaucrats running about in suits and other costumes of the elite. Like Arnold, they looked unhappy and annoyed, as if they couldn't wait to get out of the hinterlands and back to Dar on the coast. Several shiny Mercedes rolled slowly through the streets, directed by a tiny corps of policemen in smart uniforms. Otherwise, Dodoma was inhabited by the same sorts of humans I had seen since my arrival in Kigoma—Arabs in white tunics and skullcaps, women in bright robes and half-naked children. The only difference was a vague aura of relative prosperity, meaning that the people looked slightly better fed and clothed than in most Tanzanian towns. There were also fewer beggars.

I quickly grew depressed as I walked about in Dodoma, recalling something a peddler in the town of Tabora had told me. "It is like this," he said. "We are told in Tanzania to share everything with our brothers. But our country is poor, so I have nothing to share. My brother has nothing to share. So we share nothing. This is what they call socialism in Tanzania."

So what had gone wrong here? Was there anyone in these dusty, languid streets who might be able to explain?

I began my search in the Dodoma district governor's office, a dreary, air-conditioned room housed in an old British administrative building. The governor had little to say, other than that Dodoma was a "beautiful city, and will be even more beautiful when it is finished."

"And when will that be?"

"Oh, it is such a big and important project, it will take some time."

"How much time?"

"Some few years, perhaps. Would you like more tea, my friend?"

He gave me a slick, uninformative booklet about Dodoma, printed many years earlier. The governor also mentioned, as I was being politely ushered out the door, that there was another publication called the *Blueprint for Dodoma.* "This is the master plan for our great city," he said, "and if you come back tomorrow, I will see if my assistant can locate a copy for you."

"But, sir, do you mind if I ask you a few questions. . . ?"

"Tomorrow, my friend!" he said with a grin, suggesting that I try the Ministry of Development if I had any further inquiries.

Development was just down the street in one of the new buildings, a yellow, adobe-concrete rectangle that looked as if children had fashioned it in an arts-and-crafts class. After waiting for some time in a dirty waiting room—I wondered if anyone had ever cleaned it—I was led to an office on one of the upper floors. Here I was introduced to a frowning woman in a long, black dress. Her office and desk were completely empty, the walls bare except for a slogan-poster that made me wriggle after Kasama: BEWARE OF SPIES! THEY ARE EVERY-WHERE! She had no file cabinets, paper or writing utensils. Her telephone was apparently a decoration. It had no wire, unless it was a cordless model, which I doubted. She did have three used tea glasses on a small side table, and was occupied with drinking a fourth.

"You have come for a copy of the master plan," she growled, sounding like an inquisitor.

"That's right," I said.

"Well, I'm sorry, but we do not have a copy in this office. Have you tried Mr. Benara on the third floor?"

"No."

"He is sure to have a copy."

On the third floor I had no better luck. "I'm sorry," said an elderly man in another stark office, "Mr. Benara has been transferred back to Dar. Have you tried Mrs. Juba over at the party headquarters building?"

It didn't take long for me to grasp that my search was going nowhere, that I was simply wearing out a good pair of biking shoes stomping around on the crudely laid asphalt streets.

I decided that the only way I was going to learn anything about this city was to secure a copy of the elusive *Blueprint,* also known as the master plan. The best place to find it, according to unanimous opinion, was to visit an agency called the Capital Development

Authority (CDA), the group that was supposed to be in charge of implementing Nyerere's plan. "The CDA will have a copy of the blueprint," said the bureaucrats. "Yes, yes. Go to the CDA."

But there was a small problem. No one seemed to know exactly where its offices were. And those who said they did gave only the vaguest instructions. Each office I visited had a different answer. "It is to the east two streets. . . . No, it is to the *west* two streets. . . ." I felt like Dorothy in Munchkinland, looking for directions to Oz. Yet another woman bureaucrat assured me that the CDA was just around the corner and down the street and to the left and then to the right. "You then look for a certain beer shop, and you have arrived. It is so easy."

"You mean the Capital Development Authority is located in a beer shop?"

"I am telling you! You go this way." She pointed over her shoulder. "It is just there!"

I had no better luck with directions at my hotel, where no one seemed to have heard of the CDA. However, I did run into an intriguing Indian fellow at lunch, a sophisticated hawker who offered me a deal that seemed remarkably audacious, even for Tanzania. "You would like to buy a piece of Dodoma?" he asked, a fat man in a too small suit who smiled a lot and called himself a "business facilitator."

"A piece of *what*?"

"Dodoma, of course!" he repeated.

"All I want to do is find the Capital Development Authority office," I moaned. "You wouldn't happen to know where it is."

"Ah, development!" said the Indian. "That is what I am talking about! Development in Dodoma. I am in the business of development! I organize these projects. You have seen the new Ministry of Development building? I have worked on this building. Now, I am building some shops and office buildings. You have heard of the master plan?"

"I sure have," I said. "You don't happen to have a copy . . ."

"My friend, then we can do business! Do you wish to invest in construction? I give you fifty percent back on your investment in just one year. Do you know how these things work in Tanzania? You give me money now, and I take it to the minister of development, and he gives us money to build our project. Then we take this money and you get fifty percent, and I get fifty percent, and the minister gets fifty percent . . ."

"How's that? Fifty times three equals . . ."

"Yes, that's right! You understand perfectly how business is done here!" I looked at him bubbling away. Was this guy for real? Was he a lunatic? I had seen him hobnobbing the night before with the Big Men (he had gotten a beer long before I had), one of whom was rumored to be the minister of finance.

"Let me get this straight," I said. "I give you money . . ."

"Ten thousand dollars only," he interrupted.

"Ten thousand dollars?"

"Yes, ten thousand only. I think this is a small amount for an American. And you make back ten times that amount! Maybe more!"

"But you said I would make fifty percent. Fifty percent of ten thousand is only . . ."

"Yes, yes! Exactly!"

"What did you say your name was?"

With a great deal of pomp and flourish he produced a card that identified him as a development "agent" and president of an import-export company. As I studied the card, a stocky, distinguished man in a silk suit walked past, followed by several younger versions of himself carrying briefcases and boxes of papers.

"My goodness, there is the minister himself," whispered the Indian. "Shall I tell him we have a deal?"

"Have a deal!" I exclaimed, unsure if anything this fellow was telling me was true. For all I knew, he was a con man and this was an elaborate scam.* "All I want to do is find the Capital Development Authority. Do you think the minister would know where it is?"

"Tell me," said the Indian congenially, "would you consider fifteen thousand dollars?"

After lunch and the requisite afternoon nap I was back on the trail to the CDA, figuring that I might as well keep up the search for the rest of the afternoon. By now, I was asking random people on the street for directions. "Pardon me, can you tell me where . . .?" Finally, after all possible options had been exhausted, I found myself standing in front of a beer shop. That is, it sold beer when beer was

---

* I found out later that the distinguished-looking man was indeed the minister of finance, up from Dar es Salaam on business at the prime minister's office. However, I never saw a shred of evidence that my Indian acquaintance knew him or anyone else in the government.

available in Dodoma. At the moment, there was a shortage of imported cork in Tanzania—cork is used in beer caps—and there was no foreign currency to buy any more. So the beer industry had virtually stopped producing this critical commodity, an astounding inconvenience in a country where beer served the same purpose as vodka does in Russia.

I stood for a few minutes in front of the beer shop, which appeared to be abandoned, wondering if the CDA was merely a figment of someone's imagination. I stepped into a nearby shop that sold office supplies and newspapers. "Pardon me," I said to the man inside, "could you tell me where . . ."

He said to knock loudly on the beer shop door and someone was "probably" there. "Or you can go back tomorrow," he suggested, offering to sell me a three-day-old *Daily News* for six times its listed price. "We have only a few copies," he shrugged. "You know, there is this paper shortage."

Back at the beer shop I pounded my fist on the door and was about to give up when a wrinkled man in a tattered jumpsuit appeared. Incredibly, he seemed to know exactly where the CDA was located. He led me through a side door in the shop and into a colonial-era warehouse filled with thousands of empty beer bottles. I followed him through a maze of brown, stinking bottles until we came to a small room with windows overlooking the floor. This was, he said, the office of the Capital Development Authority.

Inside, several men sat around smoking and drinking tea. Again there were no pencils, file cabinets or any other items ordinarily associated with an office. Nobody got up when I entered. A young man in a yellow T-shirt asked me if I wanted tea. He sent a small boy out with a sharp order. I stood awkwardly for a moment and finally asked if anyone would talk to me about the Dodoma Master Plan. They looked at me as if I were crazy, and I had to repeat my question. Once they understood what I was talking about they began conferring in Swahili. In the end, like good bureaucrats, they opted for saying nothing, suggesting that I return tomorrow. "Tomorrow there will be someone here to answer your questions," said the man in the yellow T-shirt, who added that the blueprint also would be available then.

I decided that tomorrow, whenever it comes in Tanzania, will be an exciting day.

4 I spent the next four days banging my head against a wall trying to find someone who would say *something* about the Dodoma project. I found plenty of regular people who were willing to grumble and complain about promises unkept, of housing that had failed to materialize and numerous shortages of everything from bread to ball-point pens. A couple of Western relief workers in town told me they heard the master plan had been scrapped, or at least scaled down, but didn't know any of the details. I went back several times to the CDA, but the people there always said "tomorrow."

For all of my trouble, I ended up getting detained for most of a day when a local official accused me of trying to take illegal photographs at the Dodoma train station. (Some children thought they might have seen a *wazungu* snapping photos—BEWARE OF SPIES, said posters all over the city.) The charge was absurd, but it took me several hours to convince the authorities of my innocence. In the end, I had to "give" the official involved five rolls of unexposed film, but not before he and his police henchmen had taken my fingerprints, snapped a mug shot and threatened to lock me up.

The next morning I fled Dodoma on the back of an aging British Leyland truck headed to Arusha. With three others I sat atop several bales of used clothing and numerous crates of wretched wine produced near Dodoma. The clothes stank like fermented sweat, and nearly drove us off the truck before we had even started.

We were a diverse group. Ali was a Masai converted to Islam. Beni was an immensely fat man, a whiny trader who seemed wholly unsuited to the profession of hawking. He was carrying a satchel of rough-carved ivory statues to sell to tourists in Arusha. Ivor, a pale, stern man who looked like he would be at home in an early Bergman film, was our zealot, a born-again Christian from Norway, one of the hundreds of missionaries who still run amok in Tanzania. (Nyerere, like Kaunda, is a Christian socialist.) Thankfully, Ivor spoke only a 197 little English, although what he did know included the words "Jesus will be victorious," which he repeated constantly.

It took awhile for our driver to get the truck gassed up and ready to leave. Beni, who could not get comfortable, decided he wanted a bottle of the wine stacked under the bales of clothing. He rummaged through the stinking material, looking like a fat pack rat whose penchant for cheese frequently overcomes his usual laziness. The rest of us watched in bored amusement as Beni reached down and down until he buried his entire head in the putrid bales. At one point he nearly disappeared, his feet flailing in the air. But he was successful. "Here it is!" he shouted excitedly, drawing up a bottle of wine meant for unsuspecting tourists in Arusha. I took out my knife, pulled off the cork and took a sip of what tasted like liquid nerve gas—"God," I sputtered, "this is awful."

"Please, do not use this word God in vain," muttered Ivor, never missing a beat.

"Let me have a drink," shouted Beni. "Let me! Let me!" He took a long draft and pronounced it "excellent," glaring at me as if I had insulted all of Tanzania with my reaction.

"Tanzanian wine, it is very bad," Ali whispered to me, saying that at these moments he was happy Mohammed had banned the consumption of alcoholic beverages.

Soon after Beni had found the wine we started off. "Jesus is victorious," muttered Ivor as we rolled out of the market and onto a paved road about three miles long. Just north of Nyerere's city, the asphalt ended and the washboard began. This drowned out any chance of conversation. Each of us was left to his own thoughts and amusements. Ivor struggled to read from a Norwegian paperback Bible, which was not easy on a vibrating truckbed inundated with flying bits of dirt. Beni sat in his corner, still trying to settle his bulk while sipping his hard-won wine. Ali, being the wisest among us, fell asleep.

I wrapped a cloth around my head to keep off the dust, leaving an opening for my sunglasses so I could see the immensity of the dry Tanganyika plains unfold around me. Bateleur eagles soared above parched, tawny-colored savannahs where a drought several years old was in the last stages of killing even the most stalwart acacia. The sun, looking evil above this gathering wasteland, was rising to a fiery height as we passed distant gullies and rock outcrops poised like patties of petrified dung.

The place reminded me of the Karroo in South Africa, though there was little evidence of man here—no picnic stops, asphalt highways or traces of the Karroo's wretched fences. The only signs of Homo sapiens were occasional huts erected out of acacia branches, wire and rock, their inhabitants looking like dark toothpicks as they stood in the dust watching us pass. We were moving too fast to see their faces but I could guess at their expressions, imagining the same listless, blank stares that had so disturbed me in Zambia. Yet the situation here seemed even worse. I saw no evidence of water, crops or anything. There was *nothing*, just a few fields that once had been tilled, but whose crops had long ago turned black and blown away in the hot winds.

I longed for my bike as the landscape rushed past. I had so many questions about this land that simply could not be answered in the back of a truck. When we stopped briefly to let the engine cool down, I wrote in my journal a list of observations and questions for some future trip to Tanzania.

1. The People. *How did they survive? What did they eat? Obviously, many have moved away in this terrible drought—I see as many abandoned shacks as inhabited ones.*

2. The Land. *Ancient, like the Karroo, but more desolate—rocky, lifeless, dry, washed out. The Karroo had more colors—oranges and yellows. Here these colors only appear at sunrise and sunset. Otherwise, the earth undulates in every shade of brown. The sun, dust and mist transform the hues in a bell-shaped curve. . . .* The Great Rift Valley—*the walls appeared gradually this morning, as if God had built them to taper out nicely into the plains around Dodoma. Valley walls: at least one thousand feet high, sheer bluffs about five miles apart. Our road runs down the middle of this immense geological crack, a fault that nearly broke Africa in half. How long ago? Ten million years? How long does a crack like this take to form? This huge gully makes humans look so puny and our lives so short.*

3. The Animals. *All right, where the hell are they?* [Elspeth] *Huxley and others wrote about the great herds here, millions and millions of animals. Even* [Peter] *Matthiessen saw animals when he came through here in the early sixties. They are still up north in the parks—the Serengeti and Ngorongoro. But this whole valley used to be like that, an Eden of fauna. Has man killed them all off, or is the drought also to blame? Or are the two somehow connected?*

4. Ancient People. *The Rift is the home of the missing link—Lucy, Dear Boy and so forth—the Leakeys' discoveries. (Why do the Leakeys always attach nicknames to their bones? This is very British, this nickname business.) Why were the bones discovered here? Is it because this crack exposed them? Will my bones be so lucky to survive and grace the halls of some future museum? What will they call me? How will the little card beside my bones read? Probably "Rattled Boy" after this truck ride.*

By noon, when we stopped for lunch, I felt as if I had been attached to a vibrating jackhammer for four hours. I climbed out of the truck, shaken from my scalp to my toenails. I was baking hot. This was noontime, when the sun stood still, small and blazing, a point of fire straight up in the sky. It is not a good time to stop. After years of biking in hot places I have learned that when the sun is directly overhead, possibilities of finding shade are minimal since walls, trucks and other large objects cast no shadow.

Beni and the missionary finally found shade under a stray acacia but there was room only for two. So Ali and I took a walk, to search for shade and to escape our companions. Ali told me that Masailand began to the north, the land of his ancestors. "My grandfather lived near Tarangire [National Park]," he explained, staring hard at the horizon. "Two hundred kilometers to the north."

"What do you feel here?" I asked, feeling a certain empathy with his sadness. Even though we came from radically different backgrounds, we actually had a great deal in common. We were both men who had strong ancestral roots in the land—mine in the rural Midwest, his in Masailand—ties that had been severed by recent family migrations to the city. Because of this, I suppose we felt a shared filial instinct for open, wild territory such as this—an inexplicable bonding between a Masai in trousers and a restless nomad from America.

"What do I feel?" said Ali. "I feel that this is a place I will never know. I think about how different my life might have been if my father had remained a Masai."

"Do you wish you lived in the country?"

"Sometimes, the city is a bad place. It is dirty and loud." He paused, looked around, and took a deep breath. "But I am not a true Masai. I am Muslim. My father converted. He went to Dar and worked and became a True Believer and I was raised that way, too. But I do feel—I mean, I like this place. It is very beautiful, I think. My father, he sometimes talked about his boyhood here. He talked as if he wanted to come back. I remember once he went away for some days. My mother was so angry with him. She was not Masai. She was Swahili. She told us my father had gone back to Masailand and might not come back. She said the Masai were dirty and backward and drank cow's blood. Then my father came home, and after that he was quiet for many days. I still do not know where he went, but I think he did come back here, or tried to. It is difficult for a Masai to live in the city. He is used to the bush. I think my father was unhappy in the city. He died when I was young, only fourteen."

I asked him why he was riding on the truck, why he had left Dar to travel up to Arusha. "I am a businessman," he said. "This is my life."

"You are not going to see what the Masai are like?"

"Maybe I do go to see the Masai. But I tell you, I am a city man. I can never be a Masai and live out here. For one thing, I know nothing about cattle. To me, cattle are dirty animals. And what about the Masai houses? They live in grass huts. If my father had stayed, I would be wearing the red robes of a Masai warrior. The beads and spears. I would be prancing about showing off." He laughed. "They are so backward, like my mother said. You know they will not go to school? You will see the boys on the road. They do nothing all day, just watch cattle and carry spears."

"But they are proud," I said, "and they appear to be content. Some even seem to be prosperous, in their own way."

"Yes, but I am also proud. I am proud of my religion and my family."

"But are you content?"

He shrugged and said that he would find contentment in heaven. "Like most men, my life is difficult," he said, "but, I think that this is the way of God. These people, my father's people, they are living in the past. They must become modern."

"But why?" I asked, thinking that this was one of the more crucial questions in Africa. "Why should they become modern if they are satisfied with life? Is this not the goal?"

"Man, you talk nonsense," he said quietly, looking across the vista of ragged crags and acacia. I could sense that the more settled blood of his mother was trying hard to hold down the wilder blood of his father. "By God, they still carry spears," he muttered, his mother still speaking, "and yet . . ." His voice trailed off as he continued to gaze, and I could only imagine the struggle beating in his breast.

After lunch, the truck continued north, a roaring plume of smoke rushing down the Rift Valley. It was a lazy afternoon. I spent most of the time sleeping or lying in a half-comatose state, staring at the blur of scenery. We stopped for sticky buns and tea in the New Babiti Hotel in Babiti, another decaying British remnant that was briefly famous in the 1920s, when the Prince of Wales stopped for a drink on the way to a safari. Since that auspicious moment, the hotel had fallen on hard times. The restaurant had been stripped down to bare wood and naked lightbulbs. Most of the rooms were doorless and filled with rubble and trash. (One room mysteriously was filled with corncobs.) The sit-down toilets in back, which had once felt the fanny of royalty, had been unbolted and tossed aside. The brass plumbing had been ripped out and stacked in a corner. This left a simple hole in the ground, where heaps of dry dung stank and buzzed with flies.

At dusk, we arrived in Arusha. In the waning light I could see murky hovels leaning against one another and the glow of lanterns. I could smell fire and the stench of massed humanity. Shapes passed across the street in the gloom, roosters crowed, dogs yapped.

I was delighted to bid good-bye to the truck when we reached the town, where I said farewell to Ali and the others and began wearily hiking toward the center of town. I passed several streets of colonial-era shops, most of them catering to foreign backpackers dropping down from Kenya on their way to the Serengeti. As I approached the hotel district I sighted a species of animal I had not seen for weeks, perhaps months: *Tourists.* They were pale, Caucasian and watering in profusion at various taverns. Most were young and fashionably unshaven, adorned in an odd mix of dirt, khaki and Dinesenesque expressions.

I felt oddly out of sorts, as I was far more filthy and smelly than the fashion dictated. Not only were my clothes threadbare and torn, and my skin caked with dust, I also had managed to acquire the odors of the truck—of putrid clothing and bad native wine. In short, I was a stinking, soiled mess when I entered the first bar I could find and ordered supper and a drink. The bar happened to be The Safari, made famous by John Wayne in a dumb movie about white game managers called *Hatari.*

I approached this outpost of civilization with some trepidation. I was looking for a shower and other creature comforts, but I was definitely not looking forward to being confronted by wide-eyed tourists quoting dead colonialist writers at every turn. Call me crotchety, but I was simply too tired and run-down to face my countrymen's powerful blend of enthusiasm, rowdiness and good-natured naïveté.

Several tourists came over anyway. "Hey, dude," said a man with a New York accent, "you know where we can get some . . ." He lowered his voice. ". . . Hashish?"

"No," I replied, aghast that I looked so bad as to be taken for a drug dealer.

"How 'bout some coke?" asked his young male companion.

"Gentlemen," I said in my most measured voice, trying to appear at least shabbily genteel, "if you do not cease and desist, I will have to report you to the local drug enforcement authorities. And, gentlemen," I added, "the jails in Tanzania are no picnic."

Both youths began to protest.

"*Vamoose,*" I said sternly, waving them away as if they were mosquitoes, realizing with a frown that these boys were only the beginning of what I would see as I headed north into Kenya, last of the great Western playgrounds in Africa.

VI
Kenya
Once
Upon
a Time

Begins p.
213

Kenya is composed of twelve square blocks of America, several nice game parks and a million square miles of bush and dirty faces.
                              —Journal Entry

Africa, amongst the continents, will teach it to you: that God and the Devil are one, the majesty coeternal. . . .
                              —Isak Dinesen

1 At dawn in East Africa the sky bleeds raw swatches of color, a violent beginning for someone used to gentler North American skies. In Vermont dawn is soft and light, a pale, porcelain-colored commencement that slowly builds into stronger hues and clarity. In Africa, the sun rises with passion, like a reckless, dangerous lover. It ignites the world in reds and golds and vaporizes cool mists collected overnight. Within minutes, the passion burns itself out and the long, hazy, colorless African day truly begins.

I arrived in Arusha's central market at the bloodiest moment of dawn, hoping to catch an early *matatu* to Nairobi. At my lodgings an old clerk had suggested I look in the market for a driver named Hassan. "Hassan take you to Nairobi. He the best." After wandering about for a few minutes, past the black, looming shadows of makeshift stalls, parked trucks and sleepy children, I arrived at the spot which everyone insisted was the *matatu* stand. It looked about as promising as anything in Tanzania, more closely resembling a rubbish heap than a bush taxi stand. I had to search through a tangle of mangled *matatus* before discovering a sign of human life, a man sleeping on a car seat dragged out of a nearby wreck. He was emitting a wide repertoire of guttural snores and stank of beer. It took several shakes before he sputtered and opened one red-rimmed eye.

"Yes," he muttered, "Hassan. He go today to Nairobi. He be here in one half hour." The man rearranged a mangy blanket and closed his eye.

"Hassan comes in only one half hour?" I asked doubtfully. "You are sure?" I looked at my watch—six A.M. "There is a *matatu* leaving for Nairobi at six-thirty?"

"Yes, as I told you," said the man, reopening his eye. "One half hour only." He spoke with that pleasant sarcasm Tanzanians often use when discussing time, a tone of voice that meant it could be hours or days before any bush taxi left for anywhere.

Earlier in the trip, I might have felt frustrated, but Africa was beginning to have some impact on me at last, although I couldn't tell if what I was learning was patience or merely that characteristic 207

African resignation to the whims of fate. I was beginning to mimic the physical motions of resignation, drooping my shoulders, feeling weighted down by my rucksack. Behind a high stack of rubbish, I found a cluster of travelers huddled in a tight, friendly knot around a barrel spitting flames. A large woman with a gold tooth welcomed me into the circle, using her girth to bump a skinny teenager to one side so I could squeeze in.

The people seemed unusually excited as they chattered and fidgeted around the fire. I asked what was going on. "We are going to Nairobi!" said the boy who had been bumped. "This very morning."

"Yes, all of us are going," said a short man who said he drove trucks between Arusha and Moshi. "We are waiting for a driver named Hassan."

"Ah, yes," I said, "I know about Hassan."

"They say he will be here in just one half hour," blurted out the teenager.

O verland travel by public transport in Africa often resembles a medieval pilgrimage, particularly when the pilgrims are Tanzanians and the destination is Nairobi. In this country of suppressed mammon-worshipers there is no other place as sacred as the capital of capitalist Kenya, where it was rumored that every street had a Coca-Cola stall and every prostitute wore nylon stockings. It was a journey that nearly every Tanzanian I met dreamed about, a trek made more precious by the small number of visas allowed by the Tanzanian government, which rightly fears that a sizable chunk of its citizenry would flee if given half a chance. (Nyerere once described Kenya as a "man-eat-man" society, to which Kenyans have retorted that his country is "man-eat-nothing.") I was told that the visas cost upward of $50 in bribes and fees, a fortune in a country where the average human earns less than $200 a year.

When the pilgrims discovered I once had visited Nairobi, they asked questions all at once. Their faces shone like children's through the smoke, their eyes catching the first beams of golden sunlight as the garish reds drained out of the sky. *Is it true what they say?* they asked. *Are there many glass towers in Nairobi? Movie houses? Big houses? Is there plenty of petrol and cigarettes?*

Each pilgrim sought a miracle in the land of plenty. "I want to buy perfumed soap for my wife," said a bald shopkeeper from Moshi. "I want to buy spark plugs," said the truck driver. The fat woman, who worked as a secretary on a nearby sisal estate, said she wanted to buy twelve pairs of shoes for her twelve children. "We have no good shoes in Tanzania," she said, "except on the black market."

"And those shoes come from Nairobi," added the truck driver. He spat into the fire and whispered a question close to my ear so that no one else would hear. *Was it true the women in Nairobi were the best? Did they make a man so happy he wanted to die?* I told him I didn't know, but he nudged me in disbelief as the teenager leaned over to hear. "I am told the women are expensive," the driver added softly, "but, oooh, they say it is worth the money! They wear cosmetics even here," he pointed to his chest and made circles around his nipples.

"You! Be quiet!" said the woman who wanted twelve pairs of shoes. "Shame on you! This boy is listening." She covered the teenager's ears and made a comment in Swahili. Everyone laughed. The boy squirmed and demanded to know what was said.

"I am nearly a man," he said angrily. "I am old enough to go to Nairobi by myself. I want to know the joke."

"Tell him," said the truck driver, breaking up with laughter, "and tell our American friend."

"All right," said the woman, who didn't need much persuading. "I told this man that these women in Nairobi put cosmetics in another place and that he had better be careful, because those cosmetics in that certain place rub off during a certain activity." She laughed deeply. "And the color is so strong that it cannot be washed off. So when he returns to his wife, she will know everything!"

The teenager laughed hesitantly, wondering if this was the end of the joke. This made the group around the fire shriek even louder.

Dawn was long over and the heat of the day rising when Hassan finally arrived, a fleshy Somalian with a Safari Rally cap and a gold tooth. He laughed easily and was always hugging everyone, a vivacious personality who seemed to me more Italian than African. His gregariousness was so infectious that I could forgive the fact he was nearly three hours late, a tardiness that had strained my newfound African patience. His rig, a Toyota pickup canopied in canvas, had SUCCESS! painted in slashing strokes across the bumper. I asked him what this meant. Success for Africa? For Tanzania? "No," he shouted, a true Tanzanian, "success for Hassan!"

We pilgrims bought and shared sticky buns for breakfast while we waited for Hassan to get Success! ready. Children with dirty hair sold us tea in small plastic cups and saucers, a two-handed operation that seemed a particularly absurd holdover of imperial etiquette. As I ate, I watched Hassan fill the fuel tanks of Success! with gas. I found it strange that the gas had been stored in small, unmarked cans. "Shh," said Hassan in a tone of mock-conspiracy, "this is how we get it across the border. We tell the guards it's fish."

Hassan took his time, joking and chatting with the other drivers. I sipped my tongue-searing tea, watching the market gather energy into the morning. After a while, I became aware of a wrinkled Masai woman staring at me from a nearby stall. She was bald and wore a purple cape and multiple collars of bright beads, looking like a grand-motherly version of a punk in full regalia. Heavy earrings had stretched her earlobes into long strips of flesh. She glared un-abashedly at me, a disarming African practice. Then she began to stride across the market in my direction. When she reached me she spoke sharply in Masai. Hassan and the pilgrims grew quiet and watched, treating the Masai woman with a wary calm usually re-served for wild things. Her gait was leonine, an aging female of an unpredictable, warrior species.

I wondered if I had somehow offended her. Then she abruptly took my hand. Hers felt rough, like the pads of a dog's paw. Removing from her finger a ring of beads, she pressed it into my hand, face stern, old eyes ablaze with dignity. Then she walked away as sud-denly as she had appeared.

"That old woman has honored you," said a fellow traveler, a Masai in a dusty suit and tie. "Such a gift is a great honor among my people. She gives you a magic token. It is good luck. Wear it and they say you will come to no harm."

"But why has she chosen me for this charm?"

"Who knows? My people are mysterious. In my Western clothes, I do not understand these mysteries. Perhaps she saw something in your eyes, or in your white hair. Perhaps she thought you had magic in you that needed to be released and you required a charm to make this magic work." He spoke quietly and solemnly as the pilgrims listened in silence. "I might call this superstitious and backward," he added, "but I do not. My father was a Moran.* I have a great respect for the Masai."

---

* The Masai warrior class.

I slid the ring onto my finger and tried to imagine that I felt different, although I was not certain what I was supposed to feel. What sort of magic did I have in me waiting to be released? I thought of the possibilities of owning a magic ring. Would it improve my luck? Would I become a better person? Would I have the power to heal? Would it divert a bullet about to strike me in the heart? I didn't know, although given the uncertainties of Africa, I decided that I shouldn't think too hard about a good-luck charm delivered by an old Masai woman in a purple cape. The episode had a lyricism that might have been spoiled by too much introspection. Why not believe? I knew from years of travels that magic makes a great deal of sense where chaos and fear are most powerful.

Hassan reluctantly left his cronies in the market four hours after I had arrived there. With a holler he called us over and revved up his engine. The pilgrims and I scrambled aboard Success! I was immediately assaulted by the noxious odors of animal feces and years of accumulated human sweat. I made a huge error being among the first on board. I was progressively squashed and driven into the far left corner by what seemed an impossible number of people and several animals squeezing into Success! I was quickly cut off from any reasonable source of air and my legs somehow ended up on an upward slant, resting on a cage full of chickens. A dozen of us managed to compress ourselves onto plank benches that might comfortably have seated six. In our case five would have been better, considering the bulk of the woman with twelve children, whose rank-smelling armpit was slumped over the top of my head. Fortunately, there was a small, plastic window that I could see out of, the left side of my face being smashed against it. From this vantage point I could watch as Success! roared out of the market toward the northern grasslands of Tanzania.

We spent the rest of the morning racing across Masailand toward the Kenyan border, a cloud of black effluents swimming in our wake. There was little scenery other than grass and a few birds. Once we passed two giraffes grazing on the edge of the Serengeti. They were the first large mammals I had seen since the bull elephant in the Zambezi River Valley, a sad testament to what has been a mass slaughter of fauna over the past several decades. As we passed, the giraffes arched their necks low at the sound of Success! and trotted off toward the refuge of the park with the slow, loping gait of a slightly overweight gazelle.

Occasionally, we passed Moran warriors in red capes tending their beloved cattle. They stared at Success! in grandiose silence, insolent and proud. I marveled that at this late date the Masai still existed, a race living in a Nietzschean disregard for a modern world that had so far utterly failed to change them. I admit I gawked like a tourist, for nothing I had yet seen looked more like that image of Africa lurking in every Westerner's brain, that fantasy from the pages of tourist brochures and *National Geographic*.

Riding in Success! I had an opportunity to see one of these legendary savages at extremely close range when we picked two up for a short ride near the Kenyan border. (We had already stopped a half-dozen times to take on local passengers. One woman was carrying two live chickens that had promptly defecated on my trousers.) The Moran came aboard with their razor-sharp spears and swords, a major distraction for twelve people already concerned about space. However, no one dared suggest they leave their spears outside, not even Hassan. I later got my explanation for this behavior from a book by Beryl Markham. In *West With the Night* she makes it quite clear why the Masai prefer to endanger the lives of several innocent pilgrims rather than part with their spears. According to Markham, who greatly admired the aristocratic bearing of the Masai, the Moran's spear is nearly as important to him as his penis. She writes that to each Moran "his spear is a symbol of his manhood, and as much a part of himself as the sinews of his body. His spear is the manifestation of his faith. . . . It is the emblem of his blood and his breeding. . . ."

The other reason why no one on Success! complained is because the Masai still occasionally use their spears on outsiders, each other and anyone else who is stupid enough to violate a code of honor that suffers no provocation whatsoever. So we didn't quibble about the spears, though it was a miracle we were not impaled in the bouncing, jostling vehicle rushing at high speeds over the half-wrecked highway.

The Masai enjoyed the ride, giggling like girls at our cowardly squirmings. After we had settled into new positions I found myself pressed into the gooey shoulder of one Moran, the contour of my cheek imprinted in a lather of ocher. Pressed against the other side of my squashed body was the woman with twelve children, her skin slick with sweat that mingled with my own. Yet even in our mashed condition we were able to contract even further when the Masai and their spears disembarked. Outside, they playfully jabbed at Success!

as if it were a lion or a buffalo, or perhaps they were actors playing a role. They reminded me of Hollywood, their dress and coiffures being as gaudy as a film opening. They whooped it up as we pulled away, the Noble Savage poking fun at Sedentary Man.

The border of Kenya did not introduce an immediate cornucopia for the pilgrims in Success!, although the pocked road abruptly became a smooth blacktop with a yellow line freshly painted down the center. Up here the grass was mostly green, the result of recent, miraculous rains that had soaked Kenya while utterly missing Tanzania. ("Even the rain is against us," a shopkeeper in Arusha had told me. "The capitalists to the north must be paying off God for these rains. If only *we* had the money to pay off God.") Acacia blossomed in pinks and blues. Plovers, attracted by water, scurried from roadside gullies into the bush. Fifty years ago, Isak Dinesen described this land as being "irregularly dotted with the little marks of the thorn-bushes, the winding river-beds are drawn up with crooked dark green trails; these are the woods of the mighty, wide-branching Mimosa trees, with thorns like spikes; the cactus grows here, and here is the home of the giraffe and the Rhino."

Sadly, neither giraffe nor rhino appeared along our highway, having been long ago killed off or forced into reserves. And the mimosas Dinesen described have been chopped down and the land eroded by overgrazing. A few large mammals stood off in the distance—antelopes and cows nibbling cordgrass behind fences on private hunting ranches. Fences, my old nemesis, appeared for the first time since South Africa along the highway, their long strands of barbed steel glinting in the sunlight.

But these were my concerns alone. The other pilgrims had other matters on their minds. We were rapidly approaching their version of utopia, the great city of Nairobi. They spoke excitedly about sky-scrapers, exotic *wazungu* from across the sea and shops with glass windows selling such delicacies as toilet paper and chocolate bars. To these Tanzanians, weaned on the gray deprivations of egalitarianism, Nairobi was bigger than New York, more sophisticated than Paris, more sinful than prewar Shanghai—boundless opportunities, breathless thrills, decadence, progress and activity.

We entered the city through a vast labyrinth of concrete huts and smoky markets that spread for miles around the core city. This was an unusual portal of entry for a *wazungu*, who normally arrives in the sedate, Westernized part of town near the airport. My arrival afforded me a glimpse of this city that few Westerners see, that huge, raucous Nairobi that still retains a strong flavor of Africa—in its colors, attitudes and architecture. In the distance, I could see the glimmering international-style hotels and office towers hovering like a mirage, an Oz of glass, steel and concrete.

Success! was nearly swamped by masses of people, swirling, colorful, ragged and much busier than anything I had seen in Africa. They made even the markets in Tanzania seem primitive and lazy. People were buying and selling in a frenzy of activity, hawking a vast catalog of goods I had not seen since Zimbabwe. Like maniacs they argued over prices and shouted out bids on everything from air conditioners to freshly slaughtered chickens. At the same time the streets were choked with battered buses and gadfly *matatus* honking Star War horns; and with young men carrying boom boxes blaring tinny African rock and roll.

If prosperity can be equated with movement, then Nairobi truly was an economic miracle, although movement is one of the more effective disguises covering quieter realities. Through the dirty window of Success! I saw many people working hard, but I also saw many more in the background doing nothing, just standing and sitting and lying in the mud left by the recent rains. Peeking down side streets, I could see apparitions clad in gray rags bent over steaming kettles and huddled under soggy cardboard roofs. Scores of silent men cluttered the landscape, their hands wrapped around bottles of beer.

The pilgrims in Success! were blinded to this darker side of mecca, never doubting for a moment that movement meant prosperity. They watched the streets like anxious children as Hassan steered through the mobs and into a berth beside a ramshackle service station.

Tumbling outside with the others, I said good-bye to the pilgrims, who scattered excitedly to find friends, toilet paper and fortunes. I wished them luck, praying that their dreams would not be crushed by this vast city. Swinging my rucksack onto my back, I looked about to get my bearings amid the confusion, and then set off into the wild gyrations of what undoubtedly was going to be the most confusing city on my journey.

2   The mere thought of exploring this vast city made me weary. I had a fleeting notion of staying in one of the wild African inns near the Nairobi River, where hired thugs protected customers with knobby clubs and knives. But my reserves of curiosity were nearly depleted after five months of African travel. I needed a transfusion of uncomplicated, easy familiarity, a downtime to reenergize. I wanted to curl up in a clean bed and read a good murder mystery taking place somewhere far away from Africa—say in Bermuda or Alaska. So I set off in search of a taxi, a scarce commodity in that particular part of Nairobi.

As I walked through the hordes, I was surprised to hear a voice call out my name. It was a fellow pilgrim, the truck driver named Okingo, the man who had wanted to buy spark plugs. He hailed me from across the street and rushed over. I asked him about the plugs and he smiled broadly. "That was a trick to get a visa," he said. "No, I have come to Nairobi to stay and work." His plan was simple. He was going to strike it rich, buy a mansion and marry four women, the limit allowed by the Koran.

"How will you make this money?" I asked, stepping carefully along the crumbled edge of the road, sidestepping carts, dogs and vendors.

"I have an idea." He spoke quietly, as if one of the hordes might steal his scheme, though I'm sure they had heard it all before. "I will start a small transport business and later buy a lorry with some other men. Do you know? We each buy a part of the lorry. Partners. I will drive to the border and take goods there for the black market. Soon, I will buy another lorry and then many lorries until I am so rich."

"It sounds like a good plan," I said, impressed by his optimism, but wondering if this overcrowded, overrated city could ever fulfill his expectations.

"Maybe you can help me," he said as we sidestepped a speeding *matatu*. Its horn was rigged to play a little ditty that sounded like a Michael Jackson song.

"Help you?"

"Yes." He hesitated, and I was sure he was going to ask for money. Ten dollars, twenty dollars . . . After all, he was a Tanzanian. But he did not want money. No, what he wanted would have astounded the most insolent hawkers in Kigoma and Dodoma. Okingo wanted me to buy him an *entire truck*. And it had to be a new one, he said, the one built by the Japanese company Isuzu. "That is all I need from you," he said, looking as sincere as decency allowed him. "Just one small lorry made by this man named Isuzu. You buy, I drive. We be partners! You will get fifty percent of the profits!"

"Okingo," I said, "do you know how much lorries cost?"

"Of course, they are many thousands of dollars," he said brashly, a man who a moment earlier I had been worried about. How was he ever going to make it in this huge city? I had asked myself. Where would he live? What would he eat? I had been prepared to categorize him as one of those poor, confused rural persons who pour into Nairobi every week by the thousands, the anxious immigrants destined to join the listless men hanging about on the edges of the market, whose small dreams have been crushed under the weight of the city.

But this particular pilgrim had disarmed my stereotyped expectations. Here was a man who was not the least bit frightened by the specter of the big, mean, inhuman, capitalist city. He was in his element here and, if this city offered even a shred of opportunity, Okingo was going to take advantage of it. Okingo had no place to go, no money, no friends, but he did have a commodity that is scarce in black Africa: confidence.

"And you think that I will simply buy a lorry for you," I asked, "just like that?"

He narrowed his eyes like the hawkers in Dodoma. "Perhaps you would prefer fifty-*five* percent of the profits?"

"Look here," I said, not wanting to give him the wrong impression, "I am not about to buy you a . . ."

"You are a hard man," said Okingo. "I offer you fifty-*nine* percent, but nothing more."

"But . . . but . . ."

"My friend, fifty-nine percent is very good! I am a hard worker, a good driver. You will make your money back in just a few months. You will be a rich man. You will be able to buy a mansion, a new Mercedes, a . . ."

He spoke on, his voice growing louder as he listed the riches dangling before me if only I would buy him a truck. ". . . You can have many women," he was saying, "and a large television, and many wives . . ."

I gave up my protestations and let him bluster on as we stepped through the teeming thousands in the bazaars of Nairobi. It was a fantastic scene, this solitary, audacious pilgrim chanting his mantra to mammon and behaving as if he could take on all of Africa— assuming that he could make a decent profit.

I had not met anyone like Okingo in Africa, a man who seemed more American than African, and more nineteenth century in his huge ambitions than late twentieth century. He reminded me, perversely, of another great pilgrim who arrived in another African city as a young, penniless waif with big ideas—John Cecil Rhodes. The difference was that Okingo wasn't cluttering his dreams with a lot of dubious politics. As far as I could tell, he was following no creed at all, other than a single-minded pursuit of personal gain. This was, of course, nothing new in Africa. I have seen Mercedes sedans from Harare to downtown Nairobi filled with coiffured Africans, the princes of the realm, whose only goal in life is to amass great personal wealth. But Okingo was different. He had not been born into any dubious elite. He was no big man's cousin, son or nephew. He was a member of the underclass, a denizen of the have nots, an upstart, and possibly the best hope for Africa.

To be sure, too much can be made out of a single pilgrim on the streets of Nairobi. For all I knew, he was destined to fail miserably and become one of the ragged ones. Or, conversely, he *would* make it big, only to find that avarice, too, can exact an ugly toll. Yet it was refreshing to meet Okingo after so many dispiriting days in Central Africa. He seemed utterly *alive,* a flash of powder and color against the gray, a man filled with *passion*—pure, hard-driven, fervent passion, the sort of passion that motivates and pushes and tugs, that excites and titillates, that rushes like a thunderclap toward the future.

When I finally flagged down a taxi, I gave Okingo a twenty-dollar bill toward the purchase of his first truck—or for a bite of food, a drink, a woman or whatever else he wanted to use it for. Though disappointed that I was not buying him an entire truck, he accepted the twenty with a modesty and solemnness that seemed surprisingly genuine from a hawker and would-be prince of Nairobi. Was it possible that this paragon of ambition had managed to retain a streak of African humility?

He took the money and shook my hand, saying he would never forget me, his first friend in Nairobi. I offered him a ride to wherever he wanted to go, which he declined in the same sober voice. "You take this car and go to the rich man's city," he said. "I see you there someday when I am a rich man and can buy my own car." He gazed off toward the towers of downtown, his eyes fixed and clear, the plucky immigrant celebrating the moment of arrival. "Yes, you will see me downtown," he continued. "Look for me in just five years. I will invite you to my new house and repay this money to you. We will talk about this trip when we were young and I was poor."

Easing back into the spacious comfort of the taxi, I sped away from Okingo's Nairobi toward the city of towers and glass. The first thing I saw were several acres of multinational factories and warehouses—Dunlop, Massey-Ferguson, Bata . . . Next came a massive railway complex and a number of rocket-sized tanks marking Kenya's central coffee-roasting plant. Then came the downtown itself, a specter of straight lines, glass shop fronts, newsstands, neon and Toyota sedans.

White faces seemed to be everywhere, tourists moving about in small herds, and clusters of expatriates walking purposefully in khaki trousers and limp ties. Black faces were far more numerous, but not as obvious, as they deftly sidestepped the pale foreigners. I was reminded of London during the season when natives hug the inside edge of the sidewalks to avoid contact with Americans in plastic Beefeater hats and Harrods T-shirts.

I had my cabbie drop me off in the center of town, at the Thorn Tree Café. This is a plastic, thoroughly Western establishment that nonetheless serves a decent hamburger and very cold beer, two distinctly American vices I crave when I have been in the wilderness for any length of time. The Thorn Tree is the social hub of the young elite in Nairobi, white and black, a haven that offered a complete respite from the world I had been traveling through for the past several weeks. I had a nostalgic attachment to the Thorn Tree, a place where I had years earlier spent many hot, pleasurable afternoons in the company of fellow writers, expats and well-heeled Kenyans.

Unfortunately, as soon as I arrived at the entrance of the Thorn Tree, I knew I had made a mistake in going there. It wasn't that the Thorn Tree was physically different. There were the same expats, Kenyan students and backpack travelers fraternizing under the same gaudy green umbrellas. The problem was me. Before, I had been fresh out of America. I had been very young. I had come to this café to be with my own kind, to drink beer, to be seen—the usual things. Now, after four thousand miles of Africa—of dust, desperate conversations and ragged edges—the place seemed merely frivolous.

My reticence did not stop me from plunging into the Thorn Tree and ordering a large, bloody burger enshrouded in cheese and ketchup. Nor did it stop me from consuming it with great relish. I did, however, insist on a corner table as far away from my fellow patrons as possible. Even so, it was not far enough. The Thorn Tree was, as usual, abuzz with the sort of Western-speak I had not heard for weeks.

"We gotta get more of that Afghan weed," I heard a pale man saying at the next table. "That stuff made those lions look as big as a fuckin' house. I mean, did you see those little pigs? Man, they were like little tanks . . . vroom, vroom . . ."

"They were *warthogs*," said a woman companion in beads and Kenyan wraps. "I keep tellin' you, George, they were *warthogs*, not pigs. If you call them pigs again . . ."

"Whatever," said George. "What I'm sayin' is, that Afghan shit sneaks up on you like goddamned artillery."

On the other side of me were two Swedish women wearing almost nothing in the hot sun, poring over a map of East Africa. Abundant breasts beat against thin cotton halters and shorts were hiked up high, an incredible distraction to every male in the Thorn Tree. To my surprise, they turned around just after I sat down and asked if I would help them with their travel plans. If anyone else had asked, I might have acted as irritable and tired as I felt, but I am a mere mortal. I said I would be pleased to help them any way I could.

"You look like you travel many places," said the woman closest to me, the one who looked most like Brigitte Bardot. "Please, you have been to Masai Mara? Nakuru? Any of these places?" I told them I had just arrived from Tanzania. "Oh, then you can tell us, please. Is it possible to take a rental car across the border to Tanzania? We hear it is difficult." I was about to answer when a voice from behind me interrupted.

"Hey, did you say *rental car?*" asked a muscular American. He wore a zebra-striped T-shirt that said SAFARI UNTIL YOU PUKE. "Me and my buddy Merv are looking to rent a Land Rover," he said. "*We're* goin' to Tanzania. To that place with the animals, ah . . ."

"The Serengeti?" I ventured.

"Yeah, and we're gonna see that, ah, that mountain . . ."

"Kilimanjaro?"

"Yeah, that's it, Kill My Jell-O. Me and Merv, we were just talkin' about it. Right, Merv?" Merv had on a T-shirt emblazoned with the faces of a popular heavy metal band. He seemed to be fighting a terrible hangover, but this didn't stop him from nodding furiously.

"That is very good," said the Swede, who I was sure would dismiss those T-shirted heathens with an appropriately deprecating remark and return to our conversation. But she continued talking to the Americans and, to my surprise, asked if she and her friend could accompany Merv and the safari party to Tanzania. "Can we go with you?" she asked with that disarming innocence Swedish women are famous for. "We pay our share. We have a good time."

"Jesus, that sounds more than good to me," stuttered the Americans, suddenly at a loss for words.

After that, I devoured my burger and fled the Thorn Tree, again by taxi. I headed for the Fairview Hotel, a colonial-era inn poised on a tranquil ridge above the city, far away from safari goers and rushing Japanese sedans. The Fairview was a perfect place to recuperate. It was neither gaudy nor loud, its rooms were simple and comfortable, and it had a lovely, peaceful garden. The only drawback was that it was the favorite haunt of foreigners claiming to be "serious" about Kenya. (Kenya, having made it a policy to buy the best advice money can buy, was awash with Ph.D.'s, theoreticians and experts.) This meant one had to be very careful about choosing a seat at breakfast. The tables were long and communal, and it was easy to find oneself surrounded by several pundits at once. They come in two varieties: the new, enthusiastic first-timers and the older, more experienced cynics. They can be equally tedious, particularly when one has to endure both at the same time. Invariably, even before my eggs had arrived, I would find myself pitted between a first-timer and a cynic on such topics as modernizing the Samburu or the desirability of using animal dung to fertilize coffee trees. I do not want to give the impression that I have anything against discussing aborigines and fertilizer. It's just that I prefer these topics in easier doses, and preferably after I have finished breakfast.

Still, the experts were easy to avoid. The Fairview is a big, sprawling complex with a very large garden. It is quite easy to escape into nooks and secluded corners, where I became for a few days the most content human being on earth, drinking tea, reading novels, snoozing and wondering why anyone would be so foolish as to climb on a bicycle and pedal across Africa.

My repose lasted exactly three days, when I finally grew weary of too much tranquillity and ventured out to see friends and take a look at the city. I did not stay long. Nairobi is so much like home that I felt vaguely cheated by its towers, traffic, and bustling crowds, its fast-food burgers, teenagers with boom boxes, discotheques, panhandlers, development, progress!

Yet I was not entirely put off by this swarming, pseudo-capitalist bastion in Africa, this city where the invisible hand has been unleashed with almost as much determination as it has been confined in most parts of the continent. Nairobi is as much an experiment as Dodoma, Jomo Kenyatta's gamble that a mix of free enterprise and Western-style welfare programs could outperform the socialist ethos of his neighbors and launch Kenya into the twentieth century.

It seems pointless to offer any detailed comparison between Dodoma and Nairobi, or, say, Lusaka and Nairobi. The differences are as polar as fire and rain. One has only to open his eyes in the core city to see that the Kenyans have done something right, for not only is Nairobi a world-class city, it is a metropolis created mostly by Africans and for Africans. It has a heavy Western tinge, to be sure, and there continue to be a large coterie of foreign experts helping things along. But this does not diminish the fact that a generation of Africans has erected one of the more developed nations in sub-Saharan Africa. Gross National Product, per capita income, food production—all have been steadily improving for over two decades, a rare feat in Africa.

But this did not mean that the people of the core city were spending time gloating. They were much too busy trying to get rich. Most downtowners took the accoutrements of modern life for granted, assuming, as an American does, that telephones, electric lights and good Italian restaurants are unquestioned gifts of God to man. Far from acting smug, the typical office worker, shopkeeper, and skilled laborer tended to offer up a variety of middle-class complaints— about traffic congestion and the price of beer—that seemed trivial after the past several weeks.

However, Nairobi does have its less savory sides, not the least of which are the gross excesses of its most privileged class. Just when a visitor has decided to become impressed with Kenya, a prince of the city struts past to remind one why French revolutionaries employed the guillotine. Drenched in jewelry, tailored silk and disgusting folds of flesh, these highest of the high elites appear with great fanfare at the power spots in the city—the Intercontinental Hotel, the Holiday Inn, and various colonial-era clubs. Truly a sight to behold, they radiate arrogance, worldliness and power, like puffy, upstart Romans.

I made no effort to meet with any of Nairobi's princes, having been warned that they would view such attempts with great suspicion. "They do not talk with foreign writers," said a professor at the University of Nairobi. "In Kenyatta's day, they might have seen you. But things have changed with this new bunch. They are as secretive as the Russians in the Kremlin used to be, and certainly rival them in dullness. You watch them and see. Does [President] Moi ever smile? No—not once have I seen him smile. He merely glowers ominously, making everyone feel they had better watch their step."

Nairobians, being famous for their rumormongering, could not resist such a ripe topic as the excesses of their leadership. One only had to spend a few minutes with a Kenyan and the subject would invariably shift to the latest tale of depravity regarding the princes and princesses of the city.

There was an element of danger in such talk. People had been known to disappear after making inexpedient remarks in crowded cafes and restaurants. Like most instant aristocrats, Nairobi's princes were sensitive about how their wealth and power were obtained. Occasionally, the censored press offered the public a bone concerning a minor elite's indiscretion, but top officials were never mentioned. While I was in Kenya the papers were filled with the news that several private bankers had been embezzling millions for years. The government fumed with indignation, revealing in breathless, daily snippets new evidence of the bankers' depravity: illicit houses, jewelry and cars.

But these sensations, presumably intended to prove the government's commitment to weed out corruption, merely whetted the cravings of the rumor mill. It seemed as if half the population spent part of their day trying to guess the current net worth of President Daniel arap Moi. It was generally assumed that he was worth hundreds of millions of dollars. Some said his fortune was well over a billion dollars.

There were also stories about the other voracious appetites of the "Big Men." For example, one former foreign minister reputedly kept a large harem of mistresses scattered among his estates, women who had borne him over sixty children. (This same minister, it was said, had once been in charge of the nation's notoriously unsuccessful population control program.) And then there was a former MP who allegedly murdered a political rival for a woman who some people regarded as the most beautiful in Kenya.

I have no idea if any of the rumors were true, although they did strike me as a curious repeat of history in Kenya, where excesses have long been a prominent feature of life among certain elite in Nairobi. The only difference is that the decadent princes of today have black skin, and their names are no longer as pronounceable for Westerners as Delemere, Errol and Idina.

This is not to say that white Kenyans have completely lost the knack for excess, although the loss of political dominance has forced them to behave with more temperance. Most have adopted the less conspicuous status of the rich and powerless, living behind high, suburban walls and going to work each morning in the city. This bland but comfortable lifestyle reminded me of white South Africa, with its large houses, cozy gardens, servants, clubs, and Sundays at the race track. However, these Kenyans tended to be more sophisticated, offering a bemused, fatalistic view of life that seemed more appropriate to the position of the Caucasian in Africa.

Yet the white population is not entirely bereft of the sort of eccentrics Kenya once was famous for. There are a number of old colonial scalawags still active in Nairobi, even if many of them have retired or been reduced to operating safari operations for package tourists. As for the younger generation of whites in Kenya, most either are studying in Europe or are worrying about how to keep up mortgage payments on one of the new, flashy condominiums downtown. I found many of this younger generation to be bland reflections of their boisterous fathers and mothers, though underneath a surface of pleasant cynicism most of them seemed united by a touching devotion to improving Kenya, even if their approach was largely academic.

I spent nearly two weeks in downtown Nairobi, which was about all the good life I could bear. This place was, in many ways, a lovely and impressive little paradise—so was white Cape Town, for that matter—but it was not the *real* Nairobi. The land of clubs and high-rises represents less than fifteen percent of Nairobi's two million souls, a secluded neighborhood set aside for a small fraction of the population, most of whom lived on that darker side of the city, that abyss of shacks and squalor I had glimpsed when I arrived in town.

It seemed important before I left at least to make an effort to journey to this other side of Nairobi, if for no other reason than travelers continue to write about the core city as if it were the real Nairobi and not the anomaly it actually is. One morning I climbed aboard my bicycle—Jim had left it for me in the Fairview's storage vault—and took off on a day trip toward the outer edges of mecca.

This was not my first visit to Nairobi's slums. Earlier, I had persuaded a taxi driver friend to show me by car the way to one of the shantytowns, so I would not get lost when I climbed on my bicycle. This taxi driver—I'll call him Joseph, as he wanted to remain anonymous—was a tremendous resource, since he himself had grown up in the slums. As I bike along, I'll be referring now and then to his comments.

When I departed the Fairview, after another trying breakfast with experts discussing the morality of growing tobacco in Kenya, I headed east toward the Nairobi River. I pedaled down broad Haile Selassie Avenue, past the Kenya Polytechnic, the railway station and the district where coffee, grain and other produce are stored in large loading tanks. As the traffic became more congested and the number of pedestrians increased, I glided down an easy hillside to the small river, which an early settler compared to a gentle English brook. Today's waterway is not much larger than a brook, but it hardly looks gentle, being clogged with rubbish, refuse and perhaps a half-dozen shanties—the first vanguard of the abyss, hardly a quarter-mile away from the skyscrapers.

Crossing the river, I plunged into the insanity of Okingo's Nairobi, the frenetic swirl of hawkers, traffic, pedestrians, animals and screaming children. It was a sudden and confusing transition, the reverse of what I had experienced two weeks earlier. Before I had traveled even a hundred meters I had vendors after me trying to sell everything from plastic mirrors to machetes. Eager faces recalled Okingo's lust for riches. I was tempted to stop and try to learn more about this second city of Nairobi, this land of almost-haves that hovers just beyond the core city, serving the princes in much the same way that the four outer boroughs serve Manhattan. But I did not stop, my goal being a sprawl of shanties to the east, that outpost of the abyss known as Muthare Valley.

It took me an hour to bike through Okingo's Nairobi, past a mad collage of bleakness and dynamism that seemed, in its own crude way, to indicate that at least some of the prosperity in the core city was dribbling down to what might be termed an embryonic middle class. I had the feeling that I was glimpsing what American cities must have looked like at the turn of the century, when millions of expectant immigrants lived in a state of harsh privation in a place like New York City's Lower East Side.

I finally reached Muthare as the sun became hot about eleven in the morning. The transition was abrupt as the sloppy concrete houses and shops of Okingo's city trailed off at the edge of a large, wedge-shaped valley. Once, this valley would have been covered with thick, lovely stands of mimosa and elephant grass. Now it is the lair of a sprawling beast, a Leviathan of squalor heaped between two hillsides.

I stopped near a row of shanties to get my bearings. Filthy prostitutes in bright rags giggled at me from under a tar-paper awning. One of them fondled her breasts and beckoned me over. Meanwhile, several men holding dented tins of cheap liquor watched warily from the shade of a beer shop, their faces at midday already lost in the oblivion of alcohol and hemp.

The absurdity of my little mission suddenly became apparent. I stood staring like a voyeur into the edge of the Muthare monster, wondering what the hell I was going to do next. Part of me wanted to flee; part of me wanted to weep; and part of me wanted to rave like a madman at the horror. How could I approach such a place?

As I ruminated, I was interrupted by a great commotion rising from near the prostitutes' shanty. I craned to see what was going on and saw a policeman. And he was coming in my direction. I had been warned by Joseph the taxi driver and other friends to stay clear of police. "They will be very angry," Joseph had told me as we drove past Muthare in his taxi. "They do not like you to see these things. Maybe they arrest you." After my experience in Kasama, I did not take this warning lightly.

As I watched the policeman approach, I got a harebrained idea. He was still nearly a hundred meters away, and I was not sure that he had even seen me. He appeared to be alone and on foot. So I hopped on my bike and bolted, pedaling as hard as I could. Since the crowd was blocking the highway, I made for Muthare itself, ducking into one of the narrow shantytown streets.

The tiny street quickly became too cluttered for biking. I jumped off and began dragging my vehicle through the mud, gooey and slick from the rains. The shacks were arranged haphazardly and so close together that nearly all traces of the sun and sky were obscured. The passageways were dark and nauseating, forming a leaky, putrid castle made of paper, canvas and wood.

Most of the faces were women's. Their activity punctuated this netherworld of stillness as they tended fires, boiled watery mealies and scrubbed rags in fetid ditches. It struck me that the physical motions of poverty are nearly always domestic, as if desperate people must wash one more piece of clothing before they die.

After a few minutes, a man in an open stall hailed me in English. "What you want, *wazungu?*" he asked with a grin, his teeth yellow, his hair coated with a thin sheen of mud and water. "You buy something? Some beer? It this beer maked by us." He handed me a vile, homemade liquid in a dirty tin. Unfortunately, this intimacy brought with it a requirement of social etiquette even in Muthare. As the guest, I had no choice but to drink. The man waited as I contemplated a liquid undoubtedly infested with every infectious disease known to man. I toasted the Muthare men and drank what tasted like vomit.

I sat down on a wet bench to chat with the men, although it wasn't much of a conversation. One of the men spoke English, but he knew only a few words. This was too bad, because I had so many questions. Where had these people come from? Why did they live here? What were their hopes and fears? I did, however, have Joseph's story, which helped fill in some of the gaps.

Joseph embodied a tale of modest success emerging from the slums of Nairobi, although he was the first to admit that he had been lucky to emerge at all. In the mid-sixties, as a boy, his father had brought him and his family from a remote village in Kikuyuland. Like so many others they had come because there was no food in their village, and because his father was attracted to the supposed opportunities of the city. "Everyone was very excited at that time," he had told me as we drove around. "This was just after independence, when Nairobi was the place to be. There were so many jobs, and many men left the country."

He could remember leaving his village on a large truck with several other families. They carried only a few essentials—clothing, a few pots and pans and the hope of that heady era. "Yes, but things were difficult when we arrived. There were not so many jobs, and there was no place to live." So they had scrounged around for scraps of wood and canvas and had built a tiny shack. They ate garbage and subsidized mealies. His father grew despondent and began drinking. One day he disappeared, to be replaced by other fathers, each of whom left new siblings before moving on. Eventually, his mother, a long-suffering woman whom Joseph worshiped, qualified for a small concrete house in a government project. After that, life improved slightly for her large brood.

By the time he reached manhood, Joseph had managed to finish five years of schooling, having benefited from a brief postcolonialist bonanza when opportunities truly existed in a city a quarter its present size. He had begun hustling when he was a small boy, taking jobs ranging from loading vegetable carts to greasing chassis in a garage when he was a teenager. He then "met the right people" and became a hired cabbie, saving his money until he bought his own rig three years before I met him, on his thirty-fourth birthday. "That was such a happy day," he exclaimed with a broad smile. "On that day, I felt like a man."

However, Joseph was pessimistic about Kenya's future. He said that opportunities were diminishing all the time in Nairobi, particularly for the uneducated villagers still pouring into the city, a vast population of individuals like these men I was sharing a beer with. "I was lucky to be young during the early days of independence," Joseph said. "These new ones come to the city expecting miracles. They should stay in the village. It is no good here."

The men in the beer shop probably had similar stories to tell, of leaving their rural homes and trekking to Muthare, although my lack of Swahili foiled all attempts at meaningful communication. So after a polite interval in which I faked taking several more sips of beer, I bade the men farewell and kept walking through the streets, stepping gingerly over the ooze.

As I walked about, I thought about what all this meant for Kenya, a country I previously had been prepared to praise. The situation reminded me of India, another place of stunning contrasts between rich and poor. And the comparison hurt. For the sheer press of this underclass is likely to drag down both of these countries, even as they begin to show signs of economic growth and development. At the least they are destined to remain forever within the ranks of the Third World. A place like Muthare presents the future shock of Kenya, India and perhaps the entire world. In the West, we are raised to optimistically believe that such problems can be solved. But even as I write these words an insatiable parasite is growing in places like Kenya, consuming and making impossible demands on the organs of prosperity.

What is Kenya—and the world—going to do with all of these people? The government and international organizations annually spend millions of dollars on new housing, clinics, markets and wells. Hundreds of experts, bureaucrats and workers in the core city toil in the face of slim budgets and frequent government apathy to design and implement new schemes to improve the situation in places like Muthare Valley. As a trip through Okingo's Nairobi proves, there has been some success. Yet the entire effort is being overwhelmed by a growth rate of Malthusian proportions. Kenya's population is expanding by 4.1 percent a year—the highest in the world.

It was late in the afternoon before I finally emerged from the sea of shanties onto the edge of a road. About this time a rain shower began, falling in great sheets. It was difficult to see, and slippery going as I pushed up the side of the valley toward the highway. As I was struggling along, I saw a figure emerging out of the haze of the downpour. Yes, it was a policeman. He had noticed me and was headed my way.

The policeman asked for my papers, saying I was not supposed to be here. He demanded to see inside my handlebar bag. At this point, I knew I was in trouble, for inside the bag was my camera, guaranteed to arouse the suspicions of any African policeman. Sure enough, when I opened my bag, he practically foamed at the mouth. "You have a camera! You take pictures! This is illegal!" My poor camera, which had survived roadblocks and threatened confiscations in four countries, was abruptly snatched from its waterproof case and exposed to the rain. "You have been taking photographs!" he repeated, his tone shrill with hysteria. He banged on the camera and tried to pry it open with his fingernails. I opened it for him, grimacing as I exposed the film inside and soaked the inner workings. He took all of the film I had in my bag, but I did not argue. The alternative, I knew, might have been another sojourn in jail.

The policeman then released me with more shouted warnings. My stomach was about to heave—whether from the native beer or nerves I didn't know—as I began pedaling away from Muthare Valley as fast as my legs would take me.

3   I departed greater Nairobi some days later in another soaking downpour, late for the season. Traveling alone on my bicycle, I pedaled along the edge of the Uhuru Highway, a two-lane death trap that connects the downtown high-rises with the elite suburbs to the west. A gray spittle of oil, water and garbage kicked up from the highway as countless internal combustion engines spewed black smoke. I had heard that a Canadian backpacker had passed out from the fumes on this highway. I had no trouble understanding why.

The traffic allowed me barely an inch or two of pavement to ride on. It took considerable concentration to keep my tires from falling off the jagged edge of the asphalt. This situation was made worse by the fact that I was feeling rather wobbly trying to control fifty pounds of gear after a long hiatus off the bike.

Most of the drivers were competent in a rude sort of way, reminding me of drivers in New York City. They usually waited to veer off at the very last second, just as their vehicles were about to crush me. But these drivers were demigods compared to *matatu* drivers, who reminded me of a cross between Bostonians and Egyptians, whom I rate in a dead heat as the worst drivers in the world. *Matatu* drivers seemed keenly interested in seeing just how talented I was at avoiding the sawtooth edging of the highway. When I heard them approaching from behind I felt nothing but dread. First came the rattle and groan of the engine, then the squeaks of the grossly overloaded chassis—*rumba*—squeak-*rumba*-squeak-*rumba*-squeak. . . . Then the incessant honking—*beeeeeeeeep, beeeeeeeeep, beeeeeeeeep.* . . . Then the hoarse shouting of the driver—"Hello, meester! Hello, meester!" Finally, the *matatu* itself would appear, a fireball of energy, yahoos, gyrations, colors and screams of abandon. "Hello, meester!" the driver would holler like a madman, ignoring the road, other cars and often his own steering wheel. "Hello, meester!" passengers would scream, hanging off the truck by precarious handholds, young men laughing and daring fate to shake them off 230 and grind them under the wheels. As each *matatu* passed I could read its name emblazoned on its cab or bumper—Speed Devil, Catch Me If You Can, the Lionel Ritchie Special. Before I knew it, the whole carnival had whizzed past, leaving behind its smoke and fumes as a pungent memory.

Despite the hazards, I was happy to be back on my bike, to feel my legs pumping, to be moving under my own locomotion. But my ecstasy was short-lived. Not far from the city center was one of the longest uphills I have negotiated on two wheels. It has no passes to break the climb and no dales to rest the legs. It goes *straight up*. It beats the Rocky Mountains, the Cape Escarpment, even the Lower Himalayas—all hills I have biked. I was glad that I had chosen to travel lean, with only a few basic items strapped on my bike. But not even this did much to assuage a growing realization that this hill might never end—that this was no longer reality, that I had somehow stumbled into a biker's version of "The Twilight Zone."

It seemed inevitable with all this metal wildly rushing about that some sort of mishap would occur. Soon enough, it did. I missed the actual crash, although it must have been spectacular. At least four vehicles were involved—a truck, two sedans and a *matatu*. I saw its name still shimmering on its back canopy, which had been crumpled like a paper box. It was The Michael Jackson Special, covered with crude paintings of the singer, now squashed and broken. I recalled having seen it as it passed me a short time earlier. It had been one of the worst menaces of the day, having actually forced me off the road and into a skid on the slick red clay.

As police cars and ambulances converged and a silent crowd gathered, I could see the driver who had been laughing and screaming at me a half hour earlier, his passengers joining in with frantic gesticulations. Now this man—he was actually a teenager, perhaps nineteen—was standing in a daze beside his demolished truck. Several of his passengers sat on the ground, some bleeding and one or two wailing as a medic began to treat them. Three passengers, who a short time earlier had been as lively as the pilgrims on Success!, lay dead, their bodies lined up neatly near the shattered truck, proving that Africans ultimately require order just as much as people in the West. As I approached I noticed that one of the bodies was missing its head. All that remained was a bloody stump extending above a collar and neatly knotted tie.

By lunchtime the city had finally ended, but the hill had not. At this height—about seven thousand feet—the air was getting thin. I was thoroughly sick of the unremitting climb. I was suffering, and being alone, I didn't even have anybody to complain to.

I stopped to eat lunch near Longenet, a scattering of rust-colored roofs under a hanging ridge of palms and mimosas. The forest rose here like a huge, wet, slippery presence to tower over the drab works of humanity, a dripping, green lushness that permeated the air with a vaguely swampy odor that reminded me of northern California in the springtime, though California was never so humid.

Wanting to get clear of the highway, I found a path in a grove of mimosas and pushed my bike along a worn strip of wet soil. As I walked I disturbed a pair of fiscal shrikes in a nearby tree. Like flashes of fire they darted away, cawing madly. The path quickly angled up toward the ridge, taking me far away from the road and into the calm of a forest. I was high enough that deciduous trees and pines had taken over from the usual African foliage.

In a country as populous as Kenya, it didn't take long for a human to appear. As I laid out a lunch of cheese and bread, and worked to keep it dry under a small tarp, I heard someone singing, a boy's melodious voice that abruptly stopped just short of my leafy cave. Its owner stayed out of sight for a moment. Then he stepped into view, a boy thirteen or fourteen dressed smartly in a school uniform, shorts, knee-high socks and tennis shoes. His costume surprised me. What was a child of the elite doing out in this forest? For miles the only children I had seen were dressed in ragged clothes and tending crops or watching goats. "Hello," I said.

"Hello," he responded, sounding perplexed himself at finding a white cyclist sitting in the middle of the forest. "Excuse me," he said, after staring at me for a moment, "did you know you are on private property?"

I had to laugh, thinking about how far capitalist Kenya had come (or gone) to produce a boy whose first thought was to assert his property rights. It was one of the most un-African comments I heard on my entire journey, and said more about this country than any of my carefully chosen words. I half-expected him to summon the local constabulary or chastise me as a South African farmer would a black, but he was apparently stating a fact rather than throwing out a challenge. I guessed he was merely mimicking something a grown-up had said, for my laughter made him smile shyly. I asked if this was *his* land.

"I will one day inherit it from my father," he said slowly, still shy about my laugh and uncertain as to how I would respond. I was tempted to probe further, to ask his opinion of private ownership and the like, but I saw I might chase him off like a spooked fawn. So I smiled and invited him to join me for lunch. He nodded and sat down on the edge of my tarp.

His name was Michael. He said he lived in a nearby farmhouse. As he loosened up we came back to this idea of ownership, and he eagerly explained that his father had bought the property and the house from a former colonialist. "We live in the house the white man built," he said proudly. "It is *our* house now. The white man has gone away."

"And do you have many servants and farm helpers?" I asked, chewing on a piece of bread. "Like the white man did?"

"Of course," he said. His eyes narrowed slightly, this little aristocrat of the forest. "We have more, I think. How else could we make any money?"

I finally reached the top of the Kikuyu Escarpment about three in the afternoon, and I felt like singing one of those songs I had to learn in Sunday school—"Rise and Shine!" or "Give God the Glory, Glory!" I felt great! Monumental! The climb was over, and along with it all traces of frustration and pain.

Then came the long awaited downhill. Yeeeeeeeaaaaaahhhhh! I shouted as my nose angled downward for the first time since dawn. I shifted my gears as high as they would go, moved my hands to my lower handlebars, tucked my head down and felt my speed increase. My odometer flipped through the numbers: 30 kph, 40 kph, 50, 60, 70 . . . ! Unbelievable! Rushshshshshsh went the wind as I hit a lifetime record of 82.8 kilometers per hour, and averaged almost 60 kph for over a half hour as I rocketed down the backside of the escarpment. I was headed for the floor of the huge geological crack I had passed through in Tanzania—the Great Rift Valley—which I would be following for the next several days.

In Kenya, the Great Rift Valley has the same basic features as it does in Tanzania—the high, blufflike walls, the rolling floor, the frequent lakes. The difference is that the northern tier of the valley is considerably more prosperous, populous and—with the rain—green. The country I passed through was a smooth, broad plain of watery grass where cattle and goats grazed and a series of volcanoes pushed craggy, jagged ridges up into charcoal gray clouds. Lilac-breasted rollers and doves huddled together on power lines as shepherd boys lay in the grass watching their animals. Man was clearly in control here—the great herds that Elspeth Huxley wrote about were gone—but the control seemed gentle and unassuming. There were few fences, and most of the structures were mud and thatch *shambas* poised on distant hills. The crops were generally arranged European-style in rows, but they meandered about without being fanatical about tidiness. This made me wonder if some sort of symbiosis between Africa and the West had occurred here.

Every so often I would come to a town, which usually offered further evidence of this fusion of the old and new. Typically, they were composed of neat, colonial-era buildings augmented by post-independence additions of rough wood and concrete storefronts, often painted in bright colors. I saw little abject poverty here, although this road cuts through the rich highlands of Kenya, far from more destitute regions to the north and west. Capitalism shouted out in gaudy advertisements for Coke, Schweppes, Mobil Oil and Safari beer. On these commercial strips the truckers and people of the road sleep, copulate and eat mealie meals in taverns named Top Joy, the New Jackson Five and the Wonder of the Earth Hotel.

I met a variety of Kenyans on the road—teachers, shopkeepers, truck drivers, farmers and what seemed like thousands of children. Kids were everywhere, which was not surprising in a country where half the population is under fifteen. They would often gather to chatter around my bike when I stopped for a water break, and every so often one would try to sell me something—a wool cap or a watch. I have no idea where they got these things, although I got the feeling there was some basic training going on here for the day these children would join the migration to the city.

Women were less in evidence on the road. I often saw them hard at work tending distant crops, performing the ancient duty of their sex in Africa, proving that not everything in Kenya has been modernized. Meanwhile, their men appeared now and then along the highway, many of them lounging in the grass, their roles less clearly defined than the women's. In ancient times their job had been to wage war, plan migrations and mete out local justice, skills that have little relevance in modern Kenya. So they sit around smoking, drinking beer and waving solemnly at lone cyclists pedaling past.

One morning I ran into a farmhand who had stopped on the road to watch a rainbow spread over the valley. The brilliant hues rose like arches of colored glass, the base plunging into a small lake called Elmenteita. The water was nearly obscured by hundreds of flamingos glinting like pink diamonds. "It is a miracle," said the farmhand, who asked if I believed in omens. I said yes, and he shook my hands vigorously as if I had confirmed something he had previously been unsure of. "My son is about to give me my first grandchild," the man explained. "His wife is big, and the day will come anytime. This omen tells me it is going to be a grandson, a strong boy to take care of me when I am old."

Another afternoon I met a young teacher standing on a hill beside her school. She was about thirty and said she adored Shakespeare. Inside her small, one-room schoolhouse the bard's portrait hung in a place of honor beside an old map of the world. (Most of the Cape to Cairo corridor was still colored British red, although all references to the empire had been scratched out.) I asked her why she thought a sixteenth-century Englishman was relevant to twentieth-century Kenya and she became very put out. "My goodness," she said in a scolding tone, "why teach Shakespeare in Kenya? What a ridiculous question! Shakespeare, he wrote about life and death and good and evil. Am I correct?"

"Yes, of course, but . . ."

"You tell me. In Kenya, do we not have life and death and good and evil? These things are everywhere." She grinned slyly. "Even, I think, in America."

On yet another afternoon I was pedaling at a leisurely pace past an old man when I accidentally dropped a tube of lip balm. As I braked and turned around, the man—he was at least seventy, his back crooked with age and his front teeth missing—leaned over to retrieve the balm for me. It seemed such an incredible effort for him that I tried to stop him. "Father," I said, "I can pick that up myself."

The old man looked up at me reprovingly. I noticed that his clothing, worn nearly white and ragged at the ankles and cuffs, was an old army uniform. He told me in halting English that it was once the uniform of a corporal in His Majesty's army. I asked him if he could sit a moment and share a piece of cheese and tell me about this corporal.

"I was infantry," he said proudly, "in the world war. In Libya I fought against Adolf Hitler. We were Africans fighting the evil of this Hitler. It was very good. I spent many months in the desert. We marched much. Yeeeooo, the heat was too bad. We went to Cairo. It is such a big city, much bigger than Nairobi. You go there? It is big and dirty. I think you should stay here in Kenya."

The old soldier told me that he had eleven children, forty-seven grandchildren and "at least" thirty great-grandchildren—a total of eighty-eight people. "Eeee, may God be praised," he said. "God has been good to this old man." He thought birth control was evil. "Who would take care of an old man like me if he had no children? I am taken care of by my second son. He is a farmer. My oldest son is a mechanic in Nairobi. He sends me money. I have good children. They show respect. They take care of me."

As he spoke, the old man fingered the tube of lip balm. He dabbed his dry lips at my invitation. "It is good," he cooed. "I think we had something like this in Libya. Yes, I am sure we did."

At night I usually slept in stark, generic Third World hotels that serviced truck drivers, businessmen and other travelers from the class of Kenyans that inhabit Okingo's Nairobi. These hotels, usually situated on the edge of a small city, offer a tiny room with a cot, a thin mattress and an electric light bulb for about a dollar a night. The toilets are holes in a corner of an outdoor courtyard or at the end of a hallway. The water comes from a faucet nearby. The rooms are basically clean, although I often had to spray the mattresses for lice.

I spent little time awake in these inns. Typically, I would arrive at the end of the day feeling utterly exhausted. Only hunger (and the possibility of lice) kept me from collapsing immediately on my cot and falling asleep. With the thought of *food* foremost in my mind, I would unpeel my stinking, sweat-drenched cycling clothes, take a short sponge bath at the communal faucet and then go out in search of dinner. Usually, it was close at hand, often in a tavern adjoining the inn. Here I would sit like a zombie on a communal bench beside half-drunk fellow travelers and gorge on mealie meal, beef chunks and beer. Then, before I knew it, I was asleep, until my watch alarm buzzed the next morning at dawn.

During that first week in the Rift Valley my road remained relatively flat. However, I knew these flat contours could not continue forever, as I was in a valley surrounded on all sides by steep cliffs. Fortunately, the hill, when it came, was not quite as long as the Kikuyu Escarpment, although it was considerably steeper. I was in better shape this time, a small consolation as I began to struggle upward. The climbing was again slow and tedious as I gradually passed 7,500 feet, 8,000 feet, 8,500 feet . . .

As I got higher the land became wilderness, providing a diversion from the grueling climb. First I saw a rare long-tailed widow bird, its two-foot-long tail sailing like a black scarf across a field of tea. Then I entered a bamboo forest. The thin green shoots grew in impenetrable clumps, the spindly trunks looking like the legs of very tall sandpipers. I felt as if I had been transported to China, and half-expected to see a giant panda peering shyly behind a screen of bamboo off the road.

At just over 9,000 feet I crossed the equator and entered my own hemisphere, but the climb was still not over. With the high-altitude sun burning my skin and the thin air starving my lungs, I took it one pedal at a time, stopping frequently to catch my breath. At 9,300 feet an angry augur buzzard swooped about two inches from my head, screeching as if I had violated its airspace by climbing so high. At 9,400 feet I finally reached the Mau Summit, though I had nothing to celebrate. Almost immediately the road launched me into a series of ball-breaking ups and downs.

Toward dusk the forests grew thicker and wilder as I kept cycling, looking for a town and an inn where I could sleep. However, as the shadows lengthened on the road and the woods continued unabated, it became clear that I might not find a town at all. So I began searching for a place to camp, remembering that this was the same untamed country that had sheltered Mau Mau fighters in the fifties and Nandi rebels during a bloody uprising five decades earlier. Today, these woods are benign, but I still was nervous about sleeping out now that I was traveling alone. I preferred to pitch my tent in a farmer's yard or some other protected spot. So I kept pumping my numb legs, feeling secure in movement.

When twilight turned the landscape gray I was forced to make a move. I pushed my bike up a cattle trail and behind a row of cedars that screened me from the highway. As I entered the shadows of the trees I was startled to find myself staring over a thousand-foot cliff. I forgot my apprehensions and stood gaping at the view exposed, the expanding sun staining violet a low bank of clouds, the passionate color dripping like ice cream over distant cliffs.

I must have stood there for a half hour, watching in awe until the last light was gone and a magnificent array of stars appeared overhead. I might have stood longer if my revelry hadn't been interrupted by a sudden realization. *I was being watched.* I could feel my skin crawling, telling me that something was out there.

Who was it? What did they want? Rationally, I knew that the intruder was probably harmless. It had been thirty years since Mau Maus or any other violent persons had inhabited these forests. However, I still felt naked and exposed in my aloneness. If I had had a rifle with me I would have cocked it and called out "Who's there?" But I travel without weapons and the security some people think they bring. So I walked carefully to my bicycle, crouched low and drew out the most potent armaments I carried—a flashlight and a whistle.

I aimed the light in the general direction of the intruder and flashed it on. At the same time I held the whistle close to my lips and shouted "Who's there!" as loud as I could. What I saw made me jump. The light struck what looked like a large, looming monster out of my worst childhood nightmares. But this wild rush of fear lasted only a moment. I realized that I was looking into the dull, stupid face of a cow. Her eyes glittered yellow in the light as she softly *moooooooed.* I felt ridiculous, the seasoned traveler nearly unhinged by a marauding bovine. Then I heard a rustle behind the beast and saw another set of eyes—smaller, higher and obviously connected to a human. I jumped again. "Hello," said a voice, "what is your name? My name is Charles." I stood still as this fellow—a boy of maybe thirteen—emerged from behind the cow and came casually toward me, followed by another, smaller boy. To my relief I saw that they were simple cattle boys.

Charles introduced the other boy as David, his brother, and said they lived in a *shamba* just over the hill. I asked them about camping here and Charles said it was perfectly safe. They offered to help me unpack my panniers and assemble my camp. This became something of a show-and-tell as they perused and asked questions about everything. They ran their fingers over the slick plastic material of my tent, marveled at my portable water pump and tried to master the flick of my Bic lighter. Later, when I began spreading out food for dinner, they cooed in delight when they tasted bread I had purchased in the city of Nakuru. "It is so sweet and soft," said Charles. "Our bread here is hard and dry."

I cooked vegetable soup, thinned with water to feed the three of us, happy to have the company. The boys asked questions about America. Did we have wild animals there too? Did I know any farmers? What did our cattle look like? Did we have forests? Deserts? Pretty girls? Then they asked about Nairobi, and I could see the first throbs of desire. Is all bread in the city so good? Does every man have a lighter? A house with electric lights?

After soup and bread Charles asked if I would come and meet their father. Leaving David behind to watch my camp, Charles and I scampered over a hill and into a *shamba* a scant four hundred meters away. So much for my hidden camp. Cooking fires burned in front of several round, thatched huts arranged with an almost Western eye toward tidiness and landscaping. I could see numerous flowers planted in crude, English-style beds and round stones outlining walkways and yards in front of each hut. Charles shouted out my arrival like a herald, leading me to a large fire near the center of the compound. After several minutes an aged Nandi headman appeared in the outer light of the fire.

"Father, this is Mr. David," said Charles solemnly. I could feel the old man's power, a persona of great age, authority and unquestioned respect. Physically, he was wizened almost down to the bone. The skin of his head was wrapped taut around his skull and his hair had long ago fallen out. But the details of his appearance were only a part of a presence that seemed more spiritual than physical. The man exuded venerableness and tradition, and as I saw him looming up against the fire, I felt as if I stood in front of someone so old he seemed primordial, the murky Africa of myth and timelessness. It was an Africa I had seen precious little of on this journey.

The old man spoke to me through his son, quickly indicating in a native tongue that he was not interested in small talk of any kind. He took his seat on a worn stump—the place of honor—and launched into a long monologue about himself, his life and Africa.

"I am a Christian," he announced in a loud voice, pulling a dirty cloak tightly around his neck. As Charles translated, the old man spat the first of buckets of phlegm onto the ground. Charles had sat himself down at his father's feet and I sat on a lower stump across the fire. Several children came and sat silently.

"I am a father and grandfather," said the old man as I sat back to listen,* enraptured by his voice and the fire, the ancient symbol of Africa. I recalled the other fires I had sat around on this journey, those evenings where ancient Africa enveloped the night—on the Karroo, in Botswana, in Zeembazeemba. "I have lived for over eighty years," he continued. "I am an old man with many memories. I was a boy when the white farmers came to this place. My fathers killed the British and then later the British became our friends. This was long ago, and the whites are gone now. The black man rules us now, as it should be." He paused to disgorge more phlegm.

"But these things do not concern me. What I am concerned about are my children and my crops and my cattle. Do you see?" He raised up his arms like a magician or a priest. "We have beautiful crops this year. These rains have been good. The crops are good and the cattle are strong. I am happy, and God is happy with me to have given me these things."

He spoke for a long time in a rambling narrative about being born in a village north of here. He talked about the Nandi rebellion and the role of his father, who was apparently killed or taken away (it was unclear which). Then he skipped ahead to when he was a boy, when his village moved from place to place in search of water and good land or because the white government told them to move. It was an oral history I found hard to comprehend. He assumed I knew about certain places and people, and kept referring to dates and occurrences in terms of seasons and particular events. For instance, his village moved from the place of the two mountains in a certain dry year that occurred after a certain elephant destroyed a maize field. His form of history concentrated on deaths of important family members, good and bad crop years, and movement, always movement. I sat for over an hour, staring at the orange embers of fire and listening to the old man's voice.

Charles translated admirably, trying to fill in the titles of grandfathers and great-grandfathers until the old man abruptly stood, signaling an end to the discourse. "You have whiskey?" he asked sharply in English. The question startled me. It seemed almost vulgar to hear this man speak in my language. I pulled out a small vial of brandy I had in my coat. He smiled as I handed it to him. We exchanged sips. A moment later he stood up, which prompted a

---

* I have smoothed out Charles's actual translation for the sake of easier reading.

general scramble of those around the fire to stand with him, as if he were a judge leaving the bench. He turned to me and clasped his arm on mine, a surprisingly powerful, regal grip for such an old man. "You my friend," he said solemnly, as if this was the greatest gift he could bestow on a fellow human being.

4   The next morning, just as I was despairing that the mountains would never end, the road turned sharply downward. I upshifted, leaned low and began racing at top speeds, feeling, as always, that this downhill was particularly well deserved. I was headed for the city of Eldoret, a former colonial enclave that happens to sit in one of the more prosperous agricultural areas in Africa, the Uahan Gishu Basin. "It's a gift of God," an old white farmer had told me in Nairobi. He said he had lost his farm in the Uahan Gishu to Kenyafication, but he still reveled in his memory of the place. "You simply must see it," he added softly, his eyes turning just the slightest bit damp.

As I rushed down through the last of the high forests my road became surrounded by lush, tidy farms. Crops ran off in even rows set side by side, leaves of corn, beans, wheat, casava and oats spreading out to the sky. Blue silos and red brick homesteads sat poised on gentle hills. I had not seen anything like this since northern Zimbabwe and parts of South Africa. If I had been wearing a pair of ruby slippers, I might have mistaken the place for Kansas.

However, it soon became clear that this was not Kansas. Nor was it Zimbabwe, and it certainly wasn't South Africa. Every face I saw on the road was black—the workers, the men behind the wheels of the trucks and cars, the people running the roadside shops, the families sitting in the gardens of the big houses. As in downtown Nairobi, there was a strong Western presence here in life-style, architecture, farming techniques and the *feeling* of the place. (I kept expecting a white settler to come strolling around the corner dressed in khaki pants, knee socks and a bush hat. "Hello, mate," he would say, "mighty nice day." But no ghosts appeared.)

I arrived in Eldoret at lunchtime. It was as bustling as any city I had seen in Africa, a larger version of the many towns I had been passing through since Nairobi. There was a colonial core of British shops and converted bungalows, with more modern concrete and wood structures grafted on since independence. These included several stores, a new city market packed with produce and a restaurant where I had burgers and Coke—the New Super Sunshine Disco 2000, a surprisingly sophisticated danceteria with a computerized sound and light system. I had lunch with one of the owners, who told me they had copied the light system from MTV videos, which his cousin, a taxi driver in New York City, had sent him from the States.

After lunch I pressed on. The road outside Eldoret split into the main tarmac going west toward Uganda, and a narrower road heading toward Kitale in the north. Except for the war in Uganda, I would have turned west at this point to pick up the Nile at its source near Kampala, the capital. This had been the preferred route of most Cape to Cairo travelers since Ewart Grogan first walked the route in the 1890s. However, the city of Kampala was at that moment being overrun by the rebel forces of General Yoweri Museveni, whose ragtag army of volunteers, Baganda nationalists and boy soldiers was about to drive out the crumbling forces of the latest despot in that wasted country. It was another blood-splattered affair for a nation where normalcy and peace had long since been forfeited to lunatics. Still, I would have liked to see what the country looked like. It undoubtedly makes even Zambia and Tanzania look good. But I had no wish to get killed, so I reluctantly steered my cycle to the north, toward Kitale, the Turkana Desert and Sudan.

The Kitale road quickly deteriorated as I headed into the less developed region of the north. The edges became chewed up and potholes exposed large gashes of red soil. Fortunately, the traffic diminished, although my old nemesis in Kenya—steep ups and downs—returned with a vengeance. Yet I enjoyed the biking, for I was finally getting in decent shape again, my body hard and lean.

In Kitale, a timber and farming town, I stayed in the New Kitale Hotel, a large, crumbling colonial edifice that would have looked more at home in Mpulungu or Kigoma. A white settler named George Smith had recommended the place. "We used to go over to the Kitale Hotel for black-tie balls and other very colonial functions," he grinned. "It was quite a place back in the fifties." But no more. I doubt if anyone at the "New" Kitale could even comprehend the term "black tie."

The place was stripped of its finery and virtually empty of guests. Outside, brambles and untended vines lay tangled in the old gardens, and neglect had stained the Cape Dutch facade an unpleasant color of gray. Inside, what remained of the furniture was in shambles. Floorboards had collapsed from rot and the grand ballroom, where George once had courted the daughters of the white ascendancy, was now an empty, dusty cavern. Someone had set up two small tables off to one side for dining. Otherwise, the old room was empty.

I was shown to a large room upstairs. Like everything else in the hotel, it had been built on a grand scale, which made its current condition all the more forlorn. The only furniture in a room the size of a small tavern was a cot, an old desk and a lamp.

But the worst was yet to come. I had barely gone to sleep on my cot when a jarring noise woke me up. It was like a sonic boom, or a series of sonic booms, coming from a building below my window.

Actually, it was a disco blasting pandemonium from what must have been trailer-sized speakers. In my travels I have more or less learned to sleep through most any noise—roosters crowing, dogs yapping all night, tinny radios—but this was too much. In my best impersonation of the affronted American tourist, I stomped down to the front desk to complain. The woman on duty was sound asleep on top of the check-in counter and would only mumble in Swahili when I shook her. So I took my indignation and hiked over to the disco itself.

Inside, it was nearly pitch black, except for a few strobe lights and a red bulb in the back where several prostitutes sat and drank beer. Still the speakers boomed, as if the owners had decided to punish everyone for staying at home. I tried for a moment to find someone who might be able to turn down the volume, but only got myself a bored come-on by one of the prostitutes.

Back in the hotel, I shook the woman at the desk again and demanded that she do something. She said to come back in the morning. I kept complaining and she finally handed me a set of master keys. "You move to any room you like," she mumbled, telling me that I was the only guest in the hotel.

The next morning I was the lone diner in the ballroom for breakfast, a pathetic attempt at a British-style buffet with a single, sick piece of mango and a jar of cornflakes as hard as nuts. The milk was sour and the settings a potpourri of plastic, tin and remnants of china. The single waiter cooked my egg himself. I invited him to sit with me, but he was a holdover from the old school of colonial servants.

"Oh, no, sir, I no eat with you." He looked at me as if I had committed a sacrilege. "I am only the *waiter.*"

I got a slow start that morning, for I was not anxious to leave Kitale. Although the accommodations had been bizarre, the town itself was pleasant enough. This would be the last true city I would see for several weeks. After Kitale I would be heading for Juba in Sudan, a grueling journey across seven hundred miles of dry bush and desert. The roads would be horrible and the heat well over a hundred degrees Fahrenheit. I would have difficulty finding food and water, and if I had a breakdown I could not repair, I was stuck.

Furthermore, in Sudan I might get killed. Another African rebel—this one only a colonel—had been busy all summer blowing things up and killing people. He and his ragtag army had been shelling steamers on the Nile, shooting up government convoys and planting land mines hither and yon. So far, according to my sources in Nairobi, the colonel had not operated along my road into Juba, as this was the major route for relief convoys headed into the rebel's home district.

I dawdled all morning in Kitale, buying supplies in a small grocery—dried soups, coffee, noodles, canned beef and dried milk. In a hardware store I bought emergency flares, extra tubing for my tires and various other small items that seemed absolutely critical. I then killed more time by visiting an excellent little museum, studying an extensive collection of stuffed birds, animals, bones and several artifacts of the white era lovingly collected by a previous generation of settlers.

When I finally checked out of the New Kitale Hotel the woman at the registration desk, no longer asleep, tried to seduce me, mostly, I think, out of boredom. (There were still no other guests.) "You pick any room in the hotel," she cooed. "I like *wazungu*."

"I like you too," I said, handing her the money for the room, "but I'm off to Sudan."

If I had known what awaited me north of Kitale, I might have suffered another night at the hotel. I knew from my map that there would be some sort of uphill. Moreover, I had asked several people locally if it was a *long* uphill. As usual, I got conflicting stories. One woman—a travel agent in the Ivory Tours office—assured me the hill was not more than ten kilometers to the top. "Well, it might be as much as fifteen kilometers," she added, "but then it's all downhill into the desert."

I pedaled away from Kitale feeling a familiar blend of excitement and peril as I faced a new phase of my trip. Before this day was over I expected to be in the desert. Yet I still had a few more miles left of the Kenya I was used to. Leaving town, I passed a string of uniformed children headed for school and several gangs of men and women saw-ing trees, the damp sawdust blowing across the road. Before I was even out of town, at the edge of the suburban bungalows, I began to angle upward. I watched my odometer closely, remembering what the woman at the tourist shop had said. *Ten kilometers—maybe fifteen.*

As the forests thinned out I could see up ahead what seemed to be a massive wall of mountains. But I was not going to allow myself to get discouraged. Maybe there was a nice flat ravine cutting right through the middle. It had happened before.

I struggled on for the requisite ten kilometers, feeling my extra weight dragging me down like a bag of stones. I sang old Paul Simon songs, but got depressed by his lyrics and switched to Christmas carols. This made me think of home, so I stopped singing. It was turning into a terrible day.

After nearly two hours of biking I passed the ten-kilometer mark, but the hill kept going. I told myself not to despair. The woman had said it might be as much as fifteen clicks on the odometer, so I kept going, pausing only to change my headbands as they became soaked with sweat. This was a crudely graded hill, with no attempts at switchbacks. It reminded me of cycling in Southeast Asia, where roads go in straight lines with no deviation for even the steepest slopes. I passed the eleven-kilometer point—then eleven and a half, then twelve . . . it seemed to be taking forever and my legs hurt like hell. I stopped and took off my helmet, sweat dripping from my head and tickling my face . . . thirteen . . . fourteen . . . fifteen . . . *sixteen* . . . *seventeen* . . . For the record, it's not fifteen kilometers. It's not even twenty—or thirty, or forty—but *sixty* kilometers. That's a *six* and a *zero*.

I finally reached the top of the Cherangani Hills 2,500 feet above Kitale, nearly 9,000 feet above sea level. The Cherangani reminded me of the foothills of the Himalayas in Nepal, with their sharp ups and downs and extensive erosion. Like Nepal, this land had until recently been heavily wooded, but now it was devastated, looking as if someone had taken a giant razor and scraped the land bare. I knew that Kenya had the means to employ conservation techniques. I had seen them used in the south—neat rows of reforested trees in the mountains around the Mau Escarpment. Had someone up here got-ten greedy, or was it incompetence?

With the recent rains, the newly exposed cliffs and ridges of the Cherangani had a thin flesh of green, but this foliage would not endure long in the postmonsoon sunshine. Soon the grass, bramble and flowers would be baked black. They would shrivel up and their dead, shallow roots would loosen their grip on the soil. Come next year, when the monsoons returned, this earth, held in place for centuries by mimosa, pines and other flora, would be washed away, clogging the wild creeks and ravines and running off good soil into the great desert beyond the hills.

I first glimpsed the Turkana Desert as I rushed downward through the craggy Turkwel Gorge, a narrow river valley edged by steep ridges that stretched out like dog's paws into the desert. Soon the rain-fed sheen of green ended and the hills became rocky and parched as I followed the swift waters, frothing with red soil like blood.

I continued my mad dash down the gorge, hardly believing amid this wasteland that I could still be in Kenya. Almost instantly the soft hills had been replaced by thirsty brown rock and sand. Traffic had all but ceased, and the road had become pocked and dangerous. The occasional villages were no longer the rough, prosperous farming towns of the highlands. They were not really villages at all, but seminomadic camps, the people dressed in rags, their cattle and goats lean, their houses built out of wood scraps, acacia and grass. It was almost impossible to believe that just two days earlier I had been in Eldoret and the Uahan Gishu Basin, one of the richest agricultural oases in Africa. Now I was having to dig into the sand of an increasingly sluggish river to find water.

By dusk, still gliding swiftly on a steady decline, I had covered a tremendous distance beyond the Cherangani Hills. Despite the desolation, I felt energized as the sun tumbled into the hills at my back and the late, low-angled beams of gold shattered the road ahead. I pumped my legs hard in a regular motion, my earlier exhaustion dissipating into a mesmerizing rhythm. Every muscle and sinew worked and strained. I felt high and hardly noticed when I passed a village filled with a rather unusual sight in this remote desert— brand-new Land Rovers and a huge green truck. I thought this was so strange that I doubled back to investigate. The explanation appeared on the side of the truck: NATIONAL MUSEUMS OF KENYA.

One of the wonderful things about free-lance travel is the chance occurrence, the unanticipated accident that can transform an ordi-

nary day into an unforgettable one. When I saw those words—NA-
TIONAL MUSEUMS OF KENYA—I knew that I had stumbled onto something potentially marvelous. The appearance of a museum truck on
the desert could mean only one thing. This was an *expedition*, a
team of archaeologists sent out from one of the most famous research museums in the world. This was the museum founded by the
Leakey family, an institution whose activities and discoveries are
followed by archaeologists as enthusiastically as sports fans follow
their teams.

I approached the trucks as night fell, and was greeted by the usual
babel of village children, who led me back to a grove of trees where
several city Kenyans were setting up a camp. They gathered around
as I took off my helmet and took a drink of water. Then the crowd
split apart for a large man with a curved pipe. He grinned at the sight
of a filthy biker showing up in the middle of the desert. "I'm Kamoya
Kimeu," he said. "You hungry? Man, you look hungry. How about
some goat? We're roasting some up."

Kamoya shouted a few instructions and I soon found myself sitting on a pillow atop a fuel can with a frigid beer in my hand. Kimoya
and I leaned back against the front grille of the big Mercedes truck in
front of a fire, which felt good as the sun fell and the desert cooled off.
An American paleontologist named Kathy Stewart sat between us on
the oil cans wearing a sweat-stained safari hat, polo shirt and safari
trousers, an outfit that would have looked silly on a tourist in
Nairobi, but looked perfect on a scientist sitting in front of a fire in
the bush. As we talked, Kimoya's men bought a goat from the villagers, slaughtered it and began roasting the meat on a spit. Soon the
fat was dripping and splattering in the flames, and my stomach
rumbled at the sweet smell.

I had heard about this man, Kamoya Kimeu, from friends in
Nairobi. He was a Kenyan hero, a black archaeologist and alter ego of
Richard Leakey, the current scion of the famed family. Every Kenyan
schoolchild knew Kamoya's name, the man who helped discover
Lucy, a complete skeleton over one million years old. Kamoya Kimeu
was practically a Leakey himself, having shared in many of the
storybook adventures, brushes with death and exaltations of discovery that have long enthralled people like me, who spend far too much
time poring over *National Geographic* and watching public television programs with titles like "How Man Began."

Kamoya said his team had stopped in this village for the night.

Their destination was Lake Turkana and a secret excavation somewhere on the western shore. "We're looking for the fingers and toes of a hominid we discovered last year," Kamoya explained in a cloud of blue smoke, his voice sounding urbane and British. As we spoke he shouted good-natured orders to his team, who set up a modified bush camp resembling those I had seen on public TV—lots of canvas, bulky sleeping bags and canteens hanging from acacia trees.

With our hands we ate dripping fistfuls of goat, cut with a large knife, which seemed appropriately savage in this environment. Afterward Kamoya ordered coffee made, and we settled back for an evening of African storytelling around the fire. Kamoya, at my urging, did most of the talking, starting with his early days as a common laborer for the Leakeys.

"I started with Louis [Leakey] in the early sixties," he said. "I was a simple young man from the Kamba tribe—that's southeast of Nairobi, near the Tsavo. Louis was looking for volunteers to go to the Olduvai Gorge in Tanzania, so I joined up with some other village boys. Man, I had no idea what I was getting into! I went off and they trucked us to Olduvai and told us to start looking for bones. Human bones! My mother, when she found out, was terribly afraid of these bones. She told me to quit this job that disturbed the dead. I told her that these bones were very old, and that they were important, but I was not sure why. So I disobeyed my mother. I went back again and worked more with the Leakeys, and one year went out on an expedition with Richard. That was 1964, the year I found that ole jawbone."

"Jawbone?" I asked, trying to recall if I had read about this in *National Geographic.* "What jawbone?"

Kamoya and Kathy Stewart laughed as if I had just made a major anthropological faux pas. "That 'ole jawbone' was part of an *Australopithecus boisei,*" Kathy explained. "That's one of the missing links, a very primitive man. It was the first complete jaw of the *boisei* ever found."

"It was marvelous," mused Kamoya, taking a reflective puff from his pipe. "I was standing there beside a cliff doing some work and I looked over and there was this bone. A jaw! I was learning fast about these things, so I knew it was important. We immediately radioed Richard, who was in Nairobi. Richard was a young man then—we are all young once, you know. It was his first major discovery. We became good friends, and I got a tremendous thirst for this business of archaeology."

We talked on into the night, with Kamoya's deep voice recounting a whole series of random stories about his and Richard's adventures. His voice sounded melodic under the huge African sky. I remember the flames reflecting off his dark skin, his teeth flashing and the red dot of his pipe ember flitting through the air like an orange firefly.

Kamoya told us about the time he was bitten by a cobra in Tanzania. "I didn't die," he laughed, " 'cause I've got tough skin." In Ethiopia, Kamoya and Richard were once attacked by a deranged crocodile. "Have you ever seen a charging crocodile? Man, it scared me, it sure did." There was also a time when Richard got the ridiculous idea of using camels to search the rugged land around Lake Turkana for fossils. "I hated those animals," Kamoya grimaced. "The first time I saw one up close, I saw these teeth, big and yellow. I didn't want to do it! I told Richard I had never ridden anything that didn't have four wheels. But he talked me into it. The worst part was the way my back end felt at the end of the day."

We kept chatting, shifting from stories to conversations about anthropology, the origins of man and the relevance of Kamoya's work in modern Africa. "Some Kenyans think I am wasting my time on this archaeology business," said Kamoya. "They say we should be spending our time building factories and roads. I think these people are very shortsighted. It is important to know our history. What we have discovered makes me proud to be a Kenyan, because this is one of the first places the human race ever lived. Our race may have started here, and this is important. The world thinks this is important, and people come from everywhere to Kenya to see these wonders. I am proud to be a black Kenyan working on these things. It improves the self-image of my people. Some people in the West have this notion that blacks cannot do anything. It is wrong. Look at my team, what we have accomplished."

I joined the expedition sleeping under the sky. We laid out tarpaulins, sleeping bags and mosquito netting. Above us the stars looked as if the Manhattan skyline had been tipped sideways and raised above our heads. It was one of those moments when I felt immersed in the mystery and life-force of Africa—when I could grasp it like a beating heart and revel in its ancientness and power. It was a feeling intricately tied in with the stars, the rippling glow of the fire, the smell of goat's grease on my fingertips and the ghosts of the earliest humans, which even then were hovering over our camp, watching us sleep, whispering ancient truths that we could almost hear.

At dawn Kamoya invited me to ride with the team to Lodwar, seventy-five miles to the north. Before I could object, Kamoya's men had lassoed my bike and were slinging it up on top of the truck. I was a little annoyed that they had done this—Kamoya had simply assumed that no one was foolish enough to *want* to bike across the desert if he had another option. I felt pretty strongly about bicycling as much of the segment to Juba as possible, but it seemed that I had no choice, because the expedition was moving out. So I climbed into a National Museums' Rover with Kamoya driving on the right and Kathy Stewart on my left. A moment later we left the village and were rushing across the crags, washes and emptiness of the southern Turkana desert.

Kathy and Kamoya chatted sadly about the land we were crossing, explaining that it had not always been desert. "When I was a young man, this was still bush," said Kamoya sadly. "You talk to the locals and some of the older men remember big herds of game out here, right where we're driving. The Turkana even remember game up at Ferguson's Gulf.* Now there's hardly any left."

On the way to Lake Turkana we stopped by a police compound in the town of Lodwar, the compound where Jomo Kenyatta was imprisoned by the British after the Mau Mau emergency. Kamoya wanted to check on the security situation in the north, a wild region where the war in Sudan sometimes spills over the border, and where vicious gangs of bandits from Ethiopia and Somalia sometimes rampage. Kamoya came back with some disturbing news for me. "There has been a massacre to the north," he said, "on the Juba road, just over the border. A large convoy of lorries carrying food aid was attacked. Most of the drivers were killed. They were all Kenyan. The northern border is on alert, so I'm told."

"I'd consider changing your plans," counseled Kathy.

"With the border on alert, they won't let you through even if you try," added Kamoya, "so my advice would be not to even try."

We drove on from Lodwar in silence until Kamoya abruptly turned off the road and headed into the rocky desert. We were stopping briefly to check out a museum camp doing a geological survey of the area. Amoco was sponsoring the project, hoping to find oil. "I don't think there's any oil out here," said the team's leader, a graduate student from the University of Utah, "but we're having a hell of a

---

* My destination on the shore of Lake Turkana.

good time looking for it." He said the only problem was snakes. "I almost stepped on a saw-scaled viper yesterday. Those suckers'll kill yah in minutes." His Kenyan coleader, nicknamed Moose, complained about hyenas. "Man, they come right up here into the camp! They take food and pans and tins!"

While we stopped I asked Kamoya to unload my bicycle, because I wanted to pedal the rest of the way to the lake. "No, we don't have time," he said, distracted by a repair job in the camp that was taking longer than expected. "We've got to be to our site tonight. Sorry, but you'll have to take it easy with us in the Rover." So we took off for the lake.

Lake Turkana is the fourth largest body of water in Africa, a Rift Valley lake that has been gradually dying for centuries from a lack of fresh inflow. It was once named Rudolf, but names are slippery things in Africa. There are often two appellations for the same city, mountain or lake—the European name and the more recent name bequeathed by modern Africa. Sometimes there is a third name, the one used by the locals in their native tongue. In the case of Turkana, there are at least five names. There was the irrelevant *Rudolf,* named after a manic-depressive prince of Austria; *Turkana,* the Kenyan name; and three native names—*Aman* (Turkana), *Basso* (Sumburu), and *Gallop* (the northern tribes in Ethiopia).

As we bounced and rumbled across the desert, I looked anxiously for the first sign of the lake. The explorer John Hillaby, who had the tenacity to travel to the lake by camel in 1961, described his first sighting, which occurred at sunset across the water from Turkanaland. I recount it here because it was so utterly different from my first glimpse of Lake Rudolf-Turkana-Aman-Basso-Gallop.

It was a satin sunset of amber and oyster blue with the distant hills of Turkanaland painted in bold brush-strokes of purple water color. The Jade Sea . . . was olive green and more vast than I had imagined, certainly more beautiful than I could have foreseen. . . . It was a romantic sight. I felt romantic. . . .

My first sighting occurred during the haze of midday, when colors are blanched to pale, uninspiring shades by the intense sunshine. To me, the water ahead appeared a dull khaki color, rather like dirty brake fluid from an automobile. We were passing over gradual hills, so the water came in and out of sight. The road was paved with poured concrete, but was broken by dozens of dips into empty washes. Turkana villages appeared out among the rocks, clusters of round, grass huts shaped like squat, fuzzy oil cans. Like the Masai, Turkana warriors stood just off the road tending cattle and goats. However, these warriors had on no bright red capes and only smatterings of beads and jewelry. They had the fierce, proud expressions of their cousins to the south, but they looked considerably less prosperous. Kathy told me that these people were in a desperate state. With desertification and the gradual loss of water, cover and game, the Turkana were gradually dying off. Once, they had numbered in the tens of thousands. Now they were down well under ten thousand.

We finally arrived at midday in a small Turkana fishing village about a mile from the lake, a place that also had gone through a name change. Once called Ferguson's Gulf, it is now Kolokol. It was a tiny fleck of a town, composed of a few dusty Somalian shops, a police station and a post office all basking in the hot sun. Kamoya stayed only long enough to eat a quick lunch and unload my bicycle, giving me a warm farewell before roaring off toward his secret dig.

I was determined to ride the final mile to the lake. I strapped on my helmet, clipped in my feet and pushed off. Although it was brutally hot, I felt exhilarated to be moving, pedaling fast across a flat, scrubby floodplain covered with salt and limestone outcrops. Pink-backed pelicans flew overhead in formation, and I could see a huge, ugly marabou stork running toward the lake, where he had probably spied a dead fish floating in the surf. When the road ended I tried to ride in the sand, but found it too soft. So I dropped my bike and began to run toward the water. With the sun falling behind me, the lake was suddenly glittering and alive with color—a deep, porcelain green, the Jade Sea.

I kept running and could see the shadowy shapes of crocodiles floating like deadly logs just off shore. The Turkana, who fearlessly fish among the crocs on small rafts, believe that they are immune to the reptile's sharp teeth as long as they obey the tribe's customs, take care of their families and generally behave themselves. If a Turkana is bad, they say, then he or she will be punished by being eaten. I later heard about a boy who had been eaten the week before. He had *seemed* good to everyone who knew him, but of course he was not, because the crocs only ate bad boys. It was then discovered that the boy had disobeyed his mother. It sounded like a simple enough religion, having the devil right there in the water. I would wager that this village had some of the best behaved children in the world—not to mention faithful husbands and wives.

When I reached the waters of the Jade Sea, I shed my shoes and socks and rushed into the water up to my knees. The lake was cool and I cupped some liquid against my face. The dying sea tasted like ash and salt and was so bitter I spat it out. Then I whooped it up, splashing around and feeling a tremendous sense of accomplishment at having made it this far. A few nearby Turkana on their rafts looked at me as if I were drunk. The crocs floated in the distance, and a band of cormorants chattered as the sky turned blood-red. I remembered having seen this same sort of sky in Arusha, at the dawn of my Kenya venture. Now the sun was setting, which seemed like a neat symmetry. For not only was my time in this country nearly up, my time in black Africa was quickly running out. Soon I would pass that invisible line to the north where Africa splits in half and the land of the Arabs begins.

VII
Sudan

*Fragments
of Despair*

Tonight
in the beggar
I saw the whole
of my country.

—Bahadur Tejani

This was the country where the name makers
invented the term "potential breadbasket of
Africa." Then, a few years later, they invented
the expression "basket case." Now, with the
war and the famine, they will have to make up
a new cliché—"bone basket of Africa...."

—Journal Entry

1 Far below my jetliner, at ground level, thousands of troops blew holes in each other, civilians, giraffes, trucks and anything else that moved. Fire engulfed mud-daub villages and fields of sorghum and maize parched by the recent drought. Bombs fell from aging Russian and newer American fighters into the thick mud of the Sudd swamps, smashing rebel hideouts and spraying into the air mutilated pieces of papyrus plants, communal reeds and human flesh. Rebels retaliated by shelling trucks and Nile steamers and aiming surface-to-air missiles, mostly Russian-made and provided by Ethiopia, at passing jets like the one I was on.

In this war, however, the carnage was not happening all at once. The killing was random, slow and spread over a vast area of bush and gooey marshes. This was not the sort of war we are accustomed to in the West. It was a grinding, languid conflict of sporadic ambushes, massacres and hidden mines. It was a war of half-trained soldiers striking viciously and then dissolving like rainwater into swamps so huge they could swallow entire regions of the United States. It was a war of starvation, random slaughter, ancient feuds and suspicions, dueling despots and smoldering fury.

I strained to see evidence of the war through a scratched plastic window. At forty-five thousand feet—we were flying high to avoid the SAMs—I saw no evidence at all of war or human habitation in the green-brown smudge of land. No farms. No cities. No highways. No blood.

Above my head, next to the seat-belt sign, a voice crackled over the intercom. "To the left of the airplane is the White Nile," our British pilot announced. "This is the romantic river where all the great adventurers came and went—Baker of the Nile, Emin Pasha, Sir Henry [Morton Stanley] and poor General Gordon. Ah, those were the days . . . And to our right you might just be able to make out the Ethiopian highlands, where Mussolini got bashed rather badly by the old emperor."

I hated this. I was miserable having to travel by air, eating soppy chicken Kiev and canvaslike bits of lettuce in a *jet airplane*, for 257 heaven's sake. Beside me sat an enormous British man, a colonial servant in preindependent Kenya. He had already consumed three chicken Kievs and might have eaten a fourth except that he had dozed off. With only five or six passengers willing to brave the SAMs, we were swimming in chicken Kiev. I had suggested when he joined me that we spread out, but he said something about being "chummy," pointing out that we were the only white passengers on board. "You know, mate, birds of a feather with all these missiles flying about."

Probably, he was just nervous. Like the rest of us, he had read the newspapers in Nairobi about a civilian airliner recently shot down over southern Sudan, how the plane had disintegrated the moment a SAM struck it during takeoff. The missile had been fired from a rebel battery outside the besieged city of Malakal, which would be below us in another hour or two. According to the newspaper account, the Malakal rebels had insisted the plane was carrying military supplies. Colonel John Gurang, a rebel leader educated as an agriculturist at the University of Iowa, had explained that he was merely trying to starve out Malakal's government garrison. He claimed to have warned the government not to allow airliners into the war zone. He was sorry sixty-three people had died, but, heck, nobody said a rebellion would be pretty.

Actually, I was not completely unhappy on my perch high above the SAMs. I had wanted to travel by bike and river steamer all the way from Nairobi to Khartoum, but war is a great dissuader. In Lodwar, where I had stopped with Kamoya Kimeu, the Kenyan army had warned that travelers would be turned back if they tried to cross the Sudanese border. The U.S. embassy had said it would not take responsibility for me. Representatives of John Gurang's army in Nairobi had refused me safe passage, saying they did not control all of the armed units operating in the bush. "The south [of Sudan] is a very, very big place," a tall Dinka rebel had told me, "and there are many, many guns. Too many guns are coming from Uganda and Ethiopia. Some men claim to be with the SPLA,* but they are only bandits. Others are local men fighting about local issues. Some are soldiers from old wars in Uganda and other places. It is an unsettled place."

Nevertheless, I was terribly disappointed to be missing southern Sudan. This Alaska-sized region is a critical area of transition between black and Arab Africa, an ancient border country between the

* Sudanese People's Liberation Army.

last frontiers of the Mediterranean world and the expanses of the aboriginal interior. It is where the geography of the dying bushlands and swamps fades into the advancing northern deserts. It is the land of the tall, ink-black Dinka and the fierce, nomadic Neur, two of the more remote and undisturbed tribes in Africa. And it is the home of the largest swamp in the world, the great Sudd, that fantastic barrier of papyrus, reeds and tangled vegetation that for centuries blocked off the Upper Nile from the outside world, a natural barrier as effective against explorers and invaders as a Russian winter.

To be sure, this didn't stop most of the great Mediterranean empires of the last two or three millennia from trying. The ancient pharaohs attempted several times to penetrate the Sudd. So did the Nubians, Persians, Greeks, Romans, medieval Christians and early Muslims. All failed, and the Dinka and Neur lived and died, as they always had, only vaguely aware of the outside world. Then came the Arab conquistadors of Muhammad Ali. In the early nineteenth century, Ali's Egyptian army suddenly fell on the Dinka and the Neur, hacking through the Sudd with steel-hulled steamers and European-supplied explosives. The natives didn't know what had hit them. One day they had been living the life of their ancestors and the next they were being chased about by slavers and soldiers carrying weapons that could slaughter a whole village in a matter of minutes.

As my jet rushed over the land below, I tried to imagine what life had been like during that sordid, bloody era. I had read many books on the subject, but had found most of them replete with the same sort of hyperbole that our pilot kept feeding us over the intercom. *Danger, romance, bravura* ... aren't these the sorts of nouns that come to mind when the Nile and Sudan are mentioned? Don't we all feel our hearts beating a bit faster when someone mentions the names *Baker, Gordon* and *Ali?*

One does not have to read history very closely to grasp what the ghastly reality must have been a hundred and fifty years ago. "Probably nothing more monstrous or cruel than this [slave] traffic had happened in history," wrote Alan Moorehead in *White Nile.* As I sat in the comfort and relative safety of my Boeing 737 I read Moorehead's description:

Any penniless adventurer could become a trader. On a normal expedition such a trader would sail south from Khartoum with two or three hundred armed men. . . . The slavers would fall upon some village in the night, firing the huts just before dawn and shooting

*into the flames. It was the women that the slavers chiefly wanted,
and these were secured by placing a heavy forked pole on their
shoulders. Everything in the village would be looted. . . .*

Of course, all of this was merely history. Or was it? In rural Africa,
history is not something people discard every few years, as we do in
America. Here it remains a living force and a vivid reality, particularly among the people of the south, most of whom live a slow life
from season to season. These are people of the soil, Ecclesiastes
people—"one generation passeth away, and another generation com-
eth: but the earth abideth forever." And they do not easily forget.

Slavery and the horrors of the past were as fresh in the minds of
most southerners as yesterday's dead. Southerners in Khartoum later
told me that the ghosts of the slain were still vividly remembered in
bitter tales told around campfires in the bush. "We do not forget that
it was the Arabs who murdered our ancestors," Gurang's men had
told me in Nairobi. "We do not forget because the Arabs in the north
do not let us forget. They continue to lord over us like a colonial
power. They will not let us practice our religion. They will not let us
determine our own destiny. So we are fighting back."

Now, far down below my airplane, territories that had known only
chaos a century ago were again spinning out of control. Arabs and
blacks were again at war, fighting to win control of a huge, ungainly
nation whose borders are perhaps the most unrealistic geographic
legacy of colonialism in Africa.

The details of the conflict were fairly straightforward. Sitting in
my airplane seat, I was rereading a packet of fuzzy, photocopied
articles and wire reports that listed the particulars of each side's
demands. I also had managed in Kenya to monitor several rebel radio
broadcasts coming out of southern Sudan. The black southerners
were demanding autonomy—their own parliament and laws and the
right to practice their own religions. At the same time the Arab
northerners were calling for a united, Islamic Sudan with a central-
ized government. Splitting up the country, the Arabs argued, would
only weaken development efforts and isolate the economically destitute and landlocked south.

However, it seemed clear that this sad, sordid conflict had much
deeper roots than a list of current demands recorded on blurry pages

and shouted over scratchy radio broadcasts. Basically, the blacks hated the Arabs. It was not a blinding, consuming hate like we are accustomed to in Western movie dramas, but a slower, more grinding bitterness steeped in history, having no real beginning or end. It was an oppressive, despairing, medieval antipathy, the sort that permeates as deep as fire and sin—a mythical hatred, something Shakespeare or Euripides might have done justice to.

On the Arab side, there was aligned that other great vice of all true tragedies—pride. Not Othello's pride, but something that ran farther back in time, something that the people of the north had as little control over as the bitter folk in the south. The northerners had the blood of Ali's conquistadors flowing through their veins. This had been somewhat mellowed by blending over the years with blacks and migrants. Nonetheless, the rulers' blood remained potent enough that the leadership in Khartoum could not let go of the south. This was in spite of their oft-professed claim to be weary of the conflict, and despite the fact that a powerful dictator had recently fallen in Khartoum because he would not give up the legacy of Muhammad Ali. Was the northerner's pride religious? Was it racial? Was it an insurmountable vestige of history?

I did not know, nor was I likely to find out. For even as I wrangled with these thoughts, the south was quickly rushing past below. We had already passed the Sudd and, as the sun fell away to the west, the land below was turning rapidly from green to brown. In another few hours I would be in Khartoum, and the south would remain, for me, as mysterious as it had been before Muhammad Ali burst through the Sudd and changed everything forever on the Upper Nile.

2 I landed in Khartoum long after dark, but the night hardly mitigated the hot, balmy air that filled the airplane. When the air-conditioning shut down, my British chum burst out in sweat. He cursed the heat, hoping this stop was a short one, as he was continuing on to Cairo. When I gathered my things to go, he was incredulous. "My God, man, you are actually getting off here? In Khartoum? Trying to relive Gordon's last stand, I suppose." He guffawed. "Good luck, old boy, and watch out for those dervishes!" More guffaws as I strolled down the aisle and smelled nighttime Khartoum outside the open doorway.

Every morning at dawn God washes this city in pink watercolors, a deceptively tender color in the desert. Khartoum sits at the confluence of the White and Blue Niles, at an axis where the Nubian, Libyan and Eastern deserts converge in one of the hottest, driest places on earth. Within minutes of dawn the heat begins to rise and, at that time of year, would reach 115 degrees or higher by late morning. Yet when I stepped out of the airport, the sky was gentle, like the underbelly of a rabbit, its soft pink light reflecting off battered white taxis and men gathered outside in white tunics and turbans. The color ignited the thick haze over the city like magic dust and for a few seconds the decaying capital looked almost beautiful.

Driving through the streets I was shocked by how rapidly Khartoum had deteriorated since my last visit, in 1982. The city seemed to have collapsed into a state between makeshift and rubble, the buildings still inhabited but in an advanced stage of decomposition. Hungry dogs roamed through quiet alleys and stray refugees from the war huddled in shadows under tarpaulins. Languid pedestrians and a scattering of automobiles moved slowly through the debris, negotiating what remained of the neat grid of streets laid down by Lord Kitchener in 1899. He had designed this city (which his army had leveled after the dervish war) to replicate the pattern of the

Union Jack—an act of astounding pomposity and bluster, even for the British in Africa.

The city was in such a shattered condition that an ignorant visitor might have blamed the decimation on war. But that surmise was not literally true, as the bombs were actually falling hundreds of miles to the south. On the other hand, proximity has never prevented war from wrecking belligerents' cities, particularly when the city and country in question already have been ravaged by more calamities than the pharaoh's Egypt. These included a number of plagues visited by a natural world as wrathful as the biblical Jehovah—intense heat, little rain, rapid desertification, frequent droughts, debilitating dust storms and frequent attacks by locusts and other pests. There were also the political plagues, which pharaoh never had to deal with, a tawdry record of coups, instability, corruption, mismanagement and failed development schemes.

Sudan is such an utter disaster it makes even Zambia look successful. It owes $10 billion that will never be repaid—a sum that has contributed almost nothing to developing or improving the country.* The country's infrastructure is in shambles. Electricity in the capital failed almost as often as it worked. The few paved roads were as pocked and cratered as the moon, and government office buildings looked like slum dwellings. The standard of living had dropped into what can only be described as a free-fall. Some lists of the world's twenty poorest nations already included Sudan as a new entry, joining the destitute ranks of Burkina Faso, Bhutan and Djibouti.

Added to these woes was the painful memory that Sudan had been hailed at birth as one of the most promising, dynamic countries on the continent. At the time, it seemed to have everything required of an up-and-coming country—a plethora of minerals waiting to be tapped, vast bushlands being converted to agriculture and an ancient civilization to provide a stability and continuity rare in Africa. That hopeful cliché "potential breadbasket of Africa" was originally coined to describe Sudan, a cliché that has since jumped from country to country like a wild chimera on the loose. John Gunther, the erstwhile journalist who himself bounced around Africa in the fifties and wrote the optimistic *Inside Africa*, came through Khartoum on the eve of independence and described a city that must have

---

* The interest payments alone equal over a hundred percent of Sudan's shrinking foreign earnings.

more closely resembled the mood of today's Harare—where the chimera now furtively rests—than the wreck I visited thirty years later. Gunther wrote that "politically the Sudan is, I think, the most exciting country we saw in all of Africa. This is not a nation half-dead at birth, like Libya. It has the intense virility of something newly born and vibrant. . . . It is crowded with zest to get ahead; it boils and sparkles with euphoria. . . . I even heard one youthful Sudanese say, 'Our country is going to be like the United States. . . .' "

Obviously, a great deal had gone wrong in Sudan since Gunther's day. During my entire stay in Sudan I found no youths who were remotely euphoric. Nor could I find anyone who claimed that Sudan had *ever* been vibrant and sparkling. One middle-aged professor, who had made his reputation as a young zealot in the fifties, told me he had met Gunther when he came through. The professor was now known as a great cynic, a stocky, still handsome man who seemed filled with the weary sort of tragedy etched onto so many faces in Sudan. "Mr. Gunther, I think, was exaggerating when he wrote these things about Sudan," he recalled with a sad, intelligent, sarcastic smile. He spoke in an overstated British accent in an air-conditioned house filled with books, African art and memories. ("The refuge of an old ideologue," he said.)

"You know, Gunther was quite young at the time," the professor continued. "Perhaps he was a bit overzealous in his assessment. I say, did Gunther actually say *euphoria?* In Sudan? My God, he must have gotten his notes mixed up with some other place. There was a great deal of that disease going about in Africa at that time. But Sudan? Ah, I know where he got this silly idea. Maybe he spent too much time with the chaps in the British civil service. Perhaps they filled his head with this bit about euphoria. I have never seen a group so euphoric as those chaps were. But their euphoria really had little to do with the future of our country. It was due, I'm sure, more to their imminent departure from a rather tedious posting. We Sudanese, on the other hand, had no such prospect, as most of us would be staying on."

Before leaving the airport, I had felt a certain mood emanating from this city. I had seen it in the faces of arriving Sudanese, most of whom were returning from stints as oil field laborers in the Persian Gulf states.* Whereas airports are usually places of visible emotion—

---

* Sudan, a country of twenty million, has seen almost one million of its brightest and strongest citizens leave the country as contract laborers. One fellow returning from the Gulf said that Sudan was a "dead place for making money." He said there was not only no work and no future in Sudan, but "no good cinema."

happiness, anxiety, excitement, sadness—this place more closely resembled a morgue. Arrivals coming from Saudi Arabia and Kuwait clutched new radios, fans, tricycles as if the decay awaiting them outside was going to snatch their hard-earned treasures away like Harpies in the myth. They looked like people returning to a medium-security prison after a stint on the outside. Their faces revealed no joy of homecoming, though some had been away for years. Expressions ranged from a deep weariness to a disturbing lassitude that grew as the minutes ticked off after touchdown. The people in the airport were so laconic that no one seemed to care that customs took all night long to process about a hundred passengers. It took a great deal of effort for me to apply my recently acquired African patience to this intolerable wait. I was smoldering by the time I was released sometime after four in the morning.

To be sure, I had arrived at a particularly bad moment for the Sudanese. The country could not have been more destitute, lying prostrate after years of extraordinary bad luck. The ordeal had started in 1969, when Sudan became the personal property of a dictator named General Jaafar Nimeiri. This son of a camel trader not only spent sixteen years robbing his country blind (his enemies said he was nearly as rich as Moi in Kenya), he forced the gentle people of the country to endure a twisted, bizarre reign based almost solely on personal whim—and a healthy dose of terror. In less than two decades his political mood had shifted from communism to socialism to capitalism to Islamic fundamentalism. In the process he murdered and imprisoned hundreds, transformed his country from hope to beggary and so enraged his people that they finally threw him out in 1985.

When Nimeiri was gone and democracy restored, the people in this ruined country became uncharacteristically ecstatic. Yet this triumph proved tragically hollow. By the time I arrived a year after the elections, the new democratic government was proving to be as dull and incompetent as the dictator had been razor sharp and incompetent, a deeply distressing state of affairs for people already prone to melancholy. Everyone I spoke with—*souk* hawkers, students, beggars, politicians—displayed the same sad, puppy-dog smile, quietly muttering when they spoke. (Their eyes reminded me of winos I have seen, withered men who wake up one morning to find themselves on skid row.) "What happened?" these people seemed to say, beyond hope and despair, looking like shell-shocked mourners attending a funeral, with their own nation as the corpse.

I spent ten days trying to comprehend Khartoum, making my usual rounds of government offices, businesses and friends' homes. I head-quartered near General Gordon's old palace in a simple, comfortable inn run by a fellow named George, one of the last remaining Greeks out of a community in Sudan that once numbered over ten thousand. George's hotel, the Acropole, was the favorite haunt of reliefers and expats sent down to help salvage something from the ruins of Sudan. * They chose the Acropole because George and his family worked twenty-four hours a day to keep open telex lines, telephones, bank wires and other tenuous lifelines to the outside world. The Acropole had a private generator for occasions when the city power failed. It also had the coldest sodas in Khartoum.

There was an informal routine every morning at the Acropole, rather like a boys' summer camp. It started with a wake-up call—a gruff knock on the door by a houseboy—and then a shower to wash off whatever sweat and dust had accumulated overnight. Then each pa-tron made his first plunge outside, crossing the street from the main sleeping building to the dining hall, housed in a separate building. The street was always a shock first thing in the morning, a world of bleached and ruined buildings and alleys swarming with insistent, sometimes hideously deformed beggars. Even the most hardened re-liefers tended to hurry through this scene, dispensing piaster notes to outstretched hands and sprinting toward the protective cover of Land Rovers parked in front of the dining hall. These Rovers, which ferried the relief generals around the city, stood like a fleet of military vehi-cles amid the rubble and heaps of sand in the street, each marked on its door with a colorful decal like a battalion insignia—Save the Children, OXFAM, Band-Aid. . . .

Once inside, one was expected to pause in George's front office, the nerve center of the Acropole. This was where guests received mail and telexes and discussed political developments ("Gawd, it's de-pressing"), the weather forecast ("Bloody hot as hell"), the latest temperature of the swimming pool at the American Club (too cold) and at the British Club (too hot). The office was also the place where invitations to the frequent expat parties were distributed.

---

* The Acropole Hotel was destroyed in a terrorist bombing attack in the spring of 1988. Several relief workers and Sudanese servants were killed. No group claimed responsibility.

In such a city, these affairs were a major diversion, although most gatherings lacked much spunk, given the Muslim prohibition on alcohol.

After chatting for a while in the office, the Acropole guests moved upstairs to the large dining room, where we were served cafeteria-style in groups of twenty-five or thirty. We even dressed like campers, only the bravest wearing anything heavier than a pair of loose khakis and a thin cotton shirt. Suits among this hardened crew were a sign of stupidity.* Most of the people knew each other and spent the meal talking about whatever old reliefers talk about.

"Remember that famine in ... ?"

"Did you get *any* rain over in Darfur ... ?"

"I'm fed up with the bastards back home. Dammit, they spend more money on bloody television advertisements than on ..."

The reliefers reminded me of those at the Fairview in Nairobi, although the Acropolites were a considerably more hard-boiled group. They were divided roughly along the same lines. The younger reliefers tended to be more technically oriented and less sarcastic, occasionally revealing telling glimpses of innocence and altruism that the seasoned reliefers went to great pains to conceal. The older veterans, those who had been in the business since the halcyon days of the sixties and seventies, spent breakfast complaining, mostly about the heat and the incompetence of the Sudanese government.

One morning, I sat with an agricultural expert sent to investigate an oil seed project for the EEC. He was an old hand who had seen the horrors of refugee camps and slums but still muttered and cursed when his biscuits were served dry and hard. He apparently came out of that generation of British intellectuals which had spent its youth agitating for African liberation only to discover that liberation had degenerated into what every upper-class Briton despises most: incompetence. "Bloody fools," said the man, when our biscuits arrived, "how difficult is it to figure out that you put bread away at night? Leave it out and it gets as dry as the Sahara in this godforsaken climate."

---

* U.S. diplomats were held up for specific ridicule because they insisted on wearing full business suits, as if all of Sudan were as cool as the air-conditioned embassy offices. This policy was more than just a joke. Suits in Khartoum not only made people feel uncomfortable, it also made nearly everyone seriously question the intelligence of the American government.

The EEC man ate his food in great gulps, in a bad humor about the food, the temperature and his project. "I have just arrived," he explained, stabbing pensively at his bread, "and now they tell me I have no transport, no travel permit, no bloody anything. I'm stuck in Khartoum today with nothing to do. It may be longer, this government is so damn pathetic. People don't know what the hell is going on. The Sudanese who was supposed to be in charge of our group didn't even know we were coming. Hadn't even heard of our project. I wonder whose fault that is? Is it the Sudanese or my group in London? They're all cut out of the same mold, these bloody bureaucrats." He called over the waiter. "Dammit, can I get some coffee now, or do I have to wait until the end of the meal, like last night? Doesn't anyone in this country serve coffee in the middle of a meal?"

"Coffee at end of meal," said the Arab haughtily. He promptly scooped up my dining companion's plate, still half-eaten, before anything could be said.

"Bloody hell, I wasn't even finished. He, he . . . he did that deliberately, the cheeky bastard." The Brit threw up his hands and shrugged. "What I hate most is waiting around," he growled.

It wasn't easy to track down the people I wanted to interview. Business in the city theoretically operates from seven in the morning to two in the afternoon, and then from six to eight in the evening. I was well versed in the vicissitudes of African office hours and scheduling—Africans simply do not share our compulsions about time—but I always had been able to get my job done with a little perseverance. In Khartoum, however, time exists in an entirely different sphere, even from a spot like Lusaka. Not only did I have a hard time pinning people down for interview places and times, it became a supreme effort to find some of them at all.

Still, I tried, for I was very curious about what Sudan's leadership had to say about their country, if they had any fresh ideas. Each morning after breakfast I filled a liter canteen full of water and covered my head with a Kansas City Royals' baseball cap. (At the time the Royals, my hometown team, were playing abysmally and needed all the help they could get.) I loaded my pockets with small Sudanese pound notes for the beggars and packed an extra shirt into my bag to replace the first one when it got soaked with sweat. I then began walking. Normally, I would have set up interviews via phone, but phones seldom work in Khartoum. The other option was taxis, which were very expensive and unreliable. ("Oh, you wanted to go to the *east* side of city, mister? I thought you say west. So sorry.") This left my feet (at least until my bike was reassembled from the flight), a time-consuming method of communication that became quickly exhausting as the heat rose.

I spent most of ten days walking, drinking water and waiting. Typically, I waited in outer offices filled with bureaucrats occupying chairs and couches but doing nothing at all. Bored conversations ebbed and flowed according to the arrival of tea. (The tea man was the busiest fellow in Khartoum, I think.) These functionaries were the unlucky Sudanese among the educated class who had been unable to find work overseas. They were taking advantage of a ridiculous government policy—a holdover from Nimeiri's socialist phase—guaranteeing every college graduate a government job. This was in spite of the fact that the government was broke and could not afford anything, not even paper, erasers or paper clips. Yet somehow they managed to pay these dispirited employees a pittance each month. Some people called this system a variation on a welfare dole; others muttered that it was actually a bribe to keep these people from rioting.

It didn't take long for me to get thoroughly dejected by the specter of feckless bureaucrats hired to do nothing for a government too broke to do anything but keep an incompetent army in the field. The bureaucrats told me they wanted to work, but there was no money. I sat with a housing official who told me that no dwellings had been constructed for months. At the National Museum I spoke with one of the head archaeologists, whose file cabinet was a series of ancient Meroe pots filled with a few dog-eared papers. "I am grief-stricken," he said. "There is no money for the museum, and the exhibits are in very bad condition. Soon, some artifacts will be beyond repair."

While I waited for their absent bosses, the bureaucrats killed time speculating about Sudan's malaise. War, corruption, incompetence, the heat . . . But when I asked why they didn't do something about the problem, they threw up their hands and said, "What can we do! Allah help us!"

The irony of my whole tiresome effort in Sudan is that when I finally did see officials, they had nothing at all to say. The only interesting politician I interviewed was the leader of the fundamentalist Islamic Front, and he was interesting only because he was half-insane, a smooth-talking Ayatollah Khomeini who had some rather

grand illusions about his power and that of his movement. The man
was an Oxford-educated imam named Turabi, a fellow who was convinced that his radical form of Islam was on the verge of absolute
victory in Sudan. This was despite the fact that almost everyone
I spoke with—souk hawkers, bureaucrats, taxi drivers, politicians
and refugees—loathed and distrusted him, given his support of the
war in the south, the sharia laws and several other unpopular
causes.

I was told he had his followers among the more conservative
imams and certain disenchanted youth. But, to hear him speak, he
had great hordes of followers waiting in the wings to sweep him into
power. He seemed to have utterly missed the point that the people
were exhausted, particularly with extreme points of view, and essentially wanted to be left alone. "We are biding our time to see how this
government reacts to our demands," he said, thumping his desk impatiently, "and if they fail us, we will arouse the people to march in the
streets and demand justice!"

On my last day I conducted an interview that seemed to typify my
stay in Khartoum. I had been trying for a week to talk to the foreign
minister, and each time found him either out or "engaged." As I
wearily trudged past his office for the tenth or eleventh time, I decided to stop and give it one more try. It was nearly three o'clock in the
afternoon—the worst heat of the day, when the streets were empty
and every intelligent person was drinking a cold drink or sleeping in a
cool room. When I entered the building (it was an old British officers'
club), I found it virtually empty, even of guards. So I knocked on his
door.

"Yes?" said a voice, "come in." Inside, Sharif Zein El Abdeen El
Hindi, foreign minister and deputy prime minister of Sudan, sat
behind a large, heavy desk in a frigid, moist, air-conditioned room. I
think he may have been sleeping when I knocked. He was rubbing his
eyes and stretching as I explained who I was. He invited me to sit
down and offered me tea. A friendly man, El Hindi gave stock answers
to all my questions, joining in the chorus lamenting the
state of affairs in his country. He talked about the foreign debt,
the threats of new drought, the failure of agricultural schemes and the
collapse of the nation's currency. He said the problems were out of
control and he seemed to be at a loss for solutions. Then he said

something I had never heard a leader say. As we finished our tea, he looked up at me with doleful eyes and launched into a long, nostalgic monologue about his childhood home, which he missed terribly. He was weary, he said, and had had enough of government. "I want to retire and go home," he said, a sad man in a sad country.

3 After several more days in Khartoum, I was more than ready to climb back on my bicycle and head north. The problem now was the weather. As if the city had not been gloomy enough, two days before my projected departure a sandstorm gathered overhead, a massive, enveloping gauze of dust and grit that made it nearly impossible to see or breath without a cloth over one's mouth. These storms—called *haboobs*—come once or twice a year, rolling off the Sahara to black out life in the Nile Valley and slow things down even more than usual. Friends warned me to delay my trip. "These storms have swallowed up entire armies," George said at the Acropole, flashing his always helpful smile. So I delayed—and delayed—for three more days, fidgeting impatiently in the hotel lounge, drinking too much tea and listening to enough relief-speak to last a lifetime.

On the third day I became so frustrated with waiting I decided to take my chances. At dawn the following morning, with the tempest still blowing unabated, I took a final shower at the Acropole and carried my bicycle and gear into the ruined street below. I wrapped an Arab kaffiyeh around my head and mouth and strapped goggles to my eyes. The sun rose as I packed, though it hardly delivered its usual blast of heat in the storm. That morning it was merely a faint speck in the shrouded, turbulent sky. Sir Samuel Baker once described a *haboob* that blew into Khartoum: "I saw approaching from the S.W. a solid range of immense brown mountains, high in the air . . . in a few minutes we were in actual pitchy darkness. We tried to distinguish our hands placed close before our eyes—not even an outline could be seen."

My storm was not quite so nasty. Rather than a pitchy blackness the scene looked more like a very dusty room with a faint light struggling to break through. I could see my hand, but not much else beyond two or three meters. Buildings appeared as looming shadows and a few early cars and trucks moved like phantoms in the haze. The dreary storm seemed appropriate for my send-off, a final portent from this saddest of cities on my Cape to Cairo route.

272   I worked quickly, loading heavy bags onto my racks and checking

tires and tightening bolts. Beggars sleeping under broken colonnades peeked out from under blankets pulled tight around their bodies for the night. Their hair was white with sand. Undoubtedly, they were suffering in this long, stifling storm.

About this time the Acropole guard—a sleepy man who carried a large club—came out of the hotel, awakened by the crazy *hwage*— white man— with the bike. He tried halfheartedly to chase away the beggars, a job that seemed altogether futile in that purgatory of a city. As I finished packing, a young beggar I had seen before, an Ethiopian refugee, came over from his usual spot on the opposite corner of the intersection. I had seen him every morning for the past few days, and I knew exactly what he wanted. He had never asked for money, just for a favor. And here he was again, waving a grubby paper in my face and asking me in broken English if I would help him. The paper was an application to work as a menial laborer at the United States embassy. "Please, you take application to embassy?" he asked. I could barely see him through the stormy veil of dust, but I knew his face well. It was scarred and twisted, ravaged by some unspeakable act of war or torture. It looked as if someone had taken wire and wrapped up pinches of flesh like a tie-dye shirt. "You must help me," he said in a clear, demanding voice. "I am smart boy. I am refugee. I need help."

Just as I was about to answer him, another beggar emerged from the dust to push away the Ethiopian, yelling at him in Arabic, obviously defending his turf—this corner—from an interloper. But the Ethiopian was no ordinary beggar. He slapped the ragged man on the cheek and stunned him into silence. "These men are worthless," he said to me. "He calls *me* a beggar. I am a refugee! I am here because of the war, because they kill my family and the soldiers do this to me." He indicated his face. "In Ethiopia, I go to school. My family no poor. We have house and car the soldiers take away. I do not beg. I look for job. I ask you about this application. Please, do you help me?"

The smeared, leathery paper smelled of dirt and spices under my nose. I had looked at it before, reading the questions of American bureaucratese: "What is your official nation of origin? Why do you want to apply as a candidate for employment with the United States government?" The man's effort to fill in the blanks looked painful, each letter and word carefully and slowly drawn. I had inquired about jobs at the embassy, but had been told there was nothing available, particularly for "foreign nationals illegally residing outside their designated refugee areas." I told the Ethiopian once again that I could not help him. I wanted to tell him more, that I could not help but felt deeply moved by his plight and his motivation to work, but I was having a hard enough time trying not to stare at his horrible wounds. What more could I say to comfort a man like this? He had lost his family, his country, his friends. He would go through life wearing a mask of horror, a freak. And if peace ever comes to his tormented homeland, he will remain a pariah, a man whose very existence would bring up revolting images of a past everyone will want to forget.

I finally decided to offer the man a five-pound note, not knowing any other way to help. I mean, what could I do? Take him home with me? Adopt him? Make him my personal contribution to the betterment of everything I can think of? Would this make a real difference? Would this man *want* to be adopted?

Offering money was an error. I should have noted that he was perhaps the only ragged man on the street who had *never* asked for money—a human whose dignity hung over the pit, saved from oblivion by a single thread. No, he was not a beggar. He had said this perhaps fifty times over the past few days. He was a man, and I deeply offended him. "I do not want your money," he exclaimed, snatching away his application and looking as if I had struck him with my fist. "I told you! I am no beggar! I want to work! I deserve to work!"

I departed the Acropole at what would have been first light, except for the storm. I was no longer traveling alone. Riding at my side was a friend who had just flown in from the States, Andy Shafer, a lanky, red-haired man from New Hampshire. Since Jim Logan's departure in Tanzania, I had been inviting (imploring? bribing?) friends to come over to Africa to join me. Andy had been duly persuaded, even though he had never ridden a loaded bicycle and never had done any serious bicycle touring. However, he was something of an expert on desert travel, having spent a great deal of time trekking through the Sahara in Land Rovers. His first trip was in 1973, when he was fifteen years old. Andy's father, a college professor, had taken the whole family on a one-year expedition from Algiers across the Sahara to Addis Ababa and on to Cairo. Since then, he had come back regularly to drive about in the lonely wastelands of North Africa, a part-time nomad who knew as much as any outsider about the desert—its harshness, its cruelty, its peculiar poetry.

Leaving the Acropole was not easy. I had warned Andy that the first few minutes on a loaded bicycle would be like trying to slalom before learning to ski, but he had merely shrugged with the confidence of a seasoned traveler. "I'll get the hang of it," he had said. So he climbed aboard, his face locked in concentration.

He stayed up for all of a half-second. *Womp!* He went down into the dust, cursing and clamoring to get his legs free. "I'm supposed to drive this thing in traffic?" he moaned. "I'm gonna die."

"Don't worry," I said, "it'll get easier when we get into the sand."

"Don't mess with me," he grumbled, climbing back onto the bike. This time he stayed up, but nearly crashed into a light pole as he careened wildly down the street.

"Tallyho!" he shouted, and we were off.

As we pulled out that morning, I was feeling a bit wobbly myself. Both of our bikes were piled with gear and supplies. We were headed out into the open desert, where we would have to be prepared for anything. We had every spare part we could think of—extra tools, a plethora of medicines and first-aid equipment, a bag each of water and at least thirty pounds of food.

From the Acropole we pedaled down a series of sand-strewn streets, heading toward the river. Traffic picked up as we crossed a narrow, rickety bridge just below the confluence of the White and Blue Niles. Andy and I were no longer joking about our wobbliness. It was a serious struggle to keep control and avoid getting killed on streets where the visibility was equal to about three car-lengths. We passed through the warehouse district along the north bank of the Nile, a sprawl of British-era monoliths that until recently had serviced the river trade with the south. However, now that the war had shut down all transport on the Nile, the warehouses stood empty as they devolved rapidly into decay.

After the warehouses we passed a progression of shops and houses turning gradually more ragged and makeshift until we reached the outer ring of cardboard and tarpaulin shanties. Refugees from the southern war inhabited the newest layer of slums, phantom hovels in the dust. I had heard a great deal about these people's plight from reliefers at the Acropole, how they had fled from burning homes and soldiers and how they had struggled to reach the capital, desperate for help that neither the government nor the major international agencies could provide. Over 750,000 refugees were clustered around the city, most of them unable to receive relief aid because of a technicality in the rules that govern international altruism.* Most international reliefers provide only for refugees who have crossed a state border, not for internal refugees. Thus the irony in Sudan, where over three million foreign refugees are fed and housed by the UN and private organizations, while the Sudanese themselves must rely on a bankrupt government that can't even afford pencils for their bureaucracy.

If this had been earlier in my journey I would have stopped to investigate this endless stretch of shanties, but I was feeling dejected that morning, struggling against an oppressive storm and unable to bear the thought of traipsing through yet another purgatory of hopeless slums. How often can one go back to narrate these woes, to place names and stories on the faces of such brutal misfortune? Of course, this was a major reason why I had come to Africa. Yet that morning in Sudan I was overwhelmed by the task, drowned by Khartoum.

From the highway I could see apparitions swimming through the gloom looking remarkably like Muthare Valley, Crossroads and hundreds of other similar outposts around the world. These shades walked and carried objects and led animals and tended fires, sparked on by a life force that defies understanding. A cluster of women became clearer up ahead, and I saw that they were washing clothes at a roadside spigot, probably furnished by OXFAM or Band-Aid or one of the less rule-bound relief groups, those that call a refugee a refugee whether or not he fulfills every criterion set by the powers that be. I slowed to watch the women washing. I had seen them in every slum since Crossroads, women desperate to keep a scrap of clothing clean while their children starved.

I pedaled on, wishing for a miracle.

After what seemed like hours the dark hovels disappeared as our road swung away from the Nile and into a landscape of mud flats. Out here we saw an occasional cow or pathetic acacia, but little else. We were passing through a dead land that even a hundred and fifty years ago had been thick with acacia, *mupane* and dense underbrush. In those days hippo, lion and antelope had roamed this country, the last vestige of fauna that once covered the entire Sahara before the

---

* These rules have been organized by the United Nations, whose High Commission for Refugees coordinates most relief work in Sudan.

great sands washed it all away. It was the Egyptian-European invasion—the introduction of the modern world—that had wrecked this land. Conquest had brought with it a sudden increase in humans, camels, cattle and goats. Herders had turned loose animals that ate the delicate cover and exposed the bare ground to the sun. Farmers had cleared the land and cultivated crops, rapidly depleting already weak soil. Slave traders had cut large clearings in the bush to warehouse shifting camps of human wares, where Dinka and Neur were bought and sold. It took only a few decades to ruin the land, reducing the fertile portion to a narrow band along the banks of the Nile, replenished by the annual flood.

Outside of the city traffic thinned out to desert trucks and an occasional bus brimming with dark shapes in turbans and white robes. The paved road became choppy and finally disintegrated into a sand track at a small village called El Geili, forty kilometers north of Khartoum. This was the point where our voyage truly began, where we left behind even a pretense of normal cycling.

We stopped to load up with water at the small El Geili market. Water is obviously critical in North Africa, particularly so in the desert, where a biker consumes over two gallons a day. Yet the need for water is always balanced against its weight. Two gallons of water weigh almost thirty pounds—this in addition to the extra weight we were already carrying. We wanted to avoid carrying more water than necessary, especially if there were villages ahead where we could stock up later. Since this appeared to be the case, I suggested to Andy that we take on minimal supplies of water now, and then fill up later. Andy did not like this idea at all, telling me that he had never headed out into the desert with anything but a full water supply.

"But that was in a Rover," I insisted. "Now you've got to *carry* the stuff."

To make a long-winded story short, Andy grudgingly went along with me, saying that I was the experienced biker. He added that I better know what I was doing.

"Trust me," I said.

As it turned out, I was wrong, and not only about the water. I also made a critical error in believing the accuracy of my Michelin map, which I had long regarded as the cartological voice of God in Africa. "Maps in the desert can be deceptive," Andy had warned, but I hadn't listened. I had based all of my planning and logistics on the assumption that Michelin had correctly marked the road north of El Geili as "partially improved," meaning a graded earth or gravel road. This was, as it became immediately clear, an erroneous assumption, my second in an environment that does not permit many errors. Where the pavement crumbles away there is nothing more than a desert path, splaying off in every direction into the wasteland.

Fortunately, my companion did not suffer from the same misplaced confidence as I did. Andy's sureness about matters of the desert was genuine, so he led the way, explaining that it was critical to stay on the main track and not get sidetracked by the hundreds of false tributaries heading off toward old Bedouin campsites and dried-up wells. "If we get lost on a false path we're basically dead," Andy said in his slow, practical fashion, "especially in this sandstorm."

"That's encouraging," I said.

"Ah, cheer up, Dave. Remember what you told me when you asked me to come? This is an adventure!"

"Did I say that? My God, I must have been desperate."

At first, the main track was hard-packed and easy to follow. We felt safe being close to the Nile, although we would soon veer off into the desert around the mountains of the sixth cataract. It was comforting to see the low, shadowy buildings of villages along the river, adobe houses that meant water, food and shelter was nearby if we needed them.

Bicycling across packed sand in a *haboob* was unnerving. One never knew what was coming, or if the storm would get worse. It also had an oddly mystical allure to it. Eerie shades rose out of the haze: ancient British trucks making the Nile run, Bedouins leading camels, Nubian forts made of adobe and nomadic enclaves erected out of acacia brambles and camel skins. We struggled against a steady headwind blowing sand into our faces and mouths, though after a while I found I was enjoying myself. The heat was cut considerably by the storm, and I felt romantic, out on the Sahara in white robes riding a steel steed and doing combat with the elements. Crested larks joined us after a while, following in our wakes like dolphins at sea. Dusty white sparrows sat on bare branches, looking unhappy in the storm. The scene seemed somehow complete when a Bedouin boy rode up on his camel and asked in broken English if we had any Michael Jackson tapes. He offered to trade us two live chickens for a copy of "Beat It."

W e stopped for lunch and a midday nap in a village called Shab del el Gab, one of countless Nile enclaves of nondescript compounds surrounded by gray mud walls. There wasn't much to any of these towns. They were arranged so that the buildings were just beyond the riverbanks, reserving the rich soil for the exclusive use of crops. Each compound was surrounded by a high wall, the social status of each family identifiable by its door. The richer farmers had metal doors painted turquoise and pink (and a handful of very rich had Toyota pickups parked in front). Everyone else had doors made of wood or scraps of tin.

On the north end of Shab del el Gab we found an abandoned, doorless compound dissolving slowly into the desert. Inside was a building still relatively intact, with enough of a ceiling remaining to offer shade and a windbreak for two exhausted bikers. We set out a tarp under this roofed structure and unpacked a lunch of peanut butter and jam sandwiches, biscuits and oranges. We savored a plastic bag of gorp Andy had brought from home, and finished off the last section of a chocolate bar purchased in a New England supermarket.

We had not pedaled into the village unnoticed. Before we had unpacked our lunch a welcoming committee had arrived, consisting of an elderly woman in a bloodred dress, two younger women and a boy named Mohammed. They greeted us warmly, gave us straw mats and invited us to have our lunch in another, more "beautiful" house. "This house ugly," said one of the younger women. "It is dead." We assured them that this ugly house was fine, and offered them each a sandwich. The women began to giggle and then abruptly said good-bye, and I remembered that traditional Sudanese females, like most Arab women, never dine with males outside their families. But the boy stayed on to experience his first PB and J and ask the usual questions. Most of these were in Arabic—it took him awhile to grasp the fact that we did not speak his native tongue, although this did not stop him from talking with an enthusiasm only a boy could have mustered in the heat of the day. Finally, he asked for a pencil and paper so he could write out some English words. It was a tremendous effort for him to draw the letters, and he worked so hard at it I became very curious at what he was writing. I should have guessed.

MICHAEL JACKSON IS GOOD.

This launched him into a long discourse on the subject of Mr. Jackson, who probably has no idea how much he is revered in Africa. The boy was aghast that we, as Americans and representatives of Western Culture, were not carrying any tapes of his hero. I showed him Beethoven, Muddy Waters and the Rolling Stones. Mohammed shook his head and wrote THRILLER.

When we resumed our journey, our legs became rubbery in the heat and our heads pounded as the main track veered away from the Nile. Soon we left the villages behind and, as the mud plains turned to sand, we lost track of the main path. We had thought we were on course, but our path suddenly petered out at a small outcrop of rocks. Blackened stones marked this place as a camp, probably for truck drivers, but otherwise there was no sign of human habitation. We backtracked nearly a mile, which only got us farther off as we became lost in a tangle of paths angling off in several directions. We tried one, then another, and then got stuck in a sand-filled hollow. We had to carry the bikes to get back on hard ground. Meanwhile, the sandstorm had gathered to full force again, darkening the sky as we lost yet another track. This one ended rather ominously with a dead camel's rib cage and skull, the latter smiling with loose white teeth.

"In a Rover," Andy said, standing over the dead camel, "if you get lost, you just keep driving until you find the main track."

"Did you use the word 'lost'?"

"Would you prefer I said 'drastically off course'?" Andy looked picturesque in his torn, white desert suit, mirrored goggles and turban blowing in the wind. "We might be miles from the main track. I've seen desert roads that are literally miles wide. The trucks just keep spreading out from the main track, looking for harder sand. I remember once in the Sahel—in Niger, I think—we had to do these really huge zigzags back and forth looking for the track. We kept getting stuck, and the going was slow. We finally found the sucker three days later."

"In three days," I said, "we'll be dead."

I remembered that Winston Churchill once had come this way and gotten lost. Working as a journalist-soldier during Kitchener's dervish campaign, twenty-four-year-old Winston's horse temporarily strayed away from the Nile during a sandstorm. He eventually found his way back to the river when the storm cleared, his plight being eased by an accompanying mule equipped with a few essentials the grandson of a duke could hardly be expected to be without: a mixed case of champagne and port, tinned meats and several packets of candied dates. He also carried a tuxedo, which might have come in handy had he been invited to a black-tie dinner with a Bedouin sheik.

We did not have champagne or tuxedos, but we did have a compass, though this was next to useless. Not only did we have no fixed points for orienting ourselves, the rocks in the neighborhood were filled with iron, which deranged the magnetic needle of the compass. We knew the Nile lay ten or fifteen miles to the west, blocked by the mountains of the sixth cataract. And several miles to the east was the Khartoum to Wadi Halfa railway line, a single set of tracks that eventually runs into villages to the north and south. But both river and railroad were several hours away by bike and farther by foot, and we were running low on water with the temperature on my thermometer reading 112 degrees.

I felt like an idiot for my pomposity about the water in El Geili, a judgment Andy heartily shared. But there was no point in recriminations, not when we were lost in the desert with only four or five liters of water. We had to find a truck or a village, and we had to find one soon. Rather than blunder toward the river or railroad, we headed in what we hoped was a northerly direction, looking for the ever-elusive main desert track.

The romance I had felt that morning was squelched. There was nothing romantic about dying of thirst. Nor was there any sense of great excitement as the desert surface began to get harder to cycle across, alternating from hard-packed earth to sandy wadis—what Texans call a wash. In each of a dozen wadis Andy and I had to push and pull and carry the bikes through shallows as thick as a sandbar on the Kansas River, our seventy-pound bikes sinking up to the axles. Over the next two hours we heard three trucks pass in the fog of dust. We dumped the bikes to run toward the sounds, but missed them every time.

Finally, near dusk, we saw a flame up ahead. We pedaled and pushed through the soft sand and found a small Bedouin camp of camel skin tents, the sand covered with pellets of goat dung. Several children in skins and rags hopped about in excitement as their scraggy dogs sniffed our feet. "*Mayya?*" I asked—Arabic for water.

The boys continued to hop and shout and sing. I said what I thought was Arabic for "We are lost, can you help us?" The boys paid no attention. We started getting angry, demanding they help us, but the boys only laughed, as if they had been smoking hemp or drinking some of the wretched wine the Bedouins make clandestinely in the desert. We looked around for adults, but this seemed to be some bizarre, desert version of *Lord of the Flies*, so we kept biking.

A few minutes later we found another Bedouin village. A woman with a finger-sized scar across her face—it looked like a saber wound—came over. She understood the word *mayya*, nodding and smiling and speaking rapidly as if she were telling a story. "They have water," I shouted to Andy, who was a few meters behind. The woman led me to a blackened goatskin hanging from a tent pole. I saw that this camp was primitive—almost everything was made from skins, wood and scraps of discarded metal. She took a sandy tin can and squeezed out a cupful of vile-looking liquid. Bowing, she handed me the *mayya* with both hands extended, as if I were a prince. I thanked her and held up my two-gallon bag, indicating I wanted more. This was apparently the wrong thing to say, for her expression turned from one of respect and friendship to one of irritation. She began cackling and waving her finger at my bag as I tried to indicate we were lost with no water. I offered her money, but the woman shook her finger, even more offended. Apparently, *mayya* was worth more than a piece of paper out here. Finally, she grew disgusted with us and angrily pointed west, saying "el Niele," indicating that if we wanted to walk ten or fifteen miles, there was plenty of water in the river.

Near dusk, we scouted out a protective outcrop of rocks and erected our tent. Andy and I then laid out our total remaining water supply, a little over three liters. Even in the States, this would have been barely enough for a camp. On the Sahara Desert it was a laughable pittance. We were dehydrated from riding and needed two or three liters each just to get rehydrated. As it was, we loaded what water we had with vitamins and protein. Later Andy enhanced his stature as Desert Expert by turning out a great beef stew, an enviable feat on one liter of water in a sandstorm.

Late that night the storm, after raging for almost a week, finally cleared off. I was awakened by the absence of wind. I climbed out of my sleeping bag and stepped outside, reveling in the fresh, sandless air, the moon and the fantasy world of stars above the Sahara. It looked like a vast concert hall ablaze with burning candles. From our perch near the rocks I had a clear view of the desert for miles, and could see the distant headlights of two or three trucks making nighttime runs. None was coming our way, but it soon became clear where the lost track must be.

I stood for a long time watching the sky and the silvery light glowing off the wasteland. The desolation was stunning and beautiful, making me feel both large and small at the same time. After a while, I decided to take a walk, but was stopped by Andy's voice. He had been sitting up for a long time in the tent, joining me in a silent reverie.

"You in bare feet?" he asked.

"Huh?"

"You gotta flashlight? Take a look at the sand."

I flipped on my light and jumped back. Just beyond the edge of the ground cloth the ground was moving.

"Scorpions," said Andy. "They like warm bodies, you know. Especially warm feet."

The next day we continued the struggle across the sand, heading west toward the truck track I had seen the night before. This took most of the morning, as we moved in wide zigzags across the sand, frequently carrying our bikes over wadis. Finally, about ten, we found a string of concrete desert markers—the main track. Before long, a half-mangled bus packed with people stopped and gave us a goatskin full of water. It smelled like a blend of sewage and gasoline, but we didn't complain. Andy added iodine for purification, which worked, and sugar and powdered orange drink for flavor, which did not. The stuff tasted horrendous, but this didn't stop us from drinking a half-gallon each. We felt our energy return almost immediately. Then we filled our water bags—this time, we did not scrimp—and pushed on toward the north.

4 It took two more days to reach Shendi, the first significant town north of Khartoum. We first saw it as a smudge of dust hanging in the air. Then, through the wavy mirages of heat, the city's low, boxy buildings emerged in a bath of images looking liquid in the sun. We arrived in the middle of the afternoon, so the city seemed almost abandoned as we passed through the outer rings of bleached adobe compounds and pedaled downtown, happy to have finally arrived in a place we had expected to reach our first day out from Khartoum. But the desert had simply not cooperated.

It was a shock to pedal out of the empty Sahara and onto the banks of the Nile. Death and desolation were instantly transformed by the magic of the river. Brown became green, water replaced thirst and life-styles abruptly became slow and easy. Since leaving Khartoum we had been biking among the lean, primitive Bedouins of the desert, passing by their temporary camps and asking them to share or accept money for what little food and water they could spare. In Shendi we suddenly left the hard life of the desert and entered a balmy, ancient world of markets crammed with fruit, vegetables, cloth, goats and a thousand other things. Fields swollen with crops glittered along the Nile, while motorized pumps fed irrigation canals and gentle felucca sailboats—invented when the pharaohs reigned in Egypt—slid past on the narrow streamer of water.

We were utterly exhausted, so our first priority was to find a place to sleep. We were directed to a small, Third World hostel near the center of town, a place with NATIONAL INN scratched in a childlike hand over the doorway. It was a typical Arab inn, the sort that probably hadn't changed much since the prophet himself walked the earth. The entrance was guarded by the stereotype of the Middle Eastern innkeeper—fat, toothless and dressed in a soiled *gallebeyah*. He greeted us in a loud merchant's voice and demanded we pay everything in advance—the equivalent of fifty cents a night for a bed and about twenty cents for lunch and dinner. He then called for a boy, who shyly led us into a large, open courtyard surrounded by small rooms sealed by large padlocks. The courtyard was filled with woven straw cots arranged in the shade under a tall eucalyptus tree. Half the cots were already filled with men asleep for the afternoon siesta.

I was too tired to care much about the history of this place, although it literally reeked of age. Yet in my exhausted condition I half-expected sandy caravaners from Timbuktu and Morocco to pass through the doorway. Like us, they would have demanded cold drinks while they discarded their robes and attempted to wash off the dust of their long journey at the well under the tree. Then they would have eaten a small meal of spiced beans and sorghum cakes while sitting on their cots. The only difference was we were washing our food down with Coca-Cola instead of sorghum wine.

After our naps, Andy and I felt revived, so we set out to see what Shendi looked like. We walked across a set of ragged railroad tracks—originally laid nine decades earlier by Kitchener's army — and quickly came upon the city's *souk*, which was just beginning to activate after naptime. Shopkeepers were unlocking stalls, hawkers were removing sheets covering their wares, and camel traders were herding their snorting, sweaty beasts into wooden show pens. The *souk* was surprisingly prosperous in a primitive fashion, brimming with everything from fat mules and baskets of roasted nuts to truck parts and plastic shoes. But this stretch of river valley has long been one of the wealthiest regions of Sudan, an ancient thread of gold in an otherwise dead part of the world.

As often happened, we attracted a number of hangers-on as we strolled about, mostly students intrigued by *hwages* and curious about life in the land of "Dallas" and Michael Jackson. One of these students was particularly insistent, a Dinka from the south named Mathew. We met him in an old, British-designed park in the center of town, a place overgrown and sloppy but filled with men and boys relaxing over tea and fruit juice. Mathew offered us a lemon drink and then began telling us his story. He was staying in Shendi with a friend, though his family lived in Juba. He had been on his way home from school in Egypt when the SPLA began bombing steamers on the Nile. With all river traffic halted, the poor fellow had been stuck here an entire year with no money and with no way to contact his family.

"I hate this war," he said, mouthing the same sentiments I had been hearing from war-weary people from the moment I arrived in

Cape Town. "It serves no purpose. I do not support the north, but I also believe our leaders in the south have jumped to war too fast and many people are dying for nothing. I have an uncle who died in the first civil war.* I have friends who have died in this war. Maybe more have died since I left, I do not know. Maybe more of my family have died in this last year. I get no news. I tell you, it makes me angry that the common people want the same thing in north and south, to live in peace."

At sunset, Andy and I walked along the Nile, watching feluccas gliding like bright clouds against the palms. Diesel pumps, vibrating and stinking of foul exhaust, roared at regular intervals, sucking water up to irrigation troughs, veins flashing blue in the sun. Lean, bare-chested men toiled with hoes, shovels and machetes. Behind the crops were the walls of the wealthiest men in Shendi, those who owned the fields. The walls were made of the same bland adobe as everything else, topped with a layer of broken glass to discourage thieves. I stopped when I noticed a kitten stepping gingerly on top of one wall, a soft puff of fur against the slivers.

As I watched the kitten, afraid she was going to slash herself, I heard a man begin to laugh inside the walls. He sounded immense, a barrel-chested fellow with a baritone voice like an opera singer. Then a face appeared, peering out of a brightly painted doorway. It obviously belonged to the opera singer—a wide, beefy face followed by three hundred pounds of flesh dressed in an umber safari suit and flip-flops. The man stopped chuckling at the cat long enough to introduce himself as Hassan. "Please, my friends, you must come and eat with me," he said. "I insist!"

He led us into a small courtyard of grass and almond trees dominated by a huge bed. A covered porch led off the yard, where a woman nearly as large as Hassan lay on another bed watching television. Hassan ignored her and introduced us to a younger woman, his "new" wife—a recent addition to the family. We sat down and the young woman served us tea and cakes. She was dressed in a bright, wraparound dress, a beautiful and petite woman. I tried to imagine a three hundred pound man and her . . . no, it was too disgusting even to contemplate.

---

* 1956–73.

Hassan had invited us to dinner, but for him this was actually breakfast. Shortly before we had arrived in Shendi, Ramadan had begun, when Muslims are required to fast between sunrise and sunset. The first meal of the day was just after the sun went down. During the day no devout Muslim touched food or water, an incredible hardship in this climate, particularly for a man like Hassan, who obviously enjoyed a good meal.

As we sat down in Hassan's garden—we in turquoise beach chairs and he on his immense bed—it happened to be about fifteen minutes before sunset. Therefore, the young wife did not serve our host tea and cakes, though he looked so longingly at ours that we did not dare eat them. The food made him very anxious. He fidgeted and began an elaborate set of movements to redistribute his girth on his aircraft-carrier-sized bed. He tried to remain jolly, but as the minutes ticked by his smile became strained, sweat poured down his face and his readjustments became almost violent as he flopped about. The man was suffering horribly and could hardly wait for the call of the muezzin, which would signal the official moment of sundown. He made his torture even worse by ordering his wives to set out his nightly feast ahead of time. Not so he could cheat, but so he could look at it and anticipate it as the grand moment approached. The women went quickly to work. They brought him tin trays the size of windmills filled with spiced beans, millet bread, boiled okra, watermelon and mango. Then they brought large pitchers of grapefruit juice, sugared *kerkede* (a boiled red blossom that tastes like sour cherries) and a Ramadan drink made of fried sorghum. The dishes steamed under the fat man's nose and his face went into subtle contortions as his voice strained to keep up a conversation. Every fifteen or twenty seconds he plucked a watch out from under a nearby pillow and checked the time. I suppose he kept it under the pillow so he wouldn't have to watch how slowly the minutes ticked by. Sweat by now collected in great rivulets as it dripped down wrinkles in his cheeks. In the background the television blared and chattered, but no one was watching, an oddly American habit.

We suffered with poor Hassan. He smiled and struggled to remain calm, telling us about a scheme that would make himself and us "very, very rich men." Apparently, this man was an entrepreneur—I was glad to see they existed in Sudan—and we had been invited to "breakfast" as potential investors in his latest project. "I need only five hundred thousand dollars," he said, struggling to sound gleeful. As he spoke he slapped away a gang of flies gathering above his cherished food. "Phooey, you evil flies!" He looked horrified as one of them landed on the tip of a plantain. "Away with you!" he shouted. Then, realizing we were still there, his expression turned from loathing at the fly to a smile as wide as the mangoes on his tray. "This is a beautiful plan," he said, trying to sound like a smooth-talking hawker. "It is so beautiful. I am sure that to you in America five hundred thousand dollars is so little! But let me explain." He paused to check his watch and frown for an instant. By my reckoning, he had four minutes to go.

"I am the local representative of Agip Oil," he continued, his hand resting on the pillow as if the watch underneath it was going to spring out like a lion and bite him. "I run a single bus from Shendi to Khartoum. It has been marginally profitable in all of this sand. But you see, there is a grand new plan by the government to build a paved highway from Khartoum to Shendi. Have you heard? Is not this grand news? So naturally I want to expand my bus service. There, that is it! I want to buy five buses and build a depot and a gas storage facility. It will cost only five hundred thousand dollars."

Another watch check and a deep, painful sniff of the food. Three minutes left. He explained the details of his proposal, checking his watch, smelling his food and dripping with anticipation. He said he had lined up loans for some of the money, but thought it would be easier to get an American investor simply to write him a check. "We will make so much money!" he exclaimed, snatching at the timepiece yet again.

Hassan was in the middle of a sentence when the entire city erupted in the exotic moan of the muezzin. It came from loudspeakers mounted on minarets, from radios and from Hassan's television—which had interrupted a showing of what looked like "CHiPs." The fat man shivered with delight and gazed at the entirety of his feast, absorbing each odor and texture. Then he launched his attack, starting slowly with the large bowl of Ramadan drink, a sorghum-based concoction that he said prepared a fasting stomach to accept food. He lunged toward the meats and beans, his hands moving like a concert pianist's over his instrument. Andy and I nibbled around the edges of the feast, sensing a certain danger if we got in the way of a plowing fist or chomping jaw. He was still eating when we left an hour later.

That night we bedded down with two dozen other men in the National's courtyard. I was kept up most of the night by all those Third World noises we Westerners have spent a century ridding ourselves of: chickens clucking, dogs yapping, goats bleating and mosquitoes buzzing. There was also Ramadan to contend with. An elderly man prayed in a low monotone nearly all night, dipping his head toward Mecca every few seconds, while people in a nearby house had a radio blasting sermons half the night.

The next day Andy and I moved to a slightly better hotel, where we had our own locked room. We slept nearly the entire day, exhausted by the ride from Khartoum. When we finally rose, it was nearly dusk, and Shendi was poised again for the celebration of Ramadan breakfast. Outside the hotel we went searching for food, and ran into a young Arab, Mohammed, who invited us to have breakfast at his "school." Tall, muscular and well dressed, Mohammed spewed American slang at a breakneck speed. "Groove to the beat, man, and take it all the way to San Jose and see you later, alligator." He grinned. "In a while, crocodile, and do it every mile." He said he learned everything he knew from American novels and records.

So we followed Mohammed—he insisted we call him "Mohammed the Slang Man"—to a walled compound, his "school." Actually, it was a religious commune where disciples of a holy man gathered to hear sermons on his versions of peace, justice and holy wars against various infidels. These included Ronald Reagan, John Gurang and the SPLA, most of the West, most of Africa, the prime minister of Sudan and most of the other leaders of the world. I had heard about these communes in Khartoum. The slick-tongued leader of the Islamic Front had praised them, although everyone else in Khartoum had denounced them, calling them cells of Islamic radicalism. One journalist described them as "brainwashing centers for desperate young men."

Mohammed's leader looked quite familiar to an American who had watched the evening news over the past few years. He had long robes, a turban and a round, slightly menacing face outlined with a long, peppery beard. Yet this holy man did not seem to mind two infidel Americans appearing at his door. Speaking through Mohammed the Slang Man, he invited us to join them all for breakfast,

offering chairs while his followers finished the last few minutes of
the Ramadan day praying. This continued even after the muezzin
call. It was as if no one wanted to be the first to head for something as
temporal as a feast, though they eventually decided they had shown
enough piety and collected quietly around a blanket for their meal.
Servants then brought out the same dishes we had seen at Hassan's
house, although the quantity and eating habits were much more
restrained.

As we ate, Mohammed the Slang Man stopped speaking in slang
and politely asked us rhetorical questions about Islam. Did we not
believe that Islam was the true faith? Did we not as Christians want
to recognize Mohammed as the final and greatest prophet of God?
Did we not believe in the world brotherhood of peace offered by
Islam? He said his group favored the Islamic Code that governed
Sudan, although, like the Islamic Front, they believed these laws did
not go far enough. For instance, the disciples pointed out that the law
prescribed stoning for an adulterous woman, but the government
had no actual regulation on how these punishments were to be
carried out. "There are secular people in the government who have
actually allowed thieves to keep their hand," said one incredulous
youth.

I tried to be a good observer and keep my opinions to myself, but I
simply could not keep quiet. I finally blurted out a question of my
own, about the war in the south. "But what about non-Moslems in
your country?" I asked. "Should they be forced to abide by this
code?"

"Of course," said Mohammed pleasantly, "because these are uni-
versal laws. They are good laws."

"But they are a part of *your* culture. Take alcohol, for instance.
You believe drinking beer is a sin. The people in the south consider
beer to be part of *their* religion. Is it just to impose your religion on
them?"

Mohammed translated what I said to his fellow disciples. They
laughed with the confidence of the enlightened. The holy man
grinned like a pedagogue looking at a foolish student and muttered
his response, which Mohammed translated. "He says the black man
uses this as an excuse to get drunk, which is a sin. Even if it were not
a sin, getting drunk is unproductive. This is why our laws are
logical, I think."

Andy and I asked more questions, happy to see that their fanaticism did not preclude at least a discussion of other opinions. They calmly defended their faith, their rigid creed and their self-proclaimed right to impose it on the rest of the world, even if it meant war. Mohammed seemed to quote the Koran as easily as he had spewed slang. And, like other starry-eyed fanatics I had met on this trip, Mohammed and his friends claimed to have answers to every problem in the world, a frightening attitude I can tolerate only for a short time. Apparently, Andy could tolerate it even less, for we were barely finished with our coffee when he whispered to me that the air was getting stifling in here, and that he had to go before he said something that might get us into trouble.

After breakfast with the fanatics, Andy and I walked downtown to meet Hassan, who had insisted on giving us a nighttime tour of the city. He drove us about in a Toyota pickup, even though all the points in the tour were within easy walking distance. First stop was his brother-in-law's bakery, a surprisingly sophisticated plant that included several large, German-made stoves and elephant-sized vats for mixing dough. The shop produced enough loaves to feed most of the city, another example of this region's relative prosperity. Then, down the street we met the richest man in Shendi. He was a Scrooge-like fellow who, when we arrived in his shop, was counting stacks of money. I had asked Hassan to introduce me to some of the local politicians, and this man was Shendi's chairman of the ruling party, called Umma. It was a brief and uncomfortable meeting. "Why should I talk to foreigners?" he said with a grimace as he continued counting bills. We stood about awkwardly for a moment, with Hassan feeling deeply embarrassed. "Well, go on, get out!" said the distasteful man.

We had more luck with the leaders of the second largest party, the Democratic Union party. They were lounging on cots and blankets in front of a tea shop, gossiping and telling jokes. Everyone was smiling and laughing—old friends and political cronies tipping back teas with their mates. When we arrived, they grew more serious, answering questions about the war and the Islamic code, both of which they bitterly opposed. An intense older man named Achmed did most of the talking, though his friends tried several times to steer the conversation back to lighter topics. They seemed to be slipping in jokes here and there in Arabic, I think at Achmed's expense.

The conversation turned to the subject of Jaafar Nimeiri, the former dictator, born and raised near Shendi. At the mere mention of the despot's name, the men stopped their joking to spit in the sand. "That man was very, very evil," said Achmed. "I tell you something about him. His father lived nearby here. His father was a thief. Everyone here knows this. He used to rob the caravans on the forty days road.* He was very bad, the father, and his son was a worse man."

"Nimeiri hated Shendi," added a young man sitting on the ground. His English was careful and I sensed he was speaking to impress his elders. "You have heard of the new road coming up from Khartoum? This road was supposed to be built ten years ago, but Nimeiri did not like this area. We opposed his rule." The other men solemnly nodded and agreed. The young man, encouraged by their support, continued with vehemence. "So Nimeiri stopped the road. The Americans were building it, and they got as far as El Geili. Then the dictator told them to stop and he stole the money for himself."

"It is a fact," said Achmed, "that Nimeiri was the biggest criminal in Sudanese history." Each man then proceeded to tell his favorite Nimeiri story. Each tale got more incredible and usually ended with Nimeiri pocketing government money or throwing a hero in jail.

We finished the evening playing cards in the garden of the Shendi Club, where British merchants and officers once drank gin, toasted the queen and listened to cricket matches on the BBC. There was little left of the British presence, just an old bungalow and an abandoned bar inside. The British legacy all over Shendi was more tentative than in most of Africa. After all, this city was not created by the British, as were most cities in black Africa. It was already centuries old when they arrived, and matters such as architecture had long ago been settled. However, there were still little bits of empire strewn about, and one of them was the presence of a group of men sitting on the patio of a late Edwardian bungalow playing gin rummy.

We joined a young doctor named Sa'ad, who taught us how to play the Sudanese version of gin. Sa'ad had just come from Khartoum to manage Shendi's regional medical clinic and, as we played, he added his bit to the nation's list of woes. His particular complaints had to do with medicine in Sudan. "We have no money," he said, "so we have

---

* A nearby desert caravan route running between Shendi and Karima, another Nile town to the west. By camel, the journey takes forty days.

no medicine, no vaccinations, no bandages. It is a disaster. Here in Shendi, children die of malaria because we have no medicine."

Another man at our table—he won nearly every hand—smiled and accused Sa'ad of being overly pessimistic. He said that the problems in Sudan would take time to heal, but that democracy would eventually improve life. He was one of those fellows who dominate conversation once they have begun, and then take their leave before anyone can refute what they have said. When he excused himself, probably to find better players, the doctor said it was easy for this card shark to be hopeful. "He is wealthy and has sent his children to university in Europe. He prospered under Nimeiri and has done equally well under this democracy."

The doctor wanted to say more, but Hassan at this moment came by and whisked us away to the Toyota. "Now we go back to my home," he announced, "and I have a beautiful dessert prepared! It is a pastry of honey and wheat! We will eat and talk business! You will love it, and I will love it, I am sure!"

5   Andy and I boarded a train the next day bound for Wadi Halfa, near the Egyptian border. We had originally intended to cycle as far as Abu Hamad, three hundred miles to the north. But pedaling on this sand just to prove we could do it seemed pointless. And it was only supposed to get worse up north. Hassan had told us he had once tried running a bus service up to Atbara, but the vehicle kept getting stuck. "There are wadis up there that will swallow an entire bus, I tell you!" he had warned in his sweaty, bubbly manner. "Do not go by bicycle, my friends! It is too bad! Take the train, and that will be bad enough, I assure you."

We had arrived early at the old British station to get a chance at a first-class compartment, which Hassan said was not much, but was worth the extra five pounds. Having once traveled third-class on this very line, I readily agreed that anything was better than spending three days on a hard plank seat in a compartment filled with ten times the number of people it was intended for. Unfortunately, the ticket master insisted that he could not issue first- or second-class tickets. "Reservations can be made only in Khartoum," he said blandly. We suggested that he call Khartoum and make the reservations for us. "We have no phones working," he said. What about the telegraph? "Telegraph is down." He threatened to close his office if we didn't stop badgering him. "I only can sell third-class tickets," he said, suggesting that we board the first-class car when the train arrived. "You talk to porter, maybe he help you." He issued two third-class tickets and slammed down a wooden barrier to close his booth. The battered shutter still had faint words painted on it: POSITION CLOSED. PLEASE KEEP THIS STATION TIDY.

When the train arrived from Khartoum we discovered the source of the ticket master's frustration. There *were* no first-class compartments. To be sure, cars were identified according to class, with old markings on the outside in Arabic and English. But inside, an egalitarianism reigned that Julius Nyerere would have envied. Humans were crushed into every nook in every car, making the trains in Tanzania seem organized, tidy and spacious by comparison. Those who could not fit inside sat on the top of the train, perhaps a hundred people, their faces swathed in long scarves, their bodies wrapped in white cloth to reflect back the piercing rays of the sun.

John Gunther, when he came through in the mid-1950s, described his journey on this train as one of the most pleasant trips he had ever taken by rail. He praised the plush first-class compartments, elegant dining car, excellent food and decorous uniforms of the staff. I could hardly imagine that this half-wrecked excuse for a train had ever looked plush or elegant. The first-class accommodations had been stripped of everything that could be removed, including sinks, mirrors, commodes, doors and windows. Still, this hadn't stopped well-dressed Sudanese from reserving, paying for and occupying the formerly elite compartments. This pathetic attempt to keep up appearances resulted in the spectacle of feckless rich men sharing their bunks with as many as five other people, interlopers all. Humans were everywhere, squeezed into hallways, sprawled on compartment floors and huddled in the stripped-bare beds that the likes of John Gunther had once enjoyed. The dining car had disappeared completely, the elegant victuals and suave servants replaced by food hawkers who scrambled to sell steaming beans and tea when the train pulled into stations.

We were told that the stop in Shendi would be brief, so Andy and I hurried to load our bikes in the baggage car. We then rushed to find a spot in the first-class carriage corridor, only to find that it was already filled. We looked for a porter—I remembered the old, British-trained steward in Tanzania—but this was a fool's quest. So we wedged ourselves into one end of the corridor, constructing seats by stacking our bike packs like rickety thrones.

We should have known there was no need to rush into the train. Two hours later we were still waiting. The cause for our delay was a diesel engine that had blown a fuse. This meant we had to wait for another engine to appear from Khartoum. To pass the time and take our minds off our stiffening muscles, Andy and I played chess on a tiny magnetic board. I decided that Andy had brought this recreation with him from the States solely to humiliate me. Our game count stood at three to nothing in his favor by the time the second diesel arrived. As he was about to make it four to nothing our train finally lurched to a start, which not only saved me from further embarrassment but launched a whole new set of woes.

First was the dust, an impenetrable cloud filling the corridor to

gag and nearly suffocate even the staunchest Bedouin. Then, as the
train gathered speed on the old tracks, the carriage began to vibrate
and jerk. I was reminded of films I had seen of astronauts training in
centrifuges.

Andy and I were relieved a few stops down the line when a middle-
aged merchant from Khartoum invited us into his first-class compartment. We gratefully squeezed onto the comfort of a padded
bunk, but had to share it with two others the merchant had not
invited in. Later, as we grew more familiar with the merchant—
named Jaafar—I learned that he had actually paid more money for a
first-class ticket, almost ten dollars more than everyone else in his
cabin. I asked him why he tolerated things like no doors and uninvited guests. "What can I do?" he said. "There is no way to stop them.
Certainly, I am ashamed in front of you for the condition of this train.
But this is the Sudan. We are poor, so we cannot expect much."

Andy and I played a lot of chess on the train, but the best I could do
was a draw when Andy got bored and let me corner his king. My
losses grew more humbling as an audience drew around us to watch
the games, a steady flow of students and others who came and went
from our cabin to watch the *hwages* and to offer me advice on how to
beat the champion. Soon our games became an important amusement. Everyone cheered when a teenager named Achmed beat Andy.
The boy was so enthralled that he became a fixture in our entourage,
hardly leaving us for the entire trip to Egypt.

That night, Andy and I—joined by Jaafar, Achmed and one other
man—tried to sleep on a bunk built for one Englishman. The night
cooled off and the dust continued to shoot into my nostrils and
mouth. About ten P.M. our fourth diesel broke down in a tiny Nile
village called Kabinda.

The trouble with the engine involved that same little fuse. Once
again, no one had thought to bring a spare. Unable to sleep, I walked
up to the engineer to inquire about this latest problem. As I approached I could see that one of his men had rigged a feed line to the
telegraph running beside the tracks. However, no one seemed to be
sending any messages. Apparently, a fifth engine was required to
continue our journey, but the telegraph was down.

"So what will you do?" I asked, realizing we were at least a hundred miles from any depot.

"We must wait for another train to pass," the engineer said, "to
deliver a message to Atbara."

"How long will that take?"

"Maybe one hour, maybe five hours, maybe all night. I do not know. Maybe someone will come in five minutes, if Allah is willing."

Two days and three diesels later (total engines: seven) we reached our destination at Wadi Halfa, a cluster of shacks and military radar grids situated on the rocky desert just south of Egypt. Wadi Halfa is a new town, constructed in the seventies when Lake Nasser flooded the original, British-built city along the Nile. Egypt had provided the money for this, part of a $50 million reparations payment for river shoreline lost to the lake. I was told in Khartoum that most of this sum had gone to Nimeiri's account in Switzerland, an allegation that seemed plausible given the condition of Wadi Halfa. It was hard to believe that any money had been spent on the town, which looked like a squatters' camp. There were no truly permanent buildings, other than the train station and a small police/military complex. I saw no visible means of support in this wasteland for the several hundred residents, other than fish from the lake and the twice-weekly train.

When our train arrived in Wadi Halfa, three hundred and fifty exhausted passengers tumbled out of the cars and into the pale dawn light. We stretched our legs and tried to restore circulation, the more energetic among us strolling into town to check on the lake steamer to Egypt. This twice-weekly boat theoretically meets each train from Khartoum, although neither boat nor train was ever on schedule. Our situation was no exception. Not only were we two days late, but no steamer had arrived from Aswan for several days. "They have had a breakdown," said a sleepy shipping agent. He added that the previously scheduled ship, due in Wadi Halfa four days earlier, also had not arrived. As this news circulated, those people who knew Halfa began to move toward the town's two hotels. Others too poor for a fifty-cent bed moved to set up small tents and bedrolls beside the tracks.

Andy and I joined the migration across the heavy sands to the Nile Hotel, but found it already filled with passengers waiting for the earlier steamer. "Shit and other expletives," said Andy in a tired voice as a harassed innkeeper told us to go away. We pushed our bikes into the inn's tea shop in search of food, as we had had very little to eat on the train, catching only snacks of sticky rolls and spiced beans. Someone had painted bright pictures on the tea shop's adobe walls, depictions of our train, the missing steamer, several palm trees and a pair of blond Arabs in white tunics smoking Marlboro cigarettes.

The innkeeper found space for us after all, meaning that we got two lice-ridden cots and a room to lock up our equipment. As in the National Inn the cots were crammed into a large courtyard, although this yard was much more congested.

The lake steamer arrived two days later, about the time Wadi Halfa was running out of food. It took three or four hours to load eight hundred Sudanese travelers onto the steamer, the *Shalizar*, which had been built to accommodate perhaps two hundred people. The boat was composed of two barges attached to a central barque. This makeshift craft had seen better days, although it was modern compared to the ship I had taken across Lake Nasser on my earlier journey in 1982. That ship that had been so decrepit and unsafe it had sunk shortly after my voyage. Apparently, one of the many individual cooking fires on board had ignited barrels of gasoline being transported to Nimeiri's gas-starved country. The ship had exploded just south of Abu Simbel, killing hundreds of people. Not only did many die from fire, many more died of scorpion bites when they swam to the desert shore.

Because of that earlier catastrophe, the *Shalizar* outlawed individual cooking fires. However, in an act of unexplained stupidity, the shipping company had failed to supply any sort of alternative to personal food preparation. In fact, it had neglected to provide any food at all. Nor was there anything to drink, not even water. The onboard plumbing had long ago stopped functioning, and there were no buckets for scooping water out of the lake. To make matters worse, the ship had only one semifunctioning latrine that very quickly became awash with excrement.

When I discovered that eight hundred people had been furnished with no food, no water and no toilet facilities for a journey that might last as long as three days, my African-style patience dissolved into a huff of Yankee indignation. Personally, we had water in our bags for a few hours in the 125-degree heat. We also had snacks—*snacks*—for maybe a day, having been told there would be food aboard. As it was, the people around us, who had brought little or no water for themselves, began asking in the polite, sorrowful, Sudanese fashion for part of our water. We gave it away until a line formed and we had nearly exhausted our supply.

After a while, Andy got an idea. He tied a rope to our cooking pot, using it as a bucket to scoop water from the lake, rushing past about thirty feet below the deck. We worked for two or three hours at the bucket, pulling water aboard for at least a hundred people. Several boys helped us fill containers and toss the bucket. It became something of a game after a while to see who could throw the bucket and draw up the water without spilling a drop. Then one of the boys forgot to hold onto the rope, and that was the end of our water. At first, the boy was horrified, but all of the others thought it was very funny. Soon half the boat seemed to be in on the joke.

I was furious. "What is so goddamned funny?" I shouted at the crowd that had gathered around us. "You have just lost your only water source! Do you see this sun? Do you want to die?" This made everyone laugh harder, to see a sunburned *hwage* in such a rage.

Later, when I had cooled off, Jaafar found me and asked why I had been so angry. I told him I had been traveling in Africa for months, and had been appalled by the passivity of some Africans, allowing themselves to be kicked about like dogs. "I simply do not understand this attitude," I said. "In America, we complain constantly. Occasionally, it even gets us somewhere."

"Tell me, Jaafar," I continued, "how much did you pay for your ticket on this boat?"

"One hundred fifty pounds," he said. (This was about fifteen dollars, an enormous sum in Sudan.)

"Everyone on this ship paid one hundred fifty pounds," I said. "That means the owners are making a total of, ah . . ."

"One hundred twenty thousand pounds," said Andy, who is good at numbers.

"That means," I continued, "that they are making each year about . . ."

"A million pounds," said Andy.

"Weeeooow," exclaimed Jaafar, "is this true? That is so much money—one million pounds?" He translated this figure to the Sudanese gathered around, who passed it around in a low grumble.

"What are you getting for that amount of money?" I asked, feeling that I was finally getting somewhere with these people. "A hard deck to sleep on, no water, no food, no shelter from the sun and no latrines."

"But what would you have us do?" said Jaafar. "We are a poor, uneducated people. The Egyptians run this boat. They will not listen to us."

"Man, why not give it a try?" said Andy. "What do you have to lose?"

As Jaafar was about to answer, an old man in a dusty tunic and turban tugged on his sleeve. He asked to speak, but did not know English, so Jaafar offered to translate. The man sat down on the deck as if this were a campfire in his village, and we all joined him.

"He says he has a story to tell," said Jaafar, translating. "It is a local story about a frog and a scorpion." The old man's squealing voice spoke slowly in Arabic, his yellow eyes lively, his wrinkled hands moving in exclamation. Several others sat down to listen.

"This old father says there was long ago a scorpion who was trapped on a small island during the flood of *el Niel*, the great river. As the waters rose, the scorpion feared that he would be drowned. He saw a frog swimming past and called him over." The old man changed his voice to a hiss to imitate the scorpion, which made the children around us giggle.

" 'Frog, please come over. You must help me.' "

The old man changed to a frog's deep bleat. " 'Scorpion, do you think I am mad?' said the frog. 'If I come to help you, you will sting me with your tail, and I will die.'

" 'Frog, I will not sting you.' " The hiss was back now. " 'Look at this island. It is flooding and soon I will drown. If you will carry me to the land on your back, I will not sting you. We would both drown if I did. Do you understand?'

"So the frog agreed to help the scorpion, and took him on his back. They swam for some time. And when they were almost to shore the scorpion suddenly stung the frog.

" 'Scorpion, oh, scorpion, why did you sting me?' said the frog as they slowly sank together. 'Now we both will die.'

" 'Why did I sting you?' said the scorpion as they slid into the water to drown. 'Because, my dear frog, *this is the Sudan.*' "

The old man finished with a flourish and a wise smile. Jaafar and the others laughed. I smiled sadly and said that this was a very unhappy story. "I do not think it is funny," I said.

"You are right, of course," said Jaafar. "It is not funny, but it is true."

"Then I am sorry for Sudan," I said, "very sorry indeed."

VIII
Egypt
*Nothing
Is the Same*

All the same, Egypt is better than opium. It soothes and smoothes one's creases out with the patient weight of a German philosopher trying to be intelligible.
—Henry Adams

Certain areas of Egypt are cultivated by irritation.
—Egyptian schoolboy

Since my last visit, Egypt has begun the transformation from living in eternity to living in the present.
—Journal Entry

1 A day out from Wadi Halfa, the *Shalizar*'s diesel
engines stopped and the steamer began to list to starboard. The
captain, Mohammed, seemed unconcerned. We were sitting with
him on blankets in front of the bridge as his crewmen worked on the
engines. At noon the sun beat down hard on the thirsty, hungry ship.
Passengers huddled under canopies and tried to sleep as the captain
complained to us about this dead-end assignment.

"I hate this stinking ship," he said, telling us that he had officered
aboard numerous ships traveling as far away as the States, Brazil and
India. He was a short, plump man who looked more Mediterranean
than Arab. He wore Western clothes, spoke excellent English and
held his face aloof, like a minor patrician.

"I have taken this assignment only because my wife is complaining about long trips abroad," he said. "You know wives. They can
make life, well, let us say disagreeable. So I am doing these shorter
runs on this large, empty lake. I make the same pay—captain's pay—
but look at this disgusting ship and these dirty people." He swept his
hand over the decks and curled his lip. "The Sudanese are a pitiful
people. Like children who have been left out in the sun too long.
Look at them . . ." He shook his head. "They are pitiful."

"Actually, Captain, I think they *have* been sitting out in the sun
too long," I remarked, "and I imagine that they are quite thirsty. Did
you know that there is no water on board for the passengers? And no
food?"

"Is that right?" he said with a disinterested yawn. "Well, that is
regrettable. But this is an old ship, and it *is* Ramadan. Many people
are fasting. We would only be tempting the common people if we
provided too much food." He lay back on his blanket, closed his eyes
and continued talking. "You know, I am fasting myself, though under
the rules of Ramadan travelers are allowed to eat and drink. But I fast
anyway, for I am what you might call a reformed hedonist. Yes, it is
true. Many sailors become hedonists. But religion has saved me from
my former vices, so I follow the fast to cleanse myself. Fasting is
quite cleansing, you know. It clears out all of the bad things that have 303

collected in our bodies." He opened his eyes a crack and gave us the look of an English lord about to recommend a favorite bottle of sherry. "You really should try it, you know."

"Not in this heat," I muttered. But the captain didn't hear me. He had already fallen asleep.

The repairs took most of the day while eight hundred people sweltered. The water around the ship became littered with trash and defecation. Several people passed out from heat exhaustion. Andy and I had to administer water and salt, since the ship's paltry first-aid kit consisted of nothing for heat relief. Throughout all of this, the captain of the *Shalizar* remained unconcerned. When I suggested that the crew locate a bucket for drawing up water, he missed my point, thinking that it was Andy and me who were thirsty. He ordered a crewman to bring us Pepsis from his private stock, though they were so hot the carbonation made my stomach ache.

That night, the captain offered two more gifts—a ratty cabin near his own and a small helping of cold, gray beans in red plastic bowls. The latter were leftovers from the crew's Ramadan breakfast. We ate guiltily, thinking of our hungry shipmates. As we finished the captain suggested that we provide a monetary gift to the crew. He also indicated that a gift to the purser was in order for our new cabin, a hothouse we didn't even want, other than as a place for the safe storage of our equipment.

Then there was the matter of Egyptian pounds. The captain was willing to assist us in exchanging dollars at the black market rate, though we needed to reward the appropriate officer with a small tip for services rendered. "Everyone must have his gratuity," smiled the captain, as the beans and hot Pepsi began to percolate in my abdomen. "This is Egypt."

Later that night I woke up in a cold sweat. We were sleeping on the upper deck of the ship, behind the bridge, with about fifty other men (no women up here). Since I had gone to sleep, not long after dusk, the moon had risen to illuminate the ship. The lake was the gentle silver color of a pearl. It was probably a lovely sight, but I wasn't in a disposition to notice, because my stomach felt as if it were about to erupt. I fled down to the single latrine on the boat and found it so crammed with excrement that I could not get inside. I ran down to our baking cabin, which had once been a quite comfortable place, complete with fans, shower, sink and—there it was!—a sit-down toilet. The plumbing had long ago stopped functioning, but I was in no position to care. I was not the first to ignore the fact that it no longer functioned. Fortunately, Egypt has a very dry climate, which desiccates excrement as thoroughly as the flesh of a mummy.

I was sick for the rest of the voyage, and spent most of my time sitting on the broken toilet in that sweltering room. For toilet paper I used pages from Kurt Vonnegut's *Slaughterhouse Five*. I would read a page, tear it out and apply it to my bum, filling the toilet with the story of Billy Pilgrim and the fire-bombing of Dresden. Somehow, I think Vonnegut would have appreciated that I put his book to such good use.

We arrived in Aswan below the High Dam late in the afternoon. Being still sick and anxious to get off the boat, we began to pack up to go ashore, a notion that was soon nixed by the captain. "I am so sorry," he said, "but it is after three o'clock. Customs has closed for the day. We will be spending the night once again on this beautiful ship." He then shouted an order for his men to dock at a small, rocky island in the Aswan harbor.

I was outraged, having recovered my indignation despite my grumbling GI tract. It seemed incredible that the customs office could not stay open an extra hour or two to process eight hundred emaciated people on a ship already two days late, particularly since the authorities had little else to do in this less-than-bustling port.

I thought about going to the captain, but felt tired of asking the question "Why?" I had been asking "Why?" so frequently in Sudan that my head ached. Besides, it was time to go and read another few pages of *Slaughterhouse Five*. My only fear was that I would get ahead of myself and miss part of the story.

The next day, customs took its time, and did not finish until early afternoon. This was particularly unpleasant for Andy and me, as we were processed last. Apparently, the arrival of Westerners from Sudan was so unusual in these unsettled times that the officials at Aswan had no idea what to do with us. Andy and I sat in the hot, fly-drenched dining room on board the *Shalizar* for nearly the entire day. When we were finally allowed off the ship, we were escorted by an

armed guard to the customs office, a modern monolith that reminded me of the Chinese-built railway stations in Zambia. The
building seemed grossly out of proportion with a port that consisted
of only our steamer and perhaps a dozen fishing boats. Obviously,
whoever designed and spent good money on the project had expected
a somewhat more vigorous trade to develop on this desert lake.

We were escorted to an office and placed under another guard. He
was a young man, gawking and unsure of himself, and certainly no
match for two irate Americans fed up with authorities. Nothing
short of a shot in the back would have made us sit quietly and wait
for a gang of bureaucrats to notice we were still there. So after a few
minutes of badgering, the boy-soldier fled his post and disappeared
through a doorway, never to return. He told us to wait, but we had
been doing that since dawn. "Let's get the hell out of here," I said,
and we began pushing our bikes toward the big front doors of the
building.

Three or four guards appeared, waving guns at us. Their leader—
sergeant's stripes were safety-pinned to his ill-fitting uniform—told
us we still had to pass through customs. We said, "Fine, take us to
'em!" But he used that word again—*wait*. "Wait for what?" asked
Andy. "Until we die of thirst?"

"You want water?" asked the sergeant, to which we vigorously
answered in the affirmative. "We have water here," he said, pointing
to a nearby kiosk. A soldier was deployed to take me over, but the
kiosk was locked. I suggested that the sergeant go and fetch the key.

"So sorry, no key."

"What do you mean, 'no key'?"

"So sorry," he repeated with a weary smile I remembered quite
vividly from my earlier trip to Egypt, a smile that said, "If only it
were not so hot, and if only I were paid more, and if life were not such
a bother . . . then, maybe I would help you. But as it is . . ."

Finally, we found a sweating official in a safari suit who told us to
be calm. He sent out for hot tea—*hot* tea—and explained that we
were being delayed because the customs office had no bank forms for
us to fill out. "We get few Westerners through here," he explained,
stamping our passports and clearing us through the other formal-
ities.

"When will someone arrive with the forms?" I asked, feeling a
little better now that progress was being made.

"Tomorrow, I think," said the man.

"Tomorrow!" Andy and I exploded.

"I am so sorry," he said.

"No, *we* are sorry," said Andy, abruptly standing. "We are going into town *now.* There is no way in hell we are staying out here until tomorrow. We are going to the Abu Simbel Hotel in Aswan. Have the forms sent to us there and we will be happy to fill them out tomorrow. Good day."

He grabbed my arm and before I could say anything we were marching with our bicycles past the befuddled guards, out the door and into the street. Behind us, the official in the safari suit came jogging after us, his weary, Egyptian smile curled into an uncharacteristic expression of alarm. "Please, please," he was shouting, "perhaps we can get the bank forms soon! Today! This afternoon! They will be here just now! Please come back!" As it turned out, they miraculously appeared when the official who had them was awakened from his nap.

2   We emerged from customs and found ourselves in a raucous, squalid bazaar of stalls, bellicose hawkers and swarms of insects. After Sudan, which might be described as a man lying comatose in the sun, Egypt greeted us like a man who has just had a hit of amphetamines. One hawker nearly knocked me down in his haste to peddle a slab of rancid meat, which he dangled in front of my face like a wet, gangrened rag. Another fellow chased us like a madman for over a hundred meters, bellowing in my ear and waving a pair of bright red plastic sandals. "You buy shoe! You buy shoe!" Then there were the children, their *gallebeyahs* soiled and torn, their voices squealing hysterically, their little fingers reaching out to touch us and pinch us as if we were circus freaks.

On my previous trip, I often had pondered this proclivity toward frenzy in Egypt, this wildness that was not mean-spirited nor angry, but was nonetheless an intense, reckless sort of inquisitiveness. How could a country with a centuries-old reputation for languor be so rambunctious? I dreaded the prospect of facing all this for a second time in less than a decade, all the more so because it tended to be so random. One could spend hours bicycling peacefully along a lazy stretch of the Nile, passing lazy villages, glistening fields and quiet people when suddenly the world would explode with shrieks, pounding feet and laughter as a dozen children came spilling onto the highway—"Hello, meester . . . hello, meester . . ."

We shook off the last of the wailing kids as our road veered into the abrupt desolation of the desert. The transformation was very much like I remembered Egypt, a country where green and brown abut one another like water and fire. Roads here in the south have a way of weaving in and out between the clamor of river enclaves and the enigmatic stillness of the wastelands. It was as if the builder had a metaphysical bent, channeling travelers in and out of life and death on easy curves of asphalt.

Aswan is about twelve miles north of the High Dam, a distance that seemed very long indeed that morning. Though we had had a chance to rest in the customs building, we still felt weak and nauseous from the *Shalizar* ordeal. It was about three in the afternoon, a time at which only the most foolish people are moving about. Yet we were anxious to get to Aswan, particularly if the alternative was to wait in the wild bazaar at the dam.

After leaving customs, things went from bad to worse. What we wanted most was to find food and drink, preferably in a quiet stall, a difficult task when the desert stretched on and on. A mile or two from the dam, we ran into a government road crew laying hot, stinking asphalt. To stand anywhere near this new pavement was like getting drenched in flames. I was astonished to see these men out in the heat of the day, a gang of men shoveling asphalt onto the road, a second team steamrollering it flat and a third spraying it with tar. The crew chief explained that they were so close to completing the road they did not want to stop. "We work on this road for so long," he said, "and this is the day we finish." He beamed proudly. "We have laid one thousand kilometers since Cairo."

Later, as we pedaled north toward Cairo, I would see that these men had good reason to be proud. It was an excellent road, a testament to the fact that progress is being made in Egypt. Wide, flat and neatly tapered on the edges, it was a highway that would make cycling a pleasure for a man with memories of jagged, narrow, crowded highways in Egypt. However, the benefits of the new asphalt were mitigated that afternoon by the heat of the steaming hot surface. I measured the temperature six inches above the pavement. "My God," I said to Andy, "it's a hundred forty-five degrees!"

Aswan is typical of Egyptian enclaves along the Nile. Cities here are not arranged in the usual circle motif, with a wealthy core surrounded by rings of progressive poverty. Instead, the cities of Egypt are arranged in strips, with a thread of prosperity alongside the river and then a series of gradually more squalid strips laid side by side, spreading out into the desert.

We entered the city through a bedraggled outer strip of Bedouins, whose makeshift enclaves hovered on the edges of the settled valley.

As in Sudan, the lean, leonine Bedouin stared at us like people in Walker Evans' photos of the Deep South, their eyes dark, clear and banefully expressive. Camels bellowed mournfully as we pedaled past, their feet hobbled together by hemp rope to keep them from wandering off.

The next layer of the city, the industrial layer, took us ahead several centuries. One moment we were amid a hazy, desert world and the next we were cycling in the shadow of a phosphates factory. It looked like a boiling caldron, with tangled pipes jutting everywhere and cooling towers steaming and emitting fumes. This factory was followed by several others, part of a massive complex in Aswan that draws power from the High Dam's turbines.

I was impressed by this display of industrial virility. It was unlike anything I had seen on this continent since South Africa, and was much improved since my visit in 1982. It verified what I had heard, that Egypt was becoming a minor industrial power, manufacturing a plethora of shoddy but functional products that were exported throughout Africa and the Near East: paper, fertilizer, piping, plastics and household items. MADE IN EGYPT is not exactly a sign of excellence around the world, but it is a testament to the fact that this ancient nation is beginning to stumble into the modern world, however precariously.

However, some things hadn't changed. One was the sheer number of people. Humans seemed to be stuffed into every nook and cranny, their shacks wedged between factories, leaning against shops and clustered under palms. I'll not dwell here on Egypt's propensity for reproduction. I have had my say on this subject in earlier chapters. But I will toss out a few statistics. Egypt's current population is fifty million people—the population of California, New York and Massachusetts combined—growing at an annual rate of 3.5 percent. This means that in the five years since my first visit, the population had increased by eight million people—about 15 percent. Since Andy's last visit, in 1974, the population had increased by nearly twenty million—40 percent! The frightening thing is that all of these people are squeezed into a narrow valley whose total area is slightly more than that of New Hampshire.

Then there was the phenomenon of dust in Egypt, of which I had strong memories. It was everywhere, raised into the air in great clouds by fifty million feet, a million motorized vehicles and millions of domestic beasts. It coated factories, skin, houses and clothing, afflicting man and animal, rich and poor alike in the uniform beige that gives the country its distinctively shabby appearance.

There were a few flashes of color to break the monotony. Since the time of the pharaohs, Egyptians have coveted vivid tinctures. Ancient tombs, temples, churches and mosques are often luridly resplendent, though for most of Egyptian history color was a rare and expensive indulgence, a prerogative of rulers and holy men. This has changed with the advent of modern plastics. Today, the most modest Egyptian can attain bright hues beyond the reach of the most powerful pharaoh or sultan of days gone by: Dacron sweaters colored turquoise, washing pans blazing tangerine, plastic sandals flashing mauve in the sun.

The specter of dirt inexplicably remained as we passed from the industrial areas of Aswan into a residential neighborhood alongside a rancid canal, one of hundreds in Egypt that turn dirt into the greater scourge of mud. This black ooze, the lifeblood of Egypt, contains both nutrients for agriculture and microbes of most every disease known to mankind. Coming from as far away as Kenya and Tanzania on the shores of Lake Victoria, the mud is carried by the waters of the Nile for over three thousand miles before reaching Aswan. This particular canal was lined with a string of apartment buildings as filthy and reeking as any in Egypt, though they were of recent construction. A blue-collar neighborhood, it was part of the "new" Egypt that had also been responsible for the factories and the revamped highway. Yet it already had the look of the older quarters of town, with its stained walls, heaps of trash and mangy animals wandering about eating garbage.

This filth seemed a contradiction to the spirit of development, though I remembered what an Egyptian merchant once told me about dirt. "It is a way of life in our country," he said, "an ancient scourge that we accept. In America, you are so very sensitive to dirt. You think we are uncivilized because we do not share this preoccupation. (You are sensitive to much I do not understand, life being so short.) But you have many places to escape from the dirt. We have only our valley, which is surrounded by hundreds of kilometers of dirt. Over so many centuries, we have grown weary of fighting it."

Shortly after passing through the canal neighborhood, I convinced Andy to turn off the main road and ride around on some of the side streets near the river, a twisting, turning maze of alleyways that

represented yet another stratum of Aswan. It reminded me of medieval towns in Europe and what they must have looked like before the
imposition of concrete, street-cleaning machines and regulations
governing the disposition of animals on city streets. The roads were
unpaved, grimy and filled with goats, chickens, children and women
dressed head to toe in black. The buildings were two to five stories
tall, constructed out of adobe and weathered wood. They were
bunched together so closely that this oldest part of the city was
plunged into a mysterious shadow-world of black and gray. Every
once in a while the alleyways would suddenly end and the sky would
appear, revealing mosques standing huge, shining and immaculate
like cathedrals in ancient Europe.

After a half hour of winding our way through the dark, dank
streets we abruptly emerged onto the corniche along the river, a
world of light and enervating sunshine. With the suddenness of a
turn and a pedal we again passed through several centuries, emerging
from Old Egypt on to a broad, tree-lined avenue lined by glimmering
high-rises and bustling with Toyotas, well-dressed Egyptians and
dozens of pale faces from my own land. Along the smooth-running,
brown-blue waters was a newly built system of wharves and levees
where hotel cruisers were filled with tourists drinking cocktails and
sunning on the decks. In the middle of the river was an island
covered by lush foliage and beyond it, on the opposite bank, a bluff of
sand colored pure gold.

Andy and I headed for the Abu Simbel Hotel, an inexpensive
haven for travelers on the lam. We pushed our bikes right into the
lobby, where a group of hairy Caucasians were smoking hookahs and
eating scrambled eggs. This group was more frayed and hollow-eyed
than those fresh faces I had seen in East Africa, Aswan being a
favorite collection point for the grit and grime school of western
travel. We pushed past them and went upstairs, where both of us
collapsed still dressed onto our beds. And there we stayed for almost
twenty hours, until a worried hotel manager knocked on the door to
make sure we were still alive.

There had been a number of changes in Aswan since my last visit.
In 1982, Aswan had had a more ramshackle, undeveloped, Casbah
feeling. Now that atmosphere was partially diluted by new buildings
and modern shops brimming with numerous Western goods. There

also was a noticeable absence of soldiers, who had been as numerous as tourists, with machine-gun emplacements guarding key intersections and bridges. But perhaps the greatest change was in the people.

The Egypt I remembered was a nation of extremes—fundamentalists versus secularists, militarists versus peaceniks, modern methods versus ancient traditions. Now, after a half-decade of Mubarak's low-key, technocratic leadership, which had included a substantial loosening of economic and political bonds, the tension seemed to have evaporated. The flamboyant Nasser and Sadat were dead, the nation was at peace with Israel, and for the first time in a generation Egypt was spending its money and energy on something other than warfare, international intrigue and half-cocked economic schemes. The astounding shift from acrimony to contentment was most evident in the teahouses of Aswan, where conversations were surprisingly ordinary. In 1982, I had heard only frustrations and complaints, the conversations being almost exclusively about politics.

Part of this complacency was due to the new prosperity evident in the streets, where an entire class of people seemed to have been created, a stratum that looked almost middle class. This in a country that had once embraced socialism as thoroughly as Tanzania and Zambia. It was a rather sloppy, lower middle class to be sure, reminding me of similar groups in Mexico and India, people who were three-quarters educated and flagrantly bourgeois. (Every man owned the largest gold watch he could afford, and every young man I spoke to lusted after a boom box and a television of his very own.) Nevertheless, their presence was welcome, not only because they represented a broad-based increase in Egypt's standard of living, but because they offered proof for Africa that there was life after socialism.

Of course, there was a downside to this "new" Egypt. "Every man wants to live like a pharaoh," said a professor I met in Cairo, a Nasserite disgusted by the new hunger for money in his country. "But when he dies, he does not want to be buried with only gold statues and chariots. He wants to be buried with his radio, his car, his gold watch and, most of all, with his television. Oh, he must have his television! Otherwise, he would miss the weekly 'Dallas' episode, a thought that is unbearable, even in death."

Today, politics stood equally with topics ranging from soccer to American television. "Yes, we still complain about the government," said a businessman in one teashop, "but it is more like women complain about being cheated in the market. 'That dog, he cheated me out of a kilogram of wheat,' says my wife. But this is nothing to lose sleep over." The changes in Aswan were even more dramatic for Andy, who had last been here early in 1974, not long after the Yom Kippur War against Israel. When he arrived by Land Rover from Sudan, the country still was reeling from the war. Though Nasser was recently dead and Sadat was considering a move toward the West, the shadow of the colonel and his vision of an austere, socialist Egypt still loomed large.

In those days, Andy recalled, there were no high-rises on the Aswan corniche—no wharves, no tourists and few automobiles. The only Europeans were a few dissolute Aussies. The Russians, who had numbered in the thousands during the High Dam project, recently had been ousted by Anwar el-Sadat. This left mostly soldiers to populate a city that was considerably smaller than it is today. Andy remembered tanks lining the corniche, antiaircraft guns dotting the bluffs across the river and MiG fighters regularly flying overhead, scanning the skies for Israeli jets. Andy and his friends had been watched closely by the secret police. They had been forced to put their Rover on a flat car to Cairo because the Egyptians forbade overland travel by foreigners in private vehicles.

"All I remember is paranoia," Andy told me. "I hardly even re-member what Aswan physically looked like, except that none of these buildings were here along the river, and there was nothing Western in the stores. Yet there was this *fear.* Everyone was scared to death to talk to us. They avoided us like we were diseased. After a while we just wanted to get the hell out of here."

We lingered for several days in Aswan, resting beside the river, sailing lethargically in a felucca named *Sinbad* and sipping cocktails on the veranda of the old Cataract Hotel, where the likes of Winston Churchill and Rudyard Kipling once watched the sun drop above the ancient ruins on Elephantine Island. Unfortunately, the view was not quite what it used to be. In the "new" Egypt, the sun fell not into the desert, but into the gaudily lit terrace of a Club Med across the river. Yet the effect was still captivating as the sky ignited into great, solid bands of pink, gold and an absinthe shade of green.

At these moments, the sky over Egypt, normally a hard, sterile, unbroken cast of blue, became remarkably sensual, as if the sky were one of the fleshy, colorful courtesans Flaubert became infatuated with during his sojourn here in 1850. As I sat on the Cataract veranda in a great wicker chair, listening to the whir of ceiling fans and drinking brandy served by Nubians with polished skin, I could almost place myself in Flaubert's Egypt, land of harems and corpulent sultans wrapped in silks. It was a place where sensuality was a science more refined than war and government, where Abyssinian women were preferred because their flesh was always cool, and the young Gustave could pass a night in "dream-like intensity" simply staring at a turpentine-scented dancer lying fast asleep beside him.

It was the Egypt of Flaubert that subconsciously guided my days in Aswan. I had come to Egypt to do more than to explore the romantic fantasies of a young European, one who spent most of his time sampling the delights of Oriental decadence. It was not so much Flaubert's debauchery that intrigued me, but his appreciation of the beauty, cruelty and passion of everyday life along the Nile.

Little remains today of Flaubert's Egypt. The sultans and their great, brutal estates are gone—Nasser saw to that. The Oriental harems, opium houses and other vestiges of Turkish decadence have been expunged—fundamentalist Muslims saw to that. There is a new class of the very rich in Egypt—Sadat and Mubarak have seen to that—but they resemble Western elites more than exotic princes, and they wisely keep their pleasures to themselves, living in palm-shrouded mansions outside the cities. As for those colorful courtesans that so intrigued the young French novelist, they, too, have been squashed by modern Egypt. There were, however, the usual prostitutes hanging about, scruffy ones in the *chai* shops and more sophisticated sorts in certain tourist hotels, though none of these were the types of women one could imagine staring at all night in "a dream-like intensity."

Yet there is one element of Flaubert's Egypt still thriving in this city, one that continues to represent a vitality and excitement largely unmitigated by time. I am talking about the *souks* of Aswan, the great, frolicking, chaotic markets stretching for blocks and blocks behind the placid facade of the modern corniche. This was the living legacy of the city, the true link to the ages that the ancient monuments of Egypt could never match. It is here that living dreams and legends swirl at the edge of reality, where ghosts and the pale shadows of imagination become flesh and blood.

Part of the allure of the bazaar was its abrupt appearance just off the corniche. It was startling to step off the modern riverbank and into a tawdry, somewhat updated version of *The Arabian Nights*. There was a childlike thrill in strolling past stalls stuffed with everything from camel saddles to television sets, and with people dressed in garb as dichotomous as Bedouin robes and rayon leisure suits.

Another source of fascination was the age of this place. It seemed not only old, but profoundly permanent. Unlike most large cities I am familiar with, I could not imagine Aswan as anything but a city. It did not seem recently carved out of the landscape like most urban areas in Africa, but an integral part of it, a geological feature as natural as the desert and the river. This extended to the people as well, inasmuch as they were city dwellers, beings who seemed as imperishable as the stones and dust of the *souk*.

The truth is that Aswanians (and other Egyptian urbanites) adore being city people. They thrive on being squeezed in among thousands of other people on a narrow, crowded riverbank, whereas most people on the planet are decidedly uncomfortable in this environment, preferring at least some small measure of greenery and open sky. Of course, Egyptians have been living for several millennia in this fashion, long before my ancestors in Europe even had a word for "city."

Oddly enough, they reminded me of New Yorkers, a more recent urban breed who likewise derive their personality from their city, and who would be lost in too much foliage and clean air. Yet there is a major difference between New Yorkers and Aswanians. The latter seem considerably less frustrated than the former. To them this whole business of city life seemed as natural as copulation and praying—two activities that Egyptians excel at, being both exceptionally prolific and very religious. Urbanity to them was like a great game, something that could be enjoyed if one did not take it too seriously. Perhaps this attitude was merely a matter of experience and maturity. If Aswan were human, it would be a great-great-grandfather among cities, while New York hardly would qualify as an embryo, being at least five thousand years Aswan's junior. This should give New Yorkers some comfort that in two or three thousand years they, too, may learn to laugh at long lines and smile contentedly when assaulted by street peddlers selling futuristic baubles in the crumbling *souks* of ancient Manhattan.

I found myself wandering through the twisted streets nearly every afternoon and evening, stopping in shops and *chai* stands to talk and play long games of backgammon. Little actually happened during these excursions, and little was said that is worth recording. But it is worth imparting at least one short image of my bazaar strolls, and none is more suitable than of the afternoon I spent with a man who made ax handles.

The ax maker was middle-aged and large-boned, having the physique of a graying wrestler, an anatomical plus when one spends a great deal of time manhandling wood. I had met him during a bout of backgammon in a tea shop, and he had invited me to visit his shop, where he promised to show me everything I needed to know about his trade. Under the slowly waning sun he taught me how to clamp a raw piece of wood—about the size of an eland's leg—into an aged vise made long ago in Liverpool. He then showed me how to take a small, sicklelike tool and chop away at the ingot until I had fashioned it into the general shape. Then came more refined knives, chisels and finally a large file to smooth it down. The final step was to rub the wood with a resiny oil until it glowed dully in the sun.

While working on my ax handle, I briefly joined the world at the corner of this small *souk*. To the left of the ax man's stall was a tailor, with a massive, aquiline nose and craggy eyes. To the right was a tin vendor with a bald head and toothless grin. Across the narrow street was a grisly, sardonic shoeshiner who smelled as if he had not bathed in his entire life, though he wore a flashy blue tunic. These fellows were old friends who had spent most of their days chattering and joking together. I could not understand them—they spoke only a few words of English—but this didn't matter, for they were undoubtedly covering the same topics cronies talk about everywhere. The shoeshiner, I imagined, was complaining about the weather and the tardiness of the tea boy, while the tin man—his shop was the most prosperous on the corner—was showing off a large gold watch he had just purchased. The tailor, whose nose hovered precariously close to the needle on his Singer machine, spent most of his time snickering at the shoe shine man and telling the tin dealer to shut up already about his stupid watch.

3   I hated the idea of leaving Aswan. I was sick to death of travel. I was exhausted, a burnt out case, and felt like staying much longer to enjoy the lazy communion of the *souk*. I understood Sir Richard Burton's attraction to the peculiar sophistication of the Egyptians, their unflappable wisdom born of an ancient knowledge about human nature that we younger races can only admire. ("You Americans are such children," said a hookah dealer. "You still believe that the world is worth blowing up.") Then there was the neat contrast between the markets and the Cataract veranda, where one could still indulge in such heinous Western vices as cognac and decent food, while dreamily gazing at the Nile and the ocher folds of desert.

Yet I could not stay forever. One morning Andy and I wearily tore ourselves away and headed north. I had only one thousand kilometers left to travel to Cairo, having already covered nearly ten thousand clicks since leaving Cape Town. Being so close to the end made me want to pedal like a maniac as I pulled out of Aswan. *Pump, pump, pump* went my legs, working as if they had a mind of their own, a mind with a single thought: to finish. As much as I was interested in Egypt, including the "new" Egypt of Hosni Mubarak, I was feeling like a distance runner sniffing the end of a very long race. I knew the road ahead was flat and smooth, the food plentiful if not particularly good and the drinks cold and frequently available. All of this meant one thing—that I was about to launch myself on one hell of a bike marathon to my long-sought destination.

However, there was more at work in my haste than a simple obsession with a finish line. There also was the role of Egypt in the bigger picture of this Cape to Cairo journey. This country has long been a misfit in terms of any study of Africa, a nation at odds with most of the continent, a place whose history, people and very soul seemed foreign to nearly everything else I had seen on this trip. This was not just a matter of granite temples versus grass huts or painted tombs versus crude, wooden war masks. Nor was it simply the notion that Egypt belongs more to the Middle East than to Africa, although these all are major factors. The true difference lay in the dichotomy of attitudes between the people of Egypt and sub-Sahara Africa, attitudes of pride, tradition and dignity.

Egypt has gone through wrenching changes in the past century, but has not suffered the same utter discombobulation as black Africa. Here the people have had an all-encompassing religion to comfort them and provide them with dignity through adversity. And they have their history. In Egypt, this is a source of pride rather than embarrassment. It represents a continuity with the ages, the river and the land that provides even the lowest peasant a sense of security against profound transformations. It is this inner source of strength that accounts for the casual superiority of the Egyptian, a shrewdness about life and human nature that can be quite unnerving to an American traveler, whose own inescapable sense of superiority is a more tenuous thing, being so green in the ways of the world.

The discomfiture we in the *nouveau* West sometimes feel among those of the *ancien* East is nothing new. British imperialists, who blithely went about referring to their "Cape to Cairo Empire" as if the whole piece of real estate belonged to them, never could decide what to do about a nation that seemed at the same time barbaric and civilized. This is another element that sets Egypt apart from the rest of the Cape to Cairo corridor, the fact that the British never treated the Egyptians like other Africans. From the beginning of the conquest era, the European powers were bewildered by a nation of brown-skinned people who had such a long and impressive history. They had great cities, universities, monuments and at least superficially enlightened leaders—all of which made them seem, well, almost *civilized*—whereas blacks were classified as either savages or children and therefore fair game for colonialization and exploitation. This gave the Egyptians the distinction of being allowed *almost* to rule themselves during the imperial era—at least when they behaved themselves—a kid-gloves treatment that no other nation was allowed in British Africa.*

Our road out of Aswan was smooth and wide—a magic, asphalt carpet from the twentieth century—but the world through which it passed seemed just slightly more recent than the river itself. Bare-

* The Cape to Cairo Empire was more accurately a Cape to Khartoum Empire, as Egypt was ruled directly by Britain for only two brief periods, in the early 1880s and from 1918 to 1922. However, Britain dominated Egypt militarily and economically for at least seven decades, from before its invasion in 1881 until Nasser's revolution forced out the last British troops stationed on the Suez Canal in 1956.

chested men in loincloths chopped, dug and hauled things in fields that looked as ancient as the sky, their faces as solemn as the donkeys and camels lumbering past on the edge of the highway. Children guided water buffalo round and round in circles to power irrigation wheels, a job as monotonous and rigorous as any on this planet, as the water gurgled like black blood through intricate furrows cut beside rows of maize and beans.

Henry Adams once said that rural Egypt was better than opium. "It soothes one's creases out with the patient weight of a German philosopher trying to be intelligible," he wrote in a letter to a friend. I could not think of a better description of the sensation of heavy, thick, hot lethargy on this stretch of highway, although my personal creases were not quite as smooth as I might have liked. Whatever narcotics had permeated the air in Adams's day were now mingled with those more vital drugs I have already described as belonging to the amphetamine family. At any moment the languor might be broken by the squeal of a child dashing toward us —"Yeeeowwww! Hello, meester! Stop, meester! Yeeeowwww!"

Fortunately, the area of Egypt just north of Aswan had a relatively small population, as the ragged bluffs of the river valley pressed in too close to the river to provide much space. This was the northernmost remnant of the old Nubian Valley, a canyonlike stretch of the Nile now mostly lost under the waters of Lake Nasser. Because of the lack of available land and the comparative isolation of the area, the region was quite primitive for Egypt, with little of the development we had seen in Aswan and would see elsewhere. The villages—constructed of rugged adobe and rock and perched like battered castles in the bluffs above the highway—had no electricity or running water. Nor did I see much evidence that television and other modern amenities had made a huge impact here.

However, there was Abdul, a farmer who shared our lunch that first day on the road. He looked the classic peasant, with a dirty *gallebeyah*, rough hands and a lean, wiry frame. But he was not completely what he seemed. Though he claimed to have never attended school, he spoke perfect English and seemed astonishingly knowledgeable, a good-natured scholar of the peasantry, a Thomas Hardy character without the tragedy. As we sat under a dusty date palm near the river, he noticed a *Time* magazine attached to my rear load. I asked if he wanted to see it. "No, thank you," he said, "I have read already this week's edition." He then proceeded to cite several articles and to ask our opinion of current issues, telling us he had taught himself how to read and spent most evenings listening to a small radio in his grandfather's house.

He had a great deal to say about Egypt, both old and new, sounding like farmers everywhere with his blend of conservatism and pragmatism. He said that he believed in change but hoped things would not change too fast. "I enjoy my farming," he said. "I do farming like my fathers have always done, and it is a good way of life. Hard work, yes, but rewarding." He admitted that he was still something of a Nasserite—which in Egypt means one is a conservative—since it was the colonel who had broken up the large farming estates. "He chased out the parasites and gave respect to every Egyptian," said Abdul. "Colonel Nasser gave the land to the people. Because of this he is a hero, like your Franklin Roosevelt."

W e arrived in Idfu near dusk, a large city of twisting, impossibly dusty alleyways broken by one or two wide, almost modern streets choked with an astounding concentration of automobiles, people and animals. Andy and I valiantly steered through this melee, finally discovering a decaying hotel called El Medina in the middle of town. These digs, whose sister establishments would become a staple for us over the next few days, was another example of the unexplained proclivity toward filth in Egyptian public places. The communal bathroom could not have been cleaned for decades, and the sheets were gray with the body dirt of perhaps a dozen previous guests. The innkeeper, typecast as fat, slovenly and toothless, was a latent homosexual who hovered over us as we attempted to undress. He then offered to bathe us "if we would enjoy this thing." We declined, attaching a bike lock on our flimsy door when we went to sleep.

We did little slumbering in Idfu. The evening Ramadan festivities began at dusk and continued well into the small hours of the morning. Though we were exhausted and wanted to retire early, it became obvious that this would be impossible amid the anarchy of the worshipers enjoying their food, drink and shopping below our hotel window. Every radio and television in the city blared, and every Idfuian seemed intent on creating a new record in decibels emitted by the unaided human voice.

Eventually, Andy and I gave up on sleeping and decided to join in the fray. When in Idfu, do as the Idfuians. Outside of the hotel we rented a *tonga* horse and carriage inexplicably decorated with American flags. The driver, who seemed as hyped-up as anyone in Egypt, drove us about like a madman, pushing his poor horse to the limit as he weaved through the confusing, brightly lit streets. The dust was so thick that I was reminded of old black-and-white British movies where carriages go rattling through London's pea-soup fog, although this fog required a mask around one's mouth to prevent suffocation. I think we spent three or four hours driving about, stopping in shops and drinking a variety of sweet fruit juices mixed in blenders. At one point we decided to go on a search for beer, which was not readily available in this nontourist Muslim city. This search quickly turned into a major quest for our wild driver, despite the fact that he personally disapproved of alcohol.

We raced up and down the streets searching for beer, stopping at teahouses and canned goods shops. Finally, the driver took us out to a strange, seemingly abandoned nightclub where he said the "big men" sometimes gathered to drink. Behind the club were several streets of old mansions, most of them dilapidated and falling down. They once must have been magnificent, covered in vapid Ottoman and European gingerbread—cupids, cornucopias, eagles and other plaster facades now cracked and broken. Inside, the rooms of the old nobility long ago had been divided into crude, multi-family apartments, a fate that befell many of the great homes of Moscow after the Russian Revolution. It was in one of these houses that we finally located beer, served in a sitting room where less crude libations undoubtedly had flowed in the bad old days before Nasser. The yard was littered with bottles. Inside, the ground floor had been more or less hollowed out and the walls lined with used, reeking bottles stacked perhaps three feet thick, giving the impression of a dank fortress made of brown glass. Perhaps a dozen Egyptians sat drunk or comatose on the floor, some lying in their own vomit, a bevy of lushes whose example would be enough to make anyone become a confirmed Muhammadan and give up liquor for life.

The night ended with a visit at about two A.M. to the Temple of Horus, one of the better preserved temples in Egypt. Though it was locked tight and guarded by a soldier with a rifle, we were able to peer at it through the fence, an enormous, brooding shadow in the darkness of the night, lit only by the faint sky-glow of the city. It was an eerie, disturbing sight, largely because the old building was located literally in a hole in the ground. Thus it appeared as a sort of open grave in the midst of vitality, as if this temple were a decayed body, and we small rodents come to pick at it. I was greatly relieved when we failed to get in and returned to the living city.

Like most Idfuians, we slept late the next morning, awakened by the heat and a cloud of obnoxious flies who buzzed us at about nine A.M. For some reason, Andy and I awoke unnaturally rested and anxious to proceed, which we did after the gay innkeeper chided us for locking him out of our room. "I think you do not like me," he moaned, looking like an unhappy, blubbery, child.

That day we rushed through more of Adams's opium country, marveling at the abrupt contrast with the insanity of Idfu. We frequently stopped by makeshift *chai* stands, and were often entertained by dusty locals who insisted on buying us tea and watermelons, though they themselves were unable to indulge on account of Ramadan. They watched us greedily, encouraging us as if we could provide vicarious nourishment. That night we camped on a high bank above the Nile, protected from the highway by a thick stand of date palms. Toward dusk a gang of kids flushed us out. We were prepared for the worst, but they had come not to harass us, but to ask us to join in a game of soccer.

I played while Andy, camp chef *extraordinaire*, prepared supper. The boys were excellent players, certainly better than a clumsy Kansan raised on one of the most inelegant games in the world—American-style football. We played until sunset ignited the sky with color and the exotic voice of a muezzin drifted lazily across the valley. The boys abruptly stopped the game, as if they had been at it too long and would catch hell at home, and raced off toward their village. Afterward, with a full belly of "Andy Shafer Stew" and coffee mixed with brandy, we sat with our legs dangling over the high bank, watching bats swoop low over the river, the moon filling the land with a pale glow like soft daylight, turning the harsh world into sensuous folds of silver gray. Below us flowed the river, its waters slipping past with a steady, mesmerizing sound like a room full of whispering people.

The next day we continued through this idyllic country, enjoying ourselves despite the filth and awful food. (To be fair, it was

Ramadan.) But as we approached Luxor, the behavior of the people along the highway began to change. The tea shop men became less friendly and the children more frenetic. It was as if a great stone marked "obnoxious" had fallen in at Luxor with ripples of impudence spreading out in all directions. The closer one got, the stronger the ripples became, with children grabbing at us and asking for money while adults demanded large sums of cash for tea and sodas. When we refused, they spat on the ground and sneered with contempt. I was dismayed by this behavior. It was as if some disease had permeated the air around Luxor and other tourist sites, turning decent people into beasts clamoring for baksheesh, their lives' work devoted to a demeaning scramble for pennies and crumbs.

This obsession with money had existed in Luxor during my previous visit, but not to this extent. In '82, the town had a growing industry devoted to exploiting tourists, but it was a pittance compared to what greeted us as we pedaled onto the Luxor corniche late that morning. This was commerce gone mad, the dark side of the "new" Egypt, where hundreds (perhaps thousands) of Egyptians had embraced avarice like Faustus had Lucifer. Of course, one could not really blame them, people whose fathers had labored like buffaloes for centuries to earn a few dollars a year. A trinket salesman could earn a hundred dollars a month if he was sufficiently clever and pushy.

"What do you want most?" I asked a young man selling beads he "guaranteed" were from ancient tombs (that they were plastic did not dissuade his sales pitch).

"Money is what I want," he said. "Lots of it. And if you want to ask me any more questions, it'll cost you." I asked how much answers cost in Luxor. "One dollar U.S. for short questions, five for long questions, ten dollars for a photograph."

The place reeked of cupidity, the streets choked with tourists, vulgar hawkers, ineffective tourist police and what seemed like a small hobos' town of shacks selling "things Egyptian." These proffered such must-haves as Nefertiti T-shirts, fake death masks, pieces of "authentic" mummy wrappings, crude statues of Tutankhamen and paint-by-number reproductions of tomb paintings. At night, this gaudy spectacle was lit up in neon and yellow lights, like a faded country fair, where the games and shows are fixed and geeks bite the heads off live chickens. Poised in the middle was the ancient Temple of Luxor, its stones laid out like a broken body amid the carnival, a brooding, violated corpse shorn of its wrappings and placed on display for hordes of troglodytes.

I had little desire to linger in Luxor, and did so only because of a knee-jerk feeling that I shouldn't leave without having visited the tombs and temples of Old Thebes, even if I had seen them twice before. Andy was less eager than I about remaining here, for he could remember when Luxor was a sleepy, friendly village and the temples were free of fences, cola stands, guards, lines and visitors' fees. "You just walked up to a tomb and peeked inside," he said. "There must have been some sort of caretaker there, with keys to open up the doors. I remember it was all very eerie and mysterious, being alone inside the tombs with only a flashlight. You had the sensation that you were somehow discovering them for the first time."

After checking into an inexpensive hotel we spent two days going through the motions of seeing the sights. Yes, the antiquities were intriguing, and yes, I did feel an occasional stirring in my blood at the sight of fallen glories. But the effect was ruined by the intrusion of so many pale faces. And everything was so clean! The tombs and temples of Luxor must be the cleanest places in Egypt, kept spotless by Egyptologists obsessed with the cold, scientific sterility of the museum. I wish I had seen a place like Karnak a century ago, when sand, huts and peasants still choked the corridors and great columns lay fallen like rows of chess pieces. To me this would have been truly poignant, the ruins of a great civilization reduced to materials for peasants' huts, a place alive and dead all at once. As it is I get more satisfaction out of visiting a good museum back home, where the climate is not only cooler, but the exhibits from antiquity are arranged in a way that at least makes them comprehensible.

Andy and I quickly fled Luxor, rushing toward Cairo in a blur, stopping only to eat, drink and sleep. Cities, farms, mosques and temples rushed past in a hot progression along the smooth, flat highway. Once Ramadan was over we often lunched with Egyptian farmers, simple people whose mud brick homes were always spotless and serene in a rustic way, in sharp contrast to the public areas of Egypt. It was as if Egyptians have given up on the centuries-old struggle against dust and filth outside their homes, being satisfied with having a small, unsullied place of their own, a retreat from the masses and insanity. Even the homemade food was delicious—spicy beans, goat and warm pita bread. One day we shared tea with three Coptic priests, bearded, light-skinned men whose church served as both sanctuary and home (they had laundry drying on a line stretched between two large crosses on the roof). For them, the new Egypt meant less religious persecution, although they complained about intolerance from Muslims, whom they still refer to as "invaders" fourteen centuries after the Arab conquest.

Most nights were spent in ratty inns, although as we got closer to Cairo, modern hotels began to appear in the major cities. These hotels had a glittery, *nouveau riche* feeling to them, the walls of the dining rooms covered in red felt and the tables filled with restless young men squandering their oil field savings on foreign liquor and fancy clothes. We never stayed in these places, preferring the drastically less expensive dives. However, we occasionally stopped for a cola and a break in the frigid, air-conditioned lounges.

One night we stayed in the vineyard of a dilapidated mansion, an eerie, walled garden partially roofed by struggling vines spread out like veins against the stars. The garden was inhabited by an old gardener who roamed about in a white cloak like a ghost, a spooky fellow who spent half the night feeding the largest collection of cats I have ever seen assembled in one location.

After several days on the road, it seemed inevitable that I was about to finish my journey, a realization that added to the dreamlike quality of my sojourn along the Nile. I suppose I should have been reflecting on my long trek, upon all of those Big Questions I had pondered since coming to Africa, but the truth is I spent much of this period in a kind of trance. It was a purely physical finale that I made a point of enjoying, knowing that this probably would be my last grand expedition for a long time. This grueling sort of travel is a younger person's occupation, and life's loves and responsibilities were conspiring to end my days of uninterrupted nomadism. I felt like a man who had just run a gauntlet of fire, and had taxed his reserves to the point of exhaustion. Like Rimbaud, I will always have foot soles of wind, but unlike that energetic, bewildering Frenchman, I have made a decision to be only a part-time nomad. I treasure moments of stillness at home, even if I know the unanswered questions rattling around inside my head will always draw me back.

Our arrival in Giza on the outskirts of Cairo was marked by a rainstorm, a rare occurrence in Egypt. It was as if the gods had decided to notice our petty efforts and celebrate our arrival with a violent, glorious burst of water. As Andy and I labored up the hill on the approach to the pyramids, a lightning bolt ripped through the darkness and struck in the desert perhaps a half-mile away, sending the few remaining tourists scattering for the safety of their buses. This left Andy and me virtually alone at the base of the largest pyramid, brooding against a charcoal sky.

I would like to report that this was a magical moment for me, a deep, penetrating instant where the weight of my experiences in Africa came rushing together in a thunderclap as pervasive as the one that had just rolled across the plains of Giza. The truth is I felt very little sensation as I pedaled up to Cheops' tomb and stepped onto the ground. It was not that my mind was empty. On the contrary, it was racing with a myriad of images and emotions from the past several months—of long days spent in the bush, of jail, of war, of hate, of hope.

I slid off my bicycle at the very moment the sun reappeared and the blacks clouds blew into the desert. Carefully, I laid my bicycle up against the pyramid, and reacting to an unexplained impulse, I began to climb. I pulled myself up on top of the lowest level of stones, huge blocks as tall as a man. I thought about the people who had built this edifice: not the pharaoh, but the common people, the thousands of laborers, their families, their sons, their grandsons—the real people of Egypt and Africa (the people whose descendants I had been living among for all these months).

I reached up to the next level, found a foothold in the worn, battered stone and propelled myself up to the second level. I looked behind me and saw the city of Cairo spread out in a gray, smoggy mass below, a living, vibrant city that stood out in stark contrast to this monument to death, built by a megalomaniac who made the current crop of African despots seem like kittens.

While climbing to the third level I slipped and nearly fell. I scraped my hand as I caught myself, spilling several drops of blood, adding a small, needless sacrifice to these cold stones. As the blood became a maroon stain on the rock, I realized that nothing—*nothing*—was growing on these stones, that this mountain was incapable of supporting life. Apparently, the pyramids had paid a price for their immortality. Even birds shunned them, except as a repository for excrement.

After a great deal of pushing and pulling I made it to the tenth or eleventh level, about halfway up the Great Pyramid. There I suddenly stopped. I was high enough to be above the renewed clamor of tourists below, high enough to hear the silence of the desert that stretched out in a great expanse of ocher to the west. I was, in fact, high enough to understand that I did not want to climb any more, that I had gone far enough and was ready to go home.

Acknowledgments

Many thanks to everyone who helped, encouraged and housed this wayward traveler. First and foremost, I thank my wife for understanding the impulses of the sometime nomad she married. Next come my two compatriots—Jim Logan, who has committed this sort of lunacy before, and Andy Shafer, desert hound extraordinaire. They provided not only brilliant conversation for weeks on end, but much needed moral, technical and logistical support. Special thanks also go to Bob DuBose, who again served as an unwavering beacon of advice and inspiration; Pam Bernstein, the nicest person in New York City; and John Herman, who stuck with me.

I am grateful to my corporate sponsors: Fuji America supplied our mountain bikes; Eclipse supplied our panniers; Moss supplied the tents; and Caribou and L. L. Bean supplied the sleeping bags and packs. Special thanks to Lorraine and Punnie at Yankee Pedaler in Brunswick, Maine, for providing equipment and discounts. Weidenfeld & Nicolson and *Smithsonian* magazine helped financially.

Finally, there were the people of Africa, who assisted me with research, put me up at night, and showed me a warmth and friendliness that is the envy of the world. Specifically I would like to mention the following:

In South Africa: Elizabeth Dostal, Dr. Swart, Rodney Charles Barker, "Mathew," H. Lottering, Jonathon Abrahams, the Brandwacht Hotel, Hennie Bloem and his wife, Johan Swanejael, Peter and Connie Snyders, David Lawrenson and family, Dennis Knox, Tessa DuPlessis, Mrs. Tutu, Joy Hendron and Glen Malena.

In Botswana: Ruby Apsler, Batshane Ndaba, Neville and Debbie Peake, "Map" and Kathy Ives, Mike Durell, Alec Campbell, Jeff Ramsey, Nicolas Jacobs, Keseitse Chakaloba, "Lady Gaz," Sandy Grant and Patrick van Rensburg.

In Zimbabwe: Milo, the Bradnick family, Robin Rudd, Peter Dunjey, Mrs. Bell, Mrs. Vickery, George Palmer, Emmanuel Chileshe, Hugh Atkinson, Jim Fox, Professor Samkange, Charles Bell and Noah Koleni Dlamini.

In Zambia: the Chirundu customs man, Jan Zehner, Taxon Tembo, Michael Rank, Gelson Banda, "Phoebe," "Joe" and the Keystone Kops in Kasama.

In Tanzania: Nassar Said, George Tardois, Prosper Kashamagula, Rebecca Winchester, Dennis Arko, Kaj Arhem, Steve Mangara, V. K. Lekhi, Tedvan der Zalm, Father Stephen, Ali and Hassan.

In Kenya: Abby Kristal, Paul Smoke, Peter Stone, Don Young, Daphne Sheldrick, Eluid Muthui, Tony Seth-Smith, Joel Kinagwi, George Mathui, George Smith, Fairview Hotel, Kathy Stewart, Clare McCamy, U.S. Peace Corp workers in Naivasha, Selly Cherop, Mary Naliaka, George Olunga, Michael Silberman, C. A. Musumba, Kamoya Kimeu and Peter Siana.

In Sudan: Tom Mills, Ed Resor, Professor Mohamed Beshire, Dr. Saifel Hassan, Bona Malwal, George and the Acropole, Hassan Mohed Mustafa, Mohammed the Slang Man and Jaafar.

In Egypt: Ahmed Maher El Sayed, Jane Friedman, Reuters, Mrs. Nilly Shahin, Antel Soliman and the Church of Saint Sebastian.

In Britain: Giles Chance, Charles Meynell, Deborah Gage, Richard Hodder-Williams, Tony Wheeler and the British Library.

D.E.D.

About the Author

David Ewing Duncan is also the author of *Pedaling the Ends of the Earth* and has written numerous articles and essays for *The Christian Science Monitor*, *The New York Times*, and *Life*, among other publications. He is currently researching his third book, *Streets of America*, and is finishing a novel set in Africa and New York City. He lives in Vermont with his wife and two children.